AMONG YOU

Among You

The Extraordinary True Story of a Soldier Broken by War

JAKE WOOD

MAINSTREAM
PUBLISHING

EDINBURGH AND LONDON

First published in Great Britain in 2013 by
MAINSTREAM PUBLISHING COMPANY
(EDINBURGH) LTD
7 Albany Street
Edinburgh EH1 3UG

ISBN 9781780575728

This book is a work of non-fiction based on the life, experiences and recollections of the author. In some instances, names of people or the detail of events have been changed to protect the privacy of others. Conversations have been included from time to time for dramatic effect. They reflect accurately the sentiments shared but are not an exact record of expressions or words used at the time. The author has stated to the publishers that, except in such respects, not affecting the substantial accuracy of the work, the contents of this book are true.

Lyrics from 'Clocks' by Coldplay appear on pp. 51–3. Words and music by Guy Berryman, Chris Martin, John Buckland and Will Champion © Copyright 2003 Universal Music Publishing MGB Limited. All rights reserved. International copyright secured. Used by permission of Music Sales Limited.

An extract from 'Does It Matter?' (1918) © Siegfried Sassoon is reproduced on p. 371 by kind permission of the estate of George Sassoon.

A catalogue record for this book is available
from the British Library

Printed in Great Britain by
Clays Ltd, St Ives plc

1 3 5 7 9 10 8 6 4 2

To my mother and brother, who with
love have always been there.

To Toby, who saw us right.

And to my father, who through his own living and writing
inspired his son to live and write, but who did not live
long enough to read this.
Sleep well, Dad.

CONTENTS

AUTHOR'S NOTE

Truth is clear and absolute.

But memory is subjective and opaque.

So what follows is nothing more than what the author remembers of that truth, transcribed from diaries written at the time.

But it is also nothing less, with only the following caveat:

This story is about real people, so sexual explicitness has had to be deleted. The identities of certain people have been changed. And to further protect these persons' privacy, the laws of my country have required that some of their actions and words be omitted.

As the narrator of this story, however, I have afforded myself no such protection. My reactions to these antagonists' actions and words have been retained.

1

PRESAGE

We make war that we may live in peace.

Aristotle

Nothing good ever comes of violence.

Martin Luther

It is a still, clear night in March, and I stand alone in a wilderness.

The nearest city, or town, or village, is a very long way away. I feel the distance and it calms me; the crowding and press of city life is a world away now. Its all-pervading background drone, its pollutions of grey fumes and murky orange light that cocoon the air around you and leak away into the dirty night sky above – none of that is here.

I close my eyes. I take a deep breath and fill my lungs; nothing but clean, cool air comes pouring in. I breathe out in release and hear nothing but pure silence. At peace, I lift my face upwards and open my eyes.

The dark sky is a backdrop of true black. Perfect, clean, jet black has washed through the air hanging above me. There is no cloud, and the stars – a staggering myriad of thousands of stars – seem to weigh down the sky, piercing and flooding the pure, ink-saturated firmament with pinpricks of light from the heavens above.

The host of lights gaze unblinkingly back down at me in silence. I feel like a glimmering speck of dust in the darkness. I am just a twinkling in time.

Her face comes to me: her beautiful face, with those shining, bright sky-blue eyes; her light chestnut-brown hair flowing down to her shoulders – and a body to die for. Nine years of happy, empty, escapist one-night stands and short-term relationships, and then I have to meet her a month before I come here.

It wasn't to be. She'll have found someone else by the time I get back.

This'll be a good opportunity to forget her and get over her then.

There is a growing rumble in the atmosphere. Stealthy black shapes thunder over in the night sky high above. I follow their sound with my eyes as they make their way north, disappearing into the silence as they meld with the horizon.

Pale, star-lit Arabian sand-dunes stretch out north before me. Their pallid contours rise and roll like a frozen white sea of dust as they sweep towards where the dark sky reaches down to tomorrow's destination, with menace hidden among the stars.

We will be there tomorrow. I can see the fires burning there already. Tomorrow I will invade a country. I feel my heart quicken, and I imagine my eyes suddenly ablaze with the thought of it. I feel alive. This is life and death, here and now and black and white: I am standing on the edge of a war – maybe of my very being. This overarches anything my crushingly safe life at home can provide, an existence spent clothed in grey suits, being crammed into commuter trains to spend endless grey days in grey buildings, blindly toiling to 'maximise shareholder value'. And for what.

Will I die? The distant fires in Iraq dot the horizon, like stars brought down burning to earth. They blink silently across the desert at me with their answers. I will be among them tomorrow. Why am I not afraid? I don't believe anything will happen to me, not so much as a scratch. But what of the things I may have to do, what will they be for?

'We go to liberate, not to conquer,' the colonel had said. His Ulster accent had echoed across the sand to us that afternoon. I had listened carefully to his words; it turned out that with the winds of a sandstorm dying away in the background I was one of the lucky ones who could hear. I felt lucky because with the crowds back home questioning why we were here, he could provide some focus for us, some reason as to why we could invade and live with ourselves: reasons that the politicians and protesters could not give.

The colonel did not talk of weapons of mass destruction like the politicians did with their sexed-up dossiers. He only told us that our enemy had used them on their own people and that he fully expected them to be used on us.

'We are entering Iraq to free a people, and the only flag which will be flown in that ancient land is their own.'

He told us how Iraq is steeped in history, how it is the site of the Cradle of Civilisation, the Garden of Eden and the Great Flood. He told us to tread lightly there. We would see things that no man could pay to see and would be embarrassed by the Iraqis' hospitality even though they had nothing. 'Their children will be poor, but in years to come they will know that the light of liberation in their lives was brought by you.

'But there's going to be more fighting than at a pikey's wedding,' he grinned, before his face darkened. 'The enemy should be in no doubt that we are his nemesis and that we are bringing about his rightful destruction. There are many regional commanders who have stains on their souls and they are stoking the fires of hell for Saddam. He and his forces will be destroyed by this coalition for what they have done. As they die, they will know their deeds have brought them to this place. Show them no pity.

'As for ourselves, let's bring everyone home and leave Iraq a better place for us having been there. Our business now is north.'

Thank you, Colonel. I'm here now, and I'm going to do this for the good of some people: not the crowds pointlessly chanting about us on TV, not the journalists, not even the Queen, Tony Blair or George W. Bush. I'm going to do it for some brutalised people sitting just a few miles away from me now. I'm going to do it for the teammates I met for the first time yesterday. And I'm going to do it for myself. I don't want to be anywhere else other than where I am now.

I finish my star- and fire-gazing and head back to the tent to sleep. We invade in the morning.

*

We were taking a break beside our vehicles on the way to Iraq the next morning when a Scud missile landed close to us. It made the earth shake and everyone scrabble for their respirators. Screams of 'Gas! Gas! Gas!' echoed down the line. Black plastic muffled the high-pitched alarm in the voices, but the masks' eyepieces were windows into the soul of the man sitting next to you. Your own wide-eyed apprehension stared back at you, with each close, laboured, sweet breath sucked loud through the mask until the all-clear was given.

Later that day, the 7th Parachute Regiment Royal Horse Artillery (7 (Para) RHA) drove into Iraq, initially following in the wake of the Americans, who had entered some hours before. We drove past anti-tank mines beside our wheels and felt the heat of burning-oil fires scorch our faces. The rolling sand-dunes of Kuwait were replaced with a trench- and barbed-wire-ridden wasteland. Russian-made tanks lay scattered and charred in the dirt. I saw the defeated: the prisoners, and the prisoners burying their dead. In the scorched earth left by Saddam Hussein, I saw a smoke-blackened flag. I picked it up and carefully folded it before stuffing it into one of my pockets.

Then the five-man reconnaissance team I had joined a few days previously pushed forward alone into the desert. I saw walls of smoke reaching from the ground to the clouds outside the city of Basra and watched through the green glow of night-vision equipment as tracer fire poured up into the sky, flailing and fumbling for the tormentors above. I heard artillery shells whistle over my head before seeing them flash and burst apart over our enemy's positions in the darkness ahead.

Our two Land Rovers were quickly reduced to one after a midnight collision with a boulder, so we drove cramped through the desert, looking forward to our stops, when we would peek over the maze of sand berms that criss-crossed the country like the walls of a labyrinth.

In early April, the captain in charge of our observation post (OP) team informed us that we were the most northerly positioned British troops anywhere in Iraq. We were alone in the desert and would hold where we were until ordered on.

We hid our Rover in a dip and took turns keeping watch, day and night, with eyeballs, binoculars, night vision and radar. Soon we were joined by a small group of paratroopers with anti-tank missiles. During the day we pointed out to them the distant dark humps of dug-in tanks, and they drove out at night and put missiles into them.

It was when I came off shift one day and walked a little back from our position, looking down for a good site to dig a hole for a call of nature, that I first noticed the shells. The parched desert dirt was strewn with seashells. But they weren't fossilised and didn't look particularly old; they were just sitting on top of the sand, whitening in the desert sun. It looked like the tide had gone out on a beach that had been forgotten by the sea.

After cursing the contents of British Army ration packs while squatting and straining for an increasingly uncomfortable amount of time in wide-open flat desert on the front line of a war, I mentioned the seashells to one of the paras as I walked back in. He was stripped to the waist, sunbathing and flicking through a porn mag as he reclined in a collapsible canvas chair.

'You seen all those seashells, mate?'

'Yes, mate – mad, innit?' He turned the magazine through 90 degrees and looked thoughtful.

A pause.

'Well, where the hell did they come from?'

The magazine returned to its original position and he turned a page. His eyes were transfixed. 'This is it, mate, this is the Cradle of Civilisation.' He glanced up and noted my stare of incomprehension. 'We're in the marshlands, mate. The fucker drained them when he dropped gas on everyone round here.' He spat angrily into the dust. 'We're the fucking Great Flood now,' he beamed at me, before going back to his reading.

I weighed up his words. 'Thank you, mate. Any chance I can borrow that later?'

'Yeah, no worries.'

The war ended one morning a week later, in the middle of April. Our team drove to the nearest main road, then joined up with a convoy pulling back to a town called Al Qurnah, nestled between the fork where the Tigris and Euphrates rivers meet on their flow into the Persian Gulf.

On our way to Al Qurnah our convoy had to stop and crawl through every village it went through. There were too many people mobbing our vehicles. As soon as the lead vehicle stopped, we were descended upon from all sides. Sparkling dark eyes peered into our cabins from all around, and singing and cheering filled the air. When we got out of our vehicles, the smallest children were the boldest. The little boys and girls laughed and chatted excitedly, jumping up and down beside us with the thrill of it all. Their dark eyes seemed to light up as they gazed at us.

'Good, Mister, Good!'

It turned out to be a mistake handing out sweets; it caused miniature riots to break out around our vehicle. But the fathers were smiling, gently shooing their children away so a village elder could get to us. He carried a large silver plate on which small cups of an unknown steaming liquid were placed. He humbly beckoned to us to help ourselves. Any suspicion of being poisoned evaporated when he did that. We were the ones who were being humbled. He had nothing compared to us. That was the best, the sweetest, most delicious cup of steaming-hot poison I ever tasted.

We eventually got to Al Qurnah late in the afternoon, where the boss promptly used all of his Sandhurst officer training to get us hopelessly lost in the maze of ancient mud houses and antediluvian alleyways, trying to find a school that had been commandeered into a temporary headquarters. Eventually we found ourselves outside what had been the local Ba'ath Party headquarters, now British Army occupied. The boss went inside to ask directions, leaving the rest of us to hang around outside the main building with the vehicles.

Before long, an Iraqi man was hurriedly carried out on a stretcher in front of us. His gut was wrapped in white bandages stained with red, and one of the medics was holding a drip bag up in the air. The Iraqi's face looked pale, and he did not move or make a sound as they loaded him into the back of a military ambulance. It pulled out of the compound and then roared away out of earshot. I wandered over to a bored-looking medic standing beside the front door pulling surgical gloves off his hands.

'Who was he?'

'He's one of them. Hanged a little girl for waving at us a few days ago apparently. Doubt he'll make the heli.' He gave me a sideways look as he raised his eyebrows. 'And so what if he doesn't?'

I nodded at him.

'They're going at each other hammer and tongs here,' he continued. 'The locals are going ape-shit at these fuckers. They found one in the desert yesterday with his hands and feet chopped off.'

The boss strolled out of the front doors beside us.

'Saddle up, Jake. The school's just down the road.'

We walked back toward our vehicles together.

'This place is the Garden of Eden apparently,' he mused with incredulity. 'They've got a tree here and everything! It's spitting distance from the school – keep your eyes peeled.'

'Really?'

'Well, so the locals make out. It's near the school anyway. We might even get some sleep under a roof this evening if I have anything to do with it.'

Not if your map-reading has anything to do with it.

We drove a short distance along potholed earth streets and past more tightly packed mud-brick houses until we hit the river. Then we took a right, speeding up slightly along a dusty, tarmac-surfaced road running by the water's edge until we could see the telltale sign of radio antennas pointing up into the sky just ahead.

And it was then, as we rolled slowly past a concrete-paved enclosure beside the river immediately to our left, that we saw the tree.

It was dead. Its leafless branches were twisted upwards, silhouetted against the angry scarlet clouds that were splashed across the darkening dusk sky.

We drove into the school compound after the gates were opened for us. We parked, and I got out and banged the vehicle door shut in relief at the end of a long journey.

'Red sky at night – the wagon's on fire. Red sky in the morning – the wagon's still on fire,' someone called out in a faux country accent as we walked across from our wagons to the ops room.

Inside, we were told we had the evening to relax and sort out our lives, until we moved out again in the morning. Our eyes were directed to the mountain of mail waiting for us. There was about a sack per man; it had been piling up in the time we were out in the field. I had a whole sack and spent some time going through it in a quiet corner of the ops room.

My mother told me of her deep pride for me, while also appearing to have dealt with the stress by going on supermarket shopping sprees and boxing up the results to send to me. My brother sent me jokes and asked about kit. My father told me to watch my back. Most of my friends talked of the beers we'd have when I got home; a few of my TA mates struggled with jealousy. There were a couple of enquiring letters from officers with my unit back home, and then there was a single envelope that smelled of perfume. I opened it up and there was a card with a letter inside.

It was from her: the girl who had made my heart stop each time I saw her. The girl I thought I could only imagine being with, the girl who wasn't interested, and whose hold on me it had taken a war in the birthplace of civilisation to escape from, and begin to forget.

Cecilia.

She said the war was all over the news back home, and that every time she saw the news, she thought of me.

She said she was sorry for us not meeting up before I left. And she asked if I wanted to go for a drink when I came home.

Maybe this was why she especially asked me to look after myself out here – though she wondered whether these words would ever even reach me.

And maybe this was why her letter finished with the words: 'If it's meant to be, it will be.'

The front of the enclosed card was a black and white close-up of a suited man's face, his eyes as wide in surprise as his grin was broad. The caption underneath read: 'Alone in the elevator with the sex bomb from accounts, Jeff was delighted by her offer to go down.'

She had me with the letter. The card just blew my mind.

I needed some air. I put her card and letter back in their envelope and put it in one of the cargo pockets down my leg to carry with me. I packed the rest of the post in its sack, leant it against my kit, and walked outside.

Night had fallen. Choirs of crickets and frogs shouted at each other in the thick, humid air. The wildlife competed with the locals, though. Bursts of automatic gunfire rang out sporadically in town. None of it was incoming, however; we knew old scores were being settled and revenge exacted.

It was very dark now. The red clouds had turned into dim rolls of spectral grey shapes, blotting out the stars. I felt my way to my vehicle with outstretched arms as my eyes adjusted from the harshly fluorescent-lit ops room to the gloom outside.

The shots in town were reaching a crescendo; maybe the locals had herded all the remaining Ba'athists against a wall.

The dark shape of my vehicle loomed up abruptly. I hauled myself up onto the bonnet – and everything suddenly went quiet.

You got them all. Good, I might actually get some sleep tonight.

I pulled myself up against the windscreen, leaning back on it with legs outstretched down the bonnet. And suddenly my eyes were pulled upwards as flashes of orange and green spurted into the sky. Whoever had been doing the firing before was now celebrating. Tracer fire crackled and burst high above, waving around in the darkness. One stream of fire was replaced by another, and then another, until a filigree of gold and green was dancing against the brooding night sky.

Then, just as quickly, Eden fell quiet and dark once more.

A muffled voice piped up from one of the small sandbagged positions, or sangers: 'If any of that lands on me I swear I will go fucking mental.'

But up in the starless darkness and leaking through the thickening clouds, the moon loomed low above Al Qurnah. It glowed white and huge through the shroud gathering around it. It looked impossibly large, seeming twice its normal size, hanging unnatural and bulbous above us all, with a gigantic glowing halo of silver streaking into the darkness surrounding it.

I caught my breath and was careful not to make a sound; I didn't hear anything but silence. I felt awed in the hush; all I felt was the sudden ethereal moment of sitting at a war's end, a long, long way away from home in the Garden of Eden, watching this unnatural and celestial moon pushing its light into the darkness just above me. And all this with a promise from Cecilia tucked tight into my pocket.

I slept indoors for the first time in weeks that night. But I was woken in the early hours by the sound of thunder and rain hammering at the roof over my head. I walked to the open doorway in the dark to take a piss outside and saw the heavens opening on the earth. Forty days' and nights' worth of water poured from the sky, washing down in torrents upon the beaten-dirt ground. I added my contribution to the dark flood of waters. It was quickly swallowed up and lost, and then I went back to sleep.

Early in the morning, we turned our backs on Eden and struck on with our business north. As a regiment we drove out of Al Qurnah towards a corner of Maysan Province, bordering Iran, where we would begin our 'peace enforcement' duties. 7 (Para) RHA was headed for a place called Al Sharqi, where we would be the most northerly deployed unit in British-held Iraq.

We were careful to stay on the rain-washed tarmac of the main artery up into the Iraqi heartlands, though; the flood had given birth to a great, clotting, coagulating quagmire.

*

By mid-afternoon and halfway on our journey to the small town of Al Sharqi, we reached the outskirts of a large town called Al Amarah. A large twin arch hung across the dual carriageway, marking the town limits. But where an outsized portrait of Saddam Hussein should have hung in between the arches, there was instead a large rectangular flame-charred scar on the brickwork. I glanced up as I drove underneath it and could see the pockmarks of the bullets the locals had sprayed into the burning face of the man they were finally free of.

We carried on into town, looking for its football stadium. The Ulster battalion that we had stood among for their colonel's famous eve-of-battle speech had set up there after taking over the complex around the arena as their temporary headquarters. It turned out to be easy enough to find among the squat beige town houses, with it being painted bright sky-blue and standing about five storeys high. We parked up inside the stadium's metal fence and looked forward to a night's rest, setting up our camp beds in the shade of the alcoves running along the outer wall of the stadium. We could see a handful of Iraqi men hanging around outside the turnstiles and fence beyond. They were smiling broadly at us while the Northern Irish sentries watched them suspiciously. And after checking we were officially on downtime, I seized the moment and slipped away to write back to Cecilia.

I walked up into the open-air concrete terraces. They were deserted and silent, sweeping around the parched earth far below in a grand oval that felt more like an amphitheatre quietly waiting for its next show of blood.

Sitting in the warmth of the afternoon sun, I wrote my letter back to Cecilia. I thanked her for writing, and for thinking of me. I said I was OK, hoping and asking if she was too. I asked her for any news from home. I said that the war was over now, so not to worry about me too much. I reckoned that we'd probably be home in a couple of months, tops. And I said there would be nothing I would like more than to go for a drink with her when I got back. I said the thought of it would keep me going out here.

I walked back down to our doss area with a warm, buzzing feeling, then dropped the letter into the outgoing-post sack with a pang of heart-in-mouth hope. To have heard from her still felt too good to be true. Over to her now, though.

The handful of Iraqi men had grown into a crowd – two or three hundred of them. They congregated in and around the turnstiles. Some were sitting on top of the ticket booths; the rest pressed their faces up against the metal railings. All their attention was fixed on us; they were our fans. I could see more men arriving to join them from the town beyond. Those pressed up against the fence tried to catch the sentries' attention with a 'Mister! Mister!' before flashing them a big grin and a thumbs up.

I fished my camera out of the cargo pocket on my leg, and as I pointed it at them a great cheer went up from those who had noticed me, all waving for my picture. I took the photo and then waved back, eliciting much excited whistling, before walking back to slump on my camp bed, huddled among the rest of 7 RHA's.

The crowd of Iraqi men grew larger still as evening began to fall, and their adulation grew louder as their numbers swelled. They clapped and they chanted and they sang. They waved and they cheered us. They roared their approval of us. We felt the light of their liberation.

Against the backdrop of adoration, I saw a bare-chested, skinheaded man weaving his way towards me through the jumbled mass of camp beds holding daydreaming and dozing soldiers, all exhausted into deafness. My sleeping bag felt soft beneath my tired body. I could sense my eyes flickering shut, feeling myself sinking down to join my comrades in their death to the world.

Now I could let myself go.

'Are you Jake?' the bald man demanded, suddenly right in front of me.

The background of cheers crashed back into my ears as the sunlight shone harsh around his dark silhouette.

'Yes,' I said in surprise, swinging my legs awkwardly off the bed to sit upright.

'Mac.' He offered his hand and I shook it, standing up and blinking.

I saw Mac had his paratrooper wings tattooed onto his right upper arm, but there was a skull in the middle of the wings where the parachute should have been. The scroll inked underneath said: 'Death From Above'.

'We're dividing down infantry lines for the peacekeeping phase. You're in my section now. You're TA – is that right?'

'Yeah . . .'

He laughed and gave the para wings sewn onto my shirt a pat. 'Relax. If you've got them you're good enough for me. Orders are at seven; they'll announce everyone moving around then.'

Mac gestured at a ginger-haired, sunburnt-red-faced soldier sitting a few beds away, dividing ammunition into piles beside him. 'Go see Six Months; he's that carrot-top over there divvying up your extra ammunition now.' Then he cocked his head over to the crowd of adoring fans fenced off behind us. 'That ain't gonna last.'

'Thanks, Mac . . . Six Months?'

'Maybe . . .' Then he clocked I was talking about the other soldier. 'Ask him about it,' he said, giving me an encouraging grin.

'Six Months?' I tentatively checked with the red-headed soldier.

Six Months looked up resignedly. 'Yeah. You're Jake, then?'

'Yes, mate. Pleased to meet you.' I shook his hand and sat beside him on his bed. 'You part of Mac's crew too now?'

'Yeah. That's for you.' He motioned with the back of his hand at the extra two hand grenades and a bandolier of 150 rounds sitting between us, then dug into his chest pocket for a pack of cigarettes.

'Cheers, mate.'

Six Months smoked in silence.

What to say.

'So, what's with the name, mate?'

Six Months's resigned disposition slipped down a notch as he gave out a sigh. Then he turned his head around so I could see his left ear. It looked like half of it had been bitten off. 'Get it?' he said in mock glee.

'Um, no.' I could feel my buttocks beginning to clench involuntarily.

'Half an ear,' he said angrily. 'Half a year – Six Months.' He glared down at the ground, sucking down a long, deep nicotine drag. I nodded slowly in the silence.

'What's your name, mate?'

'H.'

'H it is then, yeah?' I stood up, picking up the grenades and rounds and cradling them to my chest with both hands.

'Yeah,' he smiled up at me. 'Cool. Oh, you're meant to have one of these as well.' H reached up to press a laminated piece of paper between my teeth.

'. . .'eers . . . 'ate.'

I dropped the ammo down onto my bed and pulled the paper out of my mouth so I could read it. It was a laminated card of Arabic phrases that someone had deemed useful for us now the war had ended – along with the extra ammunition. I cast my eyes down. It gave phonetic transcriptions of phrases such as:

Marrha-ba (Hello)
Qif wa-il-la Sa-et-leq an-naar (Stop or I will shoot)
Mean el mess-ool (Who is in charge?)
Mish fahem (I do not understand)
Ma'a Salama (Goodbye)

As the noise of adoration surged and ripped through the air, I packed the extra hand grenades, the bandolier of 150 rounds and the language card into my webbing. I took the small, smoke-blackened Iraqi flag out of the left chest pocket of my shirt and packed it into the top flap of my bergan, where it joined a small bag of dirt I had scooped up from the drained Mesopotamian marshes. And I folded Cecilia's letter into a sweatproof bag and put it into the left chest pocket of my shirt.

From now on she would be wedged in there, under the hard shell of my body armour.

*

The normal artillery dividing lines within 7 RHA were done away with. We were reorganised along infantry lines: eight men to a section, three sections to a platoon, three platoons to a company. Paras and non-paras, 'gun bunnies' and OP teams, the Regs and a TA soldier all mixed up alike.

Only about half of 7 RHA's ranks were paratroopers. The rest were 'normal' non-para soldiers. As it was an 'airborne' unit, everyone in it wore the maroon Airborne Forces beret. But not everyone in 7 RHA liked that fact. Like the small team I joined for the invasion phase, all the OP teams were made up of paras, like Mac, while most of the gun bunnies, who operated the artillery pieces, worked the radios, drove the vehicles and generally did everything else, were predominantly non-paras, like H.

The paras, as a rule, regarded themselves as having earned their maroon berets as a result of winning their paratrooper's wings, and they resented non-paras wearing their coveted maroon beret just because they had been posted in to make up 7 RHA's numbers. As a general rule, any other soldier from any other part of the Army with any other colour beret to his maroon was therefore derided by your average para as a 'crap hat', or just a 'hat' if he was attempting to be on more friendly terms. The exception to this rule were the beige-bereted Special Forces, who were what most young paras wanted to be when they grew up.

So there was an elitist schism within 7 RHA's subculture, which was enforced by the uber-class of the paras to boost their own status and self-worth and where the 'haves' with wings made a show of tolerating, or not, the 'have-nots' without wings.

The non-paras had to tolerate the paras' intolerance. Rank notwithstanding, their only hope for redemption and delivery from their status as emotional whipping boys was to join their tormentors and put themselves through the mill of the para selection course, with its 40 per cent pass rate. Then they would have the mark of a man within 7 (Para) RHA – and could tattoo it on their right shoulder if they so wanted and flaunt it in the faces of those who had failed, or had not even tried.

Even to an outsider, the unofficial divide down the middle of 7 (Para)

RHA was perceptible. On the one hand you had 7 RHA, and on the other you had 7 *Para* (RHA). As a TA para from another unit I was accepted by both camps, but in truth I was part of neither. For all their divisions I knew that ultimately they would be going home as one unit and I would be going home alone – and back to a part-time unit where I would have been the only soldier to be deployed on the ground.

*

In mid-April, 7 (Para) RHA moved on from Al Amarah into a hastily abandoned Republican Guard barracks just on the outskirts of Al Sharqi. Even if the amenities had been working it would have been basic. As it was, the place had been stripped and pillaged by looters who obviously didn't care much for Saddam Hussein's Republican Guard either, judging by the amount of wanton vandalism inflicted on the place. There wasn't a single window on the one-storey mud-brick buildings that hadn't been smashed.

Making ourselves at home, my section was given the task of clearing out the mortar store. This turned out to be a room where a few hundred corroding mortar bombs had been stored using the system of strewing them all over the floor or piling them in a big heap up to waist height. Unlike other sections, which were disconsolately wandering around sweeping or picking up rubbish, we found this job quite interesting; any accidental detonation would set off a chain reaction that would make a good effort at vaporising all eight of us and that particular part of the barracks. So there was a quiet moment when one was dropped. And then we carried them one at a time, pointlessly held at arm's length, before we gingerly laid them in a pit – which was then just bulldozed over to make way for the regimental volleyball court.

Other sections weren't so lucky. One was detailed to, in the words of their supervising officer, 'sanitise as far as humanly possible' the backed-up toilet block at the end of the accommodation blockhouse. You could almost smell it driving through the main gates. But they made no real difference. And our officer headshed condemned it as unusable, on the grounds of it just being plain blocked and because the barracks' previous occupants had rendered it too insanitary for us to safely use.

Instead, our loos became deep trenches dug just inside the main wall. Planks were laid across the trenches, with wooden commodes fixed atop for you to perch your rear quarters on. You learned to accept that clouds of flies would attack your bare buttocks from below as you pushed. If you wanted to distract yourself from this, though, you could always look down and entertain a vision of what a gate to hell might look like. You tried not to think about the structural integrity of the planks.

Occasionally a trench would come too close to having the Lord of the Flies climbing out of it, so it would be purified with the cleansing flames from having gasoline and a lighted match thrown into it by soldiers who would then run away, hooting with laughter. Then another trench would be dug and the process repeated.

On the surface, it looked like we did a good job of cleaning up the Iraqi barracks. Whoever took them over wouldn't want to scratch the surface, though, and come face to face with Beelzebub or the mother of all explosions.

Swept of shattered glass, my platoon's sleeping quarters now had glassless windows that let a breeze so imperceptible through, it couldn't even penetrate the mosquito net suspended over each man's camp bed. The beds were lined uniformly perpendicular to the wall, with a two-foot-wide space to the left forming each soldier's private space for however long he would be there. But there was, of course, no privacy.

Mac's bed was opposite mine, and both he and H had to tolerate H's bed being beside his. Overlooking Mac's bed, but overlooking H's, mine and every other bed in the vicinity too, was an A3-sized picture recently taped to the wall. It showed two figures. On the right was a depiction of a maroon-bereted para, muscular and lean in close-fitting lightweight trousers and a para smock. His left hand was down his side, clenched into a fist. The right was brought up to chest level, the index finger outstretched and ready to be pointed into the chest of the figure on the left, which was the Devil. The Devil stood bolt upright, scarlet-scaled, fork-tailed, horned and as naked as the day he was cast down from Heaven. He looked nervous. Beneath the two of them was the caption: 'And on the eighth day God created paratroopers, and the Devil stood to attention.'

Waiting for orders, Mac lounged on his camp bed underneath the poster. I lounged on mine; eyes probably appearing locked on the Devil but in actual fact fixed a few feet short, staring into middle space in a pure, comfortable trance of unadulterated vacancy.

'Where'd you get your wings, Jake?' Mac suddenly asked out of the blue. He turned on his side to look at me, bringing his head up to rest on his hand.

'Para Signals,' I replied, half truthfully.

'Oh right . . . So how come you joined the HAC?'

'Just fancied a change,' I said shrugging my shoulders. 'Radios started boring me to death.'

Mac looked thoughtful. 'Fair one . . . so what do they do, then?'

'The HAC?'

'Yeah.'

'Surveillance: living in holes in the ground, shitting in bags, that kind of thing.'

'Right . . .' Mac raised an eyebrow and then gave me the sort of smile that one would give an amiable deviant one suddenly found oneself responsible for. 'Fuck that!' he suddenly blurted, shaking his head in incomprehension, smiling at me.

'Yeah, fair one.'

'Why that – of all things?'

'Same reason we threw ourselves out of perfectly serviceable aircraft. Half the reason's the getting there, the selection process. It's proving something, I think, isn't it?'

Mac considered this before nodding. 'Fair one,' he replied. Then he stared into space for a few seconds, lost in thought. 'Get yourself to stores, Jake,' he added, lifting himself off the bed and pointing at the brown HAC beret on my bed. 'You're one of us now.'

'Thanks, Mac.'

*

'Yes?'

The storeman had finished flicking through his important ring binder and now impatiently looked up at me from his folding chair, waiting for answers.

'Sir, my section commander sent me in here to get a maroon beret while I'm attached to you.'

'Oh yeah? What unit are you from?'

'The HAC.'

'H – A – who?' he sneered back.

'H – A – C . . .'

I saw his eyes flick to the paratrooper wings on my right shoulder and then back to my face with what I took to be disgust. I imagined what he was thinking. I imagined he thought he'd got some Stupid

Territorial Army Bastard crap hat wannabe standing in front of him, wasting his bloody time trying to play at being the airborne warrior.

'H – A – T?' he sniggered at me, in a moment of inspiration.

I didn't respond. His look darkened, and he lifted himself out of his chair.

'Well there's enough crap hats round here wearing them, a STAB might as well have one too. What size are you?' He glared at the Stupid Territorial Army Bastard for a reaction, daring him to snap.

'Fifty-eight,' I said, carefully sticking to a monotone.

He turned to open a large metal box, and I caught a glimpse of his hands rifling through a vast collection of brand-new maroon berets before he fully turned his back to me, blocking my view. I stood still, but my eyes took the opportunity to inspect what other treasures were secreted in the storeman's lair. I was transfixed on an actual real-life working fridge standing in one corner when he suddenly spun round and frisbee'd a maroon beret at my chest.

'Last one I got left! Count yourself lucky.'

I looked down at the beret I'd caught in my hands. It would have been about the right size for the Elephant Man. I looked back up to him and let the desire to chuck it straight back in his openly smug face slowly subside.

'I got my wings from a Special Forces unit before the HAC, you crap hat para motherfucker,' was what I thought.

But 'Thank you very much, Sir,' was what I said, deadpan and overly respectful. It was probably just as well he didn't catch my drift. I turned my back on him and left.

'They haven't got any my size, Mac.' A whole untruth this time.

I got a half-asleep nod from a slumbering Mac and took the opportunity to push the maroon beret held clenched in my fist deep into the guts of my bergan – never to see the light of day again if I had anything to do with it.

I wanted to go out. I wanted to be on my own in the sun so I could reread Cecilia's letter and feel its warmth and promise. She was something to look forward to. She was something good.

I walked underneath a flag fixed taut over the open doorway to outside. The blue British paratrooper wings were emblazoned against a maroon background. And underneath them in gold stitching it read: '7 PARA RHA: Every Man an Emperor'.

*

My section, like all the others, began the rotation by following the day-by-day routine of guard, patrols or waiting on standby for any incidents as the Quick Reaction Force (QRF). There were some hours each day to sleep and relax, but you could semi-relax on QRF duty too.

Downtime was spent trying to sleep in buildings that appeared designed to absorb the heat of the day, sunbathing and swatting flies away approximately every two seconds, or smoking and lifting weights at our new improvised open-air gym. I would weight train every day; there was bugger-all else to do in your free time apart from tan like a local.

The lack of privacy wasn't an issue until the pressing needs of young men became multiplied by the long periods of boredom, the length of time away from home, the steady supply of porn trickling in from home, and, for some lucky ones, explicit and passionate letters from their other halves – their lifelines to cherished lives back home.

There was one place that was private, though: the condemned Iraqi Army toilets. The trade-off was between regaining some sanity and the god-awful stink that rose and fell with the heat of the day. Needs must. Every man has his breaking point, and with unofficial Army efficiency an Iraqi helmet was placed outside the toilet block entrance. Whether it was upturned or not indicated if a gentleman was inside having a moment of self-contemplation. You got used to it. You had to. I found it wasn't so unlike the early years at boarding school anyway, where the loos were the only guaranteed area of semi-privacy too.

There was no getting away from the flies, though. During the heat of the day, they infested every living space. Respite from them came as temperatures gratifyingly yet only relatively cooled into the evening. However, as Al Sharqi sits astride the River Tigris, that was when the mosquitoes and the sand flies came out to gnaw at you. And then, wildfire rumour had it that in the dark blood-starved camel spiders as large as your hand could scuttle out, working in pairs to anaesthetise your skin before chomping away at your flesh. We waited in vain for this to actually happen to any of us though, and provide something eventful to talk about.

We used solar shower bags to wash ourselves. They were filled from the shipping containers of bottled water we had delivered to us every week and left out in the sun to heat up. Shrieking like a little girl when the shower bags dribbled scalding water over your salt-filmed, sunburnt-raw skin was considered poor form.

Common sense, or a glimmer of attention to the welfare of troops, might have dictated that a cross section of the different Army-ration menus was distributed across the British Army in Iraq. However, in an inspired piece of logistical genius, 7 RHA had instead been allocated nothing but Menu 'F' individual ration packs for the entire peace-enforcement phase of operations. Your daily diet therefore consisted of:

'Breakfast': Corned Beef Hash (a stodgy mush).
'Main Meal': Pork Casserole (a squitty mush).
'Evening Meal': Treacle Pudding (it is physically impossible to eat this).

And so it came to pass that the contents of food parcels from home were torn apart as wolves would descend upon manna from heaven, or they were used by the abstemious as currency for smokes or porn.

Mud cracked as temperatures climbed, and the regiment's sole thermometer burst under the pressure. Its death reading was 54 degrees centigrade. This wasn't so good for sleeping but was excellent for sunbathing and making your own chocolate biscuits. As you cooked in the sun, you had only to leave a bar of chocolate beside you for a minute and then you could squeeze the resulting sludge onto the standard 'Biscuits Brown' contained in every ratpack. Eating these biscuits had the added constipatory advantage of granting you perhaps five or ten seconds' warning and grace during the diarrhoea and vomiting 'craze' that soon swept through the ranks of 7 RHA, a plague no doubt helped on its way by the morale-boosting visits to the condemned toilet block.

Among the patrolling duties was setting up vehicle checkpoints (VCPs) on the road to Baghdad. The twist was that we'd be doing them in conjunction with what the officer briefing my section described as 'the upper hierarchy of the local populace'. As our section leader and therefore the voicepiece of our section, Mac voiced all of our reactions to this by staring at the officer as blankly as the rest of us. It kind of made sense though, whoever this local militia was. We'd be pulled out of this area in six weeks and had to hand over to someone. So it might as well just be anyone.

The threats to watch out for on patrol were briefed to us as the odd embittered Ba'athist who might have a pop or elements of the Badr Corps seeking to infiltrate back into Iraq from Iran. We were told the Badr Corps was an Iranian-backed paramilitary organisation manned by former Iraqi Army deserters, dissidents and refugees. We were informed that Iran was trying to expand its sphere of influence and interfere in Iraq, so these people were not to be trusted.

'Yes, Lance Corporal Wood, they are anti-Ba'athist Iraqis, but they might also be Iranian agents. No more questions? No . . . Good.'

So 'the upper hierarchy of the local populace' joined us at the VCPs. There weren't many of them, but they brought suspiciously new and well-maintained Kalashnikov assault rifles, and though you couldn't put your finger on why, you felt sure they had been militarily trained. It wasn't just how they handled their shiny new weapons; it was in their posture and demeanour too – you just knew.

While languishing in the sun one afternoon on a deathly quiet VCP, one tapped the para wings on my arm. Then he pointed at his own chest, before tapping my wings and pointing at his chest again.

'Ah, OK,' I smiled and nodded to him. I guessed he was trying to tell me he was a paratrooper too.

When, though? Now? And who with?

He patted his chest with his hand, saying, 'Hamed.' That was his name I supposed.

I patted my chest in return. 'Jake.'

We smiled at each other and shook hands, and then he took a pack of red Marlboros out of a pocket and offered me one. I only smoked in bars back home but suddenly found the offer of a cigarette incredibly welcome. He lit mine before his and I nodded in thanks.

It was a comfortable enough silence; we didn't speak each other's language after all. But then I remembered the Arabic phrase card I had been given. I fished it out of my webbing and started looking for something vaguely intelligent to say to him. Hamed was looking quizzically at me, so I showed him what I was looking at.

'Ah!' he grinned. The few rows of words on the card were separated into three columns: the English phrase, phonetic pronunciation of its Arabic counterpart and finally how it read in Arabic. He ran his finger down the card as I held it, both of us collaborating to find a way we could have some kind of meaningful dialogue.

'*Laish!*' Hamed suddenly said triumphantly, tapping at the word 'Why?' on the card. But then he trailed off, vainly looking for the next word to add to it.

'*Laish* . . .' he continued.

I nodded in encouragement.

'Amreecan.'

'American?'

He nodded and then grimaced in thought before holding his palm out horizontally and making stabbing motions at the ground with it.

'Attack? Yeah, OK,' I nodded back.

Here we go.

But then he just pointed at me and said, 'Inglezi.'

'English?' It took me a second to piece it together. 'Why do the Americans bomb the English?' I said, before laughing in surprise at him. 'I don't know, you tell me, Hamed!' I shrugged my shoulders at him, smiling.

He raised his eyebrows heavenwards in exaggerated sympathy.

We puffed away on our cigarettes. The road was quiet today.

'*Laish* . . .' he piped up again.

'Yes?' I nodded.

'Faransa . . .'

'No . . .' I shook my head in incomprehension.

'Inglezi.' He pointed at me. 'Amreecan.' He pointed at the sky. 'Faransa.' He waved a pointed finger around him, before theatrically shrugging his shoulders.

'Faransa . . . France! Yeah, yeah!' I nodded at him. Yes, after the spats I'd seen at the UN on television before coming out, there certainly weren't any French troops out here.

'*Laish* . . . Faransa . . .' Then Hamed made a wanking sign, before grinning broadly at me.

I almost choked on my cigarette laughing, before clapping my hands once and shrugging my shoulders again. I had felt too much was made about the international 'airborne brotherhood' in paratrooper circles, but I could start to feel a flicker of it miming along with Hamed. I wondered if he'd been to Iran.

I saw a phrase on the card for 'I am from Britain'.

'Aanee min Bireetanya,' I read out.

Hamed nodded to me in encouragement this time.

I saw the word for 'you' (masculine singular): '*Inta* . . .' – I pointed at him, and then pointed east to Iran, just a few kilometres away – '. . . Iran?'

Hamed's expression became fixed. He shrugged his shoulders and shook his head to say he didn't understand. Then he suddenly pointed at his watch and turned round to call over the other militiaman with us for the day, who was standing beside one of our Pinzgauer vehicles. And then Hamed walked off.

He was met halfway there by his replacement, and they exchanged a few words before the new militiaman took his place beside me.

The road was still silent.

'*Salaam alaykum. Ismi* Jake,' I ventured.

The man just looked at me. Then he nodded, barely perceptibly, and turned away to stare fixedly down the deserted desert road.

We watched our backs if ever the militiamen were behind us. We didn't know them from Adam.

*

We set up a VCP further down the road from the militia one day. In two hours of searching vehicles they had let through, we found two pistols, two AK-47 assault rifles and a disassembled 'Dushka' anti-aircraft machine gun.

But we learned to make a show of cooperating together; after all, they shared real food with us in big communal breakfasts at the VCPs: huge great freshly baked flatbreads, tubs of hummus and vats of finely chopped, dressed salad. Aluminium bags of treacle pudding offered in return were politely declined.

I sat in the front of the Pinz's cab with Mac one morning after another shared breakfast and wondered aloud to him if any of the militiamen were Badr Corps.

'They're all fucking Badr, Jake,' he said quietly.

Mac handed me a fag. I had recently taken up regular smoking and he was feeding my habit. We sat smoking in silence with our feet up in the front seats of the Pinz, letting our breakfast go down, watching the militiamen waving every single vehicle through the VCP.

We would take over the running of the VCPs when we got too pissed off watching this. We politely asked drivers in our rehearsed pigeon-Arabic phrases to please vacate the vehicle while we searched it. We did not make exceptions for the shrouded women. We frisked the men, but we knew enough not to touch the womenfolk they had with them, or even to try to speak to them directly. We confiscated any weaponry we found. The British psyche usually finds it hard to accept a genuine reason why one would routinely need to carry an automatic assault rifle on a run into town.

One day I levelled my SA80 at a driver who followed Mac as he walked away with his confiscated AK-47. I didn't care what his fucking problem was; he wasn't touching Mac. I shouted '*Wagguf!*' at the man to stop, and he stared wide-eyed down the barrel of my weapon before retreating back to his car, slamming the door behind him, beating the steering wheel, screaming at us in rage. I couldn't hope to understand the tirade; I might have heard the phrase 'Ali Baba' levelled at us but couldn't be sure. He drove past us with a rictus grin of pure, black hate, and H laughed at him.

'Ali Baba' was the term we used with the Iraqis when asking after looters and bandits, now that locals were telling our officers that we weren't the only ones taking people's private property at the side of the road. With the Iraqi Army and police disbanded, a few squaddies were now the only law in the vacuum of an imploding country. We presided over this anarchy of our own making.

So perhaps it was not surprising that some of the vehicles didn't want to stop. But they thought better of it when our rifles were suddenly pointed at them. Sometimes, though, the reason turned out to be that the vehicle was in such a state that, judging by the amount of time it took the driver to restart it, it had obviously taken him numerous prayers and a sizeable portion of the day to get it started in the first place. On other occasions, the reason turned out to be under a seat or in the boot.

One afternoon back in the barracks, I was in the ops room making another fruitless check on the post for a reply from Cecilia. The bored lance corporal on radio stag there was lounging almost horizontally in a plastic chair, listening to the hiss of static.

'Check out the pick-up round the back, mate. Militia shot a bloke who didn't stop at one of their VCPs . . . well gory!' he said, before opening his mouth in a massive grin, tongue protruding.

I thanked him for the information and, as bored as he was, wandered round the back of the ops room. A white Toyota was parked outside with two gunshot holes through its windscreen. The driver's brains were spattered onto the headrest. His blood had flowed and caked dark into the light-brown velour covering the seat. I wondered if he'd thought Ali Babas were stopping him. But then I picked my way back to the block to swelter, debating whether to mix Tabasco or curry powder into my pork casserole that night.

*

The days drifted endlessly by. Sometimes we wouldn't do VCPs, though. Sometimes we'd patrol on foot round Al Sharqi and hand out pens and wind-up radios to the local schools.

Or we might drive out to far-flung villages clinging to life along the banks of the Tigris. We left our weapons and body armour under guard at the vehicles as we offloaded aid to the villagers, humping and dumping sacks of grain as we went to work on hearts and minds.

Sometimes the elders looked bemused, asking us why we were giving them all this food. But they would always thank us by inviting us into one of their carpeted front rooms, where we'd sit down cross-legged and drink their powerful sweet tea. The captain would speak to the head elder through an interpreter, while the rest of us would just grin at each other like idiots or nod sagely at the conversation we weren't part of.

It was when you walked blinking into the sunshine afterwards that you were mobbed by the kids. They just thought you were fucking great, jumping up and down to have their photo taken with you on your digital camera. Their eyes lit up and they shrieked with joy when you showed them the picture.

They looked thinner than the children in the towns, and the fathers looked leaner and more sun-beaten than their urban counterparts. Probably just a damn hard life they led out here. The mothers were nowhere to be seen.

When we left, the smallest boys and girls would run after our vehicles. We threw them our spare water bottles and food out of care and pity, and their pitiful little voices called out 'Shukran! Shukran!' as we left them behind. 'Thank you! 'Thank you!': the little words calling up to us caught me off guard once and I had to turn away to swallow the lump in my throat.

*

Late on another afternoon, in between guard shifts, I had been ambling away from a dual weights and sunbathing session when I saw a lad called Timmy up ahead, sitting on his own outside our accommodation block.

I didn't know Timmy that well, only by name really. He looked about 19. But he was in another section, so we didn't get to mix much. Ultimately, I didn't really know anyone that well.

As I got closer, I saw Timmy had just come back in from being out on the ground. He had pulled himself up to sit on the four-foot-high veranda running alongside our blockhouse. His helmet, webbing, body armour and rifle were dumped without care in a pile beside him. His shirt clung to him, soaked with sweat. His feet dangled over the ground. His right hand held a cigarette to his mouth, while his left held his face, cast down at the ground, and occasionally massaged his short, fair hair.

Timmy didn't look all right.

'You all right, Timmy? Been out on a patrol?'

He glanced up and gave me a half smile before looking down at the ground again. 'No. QRF.'

I hauled myself up beside him. 'Anything interesting?'

He looked away from me, hiding the side of his face with his hand. His heels started tapping against the veranda wall. Flies buzzed round the soles of his boots. Then his whole body went taut for a second before his legs went limp again, back to dangling over the ground, like a child's would in a high chair. The flies made a beeline straight back to his soles.

'Sorry, Timmy – are you all right?' I put a hand gently on his shoulder, and the touch seemed to sink his body down.

'I don't know how to deal with this,' he said softly, slowly shaking his head, still looking away from me.

I didn't know what to say. Not there, not then. 'What's happened, mate?'

The hand holding his cigarette started shaking, and then, without so much as a sob, I saw a single tear fall from through the fingers holding his face. It fell past the flies and landed, dark, in the pale, parched dirt. The dark spot was sucked away and evaporated before the next could join it.

He took a deep breath and it all came out in one exhalation.

'Two little girls picked something up in the desert and it went off and we got called out and I've just been picking up pieces of little girl and putting them in the back of their parents' pick-up.'

'Jesus Christ, Timmy.'

'Sorry.' He reeled away from me, rolling upright to walk quickly into his section's room.

His kit was still left outside. I picked it up and set it quietly down inside the doorway to his section's silent room. I could see Timmy curled up in the foetal position on his cot, silent, motionless and face down under his mosquito net. His section commander trod softly up to me. He gave me a thumbs up and whispered into my ear. 'Cheers, Jake, I'll take it from here.'

Soldiers know better than to go climbing over burned-out tanks lying out in the desert. Apart from the rumours as to what depleted uranium can do to you, you don't know what else is lying around there, waiting to explode.

But little girls do not know this.

I heard Timmy was bussed down to the medical facility at Al Amarah. I never saw him again.

*

There was going to be a platoon-level patrol to a town called Al Gharbi, north of Al Sharqi, on the way up to Baghdad. We had been there three weeks before, handing out newspapers, and had been well received – the townspeople just asked our officers if we could do something about the power cut that had hit them at the start of the war. In turn, they were asked to be patient; power would be brought back online. The stumbling block of thieves bringing down pylons to steal the copper wire in the power lines was also apparently explained to them.

But increasingly inflamed complaints about the lack of electricity had been travelling down the road to us, the officer told us in our pre-patrol brief. It wasn't just TV they were missing: as summer came closer and temperatures climbed, their mud-brick houses absorbed the heat of the day. They wanted their air conditioning back online, and they were looking to us for solutions.

We drove past charred Iraqi T-54 tanks on the way into Al Gharbi. I thought of Timmy and the dead children.

In town, we parked our three Pinzgauers near some open ground in the main square. In the deep-green and pleasant pastured land that was now England in my head, this area would have been a watered green bordered by flowers, or would have had a fountain trickling gently away, flanked by oak benches. Or maybe there would just be a war memorial crying for attention. But we parked up beside pools of stagnant neon-green slime, bordered by brown dirt scattered with unidentifiable rubbish.

We all debussed, checking our immediate area before taking positions around our vehicles. A crowd of young men and boys gathered about 50 metres opposite us as we went about our business. None of them were smiling in welcome, not like last time.

More than fifty men had gathered before from out of the gaggle emerged two elders wearing black and white checked keffiyeh headscarves. They walked straight up to the lead vehicle and began what looked like a fairly earnest discussion with our captain. The rest of us faced outwards, standing beside our vehicles, fingers on the safety catches of our rifles. The silent crowd looked at us and we could feel the underlying tension simmering through them. Down by the last vehicle, I stole a couple of quick glances at the exchange I couldn't hear. The interpreter looked like he was caught between two sides, struggling to keep up with whatever the elders looked determined to say.

The captain's voice flickered over our personal role radios (PRRs). 'OK, saddle up. I've told him all we can do is pass it on.'

The roar of our engines firing up suddenly cut through the hush. We all clambered back onto the Pinzs, legs dangling over the open sides, as the elders stalked back to the crowd.

'Everyone on?' Mac called down from the front seat, and our section's Pinz began to edge forwards, bringing up the rear.

H was sat beside me. And as our Pinz was about to trundle past the crowd, he brought up his right hand to wave the standard British Army, beret-wearing, non-threatening, cuddly hearts-and-minds wave that had become de rigueur out here now.

It was at that point that I saw a boy, no more than eight or nine, reach down, pick a stone off the ground and hurl it furiously straight back at him.

'Woah!' H called out in shock. The stone bounced off his body armour.

Emboldened by their friend, two other boys reached down and followed suit. One stone clattered round the inside of our vehicle and the third banged into the vehicle commander's window up front.

'What the fuck?!' bellowed Mac.

But as quickly as it had started, one of the elders rushed forward and smacked the stone from a fourth boy's hand. Everyone with a stone dropped his hand then.

Our driver eased on the accelerator, and the crowd stood motionless as they disappeared into the dust cloud thrown up behind us.

'For fuck's sake!' spat Mac. 'It's their lot bringing down the fucking pylons! What the fuck do they want us to do about it?'

But not long after, we got a tip-off about exactly when and where some thieves were going to bring down some power lines.

We carefully lay up in ambush behind a sand berm facing the targeted pylons that night, watching and waiting in dark silence. Zero Hour came and went, and when all that happened was a couple of bursts of automatic gunfire mysteriously lobbed over at us from Al Gharbi, we decided to up sticks and retire for the night.

It was only a few more days after that tip-off that we got another one. The word was that sitting out in the desert in a half-submerged shipping container were some WMDs. This was news indeed – which 7 RHA was tasked to act upon.

So we set ourselves out in wasteground desert a few hundred metres from the main road in a huge circle of perimeter security all round a rusty red shipping container sticking out of the sand.

'Don't let any locals inside the cordon,' the briefing officer had said. 'Fuck any off that get too close. And none of you goes any nearer that container than where you're put, too,' he added. 'We haven't got a clue what's inside that thing.'

So we sat rooted to our allocated spots in the desert, waiting for a chopper full of God knows who to come in and look at a container full of God knows what.

We waited for two hours on the jagged, rocky ground, searing under the sun, tapping our respirator pouches, replacing sweat with tepid water, swatting flies and smoking. And then we waited for two more.

Eventually, the buzz of an incoming chopper set off a ripple of cheers round our circle. It roared over our heads before sandblasting us as it slowed to hover and set down inside our perimeter, in between the container and my side of the circle. I glanced behind but couldn't see who got out.

But after about the time it took someone to get out of a helicopter, walk 50 metres to a container, look inside and then walk back to a helicopter, the engines wound back up to full power, and whoever it was left us alone in the desert again.

It turned out the container was completely empty, so 7 RHA went back to its barracks again and back to the repetitive grind of 'peace enforcement' that filled each day of our lives there.

So it was with a kind of drained elation that one evening in mid-May we were told we would be going home in a week. The elation was also somewhat cautious. Unfortunately soldiers soon learn that the phrase 'planned with military precision' often contains an inherent contradiction. And what elation there was was also tempered by the news that neither we nor any other unit would be getting a welcome home parade in the streets, as they had been deemed 'unnecessary' and 'inappropriate'.

I felt the acid churn inside me when I heard that. What of Timmy, an old man at 19, picking up bloody pieces of little girl? The boy went off and did his bit in good faith, just like he was told. What was he supposed to be now – a fucking embarrassment?

And then I felt like the TA soldier again, shoehorned into the Regular Army. My mood darkened, but I kept it to myself. I could feel the jaws of my previous existence stretching open around me, waiting to snap shut and swallow me back down into its stale guts. While my Reg comrades got ready to go back to another life that they shared with each other, I felt the beckoning of a solitary return to a previous life that now seemed so far away and so long ago. Maybe Cecilia would not be there waiting for me after all; all I had in reply to my letter was . . . nothing.

No one was going to relieve us at Al Sharqi; we were just going to leave it to the locals. So in preparation to abandon the barracks, we were ordered to whitewash every wall in our sleeping quarters that our officers could see squaddie graffiti scrawled across. But it did not occur to them that the most profane and depraved slogans would be branded onto the low internal walls of the guard towers – they never did guard duty, after all. These walls had formed a plastered canvas for all the bored bitterness and vitriol that any resentful or petulant soldier could muster. They jeered in sacrilege at things that would fill Allah's followers with jihadist wrath – if they happened to go up there, if they happened to read English.

The long shifts in the guard towers were spent on your own. Each lingering minute was spent staring at your appointed arcs of fire or occasionally yelling '*Imshi!*' ('Go away!') at men and boys alike who sometimes stopped to stare into the barracks from the raised road running directly beside us. We didn't want to get 'dicked' by anyone gathering information to drop mortars on ours heads while we slept at night. The men would *imshi* off straight away, but unfortunately some of the kids soon began to regard it as a form of sport. The motivation of bringing the light of liberation to some of them had begun to wear thin at times.

When you were on guard, everyone else in the barracks was relying on you for their immediate protection. During the day, getting distracted throwing boiled sweets down to kids while an insurgent rocket-propelled grenade (RPG) team might be setting up to fire on you was not top of the job description.

They gathered under your tower during the day in groups and took it in turns to call out 'Mister! Mister!' or, ingratiatingly, 'Good, Mister, good!' Acknowledging them, or even responding to the pleading of their upturned hands and cocked heads, just encouraged more of the same, but then in greater numbers and at even higher decibels.

These town kids weren't starving; in fact, some of them were just plain fat. Having seen what their fathers stuffed themselves with at the VCPs, I coveted what they ate, for Christ's sake. And I'd seen they had running water, albeit from the street, while our reality was pulling bottles of sun-heated water out of the oven of a metal shipping container.

But they probably saw us as fresh from the West, where for all they imagined milk and honey ran flowing into lakes. And our reality was that some day soon we would go back to that land of plenty. So I wasn't kind to be cruel; I didn't throw them bags of pork casserole. And I didn't throw them treacle pudding either, which wasn't 'haram' but certainly wouldn't have won any hearts or minds.

After two hours of incessant mewling and catcalling from below, swatting away equally incessant flies while sweating into gritty, stinking body armour in fifty degree centigrade heat, you began to welcome the thought of an enemy RPG team to shoot at. And when the kids didn't get your warm bottle of water, which was all that warded off heat exhaustion, or the treasured bag of welded-together jelly babies your mother had recently sent you from some place called England, they parroted newly learned English back at us: 'Mister, Mister! Fuck off, Mister!' This would then be the cue to run back and forth looking over our wall.

The kids had it worked out: the British troops were captive audiences in their guard towers. And though the British troops probably fantasised about it, they couldn't shoot you just because you were being an annoying little shit.

Some guys whacked off in the guard towers to keep awake in the small hours. You learned to be careful where you initially sat or touched when taking over in the dark. I couldn't bring myself to do it there, if only because I was aware that every open-air guard tower had telescopic night vision. Being the subject of such squaddie TV didn't appeal, but caution was obviously increasingly being thrown to the wind, as one of the standard precautionary greetings from your relief as he paused halfway up the ladder to you became: 'Are you wanking?'

Apart from the condemned loos, there was nowhere private to whack off, and if my crotch ever tightened on guard duty at night with wandering thoughts of Cecilia, my lust was soon tempered by my meandering mental shots in the dark as to why she had never written back.

Night after night, I stared at the same dark-green dogs sniffing around the same patch of flat, featureless, light-green desert. Sometimes one animal would catch the scent of another snuffling near it. Sometimes they might hump each other. The animals just shagged what was to hand. And then they'd mindlessly trot back to the same piece of dirt they were sniffing round before, scratching out their everyday existence in the here and now.

It wasn't to be. I tried to ignore the grey tinges of doubt creeping into the black and white certainty of my purpose out here. And going home . . . it would be good to see my family and friends again, but I could feel my chest tighten in apprehension at the thought of returning to the ordinary. Life in Iraq wasn't perfect – my love life certainly left something to be desired. But with all its discomforts and deprivations, the day-to-day living still felt a damn sight more immediate and meaningful in its stark simplicity than back in the easy comfort and obscurity within the guts of the Bank.

I felt I had come here in good faith and joined a fraternity with a purity and clarity of common purpose. We had watched each other's backs with one finger on the trigger as our feet walked through an ancient land, as we played at being benevolent gods. I convinced myself that the reports of a rising guerrilla campaign were of an overthrown minority who had everything to lose and that they did not represent the Iraqi people, who now had everything to gain. I denied my doubts and the vacuum we were now going to leave behind us. I wanted it all to have meant something.

I felt like this technicoloured war through Eden had taken my soul. And I didn't know how in hell I was now supposed to feel enlivened about being spat back into the pale grey for the rest of my days, day after day.

And why didn't she write back.

*

There were no cheering crowds to see us on our way when we left Al Sharqi. Through the window of my Land Rover I saw a militiaman outside our gates, AK-47 in hand, and one young boy standing beside him.

We drove in file past them. And they stared at us in silence.

2

HOME

And happiness is thought to depend on leisure; for we are busy that we may have leisure, and we make war that we may live in peace.

Aristotle

I reject your reality, and substitute my own.

Adam Savage, *MythBusters* presenter

The train clattered out of the darkness under the River Thames, bringing sunshine bursting into my eyes. I blinked to adjust to the bright summer morning invading the carriage; the rays glared round the still heads of the crowd packed inside, pressed shoulder to shoulder and back to back in total silence. All warm bodies against warming bodies in a humid, impersonal mass.

No one looked at anyone else. Some busied themselves with texting on mobile phones; some stared dispassionately at the floor. Some stared disconsolately at the floor. Others appeared to have found a piece of middle distance they could lose themselves in, just beyond the close presences rammed around them.

I leaned against my window, looking outside at the grey blur of the siding, with the stale, warm breath of a stranger on my neck.

The train braked harshly for a stop, and the unwary were thrown forward in unison, clenching onto handrails, flailing for personal space in the hot press. Then there was the automated health-and-safety electronic screech of warning that doors were opening. The crowd gathered outside my window on the platform stared miserably in at the crush on the train. No one got off, so no one got on.

I savoured the few seconds of stillness. Cool, clean air wafted in from outside. Then the train shrieked that the doors were closing and announced its onward journey by throwing everyone backwards in a synchronised jolt.

Sweat soaked through the pressed white shirt of the man next to me. I could see his eyes shut tightly, creasing his brow; he looked like he would rather be anywhere else than where he was now.

It had been four weeks since I had flown back from Iraq, but I was still enjoying the novelty of the brush of clean, laundered material against clean, washed skin. Despite the heat in the train I was not sweating, but I also felt different to the others. I felt detached. As much as I probably looked to be taking in my surroundings more than anyone else on this train, I could not feel anything in common with the white-shirted man stood wedged beside me. I looked dispassionately at him, his eyes clenched as tight as his white-knuckled fist on the grease-filmed handrail above us. His face was lined and pale, with silver flecking prematurely at his temples. I tried to reconnect with how his worries were now mine: the commute, the office, the meetings, the deadlines, the snatched evenings and the too, too short weekends to all but live for.

The train lurched to one side and he opened his eyes in irritation, and then opened them wide in alarm when he saw my face staring at his, inches away. He turned his head away in panic and busied himself with the floor.

I would have conspiratorially winked at him. As it was, I just tried desperately to stop my ribcage shaking against his in stifled laughter. I probably looked like the loony no one wanted to risk making eye contact with on public transport. Best restrict myself to surreptitious glances in the future, I thought, and I looked out of the window again as the train swung sharply round a bend to show our destination soaring out of the ground.

Towers of glass glinted in the sunshine. The central Canary Wharf tower jutted highest of all: eight hundred feet of blue-grey glass and steel. Eight hundred feet – exactly the height from which the Army used to kick me out of aeroplanes.

A passenger plane was on final approach to land at City airport. It looked like it was on a collision course with the tower, flying straight as an arrow towards the waist of the building. But instead of a 9/11-type impact and a ball of flame the plane just disappeared from view, as if swallowed by the glass giant. And then, mundanely, it emerged from the other side, continuing the descent of its human cargo into the city's beating heart.

I remembered sitting at my desk and seeing the planes flying so close a pilot would only have to bank the aircraft off course for a few seconds to collide with us. I imagined being at my desk as it hit: a split second of sensory overload as metal, kerosene and flesh smashed through glass, concrete and flesh. A split second of shock and primeval terror turning your bowels into liquid as a wall of flame and debris screamed forward to consume you. And then nothing.

I did not think like this before.

Covetous regulations by the Canary Wharf estate decreed that no other tower in the area could be higher, and my eyes swung down slightly to my bank, and my final destination. I saw the proud structure, the banking behemoth, but with a quickening in my stomach I only felt: Cecilia. I was just minutes from walking into the same building as her now.

Sweat glazed my palms as the train pulled into Canary Wharf station, and after a final scream of warning from the train, I was released from its clutches into the gush of humanity scurrying and barging past slower objects to get to their desks on time.

Footfalls of hundreds of heels echoed around me, hurriedly carrying me out of the station and back into the sunlight. Out of memory, I set a course for the Bank among the currents of people. I took the time to glance around in the pleasant, open warmth, finally free to breathe the air after the suffocation of the train.

The crowd around me surged forward, heads down, and I drifted along with the suited throng into the sun, my destination darkly silhouetted ahead, slowly filling more and more of the sky.

Closer, the Bank's outline loomed larger, like a leviathan rising out of the depths, until the air suddenly darkened and cooled around me. The Bank had blotted out the sun and stood revealed in its shadow.

Mammon towered above me, and I pulled up stock-still with a sudden, massive sense of unease. The crowd parted and spilled past me in waves.

This was it. Over the tops of bobbing heads I could see the gateway back into my old life yawning open. Back to the same, the ordinary, the mundane. Back to where Iraq was just a forgotten memory on TV screens. Back to where I would now be completely, and utterly, alone.

The revolving door chopped around angrily up ahead, sucking the crowd into its jaws to swallow them inside. I wanted to push back and swim away and fight the inevitable.

The inevitable. I joined the crowd filtering inside; what the hell else was I going to do?

It was like going through an airlock into a parallel universe. The bustling warmth of the outside world evaporated in an instant. The cavernous foyer was cool and filled with a sterile hush. Footsteps fell muffled on the dark stone floor. Polished black-glass walls reflected orange-bronzed receptionists and plasma screens scrolling up-to-the-minute stock-market updates. I walked past silent, gliding escalators and then up to a chrome turnstile that I pressed my nameless photo ID against, allowing me final access into the building's guts.

A small crowd waited blank-faced for a lift, and I joined them, fighting down the panic thumping out of my chest and soaking my hands with sweat. A quiet chime announced the doors opening, and we filed orderly on board.

The lift did not make a sound as it smoothly accelerated upwards. Mirrored walls reflected its silent cargo back in on itself.

Another quiet chime: my floor; and then one last security door to press my ID against.

I sat alone at the desk. The tinted windows drowned out the sun, which was replaced by the harsh glare of halogen strip lights. A vent pumped dry recycled air onto my face from the grey-panelled ceiling above me. I could hear the click of sensors automatically switching the air conditioning unit off and on into and out of life. I could sense its artificial whir sucking the life out of the day.

There was nothing else to hear across the large, open floor apart from the barely audible electric hum of a sea of computers around me, accompanied by the muffled clacks of pointed fingers tapping away assiduously at their keyboard interfaces. No one talked. I thought of Cecilia, just one floor away from me now.

The email from Human Resources had told me that in an act of corporate rationalisation my old team and its responsibilities had been redistributed around the company while I was away. So I had reported to the tenth floor of the Bank like it told me to and now sat at a desk my new department head had showed me, among 12 new colleagues to whom my succinct, superficial introductions were now over.

I was now a 'System Analyst' for the 'Exec-Horizon' team. I sat on the far left of a grey laminated shared bank of desks, with five of my new colleagues sitting to my right. There was a black panel, just shorter than the height of our flatscreen monitors, running along the length of our workspace. And, as if a mirror had been rested on the black partitioning wall, six more of my new team sat facing us, cloned on a cloned bank of light-grey laminated desks. Our department head sat behind me at her own separate desk, presiding over one of the floor's prestigious corners with a photocopier and a plastic pot plant for company.

Someone who knew I was coming back today had put a dark-grey name sign on top of my grey monitor. On its face was a fake brushed-brass plaque on which black letters had been printed. 'Jake Wood', it read. My Army dog tags had more personality.

I lifted myself a few inches out of the black ergonomic chair and stole a furtive look over the one sign of my identity here, just as I used to peep over the sand berms, careful to stay unseen. I didn't want people thinking I was weird or something.

A sea of monitors stretched out before me across the open-plan floor, each one with an identical name sign on top of it, like the marking of a grave. In long shot, the tops of my co-workers' heads were just visible. Closer in: eyes here, a face there. Some sad eyes and worn, grey faces, all locked numbly to white screens. I saw a petrified forest of co-workers gazing blindly back at me.

I sat back down. I noticed my charcoal-grey suit was the same shade as the charcoal-grey carpet, and I had the sudden sensation that my legs were taking root, being sucked down and assimilated, blending and fading into the grey, humming background that was the Bank's foreground.

This was it: petrified to my spot in the Bank for the long, uniform working hours of my life to tick by to the bitter end. The waves of panic reached back up from my guts to clutch at my chest, and I had to breathe deep to fight them down, bury them back down safe inside.

I stared numbly into my white, glowing screen, and then clicked on email. Five months of internal corporate spam stared back at me.

Sifting through the 668 emails, I soon felt that a hundred-odd too many were sent to the entire multinational corporation on behalf of some demigod by their PA. They announced in a suspiciously similar fashion how we were to join Whoever in warmly welcoming Somebody Else from Some Other Bank to 'the Team'.

What team? My team consisted of 12 men and a female department head sitting alongside me in total silence. Where was my email? Why should I care what over-inflated individual had joined a division of the Bank I wasn't part of, and at a pay grade so beyond most mortals' imaginations that even if they did sit loftily over me and everyone else on this floor in a hierarchy somewhere they'd have no earthly reason to have anything to do with us anyway?

Of course a gold-laden handshake for a fat cat gets a global email. And of course I shouldn't expect anything from anyone here: a welcome back, a welcome home. Along with everyone else who reads these emails in the Bank, I am a no one. And where I have just come back from counts for nothing.

I sat in silence alongside my silent colleagues. As I saw it, I had two options.

Get a complimentary coffee from the vending machine and swallow the caffeine down with the bile as I finished reading the emails from management connecting with the troops. Then just double click on my first work assignment and complete the Bank's digestion of me.

Or I could just run and fuck all of this off and go outside and buy 20 Marlboro Lights and smoke in the sun and try to think of what the hell I was going to do.

But it was at this point that she sat down beside me.

'Hello.'

I didn't recognise her at first. Her hair was tied back from a face more tanned than I remembered. But then I saw her eyes. Jesus Christ, those eyes. They shone as sky blue and bright as the day outside.

Cecilia.

I floundered through the seconds, dumbstruck. The girl of my fantasies in Iraq was now sitting right beside me. She was like a ray of light cutting into the grey around me, bringing colour streaming back into my life.

Her small, slightly upturned and perfectly formed nose wrinkled slightly as she beamed a wide, perfect-white smile of recognition.

'Welcome back.'

'Hello . . . Thank you,' I finally blurted.

'Good to be home?'

'Um, yeah. Yeah! Good to see you.'

Her smile widened a fraction just as her eyes narrowed imperceptibly.

'I'm Caroline's PA,' she said, motioning over to my department head's now empty desk behind us.

'Oh, right.'

'I look after new starters too – you're sort of one again now, aren't you? So here's a little present for you.'

She put a name sign in my hand. It was made out of dark-grey plastic and had 'Jake Wood' printed onto a fake brushed-brass front.

'Ooh, thank you,' I smiled back at her. I could still feel the brush of her fingertips lingering in my palm.

For a couple of long seconds, we locked eyes in the quiet, and we ignored the carbon-copy name sign staring down at us from my monitor.

'OK, mental busy at the moment,' she said suddenly, louder.

Then she leaned forward and, hiding the action in the fluid motion of getting up from the chair, quickly squeezed my wrist as it rested in my lap.

'Good to have you back,' she whispered. And then she walked away to the lifts, back to her floor one above mine.

And that was that.

Or I guessed it could have been, until I sent her an email asking her if she wanted to go for that drink.

*

We walked together up City Road, wending our way through suits evacuating offices at the end of their day. Up ahead, the old stone battlements of the HAC gates nestled inharmoniously among the modern glass-fronted buildings, like a gateway to another world.

I pointed my unit out to Cecilia. Then I winked at her. 'Don't worry, I'm not taking you for a drink in a barracks!'

'I should think not too!' she said, before arching an eyebrow. 'Is that where you keep your uniforms, though?' Her eyes widened in mock innocence.

'Some of them . . . I've got a couple at home too.' I returned the wide-eyed look of innocence.

I turned my back on the HAC to lead her down Worship Street. We were going to The Prophet.

I swung the glass door of the bar open for her, and the clean, perfumed scent of her filled my nostrils as she walked in front of me. My eyes travelled helplessly down the long chestnut hair flowing over her close-fitting white blouse, down the perfect curve of her waist, over her hips and lingered on the shape of tight female buttocks moving under a tight black skirt.

The Prophet was playing a laid-back funky tune softly in the background – Groove Armada, I thought. The music chimed with the dark wooden floorboards, exposed brickwork and deep distressed-leather sofas, completing the effect of a Shoreditch-trendy bar stuck too far into City territory for its own liking.

I ordered her a vodka, lime and lemonade at the bar, as requested, and a pint of strong continental lager for myself, and then we made our way to one of the low tables set beside the full-length windows overlooking Worship Street.

Cecilia sank into a sofa as I set the drinks down, then I sat on the chair opposite. As soon as I did so I chided myself for not sitting beside her. I still felt myself in awe of her.

Get a grip, Jake.

I was about to say 'cheers' when she leaned forward and asked the question.

'So – what was it like?' Her eyes were shining, bright and expectant.

I'd had this question a few times since getting back, and it was one I was finding increasingly difficult to answer. I had learned to say 'hot', which covered some of it and was a concept people could relate to. Sweating into a Nuclear Biological Chemical (NBC) suit during a gas alert while in fear of your life, however, was something they could not relate to, and was therefore something I felt was as pointless as it was uncomfortable to go into.

'Hot.'

Of course, by giving a one-word answer most people got the point that, for whatever reason, I wasn't in fact going to wax lyrical for their benefit with a sweeping narrative set among desert dunes, studded with gems of exciting stories from a strange and distant land.

Looking at Cecilia's crestfallen face, I realised that just saying 'hot' was the equivalent of saying 'fuck off'. I didn't want Cecilia to fuck off – what else was she meant to ask?

'Sorry, I don't mean to be rude; it's still just a little weird being back. You know that Coldplay song "Clocks"? They kept on playing it on the radio before we invaded. I can't listen to it now without the hairs on the back of my neck sticking up.'

There. I was sharing.

Cecilia nodded. 'Was it dangerous?' she asked quietly. The question felt loaded with expectation.

I shrugged my shoulders. 'It could have been, I guess. It turned out pretty quiet for my team, though. The closest I came to getting shot was by my own side.' I savoured a long draught of my beer.

'Really? What happened?'

I paused to think of what had actually happened. I'd pushed it out of my mind. 'Well, maybe you heard from Carl that I was doing reconnaissance?'

She nodded, and then shook her head. 'Yeah . . . I don't really know what that is though.'

'It basically involved creeping round the desert in a small team, and lying up from time to time to report back on what we could see. There were only five of us, so we had our own little routine, which seemed to work quite well. The thing was, though, because there were only five of us, towards the end of the war we were getting bloody knackered.

'Anyway,' I carried on, recollecting the events as I recounted them, 'we laid up in an OP one night . . .'

'What's that mean?'

'We stopped to have a look around. I went on stag – that means on shift – and towards the end of it I could see something moving on radar . . .'

'You had radar?'

'Yeah – a little one; it was a bit ropey sometimes, though. It kept telling me a tracked vehicle was moving around in this tight circle about a K out. Well, this could have been the radar having one of its fits, or it might have been of interest – and not just because we were five blokes on our own in the Iraqi desert. So, anyway, I woke Pete up as it was his turn to go on stag, and when he sat down beside me I briefed him and then told him I was going over to that sand berm – bank – over there to get a better look through night vision at whatever it was, or whatever in actual fact it probably wasn't.'

'So what was it?'

'Nothing, I reckon. I couldn't see anything. So I'm walking back to Pete to give him the night vision back, and it's a really dark, cloudy night, and I'm about 20 metres away from him when he suddenly swings round and points his gat – rifle – at me. He says "halt", but it's in this really panicky whisper, and I can hear him trying to get a better grip of his rifle as he points it at me and goes down on one knee into a firing position. And it's at that point that I realise that he must have been half asleep when I did the handover to him, and now he has suddenly woken up on his own in the Iraqi desert in the middle of a war with a dark figure carrying a weapon coming towards him from out of nowhere.'

I took another swig of beer.

'So what happened?'

'Oh, well, nothing; we just ended up having this sort of farcical stand-off where both of us realised that we had no idea what the password was. And then we both realised that our team didn't in actual fact have a password, so he kept on saying "halt", and all I could do was put my arms out to my side in a crucifix and whisper "it's Jake" in as loud a whisper as possible and just hope he didn't shoot me.'

Cecilia was staring wide-eyed at me.

'It's all right, he didn't shoot me!' I grinned at her.

She shook her head. 'Well, I hope he said sorry!'

'No! I never blamed him. We never talked of it again actually – but we thought it was a good idea to get a password system going in the morning.'

Cecilia shook her head ponderously this time, taking slow sips from her drink, keeping her eyes fixed on me. Her gaze seemed to bore into me, probing, questioning. And I did not like how now, from the safety of a London bar, I could feel the prickly sensation of mortality creeping up my spine. Only Pete would ever know how close I'd come.

And it was then, of course, that the opening piano riff of 'Clocks' poured out across the bar.

'Wow! How freaky is that!' Cecilia exclaimed. Her beautiful, smiling eyes opened even larger in surprise.

But the piano chords drilled into me, dragging me away. I clamped my knees together under the table as my hands clenched together in my lap. I looked down, cursing the coincidence inside.

Then the words, washing over me . . .

The lights go out and I can't be saved
Tides that I tried to swim against
Have brought me down upon my knees
Oh I beg, I beg and plead, singing . . .

I was back on the Iraqi border again, right back at the beginning, watching the distant fires burning with the colonel's words echoing round my head. My mind flew through the war and into the Garden of Eden, soaring across the scorching sands into Al Sharqi. Promise and wonder, fear and excitement, confusion and doubt: all mixed up in one bombardment. I felt lightheaded with thoughts of the invasion and suddenly felt thankful I had a table between me and Cecilia that I could try to hide my turmoil behind.

Come out of things unsaid
Shoot an apple off my head and a

Trouble that can't be named
Tigers waiting to be tamed . . .

I was dimly aware she was now watching me intently, and I felt my bowed face flush as I struggled to surface, back to where she was, back to where I wanted to be.

Confusion that never stops
Closing walls and the ticking clocks gonna
Come back and take you home
I could not stop, that you now know, singing . . .'

But now I am sitting in the blackness of the back of the Rover as we drive in the pitch of night, every light off, still further beyond the front line to our next OP. And the sudden *bang*, and gut-wrenched in a split second of terror I am being thrown across the cab like a rag doll, with no idea if we have hit a rock or a mine, or if something very, very bad has blasted into us and I am now in the last second of my life.

'Are you all right?'

I forced myself back up to her, pressing my heels into the floor to stop the tremors in my thighs.

'Sorry, yeah, OK – fine.' I nodded blankly. I took a gulp of beer.

'Did you ever have to . . . hurt anyone?'

Come out upon my seas
Curse missed opportunities am I
A part of the cure
Or am I part of the disease . . .

'Not that I know of . . . Not directly at least, anyway.'

'What do you mean?'

And nothing else compares
And nothing else compares . . .

'I don't know if there was anyone in the tanks we spotted. We just spotted dug-in tanks and then the paras went out and put missiles into them. I don't know if there was anyone inside them.'

'Oh, right.'

You are
You are . . .

'I'll bring in some photos tomorrow. They'll say a few more words than I'm managing now.'

'Yeah, I'd like that . . . Nothing too gory I hope, though.'

'No, there's only one photo with a dead body in and that's a way off, don't worry.'

'Urrghh!' Cecilia scrunched her little nose in squeamishness.

Home, home, where I wanted to go

Home, home, where I wanted to go . . .

The song was fading, melting into another chill-out track I did not know the name of. My hands unfurled as I felt myself open up to her again. I took in her perfect features: the soft, unblemished skin, the long hair caressing the sides of her nymph-like face, the delicate hands with their perfectly manicured nails stroking the long glass. Her perfume filled my senses again, and I recognised it now as the same scent that was on her letter to me. I looked into her wide, ocean-blue eyes for a few seconds before choosing my moment.

'Your letter meant a great deal to me out there, Lia.'

'No problem,' she smiled. 'I found out your address from Jill. Carl was sending little updates on you round the office after speaking with your mum.'

'Yeah, I know. I need to say hello to him. He been his usual self?'

She said that he had indeed been his usual buoyant self. And this update on my work friend came as no surprise. But as the conversation turned to other employees, and then finally to those few gods of the Bank I only knew vaguely by name, the rumours of the buoyancy of their bonuses hit me with shock.

'Jesus,' I breathed out. 'What about everyone else in the Bank? Or just in general . . . I mean . . . Don't you think that's a bit . . . obscene?'

'No. If they've been making the Bank money then they deserve it.'

'Yeah . . . Well, I guess . . . I've just been hanging out with blokes who've been putting their lives on the line for 50 quid a day, that's all.'

Cecilia's mouth hung open. 'They get paid that?'

'And less. You know that fire strike just before the war? I think perhaps the Army had enough to do at that time, but they had soldiers scooting round on sixty-year-old fire engines doing the job of firemen who wanted 30 K a year to do a four-day week!'

Cecilia shook her head.

'So you were on 50 pounds a day when you were out there?'

'No, the Army paid me my bank wage. I kept quiet about it out there, though. I didn't think it would help another lance corporal if he knew I was getting paid the same as a major. It probably wouldn't have helped me either, for that matter. You probably know how much I get paid, though, don't you?'

Cecilia leaned back into the leather sofa, holding the straw of her drink to her lips, and just smiled as she winked at me again.

Later, around eleven o'clock, I stood beside her in Liverpool Street station. She had said Jill, her team leader, was whipping her ass at the moment so she needed an early start at the office tomorrow. The large departures screen announced her train was leaving in three minutes. So our goodbye would have to be snatched, and a moment far too hurried than in any of my long, lingering fantasies of her through long months in a faraway land.

My heart beat hard and fast as I faced her, and I imagined she heard it betraying me: nerves fluttering taut, like a schoolboy leaning in, tentatively trying for his first kiss with his first love. My lips moved slowly towards hers, hovering millimetres away, savouring the moment of connection. But then she turned her head, just a fraction, allowing me to kiss her cheek instead. I pulled my head back slightly and she squeezed my hand.

'Got to go – remember those photos tomorrow.'

And then she was gone.

*

I made a point of being in at nine the next morning, but she was already away from her desk when I went up to her floor to give her the photos.

Jill was there, though. She welcomed me back home to the office before suggesting leaving the photos on Cecilia's desk, ready to look at when she came back from a morning meeting with one of her managers.

I thanked her with one word, casting my eyes from her desk to Cecilia's as I tried to avoid any further conversation that would lead to the inevitable 'so what was it like?' question. I laid the photos on the grey laminated workspace, taking the chance to furtively glance over it as one would a forbidden inner sanctum. But I was disappointed; the only sign of her personality was the uniformly grey name sign sitting on top of her monitor.

It was as I was turning to leave that I immediately locked eyes with a man sitting at a parallel bank of desks. Corporate-short dark hair speckled with grey sat atop a strong-featured face with piercing green eyes. His eyes bored into me before suddenly flicking down to the monitor in front of him.

Back at my desk, I pulled from my pocket the other item I had brought in from home. It was a 'Matt' cartoon my mother had cut from the *Daily Telegraph*. In reference to some apparent banking woes I hadn't had the slightest interest in while I was away and the Army covering for the striking Fire Service, it showed a row of desks at an investment bank, their occupants' heads in hands, while a file of soldiers ran uniformly in behind to occupy the office. At the forefront of the scene, a pinstriped boss gesticulated to another. 'Things got so bad we had to call in the Army,' the caption read.

I Blu-tacked the cartoon to the side of my monitor. This was the sign of my personality here. Said it all, I thought.

I busied myself with reading background documentation on 'Exec-Horizon' for most of the morning. But by half eleven my mind was beginning to bend under the sheer tedium of 'the key tool used by our senior client-facing executives to record and share information relating to our strategy and plans for each client and our relationship activities'.

I resisted the urge to beat my Iraq-tanned forehead on my keyboard and thought I'd go to find Carl instead. I looked up my friend from our former team on the company database, found his floor and then slipped away from my desk. Nobody seemed to notice.

After a few minutes of wandering around an equally silent carbon copy of my floor, I found him. His bored eyes lit up as I approached him.

'Jake!'

'All right, Carl. How you doing?' I grinned back at him.

Carl made a face while gesticulating at his surroundings, and I laughed as I plonked myself down in the empty chair beside him.

'Good to be back . . . ?' He smiled mischievously.

'Oh, yeah, it's fucking kicking here.'

One of Carl's new colleagues glanced up in horror at me and I made a point of ignoring him.

Carl nodded, regarding me for a moment, before continuing more quietly. 'You're looking well, mate. War obviously agrees with you.'

I grimaced a little. 'Wouldn't get too hung up on that word, Carl – it was pretty quiet really.'

Carl raised his eyebrows and flicked his eyes from side to side round the office meaningfully.

'Well, maybe not in comparison,' I ventured.

'Your mum said you requested a transfer to a more front-line unit when you were out there.'

'Yeah, I was looking at being stuck in front of a radio at an HQ. So I just thought bugger that and started pointing out to people I was OP and para-trained – I got the move the day before we invaded.'

'You mad fucker . . .' Carl shook his head, smiling at me.

'Life's for the living.' I shrugged my shoulders, returning the smile.

Carl nodded silently before continuing. 'She's very proud of you, Jake.'

I could only nod back. I was also aware of the stress I had put her through.

And I was aware, too, that Carl was an avid gamer and therefore I imagined his only frame of reference in addition to the sensationalist news bulletins were equally sensational computer games like *Medal of Honor*. My real-life experiences had been somewhat different.

Change tack.

I leaned forward, speaking more quietly to him. 'Cecilia wrote to me out there saying she liked me. She got my address off Jill.'

'Woah!' he exclaimed in appreciation, before stopping for thought and wincing slightly. 'When was that, Jake?'

'Early April.'

'Right . . .' He nodded slowly, leaning forward too so no one else could hear. 'You might want to be careful there.'

'OK . . .'

'There's a few rumours flying round about her and someone else in the office.'

The words hit like hammer blows.

'Who?'

'You'll have spoken to him before, when we were on call for trade support – James Blake?'

I nodded. I remembered a voice on a phone.

'His team works beside hers . . .'

'Green eyes, grey-black hair?'

Carl looked taken aback with the sudden curt details, before nodding at me.

I fell silent as I began putting two and two together. And maybe all these shots in the dark even added up to four. But what did I really know? I knew jack shit.

'Look, we're having some drinks tonight at Bar 38. Come along, I'll buy you all the pints you've been missing out on.' His voice sounded concerned.

'Sounds good, thanks – I'll see if I can hold on that long.' I turned my face back up to his.

'Good stuff. There's a meal coming up soon with the Back Office boys too; they'll be pleased to see you again. I'll send you the email.'

'OK, cool. Yeah, I'll be along for that too,' I answered numbly.

'Awesome, mate.' Carl winked, before adding in a hush: 'Fuck her.'
Hope springs eternal.

*

I went outside to chain-smoke three cigarettes before buying a sandwich to munch silently in a square not far from the Bank. I sat on one of the polished stone benches facing the gushing water fountains and tried to enjoy the sunshine and my hour's break from the office, like all the other ants congregated around me. But I could not. I thought of what was, what had been promised, what might be and what might have been. I chain-smoked another two cigarettes before forcing myself back to my desk.

Vending-machine coffee in hand, I saw Cecilia had returned the photos when I went to sit down. There was a Post-it note stuck to the envelope on which she had written the word: 'Interesting'.

I guessed 'interesting' was the most these photos could ever be to someone who had not been there. I opened the envelope and felt myself being drawn into the world of these photos again, losing track of the minutes as I relived each snapshot in time: the lit oil well spewing fire high into the sky; an incinerated Iraqi tank my team had designated to be killed; Iraqi prisoners burying their dead; our OP in Bible-ancient marshlands; me smiling beside a sullen Hamed.

And as I remembered the burning heat of the oil fires on my face and the acrid smell of the burned-out tanks in my nose, I also remembered the solid feel of the rifle's pistol grip and handguard, sweaty but sure in my hands. My rifle had never left my side. It was power, protection and purpose. I felt stripped bare when I had to hand it in. I fought to keep the memories real; it was all a world away from the real world I now found myself back in. Back there – that was my real world. I missed it.

I was broken from my reverie by a hand suddenly patting one of my shoulders from behind. My head darted to one side to take in the unexpected threat.

'Smoke?'

It was Asef, my new team leader. Obviously he could smell the lunchtime chain-smoking on me and now wanted to have a quiet word about knuckling down at work. And, clearly of Arabic origin, he had also caught me looking through photos of my tour in Iraq instead of staring studiously into my monitor.

Nice one, Jake.

'Yeah, sure,' I said, guiltily stuffing the pictures back in their envelope. He must have seen them.

We didn't talk on our way outside, not until he offered me one of his red Marlboros on the pavement across from the Bank. I lit his before mine, wondering how the bollocking would begin.

'You've just come back from Iraq?'

'Yeah.'

Don't ask me what it was like . . .

Asef just nodded, and he did not ask the question.

'You did a good job out there. Welcome back.'

He offered his hand to me and I shook it in surprise, thanking him. He must have meant 'you' in the plural sense.

'I'm from Jordan,' he continued, before taking a puff on his cigarette, adding emphasis to his next words. 'Saddam was a motherfucker and he got what was coming to him. They just got to catch him now his sons are dead.'

These were not the first words I expected from my new team leader. A grey face seen from inside my bubble was suddenly morphing into a real person. At five foot ten, Asef's dark eyes were level with mine, and I saw how my suntanned skin was only a shade browner than his natural colour. He had a lean, muscular build that mirrored my frame, but I put him at forty, ten years older than me. Together with his tailored black suit, rough designer stubble, shining gold Rolex and coarse language, to me he looked for all the world like a gangster on the make. And it looked like I wasn't going to get a bollocking, after all.

'Can't say I disagree,' I said, raising my eyebrows.

'And don't let anyone fucking disagree with you. They don't know fucking anything. You didn't see any Iraqis protesting against the war here because every one of them here had to run for their lives from that cunt. I mean, fuck, what all those protestors don't get is that if they'd tried pulling that shit under Saddam they'd have had poison gas dumped on them. Fucking wankers, it makes me nuts what they take for granted. They can just go home and pat themselves on the back – and all about something they know fucking nothing about. All they know is what the telly tells them, and I mean really know – like you do now.' He threw his cigarette butt on the ground and stamped on it, angrily twisting his heel into it to kill it.

I couldn't disagree; I would be the worst of hypocrites to disagree. And if my new team leader wouldn't be gunning for me as I sat through an indefinite period of not giving a damn about what drudgery stared at me from my computer, then that was fine with me.

Asef asked me what I'd done in Iraq and I skipped over the outline, keeping the details sparse. When I described the cheering crowds at the war's end, though, he nodded vehemently in agreement.

'You see?' he said in triumph.

I did not mention how I felt the liberation turn sour. I did not want to think of it.

*

Back at my desk, chest tight and head light from two too many cigarettes, I clicked on an email sent from Caroline while Asef and I had been out smoking. 'Team drinks tonight at the Cat and Canary,' it said. And Cecilia was on the mailing list.

I squeezed in an after-work session at the gym before going along, so the evening was in full swing when I approached the gaggle of co-workers drinking on the waterside terrace. Caroline was the only woman I could see, and she was in deep conversation with Asef. The other ten or so blokes were huddled in an inward-facing clump beside them. No Cecilia.

A guy whose name I was pretty sure was Rick saw me coming and raised a full pint of beer over his head. 'Jake! Welcome . . .'

Rick put the glass in my hand and moved to one side so I could be part of the group. And when he did so, I saw what they were all congregating around.

There was Cecilia, right there in the middle, holding court as she commanded the attention of all around her: one bubbly, unobtainably sexy girl in a pack of suited, slavering blokes.

'Nice of you to make it.' She smiled sweetly at me.

Everyone shut up and all eyes turned to me.

'Well, you know – bit of a workout.' I didn't know what the hell else to say.

'Mmm . . . I guess you're excused then.'

Cecilia gave me a smile and then seamlessly went back to goodnaturedly teasing two men about how 'only nerds work in IT'. And I drank as Rick asked me how I was settling into the new team, drinking in all Cecilia's beauty from the corner of my eye.

Within half an hour, the group began to thin out, people giving excuses to drunk, protesting colleagues of waiting wives, girlfriends and babies. And as more went inside to bring more rounds of drinks outside, I noticed how Cecilia was slowly gravitating round the group, place by place, towards me.

It was as I was feigning interest in a group discussion about a more technical feature of the Exec-Horizon application that I felt her foot gently push down on mine.

I gave her a warm smile. It was returned. And with that, I suddenly found myself asking her if she wanted to come with me to Carl's drinks at Bar 38.

'Yeah, let's blow this joint,' she said immediately. 'I'm meeting people there anyway.'

The two of us made our way across the footbridge to the bars on the opposite side of the water.

Carl and the rest of my old team were sitting outside Bar 38, with another group of men sitting at a second table pulled up to theirs. Several pitchers of beer and Pimm's were dotted across the tabletops, and Carl banged a chair he had reserved beside him in exaggerated impatience as we approached.

'Ah, Lord Lucan, I presume!' he called out to drunken cheers from Daryl, Hans and Andy.

'Honoured to make your acquaintance.' I nodded to them, before going over to another table to get a chair for Cecilia.

When I turned to bring it back, however, I saw her making her way to another chair reserved among the group of men on the other table. The chair was beside James Blake. He was patting it, smiling up at her. When she sat down close beside him his eyes narrowed at me.

I put the unwanted chair to one side and sat down alone at my place. Hans sloshed Pimm's into the empty pint glass in front of me. 'Get this down you, war hero!'

Only Carl noticed the look in my eyes. He gave me a soft wink.

'How you doing, Jake? Get any good kills?' Daryl chirped at me, eyes glazed.

I winced at the question and could only look at him.

'Woah! Killer stare!' Hans looked at me expectantly.

'It wasn't like that,' was all I could say.

'Yeah, right – whatever!' Daryl carried on, before giving a confidential nod to the other table. 'Tell us later then.'

I didn't have the energy to put them right. I knew they didn't mean any harm.

Timmy, sobbing into the dust.

I wondered where he was now.

And now, here, I watched Cecilia and James Blake sitting together, chatting and laughing. And I watched all the unspoken body language between them. And I saw how all this body language reeked of chemistry. And I saw how his teammates never raised an eyebrow to any of this body language – as if this chemistry was the most natural thing in the world.

I drank.

It was about ten when I saw her stand up to leave.

'Sure you don't want to stay, Cecilia . . . ?' I caught him say. I didn't know whether he meant here at the bar, or somewhere else.

'Yeah, need an early night tonight, Jamie.' She touched him once on the shoulder and then walked across to my table.

'Night night, boys – make sure you get some beauty sleep!' she said, standing directly behind me.

There were various catcalls around our table about who needed it more than the other. I didn't say anything. Then she patted my shoulders with both hands and walked off alone across the footbridge.

James's green eyes were staring through me. I stared back at him and his face cracked into a smile. 'Nice to finally meet you face to face, Jake-mate,' he called across the table, leaning back into his chair.

Jake-mate? I had to lean forward to hear him properly.

'Yeah, and you – mate.'

'I must say, you're really not how I imagined, though.'

'Oh, yeah? How was that?'

'Well, after all those late-night conversations we had about messaging gateways and suchlike, I just assumed you'd be . . . well, a geek.'

I just nodded at him. I wanted to punch the geek team leader very hard in his face.

'Heard you've been away playing at soldiers anyway – welcome back to the real world.'

Bottled-up wartime aggression coursed through beer-lubricated veins. I wondered how far his goggly eyes would pop out with my knee in his back, garrotting the purpling life out of him with the strap of his metrosexual man-bag.

He raised his glass to me and I just managed to mirror the action with mine before gulping my feelings down with some of its contents.

He didn't complete the toast, though. Instead, he placed his drink on the table and smoothly rejoined the conversation beside him, ignoring me. I took his gesture to be as empty as the untouched glass in front of him was full.

I carried on drinking with my old teammates. I downed the rest of my glass in one and poured myself another from a pitcher.

Drink and make it all go away. Fuck her and him and fuck it all.

It was when I set my glass down after downing another beer in three gulps that I saw the girl.

She was smiling across at me from another table. So I smiled back at her. She raised her glass to me and drank a little; still keeping her eyes on mine, still smiling. Then her eyes motioned to the empty chair beside her.

They were all still there at closing time when I walked off with her. I turned to Carl and the rest of the old team to wish them goodnight, and Daryl and Hans nodded appreciatively at the back of the girl walking ahead of me. James just looked at me, though, one index finger held up to the side of his face.

You may wonder why I took this girl to my bed. I can only tell you that I wanted to be wanted, and that after months away I just wanted to feel another's naked flesh against mine that night, in the same base needs that we all share. But as you know, a drunken fuck with someone you have only known for two hours will only deliver so much, and you will also know that this was not the female welcome I had dreamed of in the desert. And therefore, in the small hours, when I still could not sleep, it may not surprise you that I wished the girl beside me was Cecilia.

*

When I got into the office the next morning, the first email I read was from James. He said it had been so nice to finally meet me. And he congratulated me on pulling such a 'stunner', though he said he and his team were having a debate as to how old she was . . . 'About 19?'

Fuck off.

The second email was from Cecilia. She said she'd heard I'd pulled a '19-year-old stunner'. And she too congratulated me.

Fuck . . .

I stared at the emails and felt the rest of my world cave in. I didn't believe it had been 'so nice' for James to meet me. And there were no prizes for guessing who had told Cecilia of my dalliance with the girl last night. What hurt all the more, though, was that I had just handed him the knife and then backed onto it.

It was only five minutes later when Cecilia came down to see Caroline with some papers. She breezed straight past me without any acknowledgement.

When she walked past again to leave I went after her, catching up with her round the coffee machine.

'Cecilia . . .'

'What?' She cut me off.

'I . . .'

'Don't worry about it – good for you.' Her mouth was smiling, but her eyes were not. Then, with a little shake of her head, she turned her back on me once more, and she was gone.

I retreated back to my chair and slumped into it, anonymous and broken. I had managed to fuck things up with Cecilia before they even began. And I had no one to blame but myself.

*

July dragged by into August, and August drifted into September. Efficient and anhedonic, I carried out my allotted tasks mechanically. I became one of the worn grey faces, sad eyes locked numbly to a white screen for the allotted time each passing day.

I went along to the Back Office meal Carl mentioned and sat silent, smoking, as the evening degenerated around me into a heated argument about which team should be responsible for overseeing which piece of system infrastructure. At one point, Carl turned his plate to me, showing me cherry-red sauce smeared over the white porcelain, and leered to me about how it looked 'like brains'.

I did indeed think it looked like brains. I thought it looked exactly like the brains I had seen shot over the car seat in Iraq.

I couldn't eat any more after that. I cocooned myself and let the argument drift over me, dissipating into the air like the smoke from my cigarettes. I thought of how I just did not care about the office power playing and politics now, and how the only thing that had changed back home was me.

Before the invasion, the HAC had provided a foil to any boredom I felt in the office. I could leave it all behind in a weekend's escape of tabbing (slogging and running) with a heavy bergan over the hills, or sitting in a covert OP, pissing into a bag, reporting unseen on Land Rovers driving by with names of Russian-made tanks fixed to their sides. But this now felt empty and make-believe – because that was exactly what it was. I was not in the desert where everything you did *mattered*, where everything was *real*.

Some soldiers I shared OPs with would ask me about Iraq. But some of them said they would resign from the HAC rather than get called up to go out there, as they valued their civilian jobs too highly. So I did not talk to those soldiers about Iraq, as I felt they did not deserve to know.

The only time I felt alive was when we did a weekend of live firing under the new training captain, Max, who had just been posted to the HAC from the regular SAS. Before pairs of us went down the valley contact lane for live fire and manoeuvre, he gave us a pep talk about how he wanted to see real aggression, as if we were doing it for real.

'And I don't want to see any of you fuckers running back with both hands on your weapon and it pointing up in the air, useless, like some health and safety prick's taught you,' he finished. 'You run back with it in one hand ready to slot someone – and you pump the other in a fist ready to drop any fucker who comes out at you.'

Then he told us to take our body armour off as it was fucking useless and wouldn't stop a 5.56 round without the ballistic plates. If he couldn't have people shooting at us then this might concentrate our minds as our partner's rounds zipped past us. He gave us a grin, and I saw some soldiers go white at the instruction.

I immediately liked him.

After each pair went through, Max debriefed them: 'Good, but . . .' or, 'Get those fucking rounds on target. They'll just keep firing at you if they see you're missing them . . .'

After I went through with a guy called Dave, though, Max was a little different.

'Good initial double tap from the lead man.' He nodded to me. 'And spot on with calling "contact front" while getting rounds down – there's no point advertising to the enemy if you're not killing him at the same time. Good mag changes on the move, good communication, good use of cover, good spatial awareness, good aggression. And I know all your rounds were on target because every target fell when hit . . . Well done.'

We nodded back, all grins and still breathless from the sprinting.

'OK, get yourselves away to the pistols.'

I was about to jog after Dave when Max touched my arm to hold me back. 'That was Premier League, mate,' he said. 'You been on tour?' he continued, eyes flicking to the para wings on my shoulder.

'Yeah, Telic 1.'

'Who were you with?'

'7 RHA.'

He nodded, pausing to regard me. 'Keep your ear to the ground if you want to go away again – I'm putting something together . . .'

*

I went to a welcome home dinner the HAC put on for the six of us who went to Iraq on Telic 1. Significant others were also invited. I did not have a girlfriend, or a wife, so I took my mum along, as I thought she deserved a thank you for bringing me into this world, and for sitting through weeks of not knowing if her firstborn son would be coming back home to her in a box.

I knew some of the HAC soldiers there had done nothing more than sit in front of a radio or a desk and drink tea in the rear. I had nothing against them, but I noticed how they did not talk to me in front of their family members, as if I would sully their shine on this day – their day. I wanted to talk to them, soldier to soldier with the same campaign medal, and tell them I too had seen nothing. But I did not want to tarnish my mother's glow as she deservingly basked in the attentions of the officers around her. So I kept it to myself.

The first time I admitted my solitude was to a woman I had never met before, in the downstairs of just another Canary Wharf bar.

I was staring at a closed door when she asked me why I was so quiet. So I told her straight in one sentence that I had come back from Iraq and felt alone and that I had now lost a girl I never had. And she told me how I'd get over it and how she understood – she'd got over her divorce, after all.

'I told him if he had a problem with the hours I put in at work then that was his problem. He couldn't accept me for what I am, and if my career has to come first then he should . . .'

I stopped listening. It was only when I noticed an absence of background noise that I looked at her again.

'What's your problem?'

'I told you.'

'Oh, just get over it!' she snorted, and walked off.

I wanted to get over it. I was dead to Cecilia and so I tried to make her dead to me. I stared, fixed, into my screen when she passed by. I did not want to feel her ambivalence, or contempt, because I felt that I deserved it. But the pain of the missed opportunity did not go away.

*

'So aren't you speaking to me now, then?'

Cecilia was standing stock-still in front of me, blocking my way to the bar.

I was stunned. 'Yeah – I mean, I thought that was it between us.'

Her tone softened. 'Well . . . we weren't going out.'

'I thought you had a boyfriend too, Cecilia.'

She looked taken aback. 'Well, I don't know where you got that from.' Then she softened again, shaking her head. 'No, I haven't got a boyfriend.'

And for the rest of this night, the bar around us, and the Bank and all the rest of this world, will go away. Because this night, Cecilia and I kiss. And this night, we are finally together within this embrace.

But, of course, a kiss is just a kiss, even if it does seem to last the whole night.

And there will be ensuing evenings, and weekend afternoons, when we begin to gently push past the boundaries of just kissing. And sometimes I will think that we are taking things very slow, even that I am being cautiously held at arm's length. But though it is always unsaid, I will always know that it was I who fucked up with her, even if it had been with a girl I wished had been her. And so now I do all the waiting I feel she requires of me, because I now cannot help but want only her.

When I turned 30, just before I first met her before going to Iraq, I went with a group of friends to Amsterdam. The phrase 'when in Rome . . .' was bandied about a lot, and though I had misgivings, I soon agreed to let them spend some money on me in one of the myriad of legalised brothels there. My friends paid for two porn-star-stunning blonde prostitutes to spend a double session with me. I had never even been with one before, and after the double session I resolved that I would never go with one – or two – again. I had felt like a piece of meat on a slab: cold, and clinically dissected as they remotely manipulated me.

I mean – it was like they were only doing it for the money.

I could not regret it, though, for it was after all another life-experience box ticked. But the only satisfaction I gleaned from it was the personal realisation that for me, now, making love to one person would always be more fulfilling than having sex with one – or two. And for that I could only feel thankful.

Now, I only wanted to make love to Cecilia. And if I had to wait for when she was ready, then I would wait.

*

I was drinking with Carl and the rest of my old team in Bar 38 when I felt my phone vibrating with an incoming text message.

It was from her.

'Where are you?' was all it said.

Maybe tonight . . .

'Bar 38 – want to meet up?' I replied.

After about 20 minutes with no reply I tried calling her. I stepped to one side of our group and had to put a finger to my other ear to block out the noise of the Friday-night Halloween revellers around me. It rang out.

I gave it another ten minutes before deciding to try again. Maybe she couldn't hear her phone in the din of another bar.

I pushed my way outside the bar, through the jostle of horned braying suits, past leering masks of ghouls, witches and demons. The pandemonium suddenly cut off when the door of the bar shut behind me. I felt like I'd made an escape, breathing easy again in the clean air outside.

Then I saw them.

Cecilia was walking left to right about ten metres in front of me. She had an arm round the waist of a man. And this man had an arm around her waist.

It was James.

I heard the words come out of my mouth. 'You're not answering your phone, Cecilia.'

They both glanced in my direction, but they kept walking.

I felt anger ripple through me, coursing down my arms into my hands. 'I said you're not answering your phone, Cecilia!' Louder, walking towards them.

James looked fully towards me, confused and then alarmed by my approach. He unhooked his arm from around Cecilia and stopped, letting her walk a few more paces alone before she turned to face me. I made sure to keep him in my peripheral vision as I confronted her.

'What's this?' I gestured at the two of them. 'What's going on?' I demanded.

'What do you want me to say?'

'What?'

'What do you want me to say?' she repeated.

I felt the anger rising.

'Is that it? Is that all you can say . . . ? What about us starting to see one another?'

'We're not, though . . . Oh, I can't deal with this.'

The words smashed into me with their rejection. Rage dissolved into shock. My whole body shook. She turned her back on me and walked away.

'What's going on?'

The voice was somewhere behind me. Close, far – I couldn't register.

James appeared beside me and I looked to his face; he wasn't angry. I couldn't stop the shaking. I didn't care if he saw it.

I couldn't think of the words.

'What's the deal with you and her?' he continued.

'Nothing now . . . I mean, I have no . . . fucking . . . idea.'

James looked at me. I was now shaking uncontrollably, my words coming out in fits and starts as my childhood stammer suddenly reappeared, clamping my vocal cords.

'We've been out a few times . . . I thought we were starting to see each other. She let me think that at least.'

I could feel something breaking in my mind. The world was narrowing to James beside me and the shaking through my body.

'Are you all right, mate?' He ran his hand down my arm, concern in his voice.

I had to look away. 'No. I am really not all right.'

I looked to his face again and he gave me a nod. Then he walked off in the same direction Cecilia had disappeared in.

I lit a cigarette, but it did not calm me. I couldn't face going back home on the DLR; I couldn't face being trapped on the train while trying to hold in the distress I couldn't control.

I walked the three miles back home alone in the dark instead. I kept away from anyone else; I didn't want to see anyone else. Sometimes I heard choked sounds of anguish coming from my throat. Sometimes I felt tears running down my face, blurring the empty dark street ahead of me, my mind reeling as my feet stumbled. Pieces and fragments of past and present whipped through my mind – too many, too much.

The only thing I knew, with absolute clarity, was that all promise of something good had now broken clean away in my head – snapped off and dead.

*

Five days passed. Then she emailed me.

She said she didn't want any bad feelings between us. She said she had never considered us as going out, any more than she had considered herself as going out with James, whom she had apparently just 'bumped into' on Friday night. She wasn't ready for a relationship. And the last thing she wanted to do was hurt me.

That evening, I went into the HAC for just another Wednesday training night. Distant firework displays boomed like artillery barrages as I went through the gates: my gates to another world.

I sat numb in green among the other soldiers, crowded in for a presentation from Max.

He wanted volunteers for Iraq.

After five weeks on the Covert Static Surveillance course, the selected volunteers would spend another two months in intensive training under Max and another SAS soldier, honing our firing and manoeuvring from on foot and in vehicles, during the day and at night. We would also be trained in advanced first aid, Arabic and foreign-weapon handling.

In March 2004 we would deploy to Iraq as the Brigade Surveillance Troop, working directly under Max as the brigade commander's personal surveillance asset.

We would be mobilised seven weeks from now. And as far as our civilian employers were concerned it would be a compulsory call-up, and our jobs would be protected, and they would never know we had volunteered.

My hand went up.

3

PROMISE

Love to his soul gave eyes; he knew things are not as they seem. The dream is his real life; the world around him is the dream.

Michel de Montaigne

The goddess is well aware of me, she who mixes sweet bitterness with life's cares . . . Love is nothing but a frantic desire for what flees from us . . .

Michel de Montaigne on Catullus 68

In the cold of Remembrance Sunday morning, I marched out of the HAC gates within a detachment of fellow soldiers, all uniformly perfect in blue Number One dress.

Identical groups were going to memorials around the city; mine was going to Islington. Traffic ground to walking pace around us as we made our way through the streets, police on motorbikes halting busy junctions so we could march through them. I enjoyed the inconvenience we caused. For just one morning, on one day, I wanted the city to see, and think, and remember.

I was kidding myself, though. Engines roared into life past us in releases of frustration as we right-wheeled into the little green in Islington with its forgotten memorial. And when we stood as still and motionless as the dead names etched into the stone for the two minutes' silence, the background buzz of the city carried on in indifference behind our backs. The drivers blaring their car horns, the revellers hooting and laughing on their way to just another Sunday hair of the dog: they had all forgotten.

The intrusions jarred my silence. I stood still at attention, but my mind was anything but quiet.

When we marched back to the HAC, I felt the juxtaposition, the absurd incongruity of the city stamping its feet in impatience behind a troop of soldiers with one foot in the past. And I felt my limbo, between the light of my escape back to Iraq, in an idealised purity and elevation of purpose streaked with self-destruction, and the dark tumult of anonymity in the dearth of meaning I felt back home, all muddied by the relationship with Cecilia that never was.

Now, I knew the HAC would mobilise me. Now, I knew we had only had to wait until 27 November, when we would learn from the Secretary of State for Defence whether the 27 of us earmarked to go would be given the green light or not. Then, maybe, I could look forward to leaving all this behind.

Fate hadn't finished with me yet, though. That Wednesday I got on the DLR at Canary Wharf to travel in for just another anticipatory training night at the HAC. And in a chance of chances, or just in plain inevitability, Cecilia was there in the same carriage, standing just a few feet away from me.

She didn't appear to have seen me. But by the same measure she didn't look capable of taking in any of her surroundings. Her eyes were cast downward, her face a perfect picture of abject misery. She looked completely alone. I didn't feel anger or satisfaction. I felt pity when I looked at her beautiful, pained face. And I could not help the glimmers of warmth for her breaking out in me. She too looked lost in her own personal limbo. I, though, had an escape opening up from mine, which might very well result in my own destruction, but it beckoned beguilingly all the same – and probably all the more because of it. I'd rather go down fighting Scylla than be sucked down, drowning in the bowels of Charybdis back home.

'Danger gleams like sunshine to a brave man's eyes,' Euripides wrote. When I considered the allure of Iraq, and Cecilia, I knew exactly what he meant. But Euripides, of course, did not think to address the fine line between bravery and stupidity.

And all gleam had now gone from her eyes. So when they looked up to mine at the end of the line in Bank station, it only seemed natural that we should go for a drink together before I went in for training.

I did not mention volunteering for Iraq to her; I did not want to tempt fate to wall that avenue off when I was so tantalisingly close to taking flight through it. She in turn did not apologise for anything, though she expressed 'regret' for my hurt and for my misunderstanding as to where I stood with her.

It was while she spoke, looking at the table, that I found myself being blinded once again by the sheer physical perfection of her. And I found myself reminding myself that it was me who had fucked up first, and in hindsight I acknowledged that Cecilia and I had indeed not been going out.

For all my latent feelings for her, I was aware that Cecilia was now someone I could never have, and now I just wanted out. I hugged her goodbye and left.

But, of course, it would only be that Friday night when fate bumped us into each other again, this time within the depths of just another Canary Wharf bar. And I do not know whether it was the alcohol in my veins freeing all that flowed latent and deep within me, but when our eyes met this time I told her where I was going back to – fate allowing, of course.

But I could not tell her why I was going back any more than I could explain to myself the reasons why I needed to tell her what I did.

She gave no sign of suspecting any of my reasons. And whether her lack of reaction signalled only ambivalence, or possibly the repression of something lying latent inside of her, I had no way of knowing either. But she asked me to let her know when I knew for sure.

I said I would.

And then there was nothing left for me to do but leave, again.

*

I spent the next week away from Canary Wharf on a course learning how to tell computers what to do in a programming language called Java. I would have found it a chore to force myself to pay attention anyway, but as it was I could not take in a single thing. I was aware of the lecturer lecturing us on the clinical interaction of public and private classes, objects, applets and servlets, but nothing more. When he enthused how Java was 'high performance and dynamic', I stared emptily back at him in disagreement.

'The keyword "void" indicates that the main method does not return any value to the caller. If a Java program is to exit with an error code, it must call System.exit() explicitly . . .'

I wanted to call System.exit() explicitly and just walk out of the class. I had now lost all patience with the ordinary as my mind spun in anticipatory excitement at the thought of returning to Iraq. I felt it kicking to be released as I trod water in the present, days dragging by to when I would finally know if I could look forward to submerging myself in the extraordinary again.

And on Thursday, 27 November, I got my answer.

I was sitting at my desk with the morning coffee when I got a text message from my mate Frosty: 'Announcement on the MOD website. Phoned the HAC to confirm – we're going!'

I wanted to punch the air and scream in triumph at the top of my voice and all to hell with disturbing the silent equilibrium of the office. But I went onto the MOD website instead, clicking with one trembling finger on the link announcing an extra tranche of TA soldiers for Iraq: 'These Reservists will be employed in a number of roles: about a third in theatre at any one time will be deployed in the infantry role as force protection, a little under a quarter will provide reinforcement to regular infantry units deployed, about a sixth will be medical personnel and the remainder will provide a variety of specialist capabilities.'

That last part of the sentence sounded like a veiled reference to us. My heart was pounding; I had to phone Max at the HAC to double-check.

'Jesus Christ, will everyone stop phoning me. Yes, we're fucking going!'

I thanked him and put the phone down, just managing to stifle laughing out loud but unable to stop the grin beaming from me. I couldn't remember the last time I'd felt this happy. I closed my eyes and lifted my face to the heavens.

Thank you . . .

When I shone my happiness back to the horizontal, Rick was looking at me like I had a chicken on my head.

'You all right?'

'Oh yes . . .'

'Uh huh . . .' He nodded to me. Such gleaming happiness was clearly out of place within the humdrum of our team. And by the way Rick continued to look at me, the chicken was still evidently perched on my head.

'Sorry, got to go.'

I had to tell someone the news in jubilation before I went through the act of gravely breaking the news to Caroline, so I went upstairs to see Carl.

'But you've only just got back!' he exclaimed. 'How come you're going away again?'

I paused and thought better of mentioning my volunteering to him, just in case word got around.

'Things are going to rat shit out there – they need more blokes . . . And I'm kind of happy with that too. Not everything's been going my way back here.'

Carl nodded. 'With Cecilia, you mean?'

I nodded back.

'Well, who knows what tomorrow will bring, Jake.'

Deep in my gut I felt a flicker of the feelings I had felt in the Garden of Eden.

'Careful how you go now.'

I did not know whether he meant Iraq or Cecilia.

*

Calmer, but with insides still fluttering, I phoned the clerks at the HAC when I got back to my desk. I asked them when I could expect the formal mobilisation orders to arrive in the post so I could inform my employers. They told me the Reserves Mobilisation Centre at Chilwell was posting them to us today, so I should expect them through my letterbox tomorrow or Saturday. Now I could warn off Caroline with confidence.

I found it interesting how her attitude to me seemed to change as I told her the news. Jake Wood no longer seemed to be the System Analyst. It seemed to excite her that Jake Wood the Soldier was now calmly standing in front of her, informing her out of courtesy that she should now imminently expect his departure back to the Army – and back to Iraq.

When would I know? How long would I be gone? What would I be doing out there? Could she have my address so she could write to me? Would I be in the thick of it? It was getting more dangerous out there, she'd heard . . .

I fielded her questions deferentially, pretending not to notice the change in her, from Caroline the Manager to Caroline the Woman.

She finished with one hand holding my forearm, telling me to be careful out there and be sure to come back to 'us' in one piece. She asked me to let her know as soon as I had a leaving date and said we would have a big farewell do separate from the Christmas drinks to see me on my way.

I thanked her, and then Jake Wood the Soldier went back to sit at his desk, wondering how he could possibly now manage to get any system analysis done in the interim.

When I got home from work the next day, a brown envelope with 'On Her Majesty's Service' emblazoned across it was waiting for me on the doormat. I went outside to sit and smoke on the doorstep while reading the letter inside the envelope. In matter-of-fact black and white print it told me that I would be mobilised on 6 January.

I set the letter to one side and took a long drag of my cigarette in the quiet. I held the smoke inside for a couple of seconds before exhaling the swirling white mist back into the cold evening air. I felt certainty as to my purpose now. I felt calm. I felt complete.

I pulled my mobile phone out of my suit pocket and sent Cecilia a text: 'I'm going on the 6th Jan. Take care, Jake.'

I went up to my bedroom and kicked off my leather shoes, before taking off my suit and hanging it with my tie back in the wardrobe. I undid my cufflinks and placed them with the collar inserts back in their suede box. Then I discarded my shirt and underwear and took a shower to wash the Canary Wharf day from me.

Naked and clean back in my bedroom, I pulled the olive-green cargo bag from inside the wardrobe, untouched from where I had left it after coming back from the war. I unpacked the contents onto my bed, reconnecting with the past, sifting through what I would need again for the future.

I set my two sets of desert-camouflaged shirts and trousers to one side, smoothing out the pale sun-bleached material against the blood-red bed sheet. I inspected them for any wear and tear before, satisfied with the results, I stood back to regard them. I would be issued with new combats, but these would be my primary clothing: they had got me through Iraq once, so they would get me through Iraq again.

Then I placed my desert boots on the floor in front of them. They were stained with grime and sweat but were broken in and fitted me perfectly. These too would see me through Iraq once more.

I laid my goggles and shemagh on my combats. These would enable me to see and breathe during dust storms.

I held the black NBC respirator in my hands, remembering the Scud missile strike near us on the first day of the war. It would enable me to see and breathe in the event of an attack involving weapons of mass destruction. I would not need this, so I placed it back in the olive bag.

My para helmet still had the desert cover on it, so it was ready to go. And finally I went through my ops vest, checking through the pockets for the myriad of little items that enable a soldier to function effectively in the field: compass, tied on with para cord; mini Maglite, tied on with para cord and with black tape round its end so only a pinprick of light showed through; spare batteries for torch, PRR radio and night-vision monocle; rifle-cleaning kit; insect repellent; spoon; waterproof notepad and pens; Ortlieb map case . . . and on. Pockets to the left of my torso were left empty for nine SA80 magazines, hand grenades and smoke grenades.

When I next went into the HAC I would prepare my bergan with its own collection of larger items, but now my personal kit at home was ready, I felt ready. I packed it all into a smaller combat daysack, which I placed beside my bedroom door, ready to go.

I had not noticed the incoming text message from Cecilia. 'Are you at home?' was all it said.

'Yes' I tapped back.

The answer came straight away: 'Don't go.'

Don't go where?

I pulled on jeans and a T-shirt and went downstairs to make myself something to eat. It was around eleven when I heard a knock at the door.

It was her.

She looked up at me hesitantly from the dark outside, eyes glistening in the light shining from behind me. And then she said two words.

'I'm sorry.'

She took a faltering step towards me, trying to gauge my reaction, before suddenly pushing forward in one leap of faith to wrap her arms around me.

I hesitated to bring up my arms in return. But then I felt them lifting to hold her tight, one hand slowly reaching up to gently stroke her hair once more.

And there was nothing else I could do but take her into the warmth of my home and close the door on the world.

And this night, we were together at last.

Her head rested on my chest the next morning, listening to my heartbeat in the quiet.

'You've got a strong heart,' she said, eyes lifting up to mine.

'Think I need it at the moment.'

But the warmth of this moment was all I had waited for. Her lips kissed my chest and I forgot the past and the future. And as she fell asleep listening to my heartbeat I drifted away with her, lost in the present and the gentle sound of her breathing.

*

The first thing I did on Monday morning was to give Caroline a copy of the mobilisation letter. She said she would get on to Human Resources immediately and ask Asef to begin redistributing my work around the team. I breathed an internal sigh of relief.

Later that morning an email arrived from her to everyone in my current and past teams – and Cecilia – entitled 'Honoured Guest: Jake Wood – 18 December':

> Dear All,
> You may or may not know that Jake will be taking leave for a while again returning to a distant land to do his duty. He is likely to be away for a few months from the beginning of next year. So . . . and as if we needed another excuse this side of Christmas (?) . . . I suggest we all meet at Bar 38 after work on Thursday the 18th to wish him a safe sojourn and Merry Christmas!
> Caroline

I was as touched by her thought as I was relieved by the formalising of my sojourn abroad. However, she didn't appear to have taken on board that my 'few months' away from the office would stretch to 12.

Caroline was affording me the chance to allow my mind to focus on the future. And as my final days in the office ticked by, still just one floor away from Cecilia, I found myself wanted all the more by the girl of my dreams for slipping further away from her, back to Iraq.

I could only guess at her reasons. But my grandfather had ingrained in me from a very early age to 'never refuse a good offer', as you never knew when the next one would come along. I now had two, in Iraq and Cecilia – and if I could now have my cake and eat it, then I saw no earthly reason to question why it was now being spoon-fed to me.

Cecilia stayed round mine increasingly often. And often we were late for work as our late-night lovemaking was rekindled in the snatched moments we had left together in the mornings.

When we booked a Friday afternoon off work together, I took her into the city for a sunset revolution on the London Eye. I cannot tell you how beautiful she looked high above the dying twilight and the twinkling silhouettes of the London skyline.

When we came to Earth we walked hand in hand along the Thames embankment, through the soft pools of light cast down from iron lamps and the glittering of thousands of white fairy lights hanging in the trees. They stretched promisingly out in front of us in shining lines, illuminating our path ahead together. Beneath the starless dark of the city sky we shared our own close firmament gazing down on us. And when the beauty became too much I had to stop and kiss her, holding her tight in the quiet light.

Before long, we sat high above the lights in the OXO Tower, bathed in candlelight beside a soft reflection of us in the ceiling-high glass overlooking the river. And when I bended a mental knee and asked if she now considered us as going out together, she said yes.

*

I resolved to never tell her my final reasons for volunteering; I did not want to colour our nascent relationship with blame. And I was aware that something could very well happen to me in Iraq, so I wanted to protect her from a possible lifetime of guilt. Whether she suspected she had been the last hair trigger was another matter, but it was something we both chose never to mention.

I did think it was best to manage expectations and make her aware of the timescales involved, though. She nodded slowly and quietly as I explained that during the three and a half months of build-up training before flying out in April, I would have leave and weekends to be with her. And though I would be in Iraq for six months, I would have two weeks' R & R in the middle to come back to her in. And at the end of it all there would be the final two months' post-tour leave – when I came back home for good.

Her voice cracked and the tears came again when I said the final line. She gripped my hand with both of hers and told me to make sure I came back to her. I could only put my arms round her and say yes.

I felt a stab of guilt then, but I wanted to carry on living my dream. And when I spoke of everything on the phone to my friend Jules later, she told me not to beat myself up about it, as I was only being true to myself. She knew me too well, and I knew she was right.

A few days later, though, after a couple of hours of drinking at my Bar 38 leaving do, I went out to the waterside to smoke and gather my thoughts. I stood in the exact spot where I had seen

Cecilia and James walking by with their arms round each other a lifetime ago. I reflected on the sea change of promise that had swept over me since.

But, dwarfed to insignificance at that seminal spot beneath the giant, dark towers of glass, I also found myself reflecting on the dichotomy of my two lives complementing the conundrum of Cecilia's sudden affections. And as I remembered the anger I felt on that dark eve, my thoughts drifted inexorably to the killing aggression I would need to nurture once more for the dusty streets of Iraq: always to be held in reserve, ready to be unleashed at any time, in response to any threat. My frail mortality would depend on it.

I was still staring silently into the black water when I felt Carl beside me.

'You all right?' he said softly.

'Yeah – fine now.'

'OK.'

He was quiet for a few moments before asking the question.

'Are you sure about all this, Jake?'

I knew he meant Iraq. And Cecilia.

I looked to him and managed to sum it all up in a sentence.

'Moth to the flame, Carl.'

'I know.' He nodded, before patting my arm. 'C'mon inside. We've got you a leaving present – and there's another skinful of beers waiting for you.'

*

On the New Year's Eve of 2004, we went to a masked ball. My mask was simple and black, matching my black dinner jacket and tie. Cecilia's was a more glittered affair with a plume of silver feathers, complementing the pretty features of her lower face while highlighting her goddess-like allure. Her eyes flashed behind it.

The two of us chatted happily at the bar with my friend Phil and his girlfriend Sophie, soaking up the buzz of the anonymity with the first drinks of the night.

Even the bar staff were incognito in masks, inscrutably preparing round after round with professional smoothness. We lapped up the cocktails, and before long you only became sure of who you really were in the faceless, laughing crowd, with all personae concealed further beneath the cloak of dimmed lighting. You only knew your nearest and closest by their mask, or what they said; your sworn nemesis could be hiding beside you and you would never suspect a thing until it was too late.

After foraying even deeper into the liquid-induced haze, Cecilia and Sophie spirited away together to the Ladies, leaving Phil and I to carry on talking animatedly beside a dark riverside window.

It was after about a quarter of an hour that I noticed them return. I recognised Cecilia by her mask. I watched her lean across the bar so she could be heard by one of the barman and saw him lean towards her in return. They talked and I saw him taking in Cecilia, watching his mask-framed eyes flick down to her cleavage, which was pushed onto the bar. He ignored the other waiting customers, letting his fellow barmen take their orders. There were smiles and pauses, drawn out in contrast to the excited chattering around them. Then he leaned further into her, putting a hand on her bare arm – and she finished the distance, kissing him on the cheek.

I felt a wound suddenly rip open, and I was feeling and not thinking as I walked straight up to them. A sudden course of aggression and anger channelled through me and I stabbed a finger across the bar at him.

'Get your hands off my girlfriend!'

He sprang back behind the bar from her, eyes wide in alarm as every conversation stopped dead around us and the hush stared in. The barman looked around him for support and another pushed my enemy down the bar, away from me, holding up a placatory hand.

The fist down my side unclenched to a hand, and then I felt it begin to shake like it had on another eve. I clenched it again to stop the tremors, feeling the crowd edge away while looking in at me, breath caught in anticipation of what I might do next. Cecilia was quiet and very still, body shrunken, watching me very carefully.

Get out.

I walked out of the room, escaping downstairs to the foyer and then into the refuge of the Men's room. I pushed the mask up to splash cold water on my face and then looked to the mirror. The galvanised product of my past and my impending future looked back at me: a bubbling concoction of rising aggression as my mind turned back to Iraq, heightened by the combined fuels of insecurity and passion for a girl I now dared to call mine.

But the pull and allure of the inherent danger in both Iraq and Cecilia proved an intoxicating cocktail I could not resist. I breathed deep and let the anger simmer away to numbness before I walked out into the foyer. And I saw her there, waiting quietly for me. She had taken off her mask, and I felt the shame run through me as I saw the sadness on her face.

'Sorry, Lia . . .'

'No.' She cut me off, holding my hand. 'I understand . . . I'm sorry. But I was only wishing him a happy new year. I need you to understand I only want you . . . OK?'

She kissed me once before hugging me tight.

'Thank you,' I whispered. 'I'm sorry, I just don't want to lose you again now I've got you.'

She looked into my eyes, saying her next words deliberately. 'You've got nothing to worry about – I promise.'

'Thank you.'

'Fancy a drink, sexy?' she said, smiling suddenly up against my mouth. 'Maybe that nice barman will give us a couple on the house!'

I burst out loud in laughter and kissed her smiling mouth again, long and deep, before we went hand in hand back to the bar. And we giggled together like naughty schoolchildren as we watched the unwary barman gesture with wary eyes for one of his colleagues to serve the loony and the temptress.

At the stroke of midnight the world disappeared from the two of us, and I felt the exhilaration of one perfect moment of holding the future and new beginnings in my hands, full of purpose and promise – and Cecilia.

I cuddled her cold little body warm in the bed she had christened as ours later that night. And I embraced the realisation, banishing all fears, that I was now holding tight a girl I could perhaps, maybe, dare to love.

But from the back of my mind, as she slept tight up against me, I remembered the words a fusilier had said to me as we mobilised months ago for the invasion. It was my first tour, but his second invading a country. And in the collective buzz and reflection of soldiers having their last pint at home before flying out to do the job they wanted to do to a man, I had asked him if he'd noticed any changes in himself as the date drew nearer.

'My missus certainly has,' he replied.

'What's that then?'

'Aggression.'

*

The HAC would be deploying four five-man surveillance patrols to Iraq. And the first stage of our build-up training would be the six-week Close Observation Platoon course, run by the Regular Army at a run-down barracks beyond the arse end of nowhere on a forgotten corner of Kent shoreline. The nearest outpost of civilisation was a nuclear power station.

But this suited the nature of the course perfectly. And on the evening of 11 January, we filed into a classroom for the introductory brief. While the chief instructor waited silently for us to find our seats, I took in the first projection slide waiting for our attention.

It was the school's crest and motto: a badger's head with 'To see and not be seen' annotated below. I smiled at the deceptive badger symbolism: a furtive, unseen creature that was anything but snuffling if cornered, fighting at any cost to protect itself and its own.

The chief instructor began by introducing himself and the other instructors standing to one side of him, before giving an outline of the upcoming course and what he expected from us. He was from 22 SAS. The other instructors had similarly 'interesting' backgrounds.

Building on our existing HAC qualification as green-triangle-badged 'Special Observers', we would be advance-trained in the planning of, infiltration into, construction of, day-to-day running of and exfiltration from covert rural and urban OPs. We would leave no sign of our presence. We would be instructed in advanced photographic and video surveillance. And in the unlikely event of being compromised by the enemy, we would be drilled in aggressive contact procedures from on foot, in vehicles and out of our OPs.

On the physical side, there would be individual and team tests throughout the course which would become progressively more difficult. As with everything else on the course, these would be pass/fail. No leeway could be afforded; we were training for real now.

And lastly, we would never be allowed to talk about what we learned on the course. Not with our girlfriends, our mothers, even if they were one and the same, or our Uncle Ivan thrice removed showing a sudden friendly interest in our lives all the way from St Petersburg. End of.

As we filed back out of the classroom, the buzz among our ranks continued back to our billets. Personally, I couldn't wait to get started and was spurred on further by the prospect of being my patrol's second in command (2IC). Though I would be outranked by one of the soldiers under me, Matt, I was told I had been appointed over him because of the unit I'd come from before the HAC – and because I was the only HAC soldier mobilised among us now who had operational experience of Iraq.

As a lance sergeant, Matt was only one rank higher than me, but as a rule rank meant little in the HAC, where no matter what your previous experience you automatically started from the bottom again after passing the six-month Patrol Selection Course (PSC). And once in, the normal 'Green Army' rule of addressing soldiers by their rank was supplanted by the use of first names instead.

I still thought it diplomatic not to rub things in Matt's face, though, and resolved to never order him about. I would be friendly and strive to excel at my job; respect and willing compliance would hopefully follow.

The other two soldiers under me were Paul, a fellow lance corporal, and HR, a trooper. Along with Matt, they were both in the same squadron as me back at the HAC, so we all already knew each other well. Bonding had come in the form of getting rained on in the same hole in the ground as each other, or downing the same rounds of beers on squadron nights out, all uniformly dressed in the unofficial mufti of the loudest Hawaiian shirts one's eyes could cope with.

We were all grins as we unpacked our bags beside our beds in our patrol's room, but there was an unspoken undercurrent of nerves as we contemplated the tests lying ahead of us. We gabbled excitedly, eyeing each other's personally bought, superior kit for the tour ahead, labelling it as 'Gucci'.

Leon, our sergeant, was somewhat different, though. Our patrol commander (PC) lay silent on his bed among the activity, staring up at the ceiling with his hands behind his head.

'You all right there, Leon?' I asked after a while, putting my trainers and physical training (PT) kit on my chair ready for the first test in the morning.

He pulled himself up on the bed before looking mournfully at me, complaining of a back problem.

This was not good: it was Matt, Paul and HR's first time on tour and we were looking at being led by someone who sounded like he didn't even want to be there.

'OK – well, maybe mention your back to the DS tomorrow morning before the first gut wrencher! I'm sure if you're injured they'll take that into account.'

'Yeah, think I might do that. I just don't want to make things any worse.'

I'd never been sure of Leon from the off, when he'd been an instructor on my PSC a year and a half ago. I'd soon developed distaste for how I thought he seemed to enjoy shouting at recruits for the sake of it and zeroing in on any perceived fault at the expense of any encouragement. After passing the course, I heard from another instructor that Leon had wanted to fail me for 'attitude'. That was his prerogative, but clearly the dislike was mutual.

For the good of all of us in Iraq, I hoped he would not turn out to be the real-life personification of the bullying instructor from *All Quiet on the Western Front*: a figure whose attitude of screaming the talk while playing a position of power back home quickly unravelled when he finally had to walk the walk for real in no-man's-land.

I hoped to God Leon had a spine, for all our sakes. Iraq would be a very long and potentially fatally unforgiving tour otherwise.

*

As we lined up shivering in the freezing drizzle of the pre-dawn darkness the next morning, I did not notice Leon have a word with the Directing Staff (DS), though.

On a personal level, I thanked God I had ramped up my physical training still further before coming here. The morning's PT was an unrelenting, brutal sickener of sprints, press-ups and fireman lifts lasting till past the sun came up. I saw Leon lagging but still running, pressing up and carrying. In the few times I could catch my breath I didn't know what to think of that.

Showered and with the unhealthiest fried breakfast imaginable sitting queasily in our bellies, we began our instruction in all the chief instructor had promised. By the end of the day our writing hands ached from the note-taking as much as the rest of our bodies did from the morning's exertions.

And for the weeks before going out in the field for our first exercise, this format was repeated each day. Sometimes the morning phys was a team exercise, racing against other patrols; sometimes it was an individual timed run carrying a weighted bergan. The lessons were interspersed with monkey-see, monkey-do practical demonstrations of patrolling procedures and operating technical kit. And then there were the parts I always looked forward to: the adrenalin-filled live firing, both individually and as part of a patrol. Some of it was tweaked old ground for me, but firing from inside a car through the windscreen was not. Fortunately all the glass in the car had been removed, so we didn't blow out our eardrums along with the windows.

It was the phys sessions that were the most character-building parts of our day, though. Or character-destroying, depending on your viewpoint.

We had a dawn stretcher race. Each patrol was allocated a frost-covered stretcher with concrete-filled metal ammunition boxes welded to it in simulation of a heavy body. Then suddenly we were all set off as a oner, each patrol racing the others over the three-mile course. Each man carried a corner handle of the stretcher on his shoulder, leaving the spare fifth man to run alongside, shouting encouragement while catching his breath before going back on to one of the handles. And running alongside all of us were the DS, watching quietly, as always.

It was, of course, agony. But everyone was going through the same agony. And it was as much a brutal team-building exercise as it was a heart-thumping competition against the other patrols.

We swapped team members on the run every few hundred metres. And we were doing all right, our running legs synchronised into a rhythm of 'Left! Right! Left!' to keep us going as one and stop the stretcher from jolting out of time as we pressured the second-placed team in front of us to get out of our way along the dark, narrow-tracked road.

'*Come on!*' one of the DS suddenly screamed to us. 'Get past those fuckers!'

We surged forward onto the frozen verge, pushing past the other stretcher through the crunch of long grass before slotting in front of them. It was comforting to see the agony on the other team's faces reflected back to us as we passed them.

Then Leon suddenly came off the stretcher, calling out about his back. Our stretcher rocked wildly and our feet stumbled in lost rhythm as Matt had to suddenly lunge for the fourth handle. And as soon as we had overtaken them, the other patrol pushed past us.

The DS didn't say anything. I was vaguely aware of him watching intently to one side. I called out the time again to claw back our rhythm and lost pace, but the team in front had been stung by our overtaking and were shouting their own time in defiance.

So we began the slow process of catching them up again, every metre eaten into with each heavy stride as shoulders screamed and lungs gasped. I reckoned we must have been into the last half mile and shouted for everything from everyone for the last push to the finishing line.

But something was wrong at the back; Paul had been on the stretcher for longer than any of us now, and I could feel the stretcher yanking back from me as I willed it forward.

'Change!' I heard his breathless call behind me.

But Leon carried on running beside us. 'I can't,' he said.

I let my irritation fester for a couple of steps before calling out to the others: 'OK, just dig in lads – this is us now till the end. Let's fucking do it – come on!'

But we did not catch the stretcher in front of us. Instead, before we lumbered exhausted and one man down over the finishing line, it was our team that was caught and passed by another behind us.

I couldn't bring myself to look at Leon as I stood to catch my breath when it was all done.

Yes, it fucking mattered. Where we were going, aggression fucking *mattered*.

As the quiet DS walked past me to join his huddle of colleagues conferring secretly away from us all, I saw him give me a single nod.

*

When I was a young boy, I was brought up in hero worship of my father, a Royal Air Force pilot, and my grandfather, a multi Military Cross-decorated double world war Army veteran. My mother, too, had been in the Army – and my aunt and my uncle and my cousin. I was nurtured in a family that revered achievement in the military world. And as the eldest of two brothers, I shouldered the responsibility of living up to all the expectations I placed on myself in the shadow of these towering figures. It became my nature.

But I had a stammer: not a mild speech impediment but a strangling, vocal-cord-clenching disability that would leave the other kids in fits of giggles or groans when I had to read something out in class. Whether the pressure I placed on myself to achieve led to my stutter I will never know, but in later years I could reflect that it certainly compounded it. And the more frustrated I became at my inability to speak and socialise with my little peers, the more my stammer clamped down on me, shutting me off from them.

By the time I went to boarding school at 13, I could be described as painfully shy and semi-reclusive. I went through my adolescent years as one of those other boys orbiting the cold reaches beyond the 'cool' social cliques. My few real friendships were born out of shared banishment, or a rare, patient maturity in some that could see beyond the stumbling words that would just not come out.

I put my head down and tried to prove my worth to the father-in-my-head in exams and the RAF Cadets instead. And I took my frustrations out in the First VIII teams for shooting and cross-country running, making sure I won colours in both. I shied away from the team sports, hoping to prove something to myself in these individual fields instead. And I felt the most self-satisfaction when I ran alone in the races, channelling pent-up frustration and anger into masochistic achievement. It was towards the end of races, when everything was reduced to a mental game of how much pain you could endure, that I overtook the most people, especially uphill.

I taught myself endurance, patience, discipline and bloody-minded determination. But I was still reaching for self-esteem and speech when, aged 18, I heeded the childhood call and applied for an RAF University Cadetship.

I failed, of course. For what possible use would a Harrier pilot be who took five times as long as everyone else to talk?

But the one amazing ray of recognition they did surprise me with was the consolation prize of an RAF Flying Scholarship: a no-strings-attached award of thirty free flying hours' instruction at a civilian flying school. I didn't want to question the financial rationale behind it. Further, if you could rustle up a spare £1,000 to pay for an extra ten flying hours, you could qualify for your private pilot's licence. And in the cruel fortune that only fate can bestow, my immortal grandfather had just died, leaving me £1,000 in his will.

So in between passing my A Levels and going to university, and instead of taking the ordinary lessons in learning how to drive, I took the train to a windswept airfield in Kent to spend a month learning how to fly.

The actual flying was no problem, it transpired; I had obviously inherited something from my father. But my stammer when speaking to air traffic control fast became an impediment to progressing any further on the course and flying solo. While I could control the plane with ease, I had no control over the paralysis of my vocal cords. I would press the radio button to speak, but the only thing transmitted to the tower would be the deafening silence filling the cockpit. My instructor quickly learned to fill the void with his own words.

I knew things were fast coming to a head. And after I had landed late one afternoon, taxiing back to the school at the end of the day, I was aware of my instructor being quieter than usual in the seat beside me. I parked the aircraft in its allocated space and went through the closing-down checks as normal, the roar of the engine suddenly replaced by the whine of dying electrics, and then silence.

He paused in thought for another moment before speaking.

'Jake . . . You can fly. There's no doubting your ability, but I can't let you go solo if you can't use the radio.'

I nodded, staring mutely at the altimeter with its registered height of zero. I was going to be cut from the course.

'But I don't want to throw you off the course: it'd just be a waste – a needless waste. I want you to go back to the B&B tonight and look inside yourself. You need to talk. And you can talk – I've seen you blabbering on like everyone else when the pressure's off . . . ! But it's sink-or-swim time now. Tomorrow morning, you can be the first of the class to fly solo – or not. It's up to you . . . Relax . . . and believe in yourself – you can do this, Jake.'

I didn't go to the pub that night with the other students as usual. I sat alone with my thoughts in the little room in the seaside B&B instead, looking deep inside myself. I was on the cusp of success or failure: stammering or talking. It really was now or never: sink – or fly.

As I finished readying the aircraft for taxiing out the next morning, I took a deep breath before 'pressing the tit' to speak.

There was a long second of silence as my voice fought to be heard in that old familiar clench of tension . . . and then I just let go.

And as the breath flowed out the words poured out with it.

'Manston Tower, this is Golf Bravo Hotel Foxtrot Charlie, ready to taxi.'

'Golf Foxtrot Charlie taxi to alpha one, hold for runway two eight via taxiway alpha, QNH one zero zero three.'

There was a stunned silence in the cockpit as both my instructor and I realised what had just happened. And then he just smiled.

'Good lad . . . OK, let's take her up for a circuit.'

When I landed, he asked me to taxi off the runway and stop. And then, without a word, he suddenly unstrapped himself and got out of the aircraft.

From the ground he looked back in at me through the open door, shouting over the roar of the engine. 'You don't need me any more – you can do one on your own now! Relax – enjoy it! You've earned it!'

And then he slammed the door secure shut, banging it with his palm before giving me a thumbs up, backing away as he grinned at me in encouragement.

Quiet and alone in the cockpit, I felt a smile spread across my face in pure, unadulterated self-confidence. And after I radioed the tower for clearance to line up on the runway, I laughed out loud to myself at how easy it was. Now, I was going to fly.

I gently throttled out onto the runway, lining up on the centreline before applying the brakes. The wide tarmac dwarfed my little plane, stretching far ahead of us into the distance.

'Manston Tower, Golf Foxtrot Charlie ready for take-off.'

'Golf Foxtrot Charlie cleared for take-off, wind two three zero, nine knots.'

And I when I pushed the throttle forward I did slip 'the surly bonds of Earth'. And I did 'dance the skies on laughter-silvered wings . . . high in the sunlit silence . . .'*

Long after my wheels floated back down to kiss the Earth, the smile stayed with me; the burden of my formative years lifted up and away. And sure, I might sometimes s . . . stumble on a word, but take another deep breath, reach down into the blackness in me that feared failure, chase those rays of hope I had won high among the clouds . . . relax . . . and the words just flew out again.

Now, I was in control.

Thanks to my grandfather, I did go on to get my private pilot's licence. And I could only buy my instructor a bottle of scotch at the end to say thank you in kind to him. I liked to think he probably won a round of beers from the other instructors for it being his student that was first to fly solo, though – and for it being me.

I had learned the true value of determination. And as my saviour, I resolved to stay faithful to the trait that had borne me with success and wings into the air. And I learned that through the dogged pursuit of achievement, I could indeed find self-worth. And so, paradoxically, I no longer felt I had to retread my father's footsteps into the RAF in a skyward pursuit of self-validation. Now, I could follow my own path. And from that point on in my life, I found it even harder to give up on anything, as I felt I could do anything I put my mind to.

So as I ran gasping for breath along the Kent shoreline 12 years later, with the heavy bergan biting into my shoulders and dragging

---

*   From 'High Flight' by John Gillespie Magee Jr.

each wading step heavier down into the deep shingle stretching far into the distance, I remembered flying through the very air above me now, above this very beach. And as the dawn run turned into just another solo game of how much pain you could bear, I picked off the soldiers in front of me, one by one. It was the mind that ruled the body, not the body that ruled the mind.

I finished second in that run, the lead man determinedly keeping his lead with his own personal demons and anxious glances over his shoulder. And when I caught my mind beginning to chide me for not coming first, I stopped the thought dead in its tracks and allowed myself a wry little smile of self-recognition.

*

I was thriving on the course. And my rising confidence was buoyed further by the increasingly wistful longings of Cecilia from afar. When we finished late each evening and I switched my mobile on, there was always a text message from her crying out for attention, or a voicemail filled with yearning. My absence was making her heart grow fonder.

I felt the same longing. And I might have been torn between my desire for her and the very consummation of my being on the course – with the promise of Iraq looming ever larger. But this was not a conflict in my mind; one merely reinforced and accentuated the other. I felt whole.

When we knocked off early one day at six, I phoned to see how she was. And when I told her the news about having a whole evening off, she could only say, 'You're joking . . .' in hushed disbelief, before jumping in her car and driving for two hours round the motorways to spend a couple of hours with me.

She picked me up outside the camp gates, and we drove without direction for a while round the nearby town of Ashford on the pretext of looking for a pub. But we really just wanted each other's company.

Unfortunately it turned out she didn't want to risk being caught in flagrante delicto with her soldier boyfriend parked up in a sordid lay-by – but also because the anticipation of us finally being together at the course end would make our acts all the more 'delicious'. And as my lust died down with my tumescence, it dawned on me how the coming reality of Iraq was colouring my mental horizon. I knew I could very well die soon. But I noticed the lack of emotion I attached to calculating this probability – and how much that contrasted with, or probably was causing, my total lack of inhibition and wilful desire to risk-take and live life to the full in all the time I had left at home now.

Cecilia would not be facing death – though she did say she wanted me to pack her in my bergan when I finally came to leave. I wondered if she truly appreciated the harsh realities of how long I would be gone and what might happen to me. As we drove back to the base with Kylie Minogue playing on her stereo, planning our happy Valentine's weekend escape at the end of the course, I looked across at her sadly as she gabbled away excitedly. Reality was going to hit her hard, and sooner than she realised.

But a few days later, before our patrol went out on our first rural surveillance exercise, we had an unexpected entire night off and no early morning phys the next day to wake up to. As the team's 2IC, I sorted out all the patrol kit in double-quick time, documenting who had what with rapid efficiency. Then I packed my own kit in a blur, changed into civvies and opened my car up at full, recklessly illegal throttle along the motorway back home to snatch a full night with Cecilia.

She lay on top of me in that breathless afterwards, listening to my heartbeat again as it returned to rest in the warm, close quiet.

'I love you,' she said quietly to the heart, fingers stroking the bicep holding her tight.

'I love you too, Lia,' was all my heart could say back.

She brought her face to mine, and though she had broken out in a wide, thankful smile I saw her eyes were shining wet.

I kissed her tenderly, then deeply. And we held each other tight into the night, savouring every second of these close moments before the darkness of sleep and the cold fingers of dawn that would separate us once more.

*

Back on the course, Leon had been excused from subsequent phys sessions because of his back injury. So, come the time when we deployed from the classroom into the field, I thought maybe this rest was why he appeared to be fit again. He needed to be. I shared the patrol kit for the coming exercises equally among us, but to a man we all carried in excess of 100 pounds.

I looked forward to getting out on the ground and seeing how our patrol would work as a team, finally putting together all we had learned in two five-day exercises: the first putting in a covert rural OP and the second operating a covert urban OP.

With blacked-out faces, our team was tactically dropped off from a blacked-out van. We threaded our way across silent, white-blanketed fields beneath the vast blackness of a clear, star-studded sky. Thick snowflakes dropped like lead weights through the clouds of my freezing breath. And I caught myself thinking of my long-lost colleagues from my former life, tucked up asleep beneath the orange murk of a city sky with only another numb day in the office to look forward to in the morning. I pitied them.

But they would probably have pitied us instead, living as we did for days inside a snow-covered gorse bush. The thorny crampedness inside was as welcome as it was unavoidable, though: the sharing of our bodies' heat helped stave off the sub-zero cold. And we wanted the snow to keep falling as it did, because this would cover all signs of our ingress, and thus cover any sign of us living in this particular bush, for all those 'enemy' hunting us.

We lived on cold food and even colder water in 'hard routine' to reduce noise and the sign of steam rising from the OP. And we evacuated our bowels and bladders of said intakes into resealable bags, to repack away in our bergans.

And though feeling in our feet and hands numbed away, we whispered our spirits up with the shared warmth of our various love lives. As the days and hours descended into shivering, lingering minutes, we dug back into the past of best shags, worst shags, fittest and ugliest birds we had ever been with and how good, bad or indifferent losing our virginities had been.

And when the trickle of inaudibly whispered conversation inevitably ran dry, or we were just too tired to repeat old ground, I sometimes smiled to myself at the incongruity of sitting in a gorse bush within a snowdrift when we would encounter neither in Iraq – unless Hell had frozen over, of course.

You learned to use the biting cold to keep you alert when you needed to be, when you needed to keep your eyes fixed for hours at a time on that optically magnified target to your front, before snuggling up to a comrade in dormant Spartan man-love when you could.

We suffered as much as each other. I lost all feeling in my feet at one point, wriggling their numbness in a pathetic attempt to keep the warm blood supply flowing through them. But I kept it to myself; everyone else had it the same.

In the early days of this rural OP, our team seemed to work well. And I found myself warming to Leon as I began to think that perhaps, when it did matter, we could operate with cold, clinical efficiency.

But then I think our team stopped working well. And I do not think it worked well in the urban OP phase either.

Leon did some things well. But although I was only the team 2IC, sometimes I found myself doing the team commander's job. And when I found myself doing this job in addition to my own, I found that I had lost faith in Leon's leadership.

If this was just some weekend TA exercise, I could have ignored these misgivings. But we were not playing at being soldiers now.

So I saw I had two options: confront Leon, or carry on observing – mentally logging everything – and let him dig his own grave. And as the harshly unforgiving reality of Iraq was fast approaching, I decided to think long term and opt for the latter.

I felt Leon and I were now way past 'having a word'. I was going to have a word with the DS and our overall HAC leadership instead – and to hell with the consequences.

But, though we all thought our OPs were as covert as could be, the DS knew exactly where we were. We had radioed the grid references of our locations to them.

And until the course end, when we came in from the field bearded and stinking to thaw out and be debriefed, we would never know just how much the DS could see of absolutely everything we had said and done – or not.

*

The urban OP was the last test of the last lessons taught to us on the course. After the collective debrief had finished, we all decamped to a bar in another room we never knew existed before. And the majority of us got totally, and deservedly, drunk.

When I went into the corridor outside to phone Cecilia in between rounds, she giggled at how I slurred my words, saying how I needed to be with her now, let alone waiting till tomorrow night, when we would be flying away for our first Valentine's weekend.

She just laughed at me again before quietening.

'I've really missed you,' she whispered.

'I've missed you too, Lia.'

'Tomorrow I'm going to hold you and not let you go. The Army can't have you then – you're all mine!'

I could hear drunken calls for me in the bar. 'He's not on the bloody phone again, is he?' someone said above all the hubbub and laughter.

'Tomorrow . . . Look, they're calling my name; they're even drunker than me now. I'm going to come straight to you tomorrow. I can't wait – I love you, Lia.'

'Make sure you do; you come straight home to me – I love you too.'

It took a few moments of deep breathing and slapping my own face to lose the waistline sign of my phone call before I was able to walk back into the bar.

'*I love you!*' some of the guys shrieked drunkenly as I walked in. '*You* hang up . . . No, *you* hang up!'

I grinned guiltily as Paul presented me with the two cans that had stacked up in my absence.

'Down in two, Lothario!' he laughed in my face, putting an arm round me. And the bar blurred back into a warm haze as I sloshed the lager down my throat, deep among the ranks of friends borne up by equal success on the course, invincible with drink – and drinking for our lives beneath the shadow of Iraq, as it edged one night closer to us.

*

We spent the next morning groggily hanging onto brooms in our billets and clearing the carnage of scores of empty lager cans from the bar. And as we went through the final, drawn-out process of handing technical kit back in to the school, a rumour began circulating that Leon was not going to be a PC in Iraq. If this was true, it could only mean that our patrol was going to be split up among the other three, as we would only have three qualified PCs now. And I probably wouldn't be a 2IC any more, as the other 2ICs were already established in their teams.

If this was true, now the course was done and we were clearing away its aftermath through the fog of our hangovers, I reflected on how I didn't take any personal pleasure in Leon's failure to make PC. But it would be the right decision, I felt coldly.

Initially I found it hard to read my course report, struggling to marry up the soldier on the paper in front of me and the self-punishing little boy nurtured deep in my nature, ever driven to achieve and feeling undeserving of praise when he finally did.

It said this soldier 'LCpl Wood arrived physically and mentally prepared for the course. He was identified a very good JNCO. He passed all the mandatory fitness tests with ease and also helped weaker members of his team when needed.'

It said 'his personal skills are of a very good standard and he has proved himself to be a good, safe, confident and accurate shot on the live firing package. He has a sound understanding of vehicle and foot contact procedures and displayed good leadership qualities when in appointment. He did well on all situation awareness scenarios by taking control of the team in the Team Commander's absence and giving advice if needed.'

The words carried on praising 'LCpl Wood' during the 'arduous and cold' rural OP phase. And it was only when it came to saying that he 'must pay more attention to detail, especially ensuring to check all equipment on extraction from OPs' that I felt a stab of comfort.

Fair one.

One of my team members had lost a radio pressel while we were leaving our rural OP, but as the team 2IC it had been my responsibility to account for all equipment.

But the report ended saying 'LCpl Wood had a good course and continually worked hard for the Team. He improved considerably throughout the course and should have no problem adapting to an operational environment. Although he is recommended to assume the post of Team 2IC, he could easily step up to the Team Commander appointment if he is remobilised on a similar tour. He is to be congratulated on having an excellent course.'

I finished reading the words. And then, numb with disbelief, I turned the page over to see if there were more. But there was no more. There it all it was, the final judgement of me signed and dated by the SAS chief instructor at the bottom of the page in black ink.

Fuck me . . .

I focussed on the one criticism on the page, feeling how I'd let myself down – and then I remembered what I was doing to myself. And when I had finished chastising myself for punishing myself, I stopped that too. With a broad, grateful smile I reverently slipped the paper uncreased into the file of my course notes, packed it away on top of the rest of my kit in my bergan, and took myself and all my kit to my car, the smile spreading wider on my face.

Now for Cecilia. *I'm coming, girl . . .*

Tim, from one of the other patrols, was packing his kit into the boot of his car next to mine. 'Jake . . . !' he started, moving over to my car. 'Keep it under your hat, but I think you're in our patrol now.'

'Really? Awesome, mate,' I grinned back at him, bouncing on the lid of my protesting boot to get it closed.

'Yeah – think we've easily got the best patrol now. You'll like it; Alex is well chilled: knows his stuff, too, unlike some other PCs we won't mention . . .'

I laughed and nodded at him. Tim was now peering through the window of my car. I watched him for a second before he stood back to look at its profile.

'What size engine you got in this, then?'

'Four litres.'

'What?!' he blurted, then nodded slowly in appreciation.

I took another look at his Renault Clio beside me, noticing the air intakes, the flared wheel arches and the large twin exhausts poking out under the words 'Sport' and 'V6'.

'Nice car yourself, mate,' I ventured back. 'What's the top speed on that?'

'Hundred and fifty . . . Yours?'

'Hundred and sixty – with the wind behind it.'

We both nodded in the pregnant silence, both thinking the same thing.

'Race you back to London,' he suddenly voiced, eyes gleaming.

I smiled back at him, stabbing the button to open my driver's door. 'You're fucking on, mate!'

And, laughing like kids, we scrambled into our cars, crawling out of the base at the allocated 5 mph speed limit before shaking the sleepy Kent countryside awake with the boom and reverberation of our engines climbing higher and higher in the pitch of excited revs.

Two young soldiers with two too-fast cars on a mission, flying back in determined abandon to our waiting other halves, chasing every snatch of every last fleeting second of the time we had left with them, revelling alive in risk.

Our race sped along the M20, on along upwards towards the M25 – I felt totally alive in the screaming, vibrating cockpit, the roar of the engine feeding the flirtation with danger. Along the blur of the road, the broken white lines merging into one and past the flash of every overtaken car, there was no time to reflect, or think – only to control – and react – and feel. And the shadow of Iraq sped along over the road with us; we were only two young men trying to cheat death, because soon, it could all . . . stop.

We only slowed down when Tim blew one of his exhausts.

*

I was just in time. Cecilia and I ran laughing across the departure lounge as our names were broadcast and shamed in final calls above us. We breezed smilingly past the tutting and reproachful looks of airport officials to take the last two seats waiting for us on the aircraft. We didn't care; we had a whole weekend together in a foreign city and nothing but each other's company to look forward to.

When I looked up from her once, looking for our stop on the clean, continentally punctual train taking us from the airport into the centre of Copenhagen, I caught the eye of an old couple sitting a few seats away from us.

Cecilia and I had been whispering into each other's mouths in between smiles and fleeting kisses, lost in each other's eyes and words as we held each other's hands in our laps, fingers stroking, savouring.

The old couple were holding hands too. They warmly smiled as one across at us, still close and warm together after their many years. I hoped we reminded them of a long time ago. The old lady kissed her husband gently on his cheek and he smiled softly down to her.

'They're lovely . . .' Cecilia whispered, with her cheek resting on mine. 'I want that to be us . . .'

'It's going to be, Lia. We've found each other now.'

We didn't go out that night. We didn't want to be anywhere other than in each other's arms.

But we walked hand in hand together through the little streets the next afternoon. At the harbour, we found the statue of the Little Mermaid – and just laughed at how it should have been called 'the Minute Mermaid'. And our happiness carried on into a colonnade of Prada, Gucci and Louis Vuitton boutiques. Her eyes lit up as she shook my hand in excitement, gabbling 'Oooh . . . Can we, can we?'

I watched her with love as her eyes roved over and coveted the alluring accessories inside. She didn't know it yet, but I would be buying her something very special for her birthday – just before I went to Iraq.

And we wandered on together, sharing not a care in our escape through the antediluvian, cobbled alleyways of the medieval quarter, stopping off for indulgently cream-topped steaming hot chocolates before finding ourselves beneath the high, old Round Tower. I playfully motivated her Army-style up the 200-metre-long spiralling ramp leading to its very top, laughing as she giggled breathlessly back with flushed cheeks, telling me, 'Just you wait till I get you back to the room . . .'

High above on the open observation deck, we held each in the cold, still air. I pulled up the hood on her deep-red, faux fur-lined jacket to keep her warm before taking half a step back to take a picture of her on my phone. The fur framed her face softly against the old brown rooftops of the city, stretching far away into the distance below.

We nuzzled close to share the picture. She looked perfect. I looked up from the picture to the face beside me, smiling beside me for real, and kissed her again above the centuries-old city, our perfect moment now captured for all time.

It wasn't a surprise when we nearly missed the plane back home as well. Forgotten coffees cooled in front of us in the departure lounge as we lost ourselves in the stroke of our fingers and lingering of our eyes. With our faces pressed close together we both realised what was headlong and breathlessly happening to us. It didn't need to be said; words didn't mean so much any more.

Both of us knew our time was precious.

*

I was relieved by the laid-back professionalism underpinning my new patrol. Alex the PC, Moxy the 2IC, Dougie, Tim, Frosty and Charlie were all from a different squadron within the HAC, but I knew them all already from the same shared weekends away, the same sodden holes in the ground and the same adrenalin-filled contact lanes. And for the remaining weeks of build-up training we bonded into one tight, confidently cohesive team as we made the final preparations for Iraq, where we would get to know each other intimately.

After hearing of our race up the M20, Alex had duly appointed me and Tim as the patrol's drivers, saying he wanted capable lunatics who could boot it out of any given situation. Though he did promise he would get other members of the patrol to cover for us occasionally, if we wanted potential 'trigger time' on the back of the Rovers.

The weeks leading into April were spent learning how to untie our tongues in everyday conversational Arabic phrases – such as, 'Please get out of the car and stand with your family under the tree over there' – or laughing hysterically as we shared the blood-dripping practice of intravenously inserting cannula needles into each other's arms, or firing unflinchingly and unerringly past each other's heads through the green glow of night vision in dead-of-the-night live-firing exercises. We even learned how to use our enemy's weapons, if we should come across them and care to throw them back in the faces of those who would use them against us.

Our manoeuvres were rehearsed, honed, repeated and then repeated again and again under the mentoring eyes of our SAS instructors, Max and Rab, who would accompany us into Iraq.

Max had coined the phrase 'smooth is fast' at the beginning of this second phase of training. And we learned the meaning of his words as our contact drills flowed into oiled, rapid efficiency, reacting as one to any given situation thrown at us, from enemy flanking to one vehicle down and multiple team members down, dead. From vehicle and on foot, in the bright of day and through the pitch of night, we seamlessly operated as one, completing our transition from a bunch of former City boys into one single peak of killing effectiveness.

By April we were ready and the date was set: we would fly out on the 14th. And we wanted someone to have a go at us out there. In immortal youth, I pitied anyone who might try and take us on.

So that left us with just under two weeks to finish prepping our personal kit and to say goodbye to our loved ones.

*

Cecilia sat on my bed, watching me quietly as I finished packing the final items into my daysack – desert-camouflaged helmet and body armour – and then my bergan: fawn-sprayed and dirtied ops vest and chest rig, rifle magazines and night-vision monocle. I sealed them tight in the internal canoe bag, then clipped the top of the bergan closed, pulling the straps hard down, satisfyingly tight. Done.

I looked up to her with a smile but saw tears rolling down her face. In my detached, single-minded purpose, I hadn't noticed them coming.

I flicked another switch in my head and sat beside her, cuddling her close in my arms as her sobs suddenly let go in floods. 'Hey, hey . . . Baby, it's OK – it's going to be OK.' I stroked her hair and held her tight as she shook against my shoulder.

'I'm sorry,' she said, looking to my face. 'It's just getting too real now.' She buried her face against my chest again, pulling her arms tighter around me. 'I feel like I'm being punished for last year – I don't want you to go!'

Her little body convulsed helplessly against me as the words stabbed into my chest, sharp as a knife, piercing my guilt. I could only drop my head to hers and hold her tighter.

I could never tell her she had been the final reason I'd volunteered to go. But now I had to go. And not only was I now legally obliged to, I was all too aware of some dumb, primitive warrior call invading every fibre of my being the closer the date drew. I could feel it dragging me away from her.

'I'm sorry, baby. But I'm going to be OK – you'll see; we know what we're doing out there. And I'm going to come back to you on leave in June – and then we'll be together for two weeks – and then we'll only have to wait for October and then all this will be over . . . I promise.'

She was quietening in my arms. Then she sat up, wiping the tears from her eyes. 'Bloody Army . . . I hate the bloody Army!' she laughed in between sobs.

'I know, baby, but it'll be over soon. It's only six months, and then I'm going to come back to you for good.'

'You better!' Her words stabbed back. 'You make damn sure you shoot first!' The violence behind her words took me aback momentarily, but the tears welling up again and her quivering lip betrayed the love and fear inside her.

'OK – deal,' I said gently. I put my hand to hers and we shook on it.

I remembered the moon hanging high over the Garden of Eden when she first wrote to me. And though I had planned to give her her birthday present when we were on holiday tomorrow in Barbados, I decided the time was right now.

'Listen . . . we'll always share the same moon gazing down on us at night, Lia. Always remember I love you – and if you wear this while I'm away, I will always be with you . . . *Sadiqatee jamiliah.*'

'What's that mean?' she said, eyes widening at the Tiffany's box in my hands.

I opened it, taking the white gold and diamond-studded necklace out to sparkle in front of her eyes, before reaching slowly up to fasten it around her neck. Then I held her face gently in my hands and let one tender kiss linger on her lips . . . before holding her gaze to mine.

'My beautiful girlfriend.'

That just finished her off.

4

AWAKENINGS

It is better by noble boldness to run the risk of being
subject to half the evils we anticipate than to remain in
cowardly listlessness for fear of what might happen.

Herodotus

There's daggers in men's smiles.

'William Shakespeare'

High on the terrace of the riverside palace, there is only the gentlest
of breezes caressing my face in the warm night air. And the softness
of the sleeping bag cocoons my still body, soothing every muscle to
rest in its warm, safe embrace.

Through the flicker of eyelids I look up once more at the silent stare
of thousands of stars arcing the heavens above me. And glowing
among them is the moon, softly lighting the darkness I am slipping
away into. And with the gentle, rhythmic sound of my friends sleeping
close by and with each tender stroke of the wind, I remember the
delicate touch of Cecilia's sleeping breath on me. But now, as my
mind sinks further down, there is only the distant lullaby of the
crickets washing through me, before that too fades away into silent
blackness, as I finally drift down into the soft abyss of sleep.

*

My eyes snapped open to the sound of the explosion, the sharp clap
punching me awake into the daylight. I felt the shock wave roll over
me – then the dull reverberation of its echo, lingering for a second . . .
gone.

'What the fuck was that?' Frosty called out, camp bed creaking loudly in protest as he suddenly sat up.

But there was only silence again.

The explosion had sounded a way off to me – big, but far enough away to not be anything to do with us.

'Dunno – perhaps we're being mortared,' I suggested mischievously, then rolled over to try to get back to sleep.

'Jesus . . .' I heard him mutter in alarm, before lifting himself out of the bed.

But there was no way I could sleep. I felt my heart thumping in excitement as much as I imagined the others' were as they congregated half-naked beside the terrace's low outer wall. I gave up the pretence and lifted myself up to join them leaning against the wall, rubbing my bare arm against Charlie's as I lit a cigarette and stared with him into the city.

Basra stretched out before us in the morning light: a sprawl of sand-coloured brick and grey-concrete buildings stretching far into the distance, the huddle and clutter of uniformly low, pale, flat-roofs only interspersed in places with the green of palm trees or the gold of dome-topped mosques. Here and there I glimpsed specks of vehicles and people roving the rousing streets like ants in a hive. To close your eyes and listen in the dark to the distant, familiar background hum, it would sound like any other city in the world. But open them again and they would only see a strange foreign mass.

Running along our right was the wide Shatt al-Arab waterway, oil-slicked black and blue. I could make out the line of a pontoon bridge over it in the distance. And just beyond that, I recognised the huge white hull of Saddam Hussein's presidential yacht from news footage. It lay half-capsized on its side, shining in the morning sun like the corpse of a beached whale, rotting into the water.

And in the distance a plume of black smoke marked the spot of our rude awakening. We would later find out it was a 'VBIED attack on an IPS station'. Or, in other words, a man had taken it upon himself to drive a vehicle laden with explosives into a police station, with the one holy aim of killing himself and as many people there as he could take with him.

This was the reality of the Iraq we would now be immersing ourselves in. I looked at the smoke rising from its point of death and thought how the vast expanse of the rest of the city looked so peaceful from up here, so far away.

Only a year had passed since I had stood on a border and been rallied with hope that 'We go to liberate, not to conquer.' Did the 'light of liberation' indeed now shine down on this city, in this morning sun? I blew smoke from my lungs at the thought, letting it obscure my view of Iraq for a second before it vanished like words into the air and Basra was brought into sharp focus once more.

'Up in smoke . . .' I whispered quietly to myself.

'Say what, Jake?' Charlie asked quietly in his Australian twang.

I gave him a grin; I was aware this was new territory for me, but it was even newer for him.

'Welcome to Iraq, mate.'

He nodded quietly, looking out to the smoke.

'We'll be all right, mate,' I continued. 'We're going to stick together and take anything this place throws at us.'

Tim was now standing close beside us. 'And throw everything back at any fucker that tries anything on with us,' he added punchily.

We stared into the city and nodded as one.

*

Deep within the fortified palace complex, inside one house within a little cul-de-sac of buildings already nicknamed 'Brookside Close', the HAC patrol callsigned 'Sierra One Two Delta' spent the morning unpacking kit in an airy white-walled and granite-floored ground-floor room.

This would be our home for the next six months; the other two HAC patrols were housed upstairs, in a house within a close that was the heart of the British intelligence community in Iraq: named and unnamed units and agencies, closeted away from the 'green machine' of the Regular Army lying just outside, within a commandeered palace that lorded it over the lowly foreign city lying just outside the triumphal-arched gates.

For me, Alex, Moxy, Frosty and Tim, this room would be our corner of a foreign field that was England. For Charlie it would be Australia. And for Dougie – Maori – it would be another Antipodean home from home.

Birds chattered outside in the trees as we made beds and readied patrol kit, stripped to the waist in the rising foreign heat. But even their twittering sounded unfamiliar and strange, coming in single harsh, angry chirps just beyond the meshed windows keeping malarial mosquitoes outside.

We made shelves beside our beds from planks of wood and bricks found outside. And we filled them with the clutter of our lives, present, past and hoped for. Photos of loved ones took their place alongside hand grenades, bullets and the water we were learning to down in litres. And on the wall space above our beds, posters of pin-up girls took their place beside street maps of the city and the flags of our home countries. We made it our home, but it was not Home.

I did not have a wall space at the head of my bed on which to pin fantasies of a life left behind, or reminders of where we were now. I had a window. So at night, through the gauze of my mosquito net and the lattice of ripped mesh covering the window beyond, I would instead have the gaze of the moon and the stars looking down on me. I was happy with that; in the quiet of night before sleep came I could look up and share the same heavens with the girl I had left behind.

So while Charlie in the bed beside me set about pinning an Australian flag to his wall, I lay on mine and busied myself with teasing him how, even though he'd been born and raised in Darwin, because both his parents were British he was a closet 'Pom' really – and especially now he was in the British Army.

I chuckled as he took the bait and bantered back about how he'd rather be a closet Pom than a closet Brummy. Mind you, he had a point: I was Oxford-born but still hadn't quite shaken the occasional Midlands lilt on some words from two years working near Birmingham, especially when I was tired, or 'toy-ered' as Cecilia loved to tease me. I went quiet for a second and smiled wistfully at the thought of her.

'Jesus, Wood! I didn't mean it,' Charlie said looking at me, flag now pinned at an amusingly askew angle to the wall.

'No, no, mate – sorry, just miles away. Don't worry, Cecilia thinks I'm a Brummy too.'

'Well there you go then. She might want to have your babies, but she's got that right.'

'Oh – touché!' I laughed back at him.

One bed over from Charlie, with an *FHM* girly poster just fixed to his wall, Moxy, as 2IC, waded in with mock-authority. 'What's that Trooper Edwards is saying, Jake? Is he being insubordinate?'

'What the fuck?' Charlie squeaked indignantly, pointing a finger playfully at me. 'He started it!'

I laughed loudly and then winked fondly across at Charlie as he muttered 'bloody Poms' to himself, before cocking his head over thoughtfully at the unnatural angle of his home flag.

And then Dougie walked in from outside holding . . . something . . . in his hands. It was pole-shaped and about five feet long, the wooden shaft broad and edged at one end before narrowing along its length, just beyond a flourish of feathers, into an evil, ornately carved spearhead.

'Jesus Christ, Dougie! What the hell is that?' Moxy blurted.

'It's a taiaha, mate,' Dougie said proudly, holding the object up in both hands for us all to see. 'Traditional Maori weapon – brought it with us for luck . . . No one's got any objections to me hanging it over the door to the room, have they?'

'No, mate . . . No objections while you're holding that thing anyway!' Moxy laughed open-eyed to him.

So Dougie banged some nails in on which to rest the taiaha, before joining us inside as we sat half-naked on newly made-up beds with new lives settled in, beginning the stripping and cleaning of the weapons we would take with us into the city outside.

It wasn't long before Alex ambled amiably in from his patrol commander's briefing. 'Post!' he called out, throwing the one letter in his hand to me. I caught it in one hand – it was from her. 'You must have been apart for hours now at least,' he grinned at me before sitting heavily down on his bed, bed springs briefly protesting at the six-foot-plus body they suddenly had to contend with. 'Well, that was interesting,' he beamed across at his men. And now quiet in expectation they looked as one back at him. We were going to get our first tasking.

'OK . . .' Moxy said calmly. 'So what are we doing then?'

Some of what Alex said we already knew from prior briefs, but he needed to underline reality now our forerunners, 4/73 Battery, had left for England. So now, as of today, we were the Brigade Surveillance Troop. And he did this effectively, easily and confidently, running us through the situation in town and immediate threats to us out on the ground and back here in base.

And as he spoke the only sounds from the rest of us were the clink of barrels being pulled through and, increasingly as he continued, imaginary specks of dust being obsessively brushed and blown from working parts.

In the past few days there had been three suicide-bomb attacks on police stations in Basra and one New Zealander soldier shot dead.

My eyes glanced to Dougie, but he sat impassive, listening as intently as the rest of us.

There were daily attacks on British bases and patrols around Basra, and these bases were regular targets for insurgent mortar and rocket attacks at night. It had been three days since the palace here had been hit with indirect fire, so we were now overdue some attention.

Out on the ground, the favourite modus operandi of the insurgents was to wait for you to drive past and then hit you with improvised explosive devices (IEDs). Then, depending on how they felt, they would follow up with small-arms fire and RPGs.

The only defence against IEDs was constant vigilance against anything that looked out of place and might conceal them: a pile of rubbish or dirt at the side of the road, disturbed earth on tracks, abandoned vehicles or motorbikes – they had even resorted to planting IEDs in the carcasses of roadkilled dogs.

The suspicion was that the bomb makers were getting help from Iran, both in terms of expertise and materials. And there were reports that the technology of armour-piercing, explosive shaped projectiles had been smuggled across the border too. However, in our 'soft-skinned', cut-down and completely unarmoured Land Rovers, it would of course be academic which particular explosives were used on us.

Our electronic countermeasures (ECM), now we had it working, should guard against IEDs triggered electronically, but the 'Mark One Eyeball' was our only defence against those detonated manually by means of a hidden command wire. If anyone saw anything they were suspicious of they were to flag it up to the rest of the patrol – immediately. Prevention, not cure, was the only way forward.

'The more eagle-eyed of you Special Observers will have noticed the metal uprights sticking out of the top of each Rover,' Alex continued. 'They've been welded on after a craze the insurgents went through of tying wire across the roads to try to decapitate the blokes on top cover – so that's one thing you don't have to worry about so much any more!'

I caught Frosty's eyes bulging in reaction and we laughed silently across at each other.

4/73 . . . Alex paused at this point . . . had their way of patrolling, but ours would be different. On the familiarisation patrol he and Moxy had gone on with them yesterday, it soon became obvious that their method of dealing with the threats was to drive as fast and aggressively as possible. The rationale appeared to be that a fast-moving target was harder to hit. However, Alex said that his driver was concentrating on driving so fast and cutting up as many Iraqis as possible that there was almost a major collision as they pulled onto a dual carriageway. Also, he added, this style of driving made the gunners trying to do 'top cover' on the backs of the Rovers superfluous. There was no way they could provide any security or extra eyes; they were just along for the ride, thrown around the back of the Rovers as they struggled to hold on for dear life. Probably many of them had found God on their tour – while finding relief at the end of their final patrol that they had not met Him just yet.

We would always avoid being bogged down in traffic jams, where we would be juicy targets for an RPG, and would mount pavements to get away if need be, but it would be done at a steady, smooth pace that allowed the top covers to utilise their 360-degree viewpoint and weaponry if needed. And at a slower pace with more spatial awareness, there would be less chance of going back home in a box after colliding with one of the Iraqi drivers – who apparently had not the faintest concept of anything approaching a highway code. They knew enough to drive on the right-hand side of the road, most of the time, but that appeared to be as far as it went.

'Smooth is fast' would instead be our ethos, as instilled in us by Max.

There were silent nods of agreement from all of us.

As a key brigade surveillance asset, he continued, our patrols were currently the only ones allowed out on the ground without the prior permission of the brigade commander. And currently we were the only British unit in the whole of Iraq to be allowed out in the small 'packet' of only two vehicles – and only seven men.

So with this in mind, if it did come down to the basics of life and death in contact with enemy out on the ground, then pure killing aggression would be our only saving grace. Capture, with its only prospect of being paraded in an orange jumpsuit prior to being beheaded, was simply not an option.

Our training would see us through, but it didn't have to be stated any more that now everything was for real. So switching on from the second we left base to the moment we got back in through the gates was vital.

The patrol order would be as rehearsed in our training: Alex in the cab of the front Rover with Tim as his driver and Dougie and Frosty as top cover. In the second vehicle: Moxy commanding with me driving and Charlie as top cover. The ECM would be carried in the front vehicle, so it was up to me as the driver of the second to keep within its protective bubble.

'No probs,' I said confidently. Moxy winked at me.

Our stripped and cleaned weapons were now lying ready in our laps. I smiled inwardly at how Alex had got the message across, covertly casting my eyes around my teammates. To a man, there were only fixed, determined faces mirroring my own.

'So!' Alex suddenly said loudly, smiling easily to us again. 'Tomorrow morning's just a bimble around town to familiarise ourselves with the streets. We'll go up to the base at the Shatt al-Arab Hotel in the morning, have a bit of lunch, then take in some of the slums on our way back home to beer and medals.'

Brief over, Dougie, Charlie and Frosty went back to finishing prepping their personal kit for the patrol tomorrow while Moxy and Tim stood in front of the Basra spot-map hanging on the wall, familiarising themselves with the streets and junctions numbered and colour coded in spots, like 'Yellow 4' or 'Blue 19'.

I sidled up to Alex, now taking the chance to set about his own kit on his bed. 'Alex . . .'

'Jake . . .' he beamed up to me.

'No issues with the patrol order at all, but . . . Would it be OK if sometimes the drivers could swap round with the top covers? You know, sort of mix things up a little bit from time to time – keep people fresh?'

'OK – you worried about being vulnerable in the driver's seat?'

'No . . . Well, to be honest, I just want to get some rounds down.'

'*Loo*-ny . . . !' he laughed. 'Yeah, no worries – Tim's asked the same thing. I'll get Frosty and Charlie driving too, so you'll get your turn, don't worry.'

'Cool – thanks, Alex,' I said gratefully.

'Happy to help,' he said amiably, nonchalantly shrugging his shoulders before I felt his eyes reappraise me for a second. 'I must admit it would have been a little disconcerting having two, sane, otherwise rational men come up to me and say they want to kill the enemy,' he continued, still smiling. 'But it's what we need out here, without a doubt, so you got it – loony.'

'Just want to do my bit,' I grinned back at him.

'Your driver wants to kill people, Moxy!' Alex called across.

'Does he?' Mox glanced up from the map, smiling at me. 'That's good then.'

'*Loo*-nies!'

108

'Happy to help,' I quipped back, and then with all my patrol kit prepped and ready, I went into the downstairs communal area to get an ice-cold bottle of water out of the fridge. Matt was there, already scribbling a first letter home.

'Jake, all right, mate? I was wondering if you could do me a big favour.'

'Yeah, sure,' I said, unscrewing the bottle top before taking the first, refreshingly cool gulps down.

'Thanks, mate. It's Danni, see – I'm a little worried about her as she's on her own with no one else in her position to talk to. Would it be all right if she had Lia's number? It might be good for Lia to have someone else to talk to, too?'

It sounded eminently sensible to me. Wives and girlfriends of TA soldiers weren't used to their men disappearing for six months in harm's way, and there consequently wasn't the natural support network for them in this period that the other halves of regular soldiers might have, living on or near their partners' barracks. I said I'd double-check with Lia on the phone this evening but was sure it would be more than all right.

Tim had appeared beside us now, lifting a can of Coke from the fridge to complement the bag of his beloved Haribo clutched in his other hand. And, sitting with him at the plastic table outside the front of our house, he probed me gently about Cecilia while I enveloped myself in the security blanket of the smoke from my lovely fags.

'I know, mate . . . We had a rocky start, but she's really changed her tune now. I think that's all behind us now . . . I hope.'

'She wants it to be – if she's got any sense she'll know how lucky she is now she's getting a piece of the Woodster,' he said quietly.

'Thanks Tim . . .' I said quietly back. 'Never knew you felt that way, though!'

'No . . . You wrong 'un!' Tim shuddered, shaking his head momentarily at the thought of getting a piece of 'the Woodster' before continuing his vein. 'You know we're all here for each other, though, mate – OK?' His wide, earnest eyes were fixed on mine.

'I know, mate – thank you.'

'Cool – give me Cecilia's number as well if you like; I can pass it onto Liv so she's got someone else to get pissed with!'

And after an afternoon spent sweating out my body weight in a high-ceilinged, palatial reception room converted into a squaddies' gym, and 'scoffing' in an even more ornately decorated, cavernously huge, converted dining hall, I took myself away at dusk through the gathering swarms of mosquitoes to an outbuilding in the palace complex to phone the girl I loved.

The phone cubicles were only separated by single sheets of plywood, so privacy was not an option. The combined hubbub of soldiers' conversations echoed around the high, marble-clad room.

I entered the long identifying number allocated to me from the satphone card in my pocket, then dialled in her mobile number. I had twenty minutes; my standard allocation each week to phone anyone back home. At nineteen minutes and thirty seconds there would be a warning beep, and then the call to your loved one would be automatically terminated.

I phoned my mum first to let her know I was OK. And though I knew she would be worrying about me at least as much as Cecilia, I had to keep things short.

The automated voice told me I had 'thirteen . . . minutes . . .' to phone Lia when I hung up. I dialled in her mobile number and then waited for the call to connect and for her to pick up, pressing the receiver close to my ear while I waited, trying to close the thousands of miles that now parted us.

'Hello?'

She was too faint – she was too far away. I had to press a finger into my other ear to block out the noise around me. 'Hi, baby.'

It was hard to make out the first words she said; they were too choked up in sobs. 'I love you . . . Are you OK . . . ?' I finally made out.

'I'm totally OK, don't worry – I'm fine. I love you too . . . How are you?'

There was the sound of her breath hard in the phone as she struggled to get the words out. 'I miss you so much – I didn't realise how much I would.'

I'd feared she didn't realise quite what the separation would mean – and bar two weeks' R & R in June, she now had six months of this stretching out in front of her. I hated myself for doing this to her.

'You're leaving the Army when you get back, do you hear me? I'm never going through this again!'

'OK, baby – I promise,' I said gently, trying to soothe her, feeling the pain of not being able to hold her tight and cuddle hers away. This seemed to calm her down a bit though.

'I'm sorry, baby, I'm just finding it hard already,' she said.

'I know – it's OK, don't worry. But the first few days are going to be the hardest – it's going to get easier, though, you'll see.'

I had no idea if this was true.

And with only silence coming down the phone at me, I had no idea if she believed this to be true either.

'Look, we're going to get through these weeks to June OK – you'll see . . . I've got a window above my bed – I can go to sleep looking up at the same moon as you.'

Then the sound of a choke betrayed what I had done to her again. 'Come back to me safe, please!' she pleaded suddenly.

'We've already shaken on that baby – that's a done deal, remember.'

'OK – yeah – I'm sorry . . .'

'Don't be, it's OK – you can say whatever you want to me.'

'Like I want to live with you when you get back?'

That momentarily stunned me. But instead of an aftershock, I found I was only left with a warm glow at the thought of it. I realised I was still getting to grips with how this goddess only wanted me, now.

'That sounds good – maybe you can start looking at places while I'm away! We can look at them when I'm back in June.'

'Really?' she sounded excited.

I also thought it would give her something positive to focus on, to look forward to – if that's what she wanted. 'Doesn't scare me – I can't think of anything I want more.'

As long as I get this place out of my system first.

I heard her excited laugh down the phone and felt the ache inside of me heal over at the sound of it again.

And then the cold, mechanical beep suddenly chirped over us, sounding the one-minute-warning death knell to the closest we could ever be for a week.

'What was that?' she asked, alarm back in her voice.

I was going to have to be quick. 'It beeps to let you know you've only got a minute left – I'm sorry, baby. Look, is it OK if I give your number to Matt and Tim? They want their girlfriends Danni and Liv to have someone to talk to who's going through the same thing. It might help you too.'

'Yeah, of course – please do. Did you get my letter?'

'Yes, it was lovely, thank you – please keep writing; I'll do the same.'

'I sent it before you left so it would be waiting for you. I'm going to write every day. It feels like I'm talking to you when I do it . . . And

I can touch your necklace every time I think of you. Thank you again – the girls at work are so jealous!'

She laughed again and I let her happiness flood down the line to me – but I knew our time was fast running out.

'I love you,' I whispered.

The line went dead.

I didn't know if she heard me. I put the receiver slowly back on the hook and looked around. New soldiers carried on new conversations beside me. And behind, the first of a line of soldiers stood waiting to take my place in the time-rationed conveyer belt of telephone calls that together with post, or email, were our only lifeline back to the warmth of Home. I walked numbly out into the dark and heat of the Iraqi night, looked once at the moon above me through the swirling dark clouds of biting insects, then set out back to the house and my friends-in-arms.

*

It was still pitch dark when I was woken by the calls of '*Allaaah-hu-Akbar!*'

The tinny, amplified calls to prayer beyond the palace walls pierced our slumber, every repetition of the drawn-out phrase seeming to rise higher in pitch, volume and length. But then that might just have been my perception, born of irritation.

I pressed the light button on my watch: 0430. *Jesus* . . .

'Right – he's going to officially get on my tits,' someone said.

'Time for someone to get their first kill, I think,' Charlie croaked from the bed beside me.

And, looking up, I saw that the moon did not shine through the window above me.

*

A few hours later, our patrol's first drive into the city went uneventfully and seamlessly by. Alex navigated us faultlessly to the 'Hotel' base on the other side of Basra, efficiently calling out each turning and spot-mark in advance to Moxy over the radio.

We threaded our way through the strange streets, past battered old pick-ups and minibuses with curtained-shut windows, ancient motorbikes carrying white-robed and dark-faced men, and dog-tired donkeys hauling trailers containing entire families. Stern-faced men whipped the beasts into subservience while black-burqa'd women snapped at and slapped the cowed children sitting still in the back.

And too-small and too-young dirt-grimed children ran after every one of these at junctions, calling out pitifully as they tried to sell their wares of bottled water and fruit. But no one stopped.

Most roads were dual carriageways with crumbling-concrete central reservations in the middle and decrepit, one- and two-storey sand-bricked houses to the sides. Piles of rubbish, earth and accumulated, unidentifiable dirt seemed to be everywhere.

And then there was the smell – the high, stinking stench of open sewage festering ripe in the hot, heavy air. It was not always there, but it filled your nostrils in the slums you thought could not be any more run-down than the last you drove through.

Shining incongruously clean and high above the miasma was the occasional billboard advertising the latest Samsung mobile phone, or another seemingly unobtainable material good. Perhaps these were signs of the 'light of liberation' we had brought with us.

It was only mid-morning, but the bright, harsh sunlight was already cooking the city and broiling us inside the cabs of the Rovers. Sweat soaked the linings of our heavy Kevlar helmets and ran down our torsos in the trapped heat beneath our body armour weighed down with weaponry and water, pooling wet in the cooking pots of our groins.

My job was relatively simple, though: I had only to keep the second vehicle within the protective bubble of the ECM in front, while keeping enough of a distance that if an IED did go off, only one of our two vehicles would be destroyed. As it turned out, this did require some aggressive and defensive driving in turn to ensure a resident's vehicle didn't come between our two Rovers. And like everyone else in the patrol, laden down and sweating from heat and mental effort, my eyes constantly scanned near, far, left, right and up and down for something – anything – on the unfamiliar and foreign streets that looked out of place.

So lunch at the 'Hotel' was pretty welcome, even if it was slop. And we drank down gratifyingly icy-cool cans of pop beside one of our vehicles while Alex got our next tasking over the radio.

'Troops!' Alex called smilingly as he walked up to us. I noticed how the easy confidence exuded from him, how it flowed so easily into his men. 'Mmmm . . .' he said, spying our cold cans. 'Did you get me one?'

'*Jawohl mein fuhrer,*' Charlie said, reaching into the cold box in the back of the Rover to give Alex his.

'*Danke schoen . . .*' Alex thanked him, cracking it open to take a glug before unfolding his map on the Rover's opened tailgate.

We thought we were going to get a brief for another easy familiarisation drive back to the palace.

We were wrong.

'Just spoken to Max to let him know we're leaving the Hotel. Turns out the brigade commander's spoken with him, though, and now they want us to go back via Orange 6.'

Our eyes scanned vainly over the map before Alex pointed it out.

'OK – you know that's in an out-of-bounds area?' Moxy pointed out.

'Yep – I pointed that out to them too, but that's why we're going there.' Alex jabbed a finger at the four spots along a three-kilometre-long road, Orange 6 to Orange 9, while knocking back another slurp. 'You may as well know that's called "IED Alley" – no one's been up it for two months, for obvious reasons. So they want us to take a butcher's up it now – filming, obviously.'

Silence.

'Right . . .' Moxy filled the quiet, as our brains processed what was now being asked of us.

'So they want us to go down the three-kilometre length of IED Alley – the first callsign for two months – in soft-skinned, completely unarmoured Land Rovers?' I confirmed.

'Yep.'

'And film it – which involves going slower.'

'Yep.'

'OK!' I laughed. 'Just wanted to get things straight!'

Time for a last fag . . .

'Look – I know!' Alex said laughing with his hands in the air. 'Now's the time for anyone to put two pencils up their nose and a pair of underpants on their head and go "Wibble"!'

'No, no – that's all right,' Moxy smiled. 'I'm sure the lads were just hoping the tour would last longer than a day, that's all!'

Gallows laughter was released all round. Charlie grabbed the cigarettes out of my hand and stuffed one into his mouth. I lit it for him with a wink.

'Anyway, Max says he'll have some beers waiting for us when we get back, so let's just get it over with – it won't take long,' Alex carried on unflappably.

'Coolio – he's buying, though,' Moxy asserted, pulling his body armour back on.

'Beer o'clock – let's fucking do it then!' Tim said for us all. And we followed Moxy's cue, kitting up in kind before clambering back into our vehicles.

'Hang on, can't a condemned man finish his Fanta first?' Alex called out.

'No time for that, Alex! *Come on*, we've got beers waiting!' Tim said from his driver's door, rolling his eyes exaggeratedly in mock impatience.

'Loonies . . . I'm surrounded by loonies!'

*

No one says a word as our vehicles crawl along the narrow, pock-marked dirt road. And IED Alley is an alley. It is little more than a three-kilometre-long rat run enclosed by high mud walls so close in places that our Rovers only just squeeze through.

And over the bumps and pits in the track's surface, we have to drive even slower than anticipated, crawling along at little more than walking pace so the covert cameras can record our journey in vibration-free detail.

Heads you live. Tails you die.

The upside of our pace is that within each lingering, drawn-out second, our darting eyes have more time to search the broken road surface, claustrophobically close mud walls, bystanders, alleyways, rooftops, parked vehicles and any real or imagined movement ahead, beside or behind us.

But the flip side our thumping hearts know is that this gives even more time for one lurking, unseen man to wait for the perfect moment to press one button and for us to be blown in a split second into splinters of metal, flesh, bone and darkness.

So no one says a word as we go up IED Alley. With every primordial sense primed to mortal maximum in the knowledge that death could come at any second, each second passes by in eternities, as each metre of the 3,000 slides sickeningly slowly beneath our wheels.

But from the soaking hands gripping the steering wheel, up the arms that do not shake, to behind my scouring, flickering eyes, there very soon comes the realisation that if it is going to happen – if we are going to die at that bend just ahead – or beside this parked car we squeeze past now – or that pile of rubbish – or anywhere along the stretch of dirt surface it would be so easy to bury a rigged artillery shell beneath – then it is just going to happen, and nothing I can do is going to prevent it. If we do not see the hidden bomb that will kill us, it will simply be time.

So inside the searing heat of the cab of the Rover, through the sweat stinging my eyes and pouring down beneath my useless body armour – beyond my heart beating uselessly for its life somewhere inside me – behind my flailing, searching eyes assessing for anything that might kill, my mind detaches from the fear, because in its paralysis it is useless. And though I am now numb, I am calm: because I know I am now as much of a passenger as I am a driver.

So in coldness I smoothly manoeuvre the Rover, with its unseen, rolling camera. And I am one with it, for it is as mechanically indifferent as I am.

Fuck it.

*

Brakes squealed in delight as our Rovers wheeled slowly through the chicane at the guarded palace gate. And then, through and free, Tim and I booted the accelerators in ecstasies of relief, racing each other along the riverside back home.

I heard the high note of the engine singing in my ears, and felt the deliciously cold slipstream pouring in through my buffeting window and the wide smile of a reprieved man breaking out all over my face – alive!

'Well done, everyone; some well-earned beers tonight, I think,' Alex's voice crackled calmly over the radio. I could tell he was smiling too.

'Yeah – "key brigade surveillance asset" or "expendable STABs" – take your pick!' Dougie's twang filled our ears.

'Well, you're expendable at least, Kiwi!' Moxy transmitted back, winking sparkly-eyed at me.

Dougie turned round from the back of the speeding vehicle ahead of us and, with a wide, toothy grin, fingered us the most quintessential of English V-signs.

We both laughed loudly from our cab, and Moxy returned the gesture before quietening to take his helmet off. And for only a second he looked tiredly into it, before the wringing-wet hair matted to his head became the only sign of the strain.

*

We were watching *Love, Honour and Obey* with tins of lager in our hands when the mortars came in that night.

Ray Winstone had just walked away giggling from one of his hospitalised henchmen, who, after being stabbed, cut, force-fed LSD and dog food and finally blown up, said he felt like he 'shouldn't be in this line of work any more'.

The muffled thump of the first incoming mortar cut through our laughter, landing a couple of hundred metres away in the palace grounds somewhere. And then in the short pauses it takes someone to drop successive rounds down a mortar tube, the second, third and fourth rounds exploded in quick succession – round the cookhouse, I thought.

They were on target, but they weren't hitting us here in our little house. We all stood up from the plastic chairs in our shorts and T-shirts, looking at each other in the lengthening silence . . . No more explosions . . . No screams for 'Medic!' . . . Then we just laughed and sat back down again. What were we going to do – put body armour on and run around outside with our hands in the air? So we just carried on watching the DVD; there wasn't anything else to do. And if a mortar was going to land slap bang among us and kill us all while we slept later that night, there wasn't anything we could do about that either.

*

First thing the next morning, one of the other patrols drove out into the desert to practise their contact drills. As an interesting add-on afterwards, just for interest, they decided to test the effectiveness of the ballistic protection welded just behind the two seats in the front of everyone's Rovers. These seat-high metal sheets were the one bit of armour we had, though naturally they would only be effective if we were very specifically being shot at from behind, with the guy on top cover obviously having to hope the incoming supersonic Kalashnikov rounds somehow missed him.

Apparently they'd just put a spare sheet of this stuff up against a sand berm, walked back 50 metres and let rip at it with an AK-47.

Close inspection immediately afterwards revealed that not only did this 'ballistic protection' fail to stop any round from just going straight through it, but also that it actually spewed shards of itself out as shrapnel along with the bullets. They felt this was perhaps a cause for concern, so radioed back with the friendly advice to immediately cut this armour out of all our Rovers. And when they brought back the armour as evidence, now converted into an outsized colander, we all agreed it was indeed quite a good idea to cut this armour out of our Rovers, immediately.

With the worse-than-fucking-useless metal sheets lying on the ground beside our nakedly vulnerable vehicles, I tried to see some way of improving our survivability in the Rovers. It wasn't much of a brainwave, but with IED Alley fresh in our minds, Charlie and I spent two hours cable-tying spare body armour to the inside of the drivers' and vehicle commanders' doors. We even made sure the Kevlar ballistic plates in them all faced outwards. The improvisation might do something, though, of course, it might equally be a completely desperate gesture and not make a blind bit of difference. We didn't know; we hadn't been on the receiving end of a high-explosive artillery shell improvised explosive device before. Personally, I thought the armoured 'Snatch' Rovers couldn't come soon enough, whatever their armour was like – whenever we got them.

After hopefully waking up the bombers along IED Alley with our little jaunt down it, we spent the next few days on foot, pretending to be a 'normal' British Army patrol along the stretch of main road IED Alley adjoined. Our cover for patrolling this area was the handing out of educational leaflets about democracy to the locals we came across. In reality, we had intelligence on specific vehicles and individuals to watch out for every time we happened to have the entrance to IED Alley in eyeshot.

We didn't see any of these vehicles or individuals, though. In fact, the only thing I gleaned from these patrols was the general ambivalence among locals to the propaganda leaflets we were handing out.

Women were nowhere to be seen along the open stretch of road; it would be against local customs to approach them anyway. I felt sure, though, that at least some of the men I handed leaflets to would remember Saddam Hussein's brutal backlash against this city in 1991 – but instead, to a man, I felt we were only just being tolerated now.

Approaching a clapped-out orange and white taxi parked at the roadside, I was going to offer the driver a leaflet with my 'clean' right hand. But I saw his eyes glaring harsh, boring into me. And with this I saw how his hidden hands could so easily bring up a concealed weapon. So my clean right hand instead held the pistol grip of my rifle as I walked up to him, and it was my 'unclean' left hand that proffered the democracy leaflet to him.

It was indeed as if I'd put a piece of used lavatory paper in his hand. He glanced cursorily over the Arabic bulletpoints, trumpeting the benefits of a political system he had no experience of and which was now being imposed on him, before just angrily shrugging his shoulders. With a despairing look of incomprehension, he thrust the leaflet firmly back into my hand before removing me from his vision – staring straight ahead, slowly shaking his head.

Later on that patrol, further down the road, I came across a painted mural on a wall. I couldn't read the Arabic writing, but beneath the picture of an AK-47 with a big red cross emblazoned over it was the painting of a dead child lying on the ground, bright-red blood streaming out of a gunshot wound to his head.

Democracy doesn't mean an awful lot when your standard and security of life takes a plunge following the toppling of your dictator. And this was no one else's doing but ours.

*

We hear results are wanted from IED Alley and that a plan is being formulated to set up a decoy to lure the bombers out. And we hear the details involve us operating a covert OP overlooking IED Alley while 'someone' drives up it at the same time every day in a four-tonner lorry.

What we know is that a four-tonner is not in any way armoured. But what we reason is that the powers that be above us think that such a juicy, fat, lonely, unarmoured and vulnerable target would be impossible to resist for the bombers.

We think that perhaps it might be more accurate to label the four-tonner decoy as 'sacrificial bait'. And we think that for 'someone', at least, the plan should be christened 'Operation Certain Death'.

And we hear that, for some reason, 'someone' does not step forward to volunteer to drive the four-tonner. And we imagine 'someone' is probably fairly relieved when, after a rethink, this plan is quietly, and permanently, not put into action.

*

It was Piers Morgan and some American soldiers running an anarchic prison up in Abu Ghraib who ended our involvement with IED Alley.

In Iraq we received newspapers a couple of days after their printing in the UK, but for us the pictures printed in them were still just as striking and abhorrent as for any civilian looking at them at home.

We hadn't received training in urinating on prisoners, sodomising them, constructing naked pyramids out of them or coercing them to

119

masturbate, naked, with bags on their heads – nor did we feel in the slightest way inclined to even if we had the opportunity. But it would be us – the rest of the soldiers out here who did not lead naked prisoners round on leashes, attach electrodes to their bodies and abuse their faith – who would weather the storm of the pictures' publication.

Having your countryman dictator do such things to you was one thing – though the chances were you would have been permanently disappeared afterwards. But to welcome an occupying infidel force into your country in the guise of liberators and then perceive them to be just another devil – and cursing your sacred faith, to boot – was quite another.

It was therefore not that much of a surprise when on the morning of 7 May we heard of a prominent radical cleric in Basra offering $350 reward for the capture of a British soldier and $150 for the corpse of a dead one. Though apparently any captured female British soldier would be graciously allowed to live on as a slave, I was under no illusions why there would be a higher reward if one of us were captured. I felt pretty comfortable it would involve a video camera, some plastic sheeting on the floor and a machete in a militant's hand being the last thing you ever saw in your life, as your head was hacked off to praises of '*Allah-hu-Akbar*!'

And therefore it was not that surprising when we heard of more than 40 attacks on British forces that morning and that everyone was being 'locked down' in their bases. And that included us – though we had been only minutes away from deploying onto the streets.

One of our other patrols was still out in the city, though, still having to make its way back to the relative safety of the palace. But when we heard over the radio that they had driven safely through a contact with our enemy and would be back with us in minutes, our feelings of relief at their safe passage were tempered by frustration – because as volunteer soldiers trained and primed to fight, we wanted to fight those who would fight us. And now, 'locked down' and impotent, we could not.

So when the other patrol pulled up outside the house still on an adrenalin high, marvelling at how there was not a single bullet hole in their vehicles and how the enemy RPG had whistled in between their vehicles, and enthusing in their comparisons over how many rounds some of them fired in reply, we did welcome them home, but we soon had to take ourselves away from them.

We sat on our beds in silence with our heads in our hands, mourning the fight that had been taken from us.

Later, I overheard Max talking to the other patrol commander, John, in the corridor.

'Think I'm going to have to organise some counselling,' Max said.

'Yeah ... I guess the lads have been through quite a lot this morning.'

'Not for your patrol, you cunt – I mean Alex's!'

'Oh, right – yeah, see what you mean!' John replied, laughing back. *Har-dee-fucking-har.*

*

We did get out that evening, though – and in armoured Snatches, which were mysteriously now available to us. But in all too unfortunate fortune, no one cared to shoot at us in our scoot across town to the 'JDAM' base.

We were going to JDAM because in all serendipity it directly overlooked the Basra offices of the OMS – the Office of Muqtada al-Sadr. We had been told that (though apparently able to trace his lineage directly to the Prophet Muhammad) Muqtada al-Sadr was a firebrand cleric and newly declared Enemy Number One of the coalition forces in Iraq. And with his 'Mahdi Army' militia already causing havoc in the Sadr City part of Baghdad, his Basra deputy, Abdul al-Bahadli, had now heeded his master's rallying call to arms. So our patrol was tasked to run an OP from JDAM to facilitate an arrest operation on Bahadli the very next day.

It was as we were setting up our OP in one of the guard towers encrusting JDAM's high, thick walls that we found out how JDAM had earned its name. After apparently spending an interesting morning firing his General Purpose Machine Gun (GPMG) at insurgents trying to kill him, the now bored and drained sentry there told us that a JDAM was a type of 2,000-pound bomb.

'So what's that got to do with this place?' Alex asked him.

'Well, this place used to be the Ba'ath Party's Secret Police HQ,' the soldier replied flatly, absent-mindedly rolling a cigarette while keeping an eye on the OMS building across the road.

'Yes ... ?'

'Oh, right, yeah: well, they bombed it good and proper last year – only thing is, one of the bombs didn't go off.'

'Right ...'

'So basically we're all just sleeping beside a fuck-off great unexploded bomb here – you'll get used to it, though, don't worry.'

'So that's buried somewhere in that caved-in building behind us?'

'Yeah – that's not all, though.' The soldier's eyes briefly lit up. 'There were a load of prisoners in the basement apparently: one of the bombs that did go off hit a water main and they all drowned, trapped in their cells – nasty, eh?'

Then his tired eyes went back to watch over the OMS building, and the street, and anywhere else from where someone might want to attack him.

We all paused to take a backward glance at the tomb behind us. I couldn't work out which disturbed me more: the thought of the corpses of poor drowned buggers still trapped in their cells, rotting somewhere near us, or the ticking death waiting to blow us into oblivion at any moment while we slept.

'Oh yeah, and make sure you keep clear of the mine-taped areas round here too – that's where the unexploded mortars are.'

'OK, thanks very much for the heads-up, mate. Look, you can get yourself away now – we're all set up.'

'Right-o,' the soldier replied blankly, taking himself to the ladder leading back down to the rubble outside the guard tower. 'Oh, and watch that junction on your right too,' he said, climbing onto the ladder's top. 'They like to pop up and have a burst at you from there.'

'OK, thanks mate . . .'

Alex waited till the exhausted soldier was out of earshot before suddenly clapping his hands once, beaming at us all. '*Okay* . . . Sweet dreams, everyone!'

*

For some reason the arrest operation on Bahadli was cancelled the next day; we didn't know why. So for the next week and a bit we sweated in the OP, conducting 'pattern of life' observations on the OMS building instead.

We watched Bahadli go in and out of the building all day every day – past his Mahdi Army minions milling around outside, bold as brass with AK-47s in their hands. Though now we had the enemy squarely in our sights, it turned out they'd obviously decided to take a break from their shooting. We couldn't just shoot them; due to our 'white card' rules of engagement we had to wait for them to shoot at us first. And this they clearly knew. So we just shot photos of their comings and goings instead, logging them all in infinite detail along with their lounging around.

There is a lot of time to think in an OP. Your eyes are focussed through one telescopic lens on one particular door or gateway for hours each day. But no matter how long you have been staring through the lens, and no matter how bored, hot or uncomfortable you are, your eyes must never wander from the lens – because the second you look away, you know Osama bin Laden is going to walk through that gate – and then all your prior patience will have been in vain.

So though your body is still, bar feeling for the tepid water bottle beside you or swatting the unseen flies that constantly fly back to tickle your grubby, sweat-filmed skin, your mind is not still – because you cannot afford for it to be still.

This affords your mind carte blanche to wander while your eyes do not, because you have to keep your deadening brain awake while you stare at that blue door, or that green gateway, which has not moved for the last hour but might swing open at any second to reveal Osama bin Laden and Satan being sprinkled with confetti after a simple family service inside. Or fat, old, bearded Bahadli might just walk out instead – not that he was going to be arrested, of course.

I thought of what to write in my next letter to Cecilia that night, in reply to her latest card telling me of things that I cannot tell you about. I thought of her soft cheek against mine, the slide of her naked back and her body pressing to mine, pulling me inside her to the hilt, eyes shining to mine.

I had to stop thinking of that, though – it was too distracting; plus I didn't want Charlie, who was sitting beside me with the GPMG, getting the wrong idea.

Instead, my mind drifted over where we were now – from Iraq, to Basra, to this bombed Secret Police HQ and, ultimately, to inside this sanger. Up in the OP with my eyes focussed sharply on the insurgents across the busy road, it struck me how the daily travels and travails of the locals trying to go about their everyday lives between us was just something in the periphery of my vision. And the background hum of their vehicles and voices was merely audio wallpaper to the squaddie television I was tuned into in front of me.

We eyed the insurgents. They eyed us back. And caught in between us, overlooked somewhere down below, were the long-suffering and forgotten silent majority just trying to get by.

Up in the guard tower, it occurred to me how removed we were from these ordinary people: in culture, creed and just sheer physicality. I wondered if in taking over the installations of the deposed dictator, as we had here and at the palace, we coalition forces could be just aiding the perception of one oppressor being supplanted by another. It made good tactical sense to take them over, as they were heavily fortified with thick, high walls and guard towers – but I couldn't shake the thought that this just couldn't help our image in the local populace's eyes.

I considered that if I was an Iraqi man with a family to feed, us Brits were perhaps just as much of a problem as the insurgents. I considered that perhaps our very presence was fanning the flames of insurgency, out of the embers of the 'fires of hell' stoked for Saddam.

Good speech, Colonel, but we need you again now.

Now we had invaded, I couldn't see any option but for us to stay on until the new Iraqi government was up and running, and until the Iraqi Army and police could stand on their own two feet. We had chosen to open Pandora's Box. We had released the bottled-up tensions inherent in this artificially drawn-up country, raging like desert jinn across its sands 'with the fire of a scorching wind', to quote the Qur'an. But if we just left now without taking responsibility for the aftermath, the country would just implode further as Ba'athists, al-Qaeda, Shias, Sunnis and Kurds killed each other unabated in civil war. And the poor bloody silent majority who just wanted to get on with their lives would wade knee-deep in the crimson of their bloodbath.

This was the quagmire we sat in, now the 'shock and awe' of the waters of our Great Flood was sucking away into the earth and evaporating away beneath the Iraqi sun – now its muddying, ebbing depths were tingeing red.

So if we had to be here among all this, I finally concluded that from a personal survivability point of view it did actually make quite a lot of sense to be housed in whatever readily fortified buildings were to hand. For if this meant I had a better chance of coming back alive to Cecilia at the end of it, then for the remaining five months I was here I could tolerate the perception some people might have that I was just another supplanting oppressor.

I concluded my internal symposium of why I now sat in this sanger, inside this bombed former Secret Police HQ, in Basra. Though as an afterthought I did remember another, personal and caustic tsunami that had led to me coming to Iraq again.

I trusted her daily letters of love now, though. And, secure in the love they promised, I spared a moment to think of my previous love rival. A priori, he was only guilty of falling for the same girl I had, so I bore him no ill will. And knowing the a posteriori hurt of losing her too well, I hoped he was OK.

Perversely, she was my light at the end of the tunnel now. For when the mortars did come in most nights, my keenness for shooting action began to be tempered by a growing ingratitude to some US soldiers in Abu Ghraib – and some Brit soldiers too, according to the *Daily Mirror*, who I felt had leapt clean over the line of what was humanly and decently acceptable.

Shooting bullets back at people trying to kill you with bullets was one thing, but waiting for the next mortar to come in, wondering over the lingering seconds if it was going to blow you out of this world, was less than fun. You don't feel your mortality any more than when you have absolutely no control over it.

So when on 15 May it transpired that the photos Piers Morgan had printed in the *Daily Mirror* were fakes, I resolved to never sully my eyes on that rag of a tabloid ever again. That they were apparently victims of a 'calculated and malicious hoax' did not wash with me. Now the locals were yet more against us; now our lives here were yet further, and needlessly, endangered. Though Piers Morgan apparently resigned as the newspaper's editor immediately afterwards, it was beyond me why the Army still continued to buy the *Mirror* in bulk and send it to us out here. I resolved to throw every single copy I saw straight in the bin and promised myself the pleasure of doing the same to Piers Morgan and US Army Private Charles A. Graner, Jr if ever I had the misfortune to meet them.

Someone got hold of a thermometer and put it in the OP early one afternoon just to see how fucking hot it really actually fucking was under the tin roof and behind the sandbag-insulated walls.

Fifty-five degrees centigrade, it said.

Maybe the heat had got to my head.

*

After watching Bahadli get into various vehicles with armed cronies to be driven away at the end of each day, our patrol was tasked with following him 'for one turn', just to get a better idea of where he disappeared to each night. So we waited behind the gates of JDAM, fully kitted up in our vehicles, while Dougie ran the OP alone, watching out for Bahadli leaving the OMS building so he could 'trigger' us onto our subject.

In front of us, the excited young soldier manning the gates was like a sprinter at the blocks, wired, wide-eyed and on tenterhooks to fling the doors open for us as soon as we started our engines, so we could 'get the fucker'.

If only, mate . . .

We imagined that our controller, callsign 'Zero', thought as we did: that Bahadli would be heading home to a Basra backstreet. And, as expected, after Dougie radioed 'standby' to us and the young soldier opened the gates in world-record time, Bahadli's vehicle did make its way straight to the city outskirts. Alex radioed to Zero that we were 'mobile', and we trailed the black Land Cruiser at a discreet distance, playing the part of a routine British Army patrol.

But the 'one turn' he eventually made turned out to be onto the Route 6 motorway – ultimately leading way up north past the hotspot of Al Amarah to Baghdad. Alex tried calling through to Zero as we made our 'one turn' onto Route 6, but it was at this point, of course, that our comms went down.

After some kilometres up the motorway, we could have cautiously pulled back and returned to base. But after a week and a bit of watching the fucker swanning about with impunity, we were bored and frustrated. It was just as good to blow out the cobwebs as we barrelled along, keeping Bahadli just in sight, as it was to satisfy our piqued interest as to just where this cleric-insurgent laid his head at night. If we found that out, then maybe someone could actually arrest him without a full-scale assault on the OMS building.

After about 20 kilometres he pulled off the road onto a dirt track leading to some low mud-brick buildings. Innocent as can be, we sailed past him up Route 6 before turning off in turn after a kilometre to lay up in a roadside power station, vehicles parked out of sight. We wanted to see if his pulling off was a ruse and whether he was going further north – not that we could then follow him, though.

But after half an hour and no sign of him, it looked like his turning off on that dirt track was maybe genuine. Maybe we could put in an OP on this location. Maybe Bahadli could be picked up away from his Mahdi Army HQ in town.

When we finally managed to get through on the radio, Zero was at first a little confused when we told him that we were 20 kilometres north of Basra. Our last transmission had been that we were 'mobile' just outside JDAM, after all. But 'no worries', we were told – though we now had to get ourselves back to the palace, as 'something else' had come up.

Back at the palace, that 'something else' turned out to be all hell breaking loose in the city of Nasiriyah, with hundreds of Mahdi Army wreaking havoc in a determined offensive to kill as many of the Italian troops and Coalition Provisional Authority (CPA) civilians based there as they could. Apparently it was touch and go whether the Italians were going to withdraw from the entire city, taking the CPA and their semblance of rule with them.

We waited pent up in our room while we found out what this would mean for us. When Alex walked in from a brief with Max with a gleam in his eye, I felt the hunger inside of me, yearning for the release of action, breaking out into an evil, closed-mouth smile.

Alex started by telling us that when Max had learned of our 'one turn' taking us twenty kilometres away from Basra, he had apparently turned to Zero and asked, 'What are those lunatics up to now?'

'Don't worry, though,' Alex smiled. 'It was a compliment.'

Now our patrol had established itself as one that was quietly craving combat, we were being lined up for a job that would answer all our prayers. Tomorrow at first light we would drive up to the Shaibah logistical base and join a British armoured battle group that was being formed there. When it was released to counter-attack the Mahdi Army in Nasiriyah with overwhelming force, it was our team that would spearhead the advance into the city, as its forward reconnaissance asset.

*

We had previously only known the sprawling, disused airfield at Shaibah as the site of our acclimatisation prior to first deploying into Basra – or where our endless supply of beers came from, surreptitiously acquired by Max 'in the margins', as he labelled such grey administrative areas.

Now along its vast stretch of runway, along the vast stretch of mechanised military hardware our two vehicles sat at the front of, it was our launching point into the unknown. For the only thing we did know was that there was going to be a God almighty fight – and we were going to be at the forefront of it, with whatever that might entail for us.

We waited quietly for the off, the sun rising from its red, angry dawn higher and higher into the sky, tension simmering thick in the climbing temperature. Directly behind us were rows of Challenger 2 main battle tanks, and behind them the hordes of mechanised infantry in their Warrior armoured personnel carriers (APCs): row upon row of turrets bristling cannons and guns, all baking hotter in the glare of the new day.

We sat at the head of all this, quiet and alone in our two vehicles. But tight smiles of self-confidence were spread across our faces: all fleeting, stomach-fluttering fear buried beneath an avalanche of quiet excitement and deadly purpose. Now we were going to come into our own.

Waiting . . . Waiting for the off . . . Waiting for our baptism in blood . . . Waiting for God, for all I knew.

Come on . . . bring it on . . .

The wide tarmac dwarfed our two little vehicles, the empty expanse of the runway ahead of us drawing out far into the distance. Beyond where the pale blue of the empty sky met the shimmering waves of heat rising up from the bleached tarmac and pale sand, lost in that mirage somewhere across the barren desert and waste, lay the mirage of Nasiriyah and all that it promised – lethal and dark.

I remembered my father telling me that when he was a young man my age, he had once landed his RAF transport plane on this very runway – in another time, when Iraq was a very different place. Through the sands of time, with perhaps the last grains of my short life falling through the hourglass of mine now, I saw how the cycles of life could turn full circle. Stroke-struck and in the twilight of his life, my father now waited at home while his young son sat on the runway his wheels had kissed so many years ago. Now, his son's wheels waited to spirit him away from this place and into the cauldron of combat – and death, for all I knew. I wondered how my dad would have felt back then, if he had known his yet unborn son would come here too, waiting for perhaps the very end of his short life in the outlying sands beyond.

I hoped one day I would have a son. But though it might be the end of him and me, I needed to do this first. I needed to live.

So we carried on waiting, through the culinary highlight of lunch out of an aluminium bag and then deep into the roast of the late afternoon.

It was getting about time for another scrumptious meal of congealed fat out of a bag when I heard some called-out words, though they were too far away and indistinct down the line behind us to make out. Out of the half-doze that had taken me, my insides leapt suddenly up in reaction as my eyes snapped wide-open and alert.

'What was that?' Moxy asked.

'Dunno – listen, listen . . .'

With cocked heads, we strained our ears to hear the command that would finally release us into the fight. Then the words came again: louder, closer – I could just about make them out now.

'Stand down.'

Moxy looked across the cab in alarm at me. 'Did you hear that?'

'Yeah . . .' I said, closing my eyes and letting my head sink back against the headrest in resigned acquiescence.

'Stand down' – closer now, drifting up the line to us in relay, echoing through different mouths towards us. The two words crashed into me, crushing me with the disappointment they carried.

'What the fuck?' Charlie twanged from the back of our vehicle, suspension jumping as he leaped up to stare behind us in incomprehension.

'You are joking . . .' Frosty joined in beside him.

Moxy flung open his door, swinging fluidly onto the ground to stride up to Alex, who had mirrored his action from the other vehicle. 'Tell me that's a wind-up, Alex!'

But outside his vehicle, smiling to the last, Alex just held one finger up to his throat and pulled it across in a cutting motion.

*

Deep in the retreat of the palace that night, we sat out on our house's terrace beneath the standard spectacular starlit sky, downing consolatory beers and pizza to the familiar foreign soundtrack of choruses of crickets.

I was chewing a mouthful while absently staring into middle distance over the terrace's low wall, lost in non-thought, when suddenly there was the quick whizz of an incoming rocket shooting over our house. In a split second I saw it land about 150 metres away, exploding in open ground just inside the walls in a shower of sparks and an almighty bang.

Instinctively, we all ducked down as one in our chairs, before looking up at each other with grimaces, then grins.

'Well, that's just rude,' said Alex.

Sitting back up in our chairs, we didn't run inside the house and throw on our body armour to lie quivering under our beds, or however else the insurgents wanted us to react. With the rockets' trajectories and our terrace facing away from the launch point on the other side of the river, only a direct hit was going to kill us. So we stood up with beers in hand for the cabaret instead, looking out with interest for the next ones to come in.

We were quite disappointed when there were only two more. And it sounded like they didn't even make it across the river, the muffled explosions sounding harmlessly short.

'Is that it? Christ, the only danger's that our pizza's going to get cold!' Charlie protested indignantly.

'Yes, a strongly worded letter to Bahadli tomorrow, I think – "Must try harder!"' Moxy declared.

When we all turned round to sit back down again, cabaret over, we saw Max silhouetted in the doorway to the house, quietly watching us – though probably lured up by the sound of the one close rocket, I thought.

'Don't worry, you lunatics – the I'ties may have sorted their shit out, but you'll get your fill of incoming up in Al Amarah soon.'

'When's that, Max?' I asked, Tim handing him a spare beer.

'Soon,' he quietly nodded. 'You'll be taking over from the other patrol in a week or so. Cimic House there'll keep you occupied, don't you worry about that.'

*

As we bided our time over the next week or so before going north to the flashpoint town of Al Amarah, the intelligence push on Bahadli just seemed to have been quietly forgotten after the Nasiriyah non-event. We could only gather intelligence on targets we were tasked with, pass it up to the powers that be and see if any action was taken on it in hindsight. But now the Bahadli effort seemed to have died a death, our next tasking made me wonder quite what had to happen for any action to be taken.

Together with an infantry team, we had slipped into a courthouse in town early one night, which overlooked a designated house 'of interest'. Twelve Iraqi policemen were guarding the courthouse, and they understandably seemed quite surprised to see us. But they did seem quite happy when an interpreter explained to them that they now had the night off to sleep instead. The infantry boys were careful to take their weapons off them and shut them, guarded, in a downstairs room, though. We knew full well the insurgents had comprehensively infiltrated the Iraqi Police Service (IPS). Leaving them armed or free to go back out into the city would be asking for serious trouble, alone and out on a limb as we were, deep in the depths of the dark city.

Ground floor secured, that left the seven of us free to run our OP from the first-floor balcony overlooking our subject – a suspected insurgent house. We waited for any sign of terrorist activity that would allow us to 'trigger' the waiting patrols at the nearby 'Camp Cherokee' base onto the terrorists.

It was in the dead of the early hours that we saw some activity through the green of our night vision and the black and white of thermal imaging. A van pulled up outside the house and four men jumped out of it before running into the house. In a matter of seconds they reappeared outside, dragging a fifth figure with them – and he was not going willingly. Three of the men manhandled him forward while the fourth flung open the side door for them to bundle him inside. Then, all inside with the doors closed swiftly, the van started forward with a lurch before pulling onto the main road and driving away from us down it, tail lights glowing in our scopes.

And that, for all the world to me, looked like a hostage being moved – or even someone in the process of being 'disappeared', for all we knew.

Alex immediately radioed through to Zero so we could trigger the Cherokee patrols onto the vehicle. It was perfect for a trigger.

But nothing: Zero told us to carry on observing the house.

Alex put the radio's handset down in disbelief as we watched the tail lights slowly disappearing into the distance. Then, with a taunting last flourish of brake lights, the van turned off onto a side street and was gone.

'Poor bloke,' Alex said, slowly shaking his head.

Even when we got back, nobody seemed that interested.

*

After spending the next couple of days conducting another OP, but this time from the relative safety of the top of one of the huge arched gates to the palace, I began to wonder whether the information we gathered was even reaching the people who could make executive decisions about it.

Through the tripod-mounted telescopic lens of our cameras, we watched another house suspected of being used by insurgents. We didn't see any potential hostages being moved like at the last one but saw large numbers of men, all of fighting age, going back and forth from it at all times of the day. As per usual, we dutifully snapped every individual and time-catalogued all the comings and goings in detail.

I think Alex was trying to buoy our morale when he relayed to us the reported reaction to this latest effort. Apparently, this was the 'first proper intelligence' that the brigade commander had received.

That was nice. But what the hell about everything else we had been doing? What of Bahadli and the OMS building? What of filming the entire length of IED Alley, balls out, in completely unarmoured Land Rovers? And what of the poor fucker we'd seen just a few days ago, dragged away in the dead of night to God knows what fate? Had this stuff even reached the higher echelons of command? Or were we now supposed to accept that all these prior efforts were not 'proper intelligence'?

In the interests of team morale, I kept my feelings to myself. But I was aware I was feeling increasingly frustrated by our long, uncomfortable hours of surveillance seemingly resulting in absolutely no action being taken and, by extension, my very personal, complete impotence to pinpoint and fire back at the unseen insurgents who rained fire down on us at night and threatened to blow us up as soon as our wheels hit the streets.

I didn't think I'd reached the stage of wanting to fire 'my weapon' in a near sexual release of pent-up frustration, but if you mix in with this the undeniable sexual frustration you encounter over the long months on tour then you have some pretty potent ingredients for some pretty fucked-up dreams. Fortunately they weren't wet – that would have disturbed me probably almost as much Charlie sleeping with his own dreams in the bed beside me.

Of course, I could have taken myself away to one of the Portaloos to sort myself out. But the guys who did so with one of the plethora of ball-teasing porn mags lying around looked like they needed to be hooked up to a drip when they came back. But it wasn't so much sitting in the sun-baked oven of a Portaloo that turned me off – it was more how I felt the pure stench of festering layers of shit and piss burning your nostrils wasn't all that conducive to fantasising about Cecilia. Developing a leaning towards scatology was one thing I didn't want to bring home with me from Iraq.

In civilian life, this would probably be about the time you felt you needed a holiday or, alternatively, that you really, really needed to get laid. But I knew I only had three weeks now until 22 June and my promise of ten days' R & R at home and, all things being equal, getting laid.

I had been getting concerned at the depth of longing in Cecilia's daily letters, though. She said she stroked my jacket hanging on her bedroom door every morning before going to work – where she felt very alone, with none of her friends understanding the stress of our enforced separation. Though she said that she always touched my necklace when she thought of me, she said that she just felt so lonely.

I thanked God she now had Danni and Liv to speak to, who would completely understand what she was going through. And when her letters began to trail off in frequency, first to every other day, then to every third, then fourth, I thought it was probably a good thing that she could focus on something else, anything else, than her loneliness. She had other things to do after all, other people to see . . . But these were things I could only imagine.

And in fleeting, darker moments, I imagined things I did not want to imagine. Because though I did not want to, I still remembered the war. But I killed those fears dead as soon as I found myself selfishly worrying that she might be losing interest in me. I blocked out the memory of why it transpired she'd lost interest in writing to me here only a year ago. Things were different now, I told myself. But I could only hope she was holding on OK.

*

The threat level in Al Amarah was such that we needed to be inserted into the 'Cimic House' compound there by Warrior APCs. The 'Civil-Military Cooperation' building was meant to be the CPA's centre of authority in the town, a shining beacon of provisional law and order and cooperation with the local populace as Iraq slowly moved towards its first taste of Western-style democracy.

In reality, it was a besieged, bullet-holed bolt-hole. The flat roof of the squat two-storey main building had grown the familiar warts of sandbagged sangers. The Portakabins optimistically placed beside it to house the resident infantry company had been abandoned due to one too many direct mortar hits. And within the 200- by 100-metre-long walls that demarked the limit of the CPA's influence in this town, the only shining beacon I saw was the 50-odd-metre-high water tower towering over the building: a perfect aiming aid for insurgent mortar crews.

Due to the near-nightly mortar attacks, everyone now slept under the hard cover of Cimic's concrete roof. Our job, however, was to sit on top of this roof each night and try to pinpoint the locations of the enemy mortar crews every time they fired on us.

A sergeant who would later write a book about his time here showed us to our rooftop. He led us upstairs onto the flat, sangered roof and then up a ladder to a smaller, ten-metre by ten-metre, raised flat rooftop. This would be our OP, with its raised, 360-degree viewpoint of Al Amarah beyond the compound's high walls.

He briefed us on everyday life at Cimic, the landmarks, the areas favoured by the insurgents and the probable areas of mortar launching points. He mentioned that incoming small-arms fire and RPGs were less of a threat to Cimic now, as they'd 'killed all the stupid ones' who had tried attacking them with AKs and RPGs in plain view of the house, though they were not to be discounted altogether.

As part of the Darwinian process, we were left with trying to pinpoint the canny ones who fired their mortars from behind buildings, their hidden round-spotters calling fine adjustments to them using the big, stupid, waving hand of the water tower no doubt. Thanking the sergeant for his brief, we spent the afternoon filling as many sandbags as we could get our hands on and lugging them up to the OP, for these would be our only protection as we sat exposed on top of the hard cover that the infantry company and CPA slept beneath. We knew full well, though, that a direct hit would make all our sweat-dripping and grit-encrusted labour academic.

Then we sat quietly as the sun descended for the first of our 13 nights on top of Cimic House, watching and waiting.

I cannot tell you how many mortars came in over those nights. What I do know is that it was only a matter of chance that one did not land square on our flat rooftop.

And what I also know is that there is nothing more frustrating than being unable to reply in kind when someone is trying everything in their power to kill you.

'I'd rather be lucky than good,' Max had once said: another of his maxims. We knew exactly what he meant, because there is something peculiar to being on the receiving end of concerted indirect fire, where no matter who you are, or how good a soldier you think you may be, you have absolutely no control over where that next mortar will land.

Maybe it will flash and burst apart in a split-second clap round the water tower just down from you again – or maybe all you will see is a split-second flash before it is you that is burst apart. But as soon as you hear the dull, distant thud of the next mortar being launched, you have to swing your eyes and night vision to bear on where it came from, head clean over the parapet so you can pinpoint the launching point, so the QRF waiting below can rumble out in their armoured Warriors and get those bastards trying to kill us all. But by the time the QRF lumbers out to meet them, you know the insurgents will have long melted away into the night.

Though you know your efforts are utterly futile, you carry on spotting the flash and thud of the launch points, because it is all you personally can do on this rooftop. It is the job you have been tasked to do. And while you do this, you know full well that each incoming mortar is arcing high through thousands of feet of air on its journey towards you, before finally tipping over to plummet down on you, specifically aimed at *you*, sitting on *this rooftop*.

And when you hear the mortar whistle above you in that last second before impact; when you know there is nowhere to hide and your hands cannot dig the hole in the concrete that the primeval part of your brain and your liquid bowels scream at them to dig; when you can only curl up, small as a foetus, on the small roof that the mortar is aimed at, behind the single layer of sandbags that will not save you if the mortar's aim is true or lucky in equal measure, then . . .

How would you feel?

They only have to be lucky with one mortar to blow you out of the world that is mother and family and everything you now value beyond value at home, everything that is in your last thoughts as your eyes clench shut, praying as you wait for death, maiming, or the momentary, heavenly sweet delivery back to the life you promise you will no longer waste.

And sometimes, you will think of the delicate, tender touch of the girl you left behind at home, who will never know and never hope to understand these bowel-turning, sweating-wet eternities of terror.

The girl you were stupid enough to leave behind at home – just so that you could be here.

*

On the morning of our first day back together, Cecilia sat me down beside her on the bed, holding my hand in both of hers with gently spoken words. 'Look – you know I'm a very honest person.'

'Yeah . . .'

'So . . . I want you to know that James asked me out for a drink while you were away. And I did go.'

My mind clouded black as my face locked impassive as stone.

'I don't want you getting the wrong idea, though. He thought it was going to be a date-type drink, but we had a good heart to heart and I told him I was seeing someone else and was happy with them.'

No reaction from me.

'Oh, Anna is going to kill me; she told me not to tell you!' She took her hands from me to hold over her face, exhaling hard into them while shaking her head.

'OK . . . Look, thanks for telling me – it's OK,' I replied. I didn't know how convincing my words were – even I didn't believe them.

Her hands went back to gripping mine as her sincere, wide sea-blue eyes searched for mine. 'You've got nothing to worry about, baby,' she said. 'I care about him – but I love you.'

I didn't want to hear about her caring for James; I had only a few days with her now and then I was back to Iraq for four months and back to placing all my trust in her again. Forgotten wounds of mistrust were ripping open as I reined back an upheaval of emotions inside me. I didn't want to say anything damaging, so I didn't say anything. I couldn't say anything.

'Look . . .' she said, fishing a leather-bound book out of her bedside drawer. 'I'm keeping a diary of all the days we're apart – you can read all of it when you come back for good in November.'

If this was meant to reassure me, it did not. I carried on suppressing all my concerns, feeling that to voice them would just put a crowbar into the crack opening between us as I leaned in to return the close, reassuring hug she gave me.

A few days later, with all this forgotten by one, I imagined, and successfully repressed and internalised by the other, I waited for her to come back to me on just another night out, in just another bar.

And while I waited, I sipped the remains of my beer, nursing its contents while I took in my transient surroundings: crowds, couples and singles on the pull, all showered clean and freshly scented, laughing, dancing and chatting excitedly away without a care in the world, all to the background thump of the latest dance music.

It had only been a few days ago that I was listening to the thump of people trying to kill me. Knowing I would say goodbye to all passing in front of my eyes now, in just as few days, I felt my solitude magnifying me among the carefree throngs. I sat alone at my table:

there was no one here I could talk to, no one I could confide in, no one who would know. And why should they care anyway? It was Saturday night and they were having the time of their lives.

But now Cecilia was coming back to me down the stairs. Her small, perfect feet in their open-toed heels, then her bare, sculpted calves moving beneath the fringe of her thigh-length little black dress, the tight material caressing up past the curve of her hips into the narrow of her waist and then to the full blossoming of her breasts. And then the diamond necklace I'd given her, glittering from the base of the delicate neck from which shone the face with its sea-blue eyes, the face so shatteringly and unspeakably beautiful it would have launched a thousand ships if she'd lived in another time. But my warship had long struck east for her; she was my Helen incarnate.

I did not want to tell her much about Iraq; I did not want to worry her. As much as I thought she might try to understand, I knew she had no frame of reference from which to try to relate to what I might say. What would I say anyway? I hadn't the heart to spill my contempt for the *Daily Mirror* after she said she bought it every morning to read on the train to work. However, she did mention that she hardly ever read the 'news' pages, turning straight to the '3 a.m. Girls' showbiz-gossip pages instead.

I wanted to keep Cecilia and Iraq as separate as I could manage, too. Yes, there had been the alluring danger to her, gleaming to my eyes, but in my mind's eye now I saw her bathed in the light of happy innocence. I did not want to let the darkness of Iraq seep through into the radiance I helplessly held her in. She was my pure guiding light to the end of the tunnel and the promise of goodness at its end. I wanted that rebirth into our happily-ever-after unsullied and uncontaminated by anything in my yet-to-be-past. I would stumble and wade through any blackness now, blindly following her innocent, spritely light to wherever it beckoned.

But then on just another night, and with only a dwindling handful of nights remaining before I returned to Iraq, I could be blind to my blindness no longer. And she would fall from the pedestal from which I worshipped the idol of her ideal.

On this corporate night out in a Canary Wharf bar, I sink gulps of beer and let the worst of my distrustful imaginings from Iraq swirl and stab through my head.

I watch Cecilia and James talking together, pressed close to one another by the crowd in the bar, his arm around her waist. And as she whispers things I can only imagine into his ear, he looks me right in the eye – and *smiles*.

Floodgates of boiling rage open within me, with killing hate flooding through arteries into clenching hands. But then fury freezes into icy, methodical clarity. And in numbed-cold ferocity, I know what I will do if I walk up to them.

I will walk up to him and push her gently but firmly out of the way when she tells me to sit down again.

Ideally he would then lunge at me, as it will then be easy to use his body's motion to throw him to the floor. But I know he will not do this: he is a middle manager surrounded by cronies and superiors and he will lose his personally defining job.

So if he just stands there I will distract his eyes with a slap to them before taking my heel hard down his shin. And then, with him smarting and off-balance, I will take his remaining leg out with a hooked sweep from my other foot into the back of his knee, putting him down onto the floor.

Or he might just hold up placatory hands to me, backing away before he turns his back on me. And then all I will have to do is jab my thumb hard into the pressure point behind his earlobe and his legs will give way, down to the floor.

Or he might just turn and run, which I will enjoy, as I know I will catch him.

But however I get him to the floor, I know that once he is there I will stamp his throat and face into the hard tiles and drop-kick his head until his flailing arms can no longer uselessly reach up to protect him – until I reach down to grab his blood-matted hair and pummel what is left of his face, spitting his blood back into his death-rolling eyes.

And the screams of horror and panic from the office workers will just be quiet background noise, fading into the thump of the latest dance music.

But as he smiles at me, I know I cannot do this. And I know all the killing rage nurtured in me by the Army, and repressed in frustration in Iraq, belongs in Iraq.

So I know I cannot walk up there and confront them as they carry on talking to each other, pressed close to one another as if they are a couple. Because I *will not* lose my liberty or even my forgotten banking career because of him or her.

I could have stayed and torturously logged everything in impotent emasculation, but I did not. I walked silently up the stairs and out of the bar.

However, that was as far as I got. I stood outside in the blackness for a while. But then, in blindness, I went back.

Cecilia and I will leave together that night. But as she sleeps later, while I cannot, my lover's paranoia will read a text message sent from James to her, which will only open my eyes wider – to the extent that I will not be able to sleep that night, at all.

*

Cecilia found me in the park near her house the next morning. I was sitting on the grass in front of the pedestal of its war memorial.

A young fusilier called Gordon Gentle had been killed by an IED in Basra while I was on R & R. The paper had said he was killed on a stretch of road nicknamed IED Alley. I wanted to leave for Iraq right now; I felt I should be over there now, trying to stop young boys like him dying, and not here, dying an ignominious emotional death at the hands of my supposed girlfriend. I felt more in common with the dead names etched into the stone in front of me than with any of the banking 'colleagues' I had spent last night with. And that included him – and her.

After I had read James's text message, I had packed up all my kit, ready to go. But then I had walked out of the house to smoke, walk and try to clear my head in the silent desertion outside. I had drifted away from the harsh neon streetlights, away from the hum of the night traffic, gravitating towards the quiet, enveloping darkness of the park. I lost myself within the deep womb of its rustling walls of inky trees. They embraced me like a tomb.

Though I lay down on the grass to try to rest in peace, I could not sleep. For now I was returning once more to the threat of Iraq, my undead, dead-tired eyes were awake to the threat from home.

When she finally found me, she said a cold feeling had run through her when she realised that I had read the message from James and saw my kit packed up and ready to go at the front door.

Sitting in my lap, wrapping her arms around me, she promises that she loves me and that she only wants me.

But I can only nod as she implores me to believe her, because I do not know what to believe.

I see her dazzling, beguiling beauty. I hear the woven webs of sweet sophisms that spin from her perfect mouth, pouring like honey into my dumb ears.

I feel the illusive, elusive enticement of her lithe, svelte body wrapping itself snake-like around me, soothing my fear-filled mind and fool's heart with its lustful lullaby.

But I think that the promise of our fairy tale is a myth. And now I have led myself up this dark garden path, I discern that I am being waylaid with Siren song back to desolation in Iraq.

Once I am sped safely out of the way for twice as long as I went before, I know that the candle she burns for me at its dark end will be nothing more than a will-o'-the-wisp's promise of predestined, floundering doom. Its dancing light on my horizon will drift further away. Then it will sputter out and die. And I will be left alone in the dark – deep in the quagmire of Iraq.

5

THE WAKE

Pardon one offence, and you encourage the commission of many.

Publilius Syrus

If the fool would persist in his folly he would become wise.

William Blake

It was not a flood at first. The blood began with a thin red line in the dust.

It is just a single slender line of seeping scarlet, swelling the narrow crack in the pale paving stones below. Spilling out from the shade of my shadow, its crimson suddenly shines bright in the sunlight, glinting as it slowly trickles away from me.

But within heartbeats the blood pumps between my legs, pooling vile around my feet in a slick as thick as oil.

We had turned back into the crowded Basra marketplace because Frosty had seen weapons being loaded into the back of a pick-up truck. When a single shot rang out as we pulled up to investigate, we had instinctively debussed from our vehicles in oiled proficiency, with weapons, minds and bodies primed for fight.

And we debussed into chaos.

The mass of the crowd was dissolving into terrified individuals running left, right, away from us and past us, surging and bumping into each other – anywhere to get away from the death I could now see through the flashes of their running legs.

Death was lying on his back on the pavement. And round his groin, seeping into the pale material of his dish-dash robe, was an angry-red, growing stain.

Crying hysterically and stumbling away from him was an Iraqi policeman with an AK. Pushing the policeman further away were two of his colleagues, desperately trying to wrestle the weapon out of his hands.

Charlie was crouching on the ground, covering left and the three IPS men with his rifle. Tim was beside his driver's door, covering right. With Dougie and Frosty remaining on the back of the Rovers, keeping a height advantage to preserve an overview of the situation while maintaining their opposing 180-degree arcs, that afforded Moxy time to radio in to Zero while Alex did his patrol-medic bit – and for me to provide close security for him while all his attention was focussed on the shot man.

The most panicked of the crowd had now taken flight, taking the three IPS men along with them. Alex and I walked calmly up to the man with the blossoming, soaking stain, through those I reasoned were perhaps the more experienced, those who had waited for the stampede to rush past them before engaging their brain on the best direction to flee. Then, of course, there were the ghouls, whom you find anywhere in the world. I wanted to ignore these lower life forms, but I could not afford to, for I knew they could just as easily be insurgents waiting for our backs to turn.

Alex kneeled down beside the motionless man and opened his medic bag. The blood was spreading across the man's dish-dash, the thin material hanging sopping wet with it between his legs and clinging taut against his abdomen.

I turned my back on them to begin my vigil, kneeling down at the man's sandalled feet with eyes and rifle searching for anything that would threaten our lives.

Just to my left, my eyes scanned over a man with two young boys. I had seen him gather them to him when the panic began, kneeling down to put his arms round them, waiting for the rush and push of stamping feet to pass before taking them away to safety. He was trying to catch my eye. My eyes fixed on his and I saw the consternation in them. Then, with a sideways flick they directed mine down an alleyway to my front.

The alleyway was empty of people but cluttered with wooden crates and metal boxes. I felt I knew what he was trying to warn me of, but when I looked back to him and saw his son's outstretched hand there was no mistaking the hidden message. Like his smaller brother, he was clutching onto his father's trousers as they edged fearfully away. He looked up to his father before looking to me. And then he lifted his free hand to point one little finger down the alleyway: *that's where the bad guys are – watch out . . .*

As soon as the father saw the hand of his son reached out for all to see, he reached down to hold it, protectively hiding in his paternal hand the dangerously overt sign of help to the British soldier.

With a minute nod of thanks, imperceptible to all but the three of them, I gestured with my eyes to the father to immediately take himself and his two sons away from this place. They disappeared behind the building immediately to my left, and I tucked myself closer to its beige-bricked wall, pulling the butt of my rifle tighter into my shoulder.

My weapon points everywhere my eyes do: along the facades of empty shop fronts, down the cluttered alleyway directly in front of me, into the dark open spaces of the first-floor windows and along the low walls of the flat rooftops above. I know that we are sitting, completely exposed, in the middle of a potential killing ground.

I click the safety catch of my rifle to 'Fire' and my index finger rests alongside the trigger, watching and waiting for the glimpse of a dark figure with a weapon, or a muzzle flash from anywhere out of the periphery of my vision, as my eyes dart left, right, up and down, and my weapon swivels in synchronicity with them.

I hear the tearing open of first field dressings (FFDs) just behind me, but I do not look. All of Alex's attention is focussed on trying to save the Iraqi man. And my body placed squarely between them and the alleyway, windows and rooftops to our front is the only protection he has. I am his bodyguard. I know that if I do not see the first burst that hits me from the gathering, unseen threat, then I will at least have given Alex some seconds to react and keep his own life.

It is then that I glimpse the blood trickling between my legs – bright-red, oxygenated arterial blood. It rolls along the gap between the sand-grey slabs of the pavement beneath me, channelling down the dirt-filled crack on its journey to the gutter. I have to ignore it; my eyes are burdened enough already. But I can feel the life of the man behind me ebbing out as his lifeblood runs beneath me.

My eyes and weapon continue to swivel smoothly so that my blood and Alex's do not join his. My eyes dart and seek over the top of my rifle's sight, its barrel pointing everywhere I look: along the facade of empty shop fronts, down the cluttered alleyway, into the dark open spaces of the first-floor windows and along the low walls of the flat rooftops above.

But from the bottom of my eyes I see the dying man's blood now overflowing from its course in the pavement. It is pooling red and thick around the pale sole of my left desert boot – scarlet and sun glinting on its journey to the sewers. I know that the longer we sit completely exposed in the middle of this killing ground, the more likely it is that our blood too is going to be spilled.

Moxy's voice crackled over the PRR. 'Al – got through to Zero . . . They've said we're not to administer any first aid to the locals . . . Regardless of that, mate, I think we want to get out of here sooner rather than later.'

There was a quick pause of reaction.

Nothing like being fucking appreciated.

'Yeah, roger that,' Alex replied. 'Almost done here – just need to get him away.'

Someone else was going to have to take him to hospital then. With two FFDs now strapped to the man's groin, Alex press-ganged three Iraqi men from the gaggle that had congregated round, lifting the man onto a stretcher-sized piece of corrugated metal that one of them had helpfully found. They carried him to the roadside and set him down while Alex tried to flag a taxi, or any vehicle, that could take him away. The man lay motionless on his back with his eyes closed, his deathly pale, waxen face turned towards me, his pale dish-dash now soaked with blood.

'He's fucked,' Dougie helpfully suggested from the back of his Rover.

I had no doubt that was the case, but I was relieved that Alex was going to see this through. No matter what Zero said, we were human beings, not fucking animals.

First one vehicle and then another drove straight by Alex as he tried to wave them down – they weren't interested either. The third, a battered white pick-up, only stopped when Alex placed himself directly in its path and pointed his weapon at the driver. With that, the man's body was quickly slid onto the back of the pick-up and driven away.

Then, quickly mounting our Rovers, so did we.

And when just a few hundred metres later we came across another body lying at the roadside, we did the same as the rest of the locals and carried on past it, without comment, as you would the carcass of just another roadkilled animal.

*

Alex was quiet when we got back, but I could tell he was fuming inside. In just one patrol, we had seen how cheap life was in Iraq.

He hadn't seen the father and his two young sons.

'None of those fuckers are going to get me,' he eventually said. I didn't know whether he meant the Iraqis who wanted to kill us or the Iraqis who drove past him without stopping to help. I thought it was probably just Iraq and everyone in it – and maybe even Zero to boot.

His wife Ems and equally beloved Jack Russell bitch Goose were waiting for him back home at his farm, deep in the green of the Hampshire countryside – deep back in God's country. He was my PC, and I would do everything I could to make sure he didn't come back to them in a flag-draped box, for I knew he had more to live for than me. I had no wife. I had Cecilia.

While I washed the blood from the soles of my desert boots, I remembered Timmy, his tears and the flies feeding on the blood of the young Iraqi girls that was smeared over the soles of his desert boots. And I remembered her first letter to me. And I remembered why she did not write back.

Now – again – I had told her I would place all my trust in her. But I could not tell her that my trust was now just a dead, empty husk. I felt this last leap of faith as a plummet into oblivion.

So why did I not give up on her. Why did I still want her.

It didn't help that she was flawless, car-crash-causing physical beauty. In the soft light of my mind's eye, she was more beautiful than ever. Beyond A-list actress picture-perfect, she was danger and allure. And lulled and lured in by her Siren song, I knew she might well leave my bones bleaching in the sun after the final spitting-out.

But since my teens, the Army that had finished shaping me had reinforced my mind to rule my body, to mentally, physically and emotionally endure – to never give up.

After I graduated from university, the wings that had borne my teenage confidence high into the sky had been supplanted by those of a paratrooper. And I descended back to earth as part of an elite airborne brotherhood – with my success breeding burgeoning self-confidence.

Now I had tasted success and self-worth, I never wanted to go back to that childhood darkness of self-worthlessness, with its plague of symptomatic, causative and compounding stammering. Every achievement bore me upwards, spiriting me further away from the darkness that I still ran from – or still fought against when my vocal cords occasionally clenched in ambush.

So I could not give up on anything – I didn't know how to give up on anything. Though Cecilia had soon recognised this part of me, playfully labelling it as 'stubbornness', the Army on the other hand classified it in my annual reports as 'determination'.

Before I transferred to the HAC, my previous unit had selected me for an eight-man team as part of their entry into an Army-run, forty-mile race over the South Downs hills, with each man carrying forty-pound bergans.

Due to the cachet the name of my unit had, our team was expected to win. In fact, it was made clear to us by our non-running superiors that failure to achieve anything other than victory would be a mark of shame, which each man would have to carry from then on.

And we won. We had to. But in those final miles to the finish, when the next team was still doggedly keeping only one hill behind us, I remember picking up the pace to a faster run, my mind screaming at my screaming body. From pacing myself in the middle of our team, I found myself beyond the front of it, pulling away from my teammates up the slog of the slopes and down the pounding sprints the other side, willing them to dig into the pain and use it – but then having to rein myself back in when I saw the hours-long agony on some of their faces.

After we had crossed the finish line, the first thing one of them said to me was: 'There's something nasty deep inside you, Jake.'

In the context of the Army I took it as a compliment. But he was right. The force that drove me to achieve was the same that propelled me from failure. It was this fear of failure – the mire in the darkness that my childhood words had stumbled through – that I was running from.

The Army had taught my mind to conquer the weakness of the body. But my Army had issued no training in the mind ruling the heart. There were no standard operating procedures to combat beguilement.

I had no prior experience of one person triggering such conflict and desire in me. And while she was still nominally mine, I could not give up on her – for any admission of failure would cut to the bone of the childhood weakness I still carried with me. I feared failure, in anything, more than anything else – more than my body being ripped apart without warning here, or a single methodical bullet bolted through my brain, cutting through everything and ending it all.

But the final, inescapable truth was that I still, helplessly, loved her. She was my first thought in the light when I woke and my last before the dark of sleep.

And with this I learned that the mantra stating that you cannot truly love someone if you do not implicitly trust them was as lazily complacent and simplistic as it was naive.

*

About three weeks after my return to Iraq, I try calling Cecilia's mobile one evening, but it rings out. And though I try again a couple of hours later, she doesn't answer that call either. So I try her home number instead.

'She's spending the night with a friend,' her mum tells me.

'OK, thanks . . . Yeah, I'm all right, thank you . . . Hope you are too? . . . OK . . . Take care, bye.'

But I am not all right.

*

The next morning we were driving up Route 6, as part of our latest mission to gather intelligence on the roadside bombers who liked to lace the carriageway with IEDs.

Alex had by now put me on top cover, recognising a 'resigned eagerness' in me, as he put it, to pull the trigger of my weapon and kill those who would do the same to us. So from my raised vantage point on the back of the second Rover, I had a good view of why our vehicles were slowing to a halt as we approached the outskirts of a town named Ad Dayr.

An Iraqi police car was driving towards us down the wrong side of the road with its roof lights flashing. Between it and us, dotted along and hunkered down in the roadside ditch to our right, were the dark, crouching shapes of men with weapons. Knowing full well that the IPS had been well and truly infiltrated by the insurgents, our Rovers stopped dead, expecting an ambush.

But the IPS car drove straight past the men in the ditch, slowing to a stop just in front of us – which didn't make any sense if it was an ambush. It would have made more sense to try to stop us when we were alongside the men in the ditch, where they could have given us the full broadside of their firepower.

Peering closer at the figures in the ditch, I saw they were wearing the uniforms of the Iraqi Civil Defence Corps (ICDC). And instead of ploughing a vehicle-borne IED into Alex's lead Rover, the IPS driver got out and ran towards Alex's door, waving his hands in the air.

Just what was going on became clearer when I saw four dark figures run from right to left across the road about three hundred metres beyond the ICDC soldiers to our front. The ICDC soldiers loosed off of a volley of shots at them.

We instantly debussed from our vehicles in reaction and anticipation, fanning out on either side of the road in a baseline facing the town.

I had only just clambered into the same ditch the ICDC were in up ahead when an RPG shot out from beside the building the four figures had run behind. It whooshed left to right and exploded in a cloud of dust just short of the Iraqi soldiers.

Fuck!

Crack-cracks of more incoming and outgoing small-arms fire rang out up ahead for a few seconds before there was a lull. But I was not scared. Instead I found I had the first real smile on my face for weeks. Now I felt we could take direct action against those fuckers – now I had control over something.

'Moxy – going forward to those ICDC to get the lowdown!' I shouted to the ditch on the other side of the road.

'OK, mate – get back here soon as you can, though,' he called back.

I ran along my ditch to the first Iraqi soldier, stooping to keep my head below its top. '*Salaam alaykum.*' I greeted him with a grin, setting myself down in the dust beside him.

He just nodded at me with his mouth hanging open, his eyes lit up like the fucking cavalry had arrived. He was wearing an antiquated metal helmet, the same that American GIs wore in the Second World War. And worn over the top of his flimsy-looking body armour was a small chest rig holding four magazines for the battered old AK-47 in his hands.

The British soldier that had materialised out of nowhere to sit beside him looked somewhat different. When I took a sip of water from the hose of my CamelBak, I realised he didn't even have a water bottle. My Kevlar helmet had ballistic goggles and a mounting for a night-vision monocle strapped to it. Over the top of my body armour was my bulging ops vest, carrying a pistol and smoke and hand grenades, as well as nine magazines and grenades for my telescopically and laser-sighted SA80 A2, with its under-slung grenade launcher.

On top of all that, I was grinning at him.

'Al-Qaeda,' he said nervously, peeping over the top of the ditch, pointing at where the RPG had been launched from.

'*Na'am*,' I nodded to him. 'Al-Qaeda.'

'*Arbaa*,' he continued, holding up four fingers.

Four of them – cool.

'*Shukran*,' I thanked him, before peering through my optical weapon sight (SUSAT) at the roadside building they had disappeared behind.

With the ICDC on the right-hand side of the road, the insurgents were clearly pulling away to our left. There was a low wall to the left of the building, leading away from it for about a hundred metres before that in turn led into a higher walled compound. Left of that, there was just open desert. So they were probably going to be behind that wall or in that compound – and hopefully not already filtering into the town beyond, because I wanted to get them.

'*Ma'a salama, sadeeq*,' I said to the soldier, taking my leave of him to crouch-run back to my friends.

I followed the ditch back down to our Rovers, looking for Alex. When I drew level with the rear of his Rover, I saw him standing just behind it, surrounded by a gaggle of IPS and ICDC as he finished making a call on the satphone. It was as I was climbing out of the ditch that I noticed my ICDC *sadeeq* had followed me puppy dog-like back along the ditch –with five more of his *sadeeqs* in tow.

'Fucking radio's out of range, obviously,' Alex said amiably to me as I pushed through his hangers-on, adding mine into the mix. 'Got through to Zero on this, though,' he added proudly, holding up the satphone in his hand, before looking quizzically at my entourage. 'You found some friends?' he smiled.

I shrugged my shoulders and smiled back. 'No more than you,' I said, looking bemusedly round at his retinue. 'They reckon there's four insurgents – probably pulling right to left beyond that wall ahead.'

One of the older ICDC soldiers suddenly addressed Alex. 'Captain!'

Alex shook his head. 'No – not Captain.'

'General?' the soldier hesitantly suggested.

Alex shook his head again, before shrugging his shoulders and nodding at him to continue.

'General!' the Iraqi exhorted, eyes suddenly ablaze. 'We kill them, General! You and us! We kill al-Qaeda!'

'Yeah . . . Come on, General,' I grinned at Alex.

Alex looked first at me and then into the expectant eyes of the Iraqi soldiers. 'OK – why not?' he smiled back gloriously.

Fucking game on.

Alex called the rest of our patrol to the back of the Rover, while the ICDC soldier who had now got it into his head that he was going into action with a British general barked unintelligible orders in Arabic to his nine men. Alex broke the news to Charlie and Tim that as our drivers they would have to stay behind to guard our Rovers and maintain comms with Zero. They took the news stoically enough, but I could see the pain of disappointment in their eyes. So I resisted raising mine heavenwards in a 'thank you' that now, as one of the top covers, I wasn't going to miss out on this.

Alex split the rest of us into two teams: him and Dougie as 'Charlie' fire team and Moxy, Frosty and me as 'Delta'. We knew where we were going and what we doing; I felt the hot surge of anticipatory killing aggression flowing through me, tempered only by the cold confidence of our training. I caught Moxy's eye and he gave me the same tight-lipped, confident smile that I gave him.

'OK?' Alex said curtly to the ICDC.

'Good, General, good! We go!'

And they did go. They launched off as one ahead of us.

The difference in tactics between us soon became apparent. The ICDC walked steadily in one extended line towards the enemy, with five or six metres between each of them and without stopping once.

Our two fire teams trailing behind them had been drilled differently. As a patrol, the five of us were spread out in a similar extended line, but with over twenty metres separation between each man to mitigate the effect of any high explosive incoming. And we always had 'one foot on the ground', with one team always firm and covering the enemy with their weapons, while the other bounded forward thirty metres or so before going firm itself – providing the cue to the trailing team to make their own vulnerable bound forward. It is in this way that we can always return fire on the enemy if they fire on us.

But across the 300-metre expanse of open wasteland leading to the low wall and compound we expect the enemy to be in, there is no natural cover to shelter behind if we are fired upon. We are horribly exposed. There are only centimetre-deep depressions in the baked earth in which we can go firm. And with the ICDC walking in front of us, we have to kneel out of this non-existent cover to ensure any rounds we fire won't crack through the backs of their heads.

In one fleeting moment, they remind me of First World War soldiers at the Somme, advancing slowly forward in extended line while waiting to get mown down by machine-gun fire. But the truth is that the closer we advance to the enemy over this bare-arsed open ground, the easier it will be for the enemy to mow us all down.

This truth becomes clearer with each bound we take towards the low wall and its neighbouring compound: the compound with its dark, open windows that can so easily hide the barrels of unseen, cocked and readied weapons, the weapons that have only to wait for the perfect moment to slice through us as we draw ever closer, completely exposed in the wide-open killing ground below.

The seconds stretch into senses-primed lifetimes – hearts thumping from effort, adrenalin and fear as we eat into the 300 metres with our bounds.

And though I feel our terrible, naked vulnerability over this exposed ground, I find the fear is diluted in the channel of my cold, aggressive purpose – into what I will do to those insurgents if I make it across to them alive. I hate them for what they would do to my friends and me.

My very being is committed to killing – it is now kill or be killed. And I welcome this wide-open opportunity as I run and go firm, and run and go firm, across the wide-open ground, as I let slip and embrace the aggression that has coursed through my body since *that night* when *he* looked to me with his arm around *her* . . . and *smiled*.

Run and go firm – run and go firm – closer and closer the sand-coloured walls loom. I will them closer with each running step – closer to the promise of killing and death and release.

But Alex's voice suddenly calls urgently over the PRR. 'Woah! . . . Hold up! Everyone go firm – go firm!'

Fucking . . . what?!

I dive onto the hard ground and scan along the low wall and into the compound's dark windows with my weapon, now barely a hundred metres away. Just a few more bounds and we'll be *there*!

'Check right.' Alex's voice comes up again.

And with a grief that makes me want to sob dark tears into the pale dust below me, I see why we – and the ICDC just in front of us – have stopped dead.

Two hundred metres to our right, clearing past the roadside

building that the insurgents had run behind and coming up the low wall that we are aimed at, is what looks like an entire battlegroup. Hordes of infantry swarm between the manoeuvring shapes of APCs, converging from a right angle on the same point we are aimed at – coming right at us.

The APCs are Danish. This is their area of operations (AO) – their turf – and we have no way of communicating with them. And they have no idea who we are, or what we are doing. At best they will peer through scopes and establish we are fellow coalition forces soldiers – and then wish our comparatively puny numbers would get the hell out of their way. But at worst, they will only see an inviting little group of armed figures in the vicinity of their objective, and kill us all in chain-gunned 'friendly fire'.

The ICDC are already running towards us on their journey to get the hell out of there.

Alex's voice comes over the PRR with English understatement: 'Bit of a potential for a blue on blue here. Let's leave them to it – Delta move.'

So my fire team took the first disciplined bound back to the dull, deadening safety of our vehicles. The ICDC just ran past us and away.

Back on top of my Rover, I silently swallowed down the frustration and rage. There was no outward sign of the grief and raw ferocity I had to repress, churning from my mind down to my guts. No sign, save for the imperceptible shaking of my fingers, before that too disappeared as they clenched around my unfired, impotent weapon, finishing my journey back to numbness, then calm.

I know that although the aggression I feel belongs here, the frustration, rage and grief it is now born of comes from Home.

*

I shouldn't have phoned her that night when we got back to the palace.

But I did.

She picked up this time. She was in a crowded bar; I could barely hear her over the shout of voices and music in the background. She went into the quiet of outside.

'I tried calling you last night.'

As soon as I'd said the words I realised too late how they sounded too terse, too confrontational – too aggressive.

I shouldn't have called her. Not tonight.

'I was at a party on the river – on a boat.'

I knew the ones she was talking about; on summer evenings from the riverside in London, you could hear the bass of their music thumping across the water from half a mile away before the raised, hollering treble of packed, excited voices motored by.

I wanted to tell her how we listened to the thump of mortars being fired across the water at us here.

But I did not.

'OK . . . And . . . you stayed at a friend's afterwards?'

'Yeah.'

There was a short silence, dripping with all that was unsaid. Then her voice ran cold.

'You think I'm doing the dirty on you, don't you?'

'I'm not saying that.'

'Right . . .' she replied. 'What do you expect me to do . . . Just sit at home waiting for you to call or something? Or constantly have my phone with me – staring at it all the time, just in case you call?'

I suddenly felt very tired. 'I'm not saying that either.'

'There's no point to this any more if you can't even trust me.'

'What do you mean by that?'

'Oh, I don't know . . .' Her words drifted off.

And the phone line, the most personal link we had over the yawning gap of time that still sat in front of us, bridging the thousands of miles between us, was filled with the deafening sound of silence. It was the sound of the long-distance connection between us stretching to snapping point, with a void of aeons now between our two alienated worlds.

She stopped writing after that.

In the times when I phone her again, though I try to apologise, and though I hate myself for doing it, she only repeats the words 'I don't know' to my attempts to find out what is wrong. She repeats these words over and over, like she had once only repeated 'What do you want me to say?' when I had once tried to find out what was going on then.

But I read through her cold distance. And my suspicions tell me that she does know.

I know. I connect the dots in my head. And these conjoined, malignant points of personal reference and history plague my mind, cankerous and black.

I don't need the brains of an archbishop to decipher why she recants

153

my ministrations to the diseased, dying remains of our relationship. But it is not anger that now fills my mind with darkness but a consuming, resigned depression, knowing that I can do nothing to change the inevitable, irrefutable truth.

For I know that even if she is not cheating on me right now, she does not want me. And there is nothing I can do to change this fact, trapped thousands of miles away in the tomb of my final months here, in this doomed escape to a distant world.

*

Eye-stinging, lung-choking, thick clouds of dust billowed up from behind our vehicles as we slowly crossed the dead, deserted no-man's-land from a forgotten war. Facing rear on the back of the second Rover, I had to wear goggles with a shemagh covering the rest of my face just so I could see and breathe.

Twenty years ago, this meandering dirt trail would have been a logistical artery to the Iran–Iraq border, into the mass slaughter of just another senseless war, tearing through the ghostly landscape we now drove through.

Dark hulks of abandoned APCs and main battle tanks lay littered and forgotten behind earthen revetments. Rolls of rotting razor wire, corroding in the sun, stretched along parapets of deserted trench complexes. Bunkers, mortar pits and machine-gun nests that had once sought to stem the tide of Iranian human-wave attacks now lay empty and silent.

Now, our long-range reconnaissance patrol was sniffing for the smuggling routes of more modern arms being run across this border.

But from my solitary vantage point into the cloudy past we left behind us, I caught glimpses of our churned-up dust drifting back to earth in our wake. And I saw that the only sign of our having ever been here would be the tracks left by our wheels, before the winds of time erased even this trace.

Million-strong armies no longer killed each other here, but death was only lying dormant, just beneath the surface. Here – everywhere – were countless hidden mines, sleeping as they patiently waited to be triggered into life. So we did not stray from the dirt track, for the peace of this necropolis was only an illusion. Cautiously, quietly, we slowly threaded our way through the minefields and the ghosts of battle past.

We followed the border north for the rest of the day, till come sunset we had left the graveyards behind. We lay up for the night in the desert expanse that marked the limbo between them and the Garden of Eden marshlands we saw marked on our maps for tomorrow: the marshlands that had been drained dry and dead when I walked through them in an invasion that felt like a lifetime ago.

We slept beneath a sea of stars and, among them, a single glowing moon, gazing silently down on us. But the beauty above meant nothing to me now. It was no longer something I shared with an earth-bound beauty while she slept thousands of miles away from me. It was only a reminder of what I was losing, as each minute slipped by of my remaining months here.

But in the morning, we drove into Eden through the sunlight of a new dawn.

And from out of the dust, life suddenly burst from the ground beneath us. The ancient wetlands had been flooded to become Eden once more.

Our vehicles bounced slowly along a pale packed-earth causeway, bearing us safely past vast reaches of sky-blue water either side, its shimmering surface reflecting the clear expanse of brilliant blue above.

The water shone beneath the sun, lapping in gentle waves against lush green reeds lining the shore below. Skimming just above the sparkling surface, flocks of bright-pink flamingos and black and white terns swooped languorously by, their chirps and calls to one another floating gently by on the wind.

Rivers of emerald grass meandered through the water's clear lifeblood, stretching out from us as far as the eye could see. And dotted here and there – like their tiny fishing boats, punted along by dark, solitary figures – were the floating islands of the Marsh Arabs, the people who had inhabited this place since before the Bible had even been thought of.

They waved at us from their narrow little boats. And they waved at us from their little mud huts on their green, floating islands, as they tended to their water buffalo, grazing peaceably beside them.

They waved because, if only in their eyes, we were not invading infidels. They would know it was we who had toppled the man who had tried to destroy their ancient way of life. They would know it was we who had removed that man who had purposely set out to cleanse them from these lands with his draining dykes, drought-bringing dams, and direct blood-letting and killing . . . the killing of these defenceless people – in their tens of thousands.

We had finished this genocide. And with its architect swept away, the dams and dykes had been broken down, bringing life gushing back into this Eden. And with their Promised Land teeming with life once again, its people had returned here to live their lives in peace once more.

We were the harbingers of this flood. This Great Flood that had resurrected this most ancient way of life in this, the Cradle of Civilisation.

If only those chanting war demonstrators back home could have seen this. But they'd never set foot in Iraq as long as they lived. They could only form their opinions from what the television or papers told them. And how many of the news reports they lapped up or ignored in favour of *The X Factor* or *Big Brother* reported on this anyway?

No – it was better to focus on the killing; it made better news.

As we carried on our way down the causeways wending through the heart of the Mesopotamian Marshes, we came across the most pointed sign of what had passed, and what was now, in this most secluded, beautiful and peaceful corner of the world. We almost missed it; it was so lost among the life and flourishing green. But there, far into the deep-blue expanse of water, with their muzzles just raised out of the rippling surface lapping around them, poked the pale barrels of abandoned artillery guns.

They pointed accusingly at the heavens, as if the flood that had swept over them had come in deluges from above. And ultimately, of course, it had.

They were the gun barrels of a deposed dictator's genocidal war machine. And now they lay silent.

They lay drowned beneath the very lifeblood of the land.

*

Back at the palace, I lay on my bed in our quiet, dark patrol room. As still as a corpse, I listened to the gentle rise and fall of my friends sleeping around me.

I thought of the dead no-man's-land we had driven through, with death still laying insidiously beneath the surface. And I thought of the flood of life we had seen immediately afterwards.

But now, immersed back in the reality of the insidious threats of Basra, Al Amarah or wherever else we might go, I remembered that some things could not be so simple. I saw that contrasts of black and white could merely muddy to produce shades of grey.

Against the backdrop of this quagmire, I thought of Cecilia. I thought of her not being everything she had promised. And I thought of the insidious threat to 'us' remaining 'us' back home. But while I still felt mired in depression at her imagined infidelity and at my helplessness to have any influence over it from here, I also saw that things were not that simple.

It could just as well be seen that it was my mistrust of her that was killing our relationship.

But I did not trust her.

But I still loved her.

The thoughts meandered through my mind until I had to go outside to smoke alone – just so I could stand any chance of sleeping.

Beneath the silent, glowing moon that now held no meaning for me, but still with thoughts of her scraping through my head, I considered that perhaps our patrol to the Iranian border was not everything it seemed either.

The purpose of its long-range reconnaissance had been to reconnoitre and photograph the tracks and causeways coming across the border into this part of Iraq. We had been briefed to assess which routes could hold vehicles – and could therefore be used as smuggling routes for insurgent weaponry from Iran.

But it struck me how the information we gathered could just as easily be used by military planners to gauge which routes could be used to go into Iran – should a re-elected neo-conservative politician deem this the right thing to do. They needed to look at the border themselves if they were thinking that, though. I mean, Jesus, there was already enough carnage *here*.

I thought even for George W. Bush those causeways might be bridges too far – just this invasion had engulfed us. There sure as hell weren't any white doves carrying olive branches of peace in the skies here; the ravens were still getting their fill of carrion flesh.

*

Some months ago, I had been a suited employee of a bank, masquerading as a soldier. Or maybe it was the other way round.

But now I am wearing the uniform of a Danish soldier, though I am not Danish. The two US Marines with whom I am slipping through the night wear the uniforms of Danish soldiers too, though they are not Danish either.

The reason I am now on my own in the middle of the night with two Americans is that Moxy, Tim and I have been attached to a US Marine 'Force Recon' team.

And the reason we are masquerading as something we are not is that we are operating in a Danish area of operations in Iraq. And British and American troops being driven out of a Danish base by Danish troops in Danish vehicles in a Danish AO might attract attention from the local Iraqis. But we did not want to attract any attention as we drove out of the gates in the late evening.

So we had played the part of a routine Danish patrol, bumping along earth roads as the gathering darkness descended on the rural hamlets and expanses of arable land we drove through. We waved standard, friendly right hands at the few locals we saw.

But when it was dark, the pretence ended. The vehicles were parked out of sight from the road behind a sand berm. And from out of this harbour area, seven US marines and I walked off into the night.

We were heading towards an isolated group of buildings tucked away in the middle of nowhere. But this part of the middle of nowhere happened to be within spitting distance of the Iranian border.

The buildings were huddled beside a waterway that flowed from the east. We had seen from aerial photographs that there was a small jetty beside these buildings, and the suspicion was that the boats that came in the night to offload at this jetty were offloading arms shipments.

We walked in silence through the darkness towards our target. There was only the soft sound of footsteps in dust. Night was day through the green glow of my night-vision monocle.

The buildings appeared on our horizon. For a few minutes we walked closer to them, before five of the marines went firm on the ground.

Without words or stopping, the lead scout, the patrol commander and I leave them behind.

The three of us begin blending into tree lines. Our crouched bodies steal through the dead ground of darkness-filled dips in the ground. As we draw closer to the target our steps become soundless, as our pace slows to that of a predator stalking prey.

Each step is now measured, with dead undergrowth felt for, before it is placed. This is because the deafening snap beneath the weight of your body will alert the unknown numbers of enemy to your presence: the enemy who is now just tens of metres away – who wants nothing more than to kill you.

Before you came out on this close-target reconnaissance patrol, you checked your light-scale equipment to ensure it did not jangle, knock or make any other sound that would give you away to the enemy. But in these final metres, when the slightest accidental sound may decide life or death, you now find yourself checking your breathing.

For you do not know how many of the enemy lie just in front of you. At this point, all you know is that you are one of only three men, and you are creeping as far as you possibly can out on a limb, with every sense primed for it giving way beneath you. The reason for your tiny numbers in such close proximity to the enemy is that you can be as stealthy as possible. Of course, the flip side to this is that if you are 'compromised' and the limb snaps clean beneath you, you will plunge, outnumbered, to drown in a world of shit.

But you accept this trade-off as you stalk closer, and closer still, to the enemy, because it remains your best chance to remain undetected.

It is when we are about ten metres away from the first mud-walled building that I realise the British and American definitions of a CTR might differ.

As I had been taught, 'close target reconnaissance' meant stealthily orbiting around a target, with a series of probes and withdrawals as you seek to gain a 360-degree intimate knowledge of your target and whatever is going on there – all the while remaining unseen and unheard.

But as I cover the rear of the two Americans slinking inexorably forward in front of me, with the first building now only five metres away, I now suspect that this CTR is in fact just going to be one probe – straight into the target.

The flirtation with danger makes me feel alive. And I am with them, as we silently skulk as one through the shadows – straight up to the door of the first building.

Kneeling, we listen as we pause to scan the area through the night sights on our weapons.

No sign of life.

We flit over to a small sand berm and lie behind it, scanning the night with our weapons and night vision again.

Up ahead, we see that the next building has light shining from underneath its doorway.

Keeping our bodies low behind the sand berm, we creep closer to the building with its sign of life.

Now we are opposite the doorway. It is just a few metres to our fronts over the berm we crouch behind.

The lead scout covers the 180 degrees to our left, leaving the PC to focus on the doorway while I cover the 180 degrees to our right.

We stay there for some minutes while the PC watches the building with the blacked-out windows and light shining from beneath its door.

I can hear several men's voices inside.

And then, with a tap on my shoulder, the PC signals me to follow them once more and we move further along the berm and into the target.

A much larger two-storey building appears from behind a line of trees.

We go firm behind the berm again while we search for any signs of life within it, but its hulk looks dark and lifeless.

We carry on up the berm until this building is perpendicular to us. Bringing up the aerial photos in my mind's eye, I remember that this largest building lies close to the water, with a track leading straight past it to the jetty: the jetty that is the reason we are here.

We crawl over the top of the berm towards the building, then slip quickly across the open metres towards it.

Its forbidding black windows gaze broodingly down on us.

Now we are against its bricked wall. And inching along to its end, we turn the corner to find the track to the jetty straight there in front of us.

The water and the jetty are just thirty metres along the gloom of the track. The right-hand side of the track is lined by a thin copse. Immediately to the track's left is another low building – and, again, this has light shining from beneath its door.

Now we sneak even slower, every light footstep feeling its way forward in silence as we filter into the relative cover of the copse.

The low building is now on the opposite side of the track to us, its front door no longer visible. As we edge through the sparse vegetation towards the jetty, I can now see the dark lumps of cargo crates up ahead.

Suddenly, a dog begins barking.

The bolt-out-of-the-blue noise makes my heart leap, a cold rush of alarm shooting up my back as I instinctively kneel and point my weapon at the sound. I can't see it – it sounds like it's just the other side of the low building.

The two Americans kneel as motionlessly and silently as I among the saplings of the copse.

We wait.

But the dog does not shut up – its piercing, angry bark gets louder instead.

Now its gutturally aggressive raising of the alarm is spreading to every other dog in the vicinity. The air is filled with their close and distant bayings and snarls coming from every direction around us.

Now there is the sound of men's voices. I can hear them back from around the first occupied building we had seen.

And then, just 20 metres away, from round the corner of the low building on the other side of the track, there is the sound of its front door banging open and a gabbled discussion between more male voices.

But then, as one, they fall silent.

The dogs continue their angry compromise of us.

We remain silent and motionless in our copse.

Through the green of my monocle, I now count eight men appearing from round the corner of the low building to our fronts.

They are silently fanning out from it.

They are hunting.

And they are all carrying weapons.

Four of them walk directly away from us, disappearing over a sand berm and out of sight.

Three walk to the edge of the largest building we had skirted round, disappearing in turn behind that.

And the last one, all on his own, heads directly towards us – right along the track we are kneeling beside.

The dogs are quieter now. I can hear the man's feet crunching against the small stones of the track as he draws closer.

He is holding his Kalashnikov in two hands; its muzzle points at rest towards the ground.

Muffling the sound between the index finger of my right hand and the thumb of my left, I click the safety catch of my rifle to 'Fire'.

He is five metres away and closing.

My weapon is aimed at his chest; I wait in silence for the moment that he sees us.

But he walks straight past us, up to the jetty.

My weapon follows him to the right, and with a quick glance to my side, I see that the two Americans also have their weapons lined up on the man.

He pauses at the waterside, taking a moment to look around the jetty.

Then he doubles back on himself, walking up the track towards us.

This time he is coming slower. He is peering into the saplings and vegetation to the side of track as he draws closer to us.

He is peering straight into the copse we are kneeling in.

My body is beginning to complain about being in the same position for too long. But I must not move or make a sound, so I ignore it.

He edges past the first American, giving no sign of having seen him.

And he is just passing the next when he suddenly stops.

He stares into the murky darkness we sit in.

Then he edges forward a few more feet before stopping again to stare hard into our copse.

He is now directly in front of me – two metres away – staring directly at me.

I can hear him breathe as I silently inhale and exhale.

My heart thumps somewhere below me; everything in the world has now narrowed to the man in front of me and my weapon pointed straight at his heart.

But now I do not hear him breathe. His body is still and he does not move a muscle.

He is listening.

My trigger finger moves from the trigger guard to the trigger.

The soft flesh of my fingertip rests lightly against its hard surface. I feel a frisson at the touch. The patient, deadly purpose within me and the lethal power waiting patiently in my hands are silently focussed as one.

The weapon itself incites violence. From muscle memory, my finger takes up the millimetres of slack in the trigger, pressing gently back against internal springs. Now on a hair trigger, I wait to squeeze just those final millimetres more.

I see that he is not wearing night-vision goggles. And I see that the moonless night and murk between the copse's thin branches is so far all that is preventing him from seeing me.

But through the green of my monocle I see him as clear as day, staring right at me. I see his dark clothes, dark hair and dark beard. And I see the dark shape of his AK-47, still pointing at the ground in front of him.

I do not use my rifle's infrared laser to sight on the man; its invisible beam will betray our position to any of his comrades who have night-vision equipment. And at two metres range, I do not need it.

I wait for the split second he brings his weapon up, calls out, or gives any sign of having seen us.

Then I will kill him.

I will squeeze my trigger finger twice in quick succession. And there will be a night-vision-blinding muzzle flash from my weapon and the deafening report of its double tap ringing out.

But in the quiet, ear-ringing seconds afterwards, he will be lying on the ground, dead. And the two marines and I will not.

In buying these seconds of life, though, the two marines and I will then be in a world of shit. And from sneaking in here unseen at the pace of a predator stalking prey, we will then instead become the hunted. It will be the three of us against however many of them there are – on their hunting ground.

So I wait with my finger on the trigger while the man in front of us unwittingly decides his own fate and those of the hidden infidels in front of him.

I wait to kill or be killed.

But now he is looking just to my left.

Then, with a turn of his body, he slowly carries on his way up the track – still peering into the dark foliage at its side.

My weapon follows him.

We wait as his dark form gradually moves metres, then tens of metres, from us, until he disappears behind the corner of the largest building. And then we lift ourselves up to our feet, bitching limbs free to move stealthily at last, and make our way silently through the undergrowth to the water's edge.

We turn right to handrail its bank. And we creep through tall reeds to begin our shadow-hugging journey to get the hell out of there.

As rear man, I now have my work cut out covering our arses as we withdraw from the target; for if the enemy that is now looking for us sees or hears us, it will now in all likelihood be a 'contact rear'.

Walking backwards in the darkness while you look behind you is just asking to trip over and alert the enemy to where you are. So every few metres I stop to scan our rear with my weapon, then slither back up to the PC in front of me.

I do not want to be left on my own in a dark place where everyone wants to kill me.

We slink past the buildings. Putting more distance between the target and us in the ground beyond, we blend into tree lines. Our crouched bodies steal through the dead ground of darkness-filled dips.

I see no sign of us being followed.

Now hundreds of metres away, we silently link up with the five other Americans. Together once more in the safety of numbers, we begin our journey back to the Danish vehicles.

The buildings disappear behind us.

My feet place themselves mechanically in front of each other. They are sure-footed in their direction as they home in on the pick-up point with its promise of life and home. And the world opens up again as we spirit further away from the target, deeper into the desert night.

But my mind is lost. And I am on my own within its dark labyrinth as I wander at a loss through its myriad of fears. For it is not the promise of warmth in the hearth of Home that now fills my mind, but the myriad of splinters that stick and catch there about *her*, and what I imagine she is doing with *him*, at this very *second*.

*

'It's going to really piss her off if you don't trust her.'

With our patrol reunited back at the palace, Frosty, Tim and I were respectively sunbathing, drinking pop and smoking outside our house. And in noticing my withdrawn nature since coming back from R & R, the conversation had turned to Cecilia.

Frosty looked at me for a reaction.

'I know, mate,' I replied quietly.

'Look, we've got fuck all control over what goes on at home out here. So all I'm saying is that if you still want her, you're going to have to trust her.'

'I know.'

Tim had been listening quietly. Then he piped up. 'Yeah . . . Maybe, Frosty, but she's not returning Liv's calls any more. And Matt's girlfriend is getting the same treatment – Matt says Danni's flummoxed by it. And that goes for Liv too – how she's just shut off from the girls – and Jake . . . it's just shit.'

Dougie appeared from inside to sit beside us. 'We on about Jake's bitch?' he broadcasted breezily.

'Yeah, group therapy session!' Frosty said, rolling his eyes and laughing.

'Mag to grid – get rid,' Dougie stated flatly. 'And do it before she does it to you . . . Or just kill her when you're back,' he grinned.

'Yeah, there's an idea,' Tim said, eyes widening in enthusiasm. 'We'll give you a hand too; our lives are being made hell, let alone yours!'

'Oh God, don't send him more loony tunes, he's on a knife edge already!' Frosty laughed.

I smiled and laughed with them.

*

I had done my apologising. And I had told her I would place all my trust in her.

Maybe we were making progress: the next time I spoke to her on the phone, though it was the usual depressingly stilted affair, she told me that she had sent me a parcel. This would be her first post to me for two months.

But when I finished the call with a ventured and thankful 'I love you', she only said: 'OK.'

When the phone line went dead immediately afterwards, with my deepest feelings now divulged and unreciprocated, I felt the balance of power in our relationship had now tipped finally and fully to her.

But she had promised she had sent the parcel. And I clung to the hope of this promise. With less than five weeks now before we all returned home, I thought that maybe her thoughts could be returning to me.

From the day she had said she sent the parcel, and on the basis of how long it had taken me to receive her long-previous ones, I worked out when it should arrive. Give or take a day either side, they had all taken ten days.

But after ten days it did not come.

It had probably been delayed in the post.

But over the next few days, as I divided my time between the threats of the Iraqi streets and the minute-by-minute gathering darkness in my mind afterwards, it still did not come.

At the 17-day mark, when we had a patrol scheduled up to the Shatt al-Arab Hotel base – which also happened to be the Army's post-sorting office in Basra – I decided that it was today or never.

Cautiously, as always, we made our way across Basra. And then, safely inside the hotel compound, we parked our two Snatches outside its front door.

Alex went inside for a briefing, leaving the six of us outside to drink cans of Pepsi and shoot the shit in banter behind the rear vehicle.

But I sit apart from my friends, silent and alone in the driver's seat of the front vehicle. I am preparing myself for going to the sorting office: for then, I will know.

I smoke a cigarette in the quiet, one leg pushed against the driver's door to keep it open. From across the river, a cooling breeze wafts across my face, clearing the smoke from my eyes.

Quiet.

I put the cigarette to my side and close my eyes. My head settles back against the headrest. I inhale a deep breath of fresh air, holding it within me for a second – feeling it tight inside.

And then I exhale . . . and with the breath that pours forth, I let the months of pent-up angst pour out along with it.

Calm.

The only sound is of the birds singing in the trees.

Peace.

Behind the dark of my eyelids I listen to their gentle lullaby.

My head sinks heavier against the headrest. And my fingers unfurl, letting the cigarette drop to the ground.

Sleep.

But now, cutting through the fading birdsong and into the blackness, is a strange high-pitched whistle.

From out of my slumber, my brow furrows slightly as I try to identify the noise . . . and then my eyes snap open in recognition.

The deafening *bang* of an explosion punches my eardrums.

It is so close that the blast wave slaps an invisible hand across my face and rocks the door back against my foot.

Now I hear the whistle of another mortar – and in the second I have before it lands I only have time to consider closing the door of the vehicle, while simultaneously hoping it doesn't land on me.

The crash of it detonating fills the air. It is just as close – 30 . . . 40 metres away? I can't see from inside the cab. All I know is that they're fucking big and too fucking close.

'*Incoming! – Get inside! – Get inside!*' someone screams nearby.

I'm way ahead of him. I've got my helmet and weapon in my hand and I'm sprinting to the front door like the rest of my patrol.

Another explosion punches the air behind me.

Just as I get inside behind my friends, there is another. Its sharp clap reverberates along the corridor we find ourselves in.

Like them, I fasten up my body armour and pull on my helmet with feverish fingers.

And then, because there is nothing else we can do, we wait.

Moxy sits opposite me on the tiled floor. He is quiet and his eyes are wide. But when I look round to the others, he only looks like the rest of them – and probably me. That was way too close.

Over the seconds, then minutes, we wait for more mortars. But there are no more.

Faces begin to ease. And wisecracks about the soldier shitting himself begin as we wait for the all-clear and clearance to go back outside – if we so choose.

Then, just up the corridor, I see lines of blue postal sacks leaning against its walls. I lift myself up and walk along to them. Flicking through the labels tied onto each of them, I find the sack that is marked 'HAC'.

I drag it back down the corridor to my friends. Then, sitting back down, I open it up to start divvying out the mail to them.

Their eyes light up when they see what I am doing, for post is a soldier's lifeline to everything he loves back home. It is an escape to read these letters of love from those who love you back home. You can keep these letters to reread in dark times, when you need to remind yourself of what goodness is waiting for you back home, when this tour is finally done. This is because the love of your loved ones is nothing less than the light at the end of your tunnel.

I divide the mail into piles: small ones for each of my patrol and a bigger one for placing back in the sack, for all the mail addressed to the other patrols. But it has only been a few days since the last mail delivery, so at most there are only a couple of letters per man.

When I reach the end of the blue sack, I see that there is no parcel.

I hand the letters out to my friends then sit back down against the wall.

And while I numbly wait for the all-clear, and for my friends to finish reading the letters from their other halves, I can reach no other inexplicable conclusion but that Cecilia is now outright lying to me.

*

When the all-clear was called, we were told to stay well clear of an area cordoned off by mine tape outside, as there was an unexploded mortar lying embedded in the ground there.

This would prove difficult, though, as the orange mine tape was right beside our front vehicle.

The unexploded mortar had landed 12 metres from where I had been sitting.

*

Being a Quick Reaction Force sounds exciting, but it is not.

Outside our patrol house, we sit and wait in full kit beside our readied vehicles. We are on standby to be crashed out in support of one of our other patrols in the city, should they suddenly find themselves in the proverbial *world of shit*.

We will receive a panicked radio call and then at that very second we will spring to our feet, jump into our vehicles and charge into the city, like the fucking cavalry to the rescue.

But this has never happened yet. Though our patrols may well have been well trained, we have also been lucky. Our unit is now one of a dwindling number that has not had one of their patrols tick the life-experience box of being blown up from the roadside.

So though you're fairly sure you got all dressed up for nothing, you do not know for sure – because you are in Iraq. And in Iraq you have learned to expect the unexpected. And *because* all tour long your unit has not had part of it wiped out yet, now, in these final weeks, you feel the increasing danger of the unexpected becoming the expected.

And because the expected will in all likelihood kill you, you know you cannot afford to relax.

So your vehicles are filled to the brim with fuel. The lubricants, oil and tyres have been checked. The keys sit in the ignition. You know it will start first time because you have checked even this.

Your cleaned, loaded and made-ready weapon waits for you on board. You will only have to click off its safety catch to begin firing.

And now, sitting just feet from your vehicle, you have fastened your body armour tight to you. Your chest rig is secured over the top of it. Your sweat pours beneath it into your shirt, because even in September it is over 40 degrees centigrade in the shade.

So you sit with a bottle of water on the table in front of you to replace your body fluids, as the CamelBak strapped to your back is only for when you are out there – *in the shit*.

When you are scrambled to your vehicle to be in this shit, the only thing you will have left to do is put on your helmet – and then you are gone.

You wait like this for hours.

We play poker to pass the time.

We are using explicit pornographic playing cards. I do not know whose they are; they had just appeared in our patrol room. All 52 of them depict approximately 52 sex acts (once all positions, variations and nuances are accounted for).

I hold two in my hand, but I am fixated on one. It is the three of diamonds.

The woman in it is a doppelganger for Cecilia. Eyes closed in desire and with anticipation, she is about to close her mouth over a man's erect penis.

But I do not remember this act she used to perform on me. I imagine her now doing this to *him*.

Every card and sex act laid out in plain view on the table stabs into me with torture, at what I am losing and what they might instead be doing to one another, as I sit powerless to intervene here in my plastic chair, in Iraq, thousands of miles away.

The beauty of the woman on my three of diamonds only twists the knife deeper.

'Wood!' Charlie blurts. 'Stop dawdling, man – I raised you ten.'

'Sorry, mate . . . Fold.'

'Fucking hell – after all that!'

He smiles and rolls his eyes at me. I smile back.

I put my cards face down on the table and light another cigarette. The game goes on without me.

But I cannot get the image from the three of diamonds out of my head. Superimposed in my mind's eye, it is her face – there – now – with him.

Her despicably eye-catching, head-turning, car-crash-causing, beautiful face.

And I can feel the crash coming; it is more than on the cards.

I am at the moment when you know you have lost all control and can only watch the end as it screams towards you.

But then all of a sudden the seconds slow to eternities. And there is a moment of peace running through your drain of fear – as you realise that there is nothing you can do.

You just give up.

But you know the end will be horrific. There will be a rush of final realisation in the last moment before it happens – and then the final, sickening impact will hit you . . . followed only by shock, in the quiet hush of the aftermath.

Though I know this is coming, I do not know when it will suddenly hit me. So my slow seconds have ticked by into eternal minutes, drawn out over every hour, of every day, as they have stretched into weeks – and now months.

She holds all the cards now.

And I know I am reaching the point when I cannot handle this any more.

Maybe you think me weak for this admission. And if you hold this point of view and you have served in Iraq, on the ground, and walked a path of heightened emotions born of mistrust with the only partner you have ever loved, then you are entitled to this point of view.

But if you have walked this path, then maybe you will understand, too well, the limits of what one person can withstand.

And if you have not walked it, then I can only ask you to try to understand.

Life deals you certain cards. When you are young, you have no control over what you are initially dealt. But as the game goes on – if its rules so allow – you can adapt your hand by discarding old cards and electing for new, as yet unknown ones.

As 'fortune favours the brave', you may well be able to make your own luck and 'raise' in confidence – or alternatively just try to bluff it. And you might well find yourself on a winning streak.

But as to what is hidden in the other player's hand . . . You can only make an educated guess on the basis of the cards you have been dealt.

You might suspect they are cheating. But if they are sly enough, or you are stupid enough, it will have to remain a lingering suspicion.

And too late through a particular game, when you have staked too much and stand to lose it all, you may realise that you do not, after all, have a winning hand.

Then you are presented with two choices. You can either give up, or you can carry on gambling – and try to turn your loss into a gain.

But we are playing poker here in Iraq. And the rules of this game dictate that I am stuck with the cards in front of me.

They torment me with how she is defiling the corpse of our relationship.

So I am folding.

*

I do not want to play football, or volleyball, or do any of the activities that my friends do to pass the time between patrols on the ground.

Though I do not want to, I find myself withdrawing from my friends, as I feel too emotionally drained to join in the lively interaction among them.

I feel dead.

All my thoughts are on her.

And the further I withdraw into myself, the more my friends do not know how to help me.

I am my own worst enemy.

I have brought all this on myself.

I have only myself to blame.

Charlie spends the most time with me. I am thankful to him, because outside the times I force myself to concentrate on the Iraqi streets, I am now god-awful, catatonic company. But late at night, when it is just the two of us, he listens. And he talks. At those times, he helps. I stand some chance of sleep.

But she is always my first thought when I wake up, before Groundhog Day begins again.

If a psychiatrist were here, he might perhaps opine I have 'depression'. But there is no psychiatrist here.

But I do hear that Max has revised his previously high opinion of me. Apparently he now opines that I am 'cunt struck'.

In incisive squaddie vernacular, this is undoubtedly true.

As he stood beside our vehicles as we dismounted from them after another patrol, I noticed him watching me.

I unloaded my weapon and made it safe in the unloading bay. My automaton's hands moved rapidly over its working parts; the countless drills of hand interacting with weapon were by now automatic.

He was standing behind me when I turned round. 'How's it going, Jakey – your missus fucking someone else or something?' he asked jocularly.

In a flash of anger I wanted to rifle-butt him in the face. But I let this quickly die inside me, along with everything else.

'Yeah – just like your missus is fucking someone else right now,' I said flatly.

He just looked at me with his jaw hanging open, shocked by my reaction. I didn't care what rank he was, what part of the Army he was from or what he'd done in it. It probably showed.

I walked past him and away.

Late that evening, though, he came to find me.

I was in the dark outside the house, smoking. I thought I was going to get a bollocking for insubordination or something. When he raised a hand as he drew close, I even thought things would now have to dissolve into a fistfight – 'in the margins'.

But instead he placed his hand on my shoulder. And his tone was gentle.

'Let's see if we can't sort this out, Jake, OK?'

'OK . . .'

'I've done some admin this afternoon; you can be on a plane back to England this Friday. Then over the weekend you can sort things out either way with your girlfriend, and fly back to us to crack on from the Monday . . . How does that sound?'

I was dumbstruck.

'Jesus, Max. I don't know what to say . . . Thank you . . . But what about the guys, though? They're going to be one man down . . .'

'Don't worry about that,' he said, holding up a placatory hand. 'I've talked it over with Alex. And your patrol's long overdue some downtime anyway.' I caught the outline of his mouth smiling in the darkness as he continued. 'I might send them down to Kuwait, come to think of it. You could always hang out with them beside the pool there if you want instead – rather than spend it with that idiot back home.'

I laughed and then shook his hand earnestly. 'Thank you, Max . . . I probably need to sort things out with her, though.'

'I know.' He patted my shoulder and turned to go, before stopping to add an afterthought. 'Come back to us, Jake.'

Then he walked away.

I watched his back disappear inside, feeling waves of warmth towards him. Then I took a last drag of my cigarette and blew its cloud of smoke into the still night air.

Now all I had to do was phone Cecilia to tell her the news.

*

I heard her breathe out. It made her sound impatient. It didn't bode well.

'It's pretty short notice – I've already made plans for this weekend.'

'What . . . What plans? . . . All weekend?'

'We haven't got anything to talk about anyway.'

'What do you mean we haven't got anything to talk about? I'm going out of my fucking mind out here!'

'Look . . . I was going to wait till you were back, but with the way things have been going . . . I think it would be fairer to just end it.'

The final words sliced cold through me.

And in the quiet, dizzying seconds afterwards, I realised that it had finally happened. And suddenly, I was now in the quiet emptiness of the aftermath.

But it was at that point that all the months of bottled-up fear, rage and aggression suddenly exploded from me to be channelled down the phone in one tirade at her.

I cannot remember exactly what I said. But I know that the phrase 'you fucking bitch' featured heavily.

What I do know I told her was that I took massive exception to being prepared to fly thousands of miles from Iraq just to talk and sort things out either way with her, while she could not even spare a few hours from her busy weekend to drive a few miles down the road and tell me face to face.

'I didn't plan this,' she said meekly, while I paused to take another breath.

I shouted something about taking responsibility for one's actions. And I think I added something about lack of trust and lack of communication killing our relationship.

I know she said: 'If you don't stop shouting, I'm going to hang up the phone.'

And I know how the call ended.

Calmer from my venting, and more resolute, I quietly said: 'I'm going to be all right, Cecilia.'

'So . . . What . . . That's it? You're not going to phone any more?'

'You've just dumped me on the phone in Iraq!'

I slammed the phone down.

End.

I walked out of the dark cubicle, through the harsh strip light of the Portakabin corridor and then into the quiet blackness outside.

There was another soldier waiting outside for one of the phones. He looked awkwardly away when I glanced at him; he must have heard me all the way outside.

I walked to be away from him, reaching into my pocket for another cigarette.

The glowing flame from my lighter danced in my hands while I lit it.

Then it died. And I was alone in the dark.

I had told her, and myself, that I would be all right.

But I am not all right.

*

I sit alone in the dark bunker.

I do not fear the pistol held in my hands.

Nor do I fear the single bullet it will bolt through my brain.

It will cut through everything and put me to sleep. And this will be a release from the hours I try to escape in sleep here, but cannot.

I slowly cock the pistol, sliding the working parts back and then forward.

The bullet is now in its chamber.

The safety catch is off.

I feel the weight of the pistol in my hands, tracing my fingers over its hard edges.

And in these final moments I feel I probably should feel something, but I am tired of feeling. I do not want to feel any more.

I raise the pistol to lodge its muzzle under my chin, adjusting its angle so the bullet will pass through the back of my head.

Comfortable that I will sever the brain stem connecting my mind to my body, my trigger finger moves from the trigger guard to the trigger.

The soft flesh of my fingertip rests lightly against its hard surface.

Finally I feel peace: my eyes close and my finger begins to squeeze, as I finally take leave of this world that is Mother and family and everything I value beyond value at Home.

But in those final millimetres, I think of my mother.

And I think of my brother – and my father.

I cannot do this to my family.

I cannot condemn them to a life of guilt, blame and torment, just so I can release myself from this purgatory.

And as I slowly release my finger from the trigger, I also think of my friends here, and what this would do to them.

They'd have to clear up the mess.

So I numbly set the pistol down beside me.

I tell myself that *she isn't worth it*.

And I light another cigarette.

*

The patrol is almost over. We have only one last junction to cross before we are on the home stretch of riverside road that leads straight to the palace gates.

I am on my own on the back of the rear vehicle, covering left, right and rear as we barrel along. The wind blasts hot against my neck and roars loud in my ears. But the noise and buffeting die away as Charlie slows the vehicle in preparation for the junction. I glance up ahead – it looks busy.

I swing my weapon from facing rear to check right. The decaying Basra street comes into sharp focus as we slow to a halt. Now that our vehicles are stationary, they are ripe for picking off with RPGs or IEDs. So right to left and left to right, I scan near and far through the 180 degrees to our rear and sides.

Child beside vehicle – nobody in the windows or alleyways – no vehicles behind us – no suspicious heaps of rubbish.

I steal another glance up ahead. The street behind my vehicle feels unnaturally quiet compared to the bustle of the crossroads up front. Tim is trying to edge the lead vehicle into it.

I begin my right-to-left scan again.

Child beside vehicle . . .

The child just below me is an Iraqi boy, aged about eight. He is wearing a dirty grey dish-dash, but he stands barefoot on the sun-baked pavement.

And, smiling widely at me, he is pointing a pistol at my face.

Only I have seen him; this moment is now private between us.

I can now kill an eight-year-old.

I turn all my focus down upon him and look into his eyes. The chug of my vehicle idling fades away into silence, as the rest of the world drains from around us.

Now, I can be totally justified in pulling a trigger. But I will be killing a child to save my own life.

I cannot justify this.

And in an instant of clarity, I see that he can save me by pulling a trigger I could not. He can take everything away. With this taken out of my hands, there will be no guilt, blame or torment afterwards, because the end will not have come from my hand.

So I do not raise my rifle to kill the boy. Instead, with dispassion, I look deep into his eyes.

The seconds stretch out in peace between us.

His smile fades.

With relief, I feel the final *coup de grâce* coming.

Do it . . .

But the little hand holding the pistol is beginning to shake.

The boy's brow is creasing. And now I see fear and distress across his child's face, as the British soldier looming over him just stares deeper still into his eyes.

Suddenly, with a lurch, my vehicle pulls away.

Charlie is gunning the throttle across the junction, and as the slipstream begins to roar around me again, I look back to the boy.

He stares after me from the side of the road, the hand with its pistol held limply down to his side.

He stands there, motionless, as his small body becomes smaller still.

And when he is almost too small to see, my vehicle turns a corner. And he is gone.

*

Some days later, I forced myself to write Cecilia an email.

Within its small body, I told her in resigned terms that I was glad there was now some form of resolution. In an attempt to exorcise the darkness within me, I wished her well with the rest of her life.

But her same-day reply said that she was so glad I had emailed. And it told me that maybe we could put all this behind us when I was back.

So I did not have resolution. Consequently, I didn't know whether I was coming or going – any more than she appeared to.

There was scant love in her subsequent emails, so I did not know what to believe.

The last weeks of our tour were spent whiling away the time on an OP from the front gate of the palace. Though this was physically safer than being out on the streets, it was by the same measure mind-blowingly dull. And the long, uneventful hours just afforded my mind even more time to dwell on her.

I just wanted to get back and sort things out either way with her; I was tired to death of this drawn-out Limbo – one foot in Hell – in a tour that had its origins as a Heaven of escape.

In the final days of October, with just six days of the tour left to go, I received a parcel from her.

Inside was the book on wine she had said she would send four months ago. And enclosed with it was a short letter, in which she wrote that she had 're-sent' this parcel after the other one 'obviously got lost in the post'. The rest of it was spent telling me what she had been doing at work.

But it did not end with 'I love you', 'Love' or even 'Your Lia xxx' as she used to say.

She ended it with the words:
'Stay positive.
Lia.'

*

Amid the afternoon rush of demobilising back in England, we had a leaflet entitled 'Homecomings and Reunions' pushed into our hands. Under the heading 'So Make Homecoming a Joyful Time!' I saw there was a bullet point saying, 'Communicate your Feelings'.

In another leaflet, entitled 'Dealing with Traumatic Experiences', I saw there were more bullet points to take note of. '*Don't* bottle up your feelings,' it emphasised. '*Do* express them and let your partner know how you feel. *Don't* avoid talking about what happened.'

But over the next five weeks of leave, while I am meant to be 'readjusting' from life in Iraq to life back Home, I spend my time as I spent it in Iraq.

I spend it not sleeping, as I waste it trying to make sense of all that has happened.

And there is no partner to 'communicate my feelings' to, because my partner is now seeing the person whom she promised me I had nothing to worry about.

But when Fate will again decree that I see them out together, I will realise that this is the only logical conclusion to our relationship.

It is no surprise.

And with this homecoming, I realise that I have returned to nowhere other than square one.

6

RESURRECTION

The mind is its own place, and in itself can make a
heaven of hell, a hell of heaven.
> Satan in John Milton, *Paradise Lost*

Our torments also may, in length of time
Become our elements, these piercing fires
As soft as now severe, our temper changed
Into their temper . . .
> Mammon in John Milton, *Paradise Lost*

The sun is sinking beneath the horizon, and the fast-reigning twilight is submerging me in shadow.

I lie face down on the flat rooftop. My body is cold and still.

The gathering night washes around me.

But the concrete beneath me is warm. I can feel the heat of the dying day still lingering within it. I can feel it exuding into me.

Hidden, glimmering embers within me are being gently fanned alive. My heart reawakens with a stammer, faintly beating once . . . twice . . . then suddenly surging in confidence, fluent in its rhythm, pumping life back around my thawing body.

My eyes can see.

I raise my head.

In the low wall enclosing the small rooftop, towards its bottom and in one of its corners, I see a fist-sized hole. A fading orange beam is streaming through it, trickling light into the darkness. I see I can look unseen through this hole onto the street below. My limbs unfreeze to begin my crawl towards it.

But the rooftop continues to fill with blackness.

The orange beam seems to gleam brighter the nearer I get to it, but the closer I draw to it, I realise this is only an illusion.

The sheer weight of the darkness immersing me is drowning the forlorn ray of light. And the nearer I get to its warm glow, the more it only retreats further through the hole. The dark does not drain after it. Its surface is above my head by the time I reach the corner.

Holding my breath in expectation, I place my rifle silently to my side. Resting my head on my forearm, I peer down at the street.

Its deserted expanse is bathed in a dying orange glow. Only lengthening shadows walk its void.

But now, just below me – I catch sight of someone.

Her.

She is with a man. But he has his back to me and I cannot see his face.

She turns her beautiful, perfect face up to where I am looking down at her.

Her wide, ocean-blue eyes look deep into mine.

And then, smiling widely at me, she slides an arm around the man's waist.

I feel a stab of sickness deep in the pit of my stomach – but I can also feel something pressing against my waist. I tear my eyes away to look down my side. Through the swelling blackness and waves of nausea, I see it is a corpse.

I kick against it, reeling away in horror. But I only roll against another. And I only catch a glimpse of the roof littered with the dead before another carcass slumps on top of me, pinning me down, before I feel the crush of more – then more – falling in on me.

Rotting flesh and liquid darkness fill my nose as I fight to surface from the crush. But I cannot see or breathe. I am trapped – I am drowning.

Black.

Wake.

Her Siren's eyes do not gaze into mine through the soft morning light.

My sweat-soaked bed is empty of the 'heaps of corpses rotting away, rags of skin shrivelling on their bones'.

And on the pillow beside me, there is only the half-read book of another man's 'Odyssey' of a homecoming.

I swing my legs out of bed to sit on its edge.

But that is as far as I get. With a pang I see the ironed shirt, tie and dry-cleaned suit hanging on my bedroom door, waiting to enshroud me. I chain-smoke two cigarettes, rubbing my temples as I summon the wherewithal to re-enter my previous life.

Nothing has changed in my absence but me.

I smoke a third before forcing my naked body to the bathroom.

Closeted inside the shower, I do not want to turn off the cleansing water cascading over me. I do not want the sensual escape of its warm, soothing embrace to end. I can feel its deluge beginning to wash the detritus in my mind away.

But this escape must end – otherwise I will be late for work and banks of blank mouths will silently tut in disapproval.

I savour the last tranquil moments with closed eyes and last deep breaths. Then I shut off the water.

I swallow down my panic in the sudden dripping silence.

Now washed numb, I walk back to my bedroom to mechanically wipe myself dry.

I put my suit on.

From muscle memory, my fingers do up my tie.

And I go to work.

*

Her email was waiting for me among the hundreds of corporate spam that had stacked up in my absence. We were just wrong place wrong time, it said. She found talking to me after I went back to Iraq a strain. There were never any laughs and we had distanced ourselves.

She had been out with one person in particular in the last month. She hoped I could respect her decision. And she said she was sure I could guess who it was, so there was no need to spell it out.

But what she did spell out was that if she really had felt about me how she said she did, would she have acted as she did on that night during my leave?

Her answer was no.

*

'Who the *fuck* are we?'

Charlie's rhetorical question lingered, unanswered, in the smoky air between us.

Beyond the moment of reflective silence permeating our little group, the City nightclub heaved and whirled around us: a mass of pointy shoes, sharp suits, loud shirts, louder ties and salon-styled, spiky hair rubbing shoulders with murderously pointed heels, short skirts, fake tans, fake nails and straightened, bleached locks.

There weren't that many women, though. However, I considered this might have something to do with the male clientele frequenting this place, who might only attract a very particular kind of woman.

I watched the rounds of ostentatiously ordered champagne at the bar, marking out the latest big man who had just hit his latest big target with all that make-believe, electronically traded big money.

I wondered who had really paid for that bill, as they fought to mark themselves out from the rest of the rats they no doubt saw as beneath them.

For all their puffed-up posturing and braying, I couldn't get over how they now looked so pallid, bloated . . . and *soft*.

So why in hell had Tim, Charlie and I come here?

We came because these people were now our peers again. We didn't personally know any of them, but that did not matter. They might work for different companies, with different job titles, but they all inhabited the same corporate world we now had to reimmerse ourselves in. From our estranged perspective, they represented it.

It was up to us to refamiliarise ourselves with this world. No one else was going to help us. Because as Iraq veterans, there would be no homecoming parade for us through the streets of London, any more than these bankers would line the same streets to welcome us home.

Walking these streets alone, weeks out of Iraq, I was anonymous. At times I even felt forgotten. But this was an inaccurate assessment, because the British public I walked among hadn't taken the time to remember their soldiers serving in Iraq in the first place. Celebrity gossip and reality TV shows seemed far more interesting.

Before I had gone to Iraq, walking the city streets had just been the same everyday experience that everyone experiences, in the crushing anonymity that only a metropolis can provide. But after Iraq, I felt this natural sense of solitude within a sea of people increasing to unnatural proportions.

On the tube I would read of soldiers killed in Iraq, but their deaths were consigned to the back pages of newspapers – and from all I saw, the backs of people's minds. I saw strangers sitting beside me flick straight past these stories in their own papers to engross themselves in whatever the remaining pages had left to offer, which was usually the star signs, or sport.

I considered this might be because being an Iraq veteran was not a badge to wear with pride. You were just part of a problem. You were an embarrassment.

Why should someone read about the reality of a young man's death in their name, when they are doing their utmost to distract themselves from the routine of their everyday, safe and secure existence?

Star signs and sport were far more interesting.

But if anyone were to somehow see the thoughts you felt spinning around your head, then you will have learned by now that you will only be a passing oddity.

Briefly curious eyes will peer in at you, asking: 'What was it like?'

But they will only want to hear certain things – and not what is on your mind now, now you are back and recaged among them.

So you do not tell them. You only speak of Iraq to the people who went there with you.

And you huddle together on nights out, mentally holding each other's hand as you try to reintroduce yourselves to this place called 'Home'.

There were many watchwords we had lived our lives by while we were away. But I could not see any of them reflected in the mass of suits now around us. The bankers raised their flutes of champagne to themselves, toasting their own success in hitting their metaphorical targets.

Among them we quietly drank down our pints, after having been targets.

I wondered if Cecilia's new boyfriend would have the same swagger to his walk in different circumstances – like in downtown Al Amarah, for instance.

But he'd never know – any more than she would.

And why should any of these people ever care?

Who the *fuck* are we?

Tim broke the silence.

'Fuck that. Who the fuck are they?' he scowled at the throng around us. 'And who the *fuck* – is *he*?' he suddenly blurted.

Charlie and I looked at the man Tim was now staring at, his eyes wide with indignant rage.

The man was about our age and dressed in the uniform dark suit. Standing with another dark-suited man on the other side of the table our drinks were rested on, he was steadily drinking from a pint glass.

My pint glass.

'Oi!' Tim snapped at him. 'That's my mate's drink!'

The suit glanced at Tim before exchanging a smirk with his colleague. 'Oh really? So where's your mate then?' He drained another long slurp of my pint before placing it back on the table, looking down his nose to shake his head condescendingly at Tim.

'Who the *fuck* do you think you are . . . you fucking dick!' Tim growled, edging closer to the suit.

'Piss off,' the suit sneered.

Maybe the two suits felt safe in a nightclub full of suited bankers, where physical violence really just wasn't the done thing. Or after another ego-inflating day of trading equities, maybe they had just quaffed too much Dutch courage from another man's pint.

Because how often in a nightclub within the heart of London's financial district, really, do you find yourself unwittingly standing beside a group of alienated soldiers, just back from the frustrations of Iraq?

The suit's colleague reached up a hand to push Tim away.

But Tim grabbed his arm, pulling the man's weight toward and past him. And in a move of such fluidity that it would have me giggling about it for days afterwards, he took a single foot to the man's off-balance legs and planted him hard on the floor.

I did not see what happened between them after that, though, because I was backing Tim up – straight into the original suit's face – grabbing his lapels to bring his face right up to mine.

'*Here* is his *fucking mate*!' I screamed into his widening eyes.

Then I threw him across the bar.

I was as surprised as I imagined he was at how far he flew. Whether it was all the months of rage, fear and frustration suddenly being explosively channelled through muscle, or all the months of weights to try to deal with those emotions, I don't know. But he got a really satisfying – and really quite surprising – amount of air.

He landed heavily against the wooden panels of the bar with a loud thud and a squeal, sprawling across the floor.

But his legs connected with a couple quietly minding their own business in front of the barman. Their drinks were knocked clean out of their hands, crashing onto the floor. They looked scared out of their wits.

Fuck. Not so cool, Jake.

As if a valve had been suddenly turned off, my stream of aggression stopped.

The offending suit, now with someone else's drink serendipitously all over him, was crawling to his feet to run away. All that was left was the mess I had made.

Keeping an eye on the suit to ensure he was indeed fleeing, I started towards the innocent couple, holding up two placatory hands. They shrank from my approach; the girl was shaking and looked close to crying.

'I am so sorry,' I said gently. 'What were you drinking?'

They seemed to calm a little when I said that. But I was still ashamed.

The barman was just staring open-mouthed at me. I asked him for two rounds of what the man had asked for. And after passing the four drinks to the couple with another apology, I thought I might as well get another round for myself, Tim and Charlie.

The crowd that had thrilled to the brief gladiatorial combat gave me a wide berth as I walked back through them with our drinks. I wasn't sorry their entertainment had finished as soon as it began.

For reasons I will never know, the bouncers never came for us.

We kept to ourselves for the rest of the night. But our mood was lighter. I thought it was perhaps a measure of the blackness inside all of us that after a venting, we could be less troubled.

I saw that all of us coming back were going to feel alone being reimmersed in this environment. But come the day's end, all of us could have each other to back one another up.

And I learned that I could have control over the darkness within me, even if it was only a stemming of its tide and not the lifting of its waters.

*

Maybe some clichés become clichés because they can also be truisms.

One cliché of subjective truth goes along the lines of: 'If you can't beat them, join them.' In my circumstances, though I did indeed want to beat some individuals to the very edge of life, I could see no other option but to rejoin the Bank.

There were a number of grounds for doing so. Firstly, and inescapably, there was the overriding money issue: I had the same bills to pay as everyone else. And secondly, now more than ever, there was an undeniable need for some sense of stability and security in my life.

These considerations tapped into the safe, middle-class psychology of my upbringing. But they were not *the* reason. And this single reason overrode all the poverty of purpose I felt in that office, and all the emptiness pervading me.

I could not give Cecilia or James the satisfaction of seeing me run, either to another company or another career. And I would not be able to respect myself if I ran away; I would only be disappearing to be swallowed into the bowels of another bank. After running away once already, albeit to Iraq, I felt I simply had to face down my demons now.

'Short-term pain for long-term gain,' I told myself, in what I hoped would be a truism.

But this would prove more painful than I had anticipated.

My scanning for threats in Iraq was immediately replaced at the Bank with steeling myself for the threat of seeing her, him or – worse – the two of them together.

When I did see them walking off to lunch together, shoulders rubbing against each other's in the bright winter sunshine outside the Bank, I was left shaking uncontrollably. My body still reacted with shock, though a distant and too long repressed part of my mind knew this reversal of everything she promised was not any kind of shock.

I thought maybe that could be the end of everything, allowing me the emotional energy to slowly reprogram my soldier's head with the long-lost mentality of computer programming.

But it was not to be.

My department head, Caroline, had apparently left the Bank while I was in Iraq. So now I had a new department head, called Ken.

I could only speculate that Ken hadn't expected me to make it through Iraq or something, because when I returned to my long-lost desk, there was nothing allocated for me to do. And when I say nothing, I mean *nothing*.

Everyone else around me appeared to be active – though admittedly only as much as tapping away at a keyboard about something you're just doing for the money counts as 'active'.

They tapped away in programming languages instigated in my absence. This turned out to be the reason for my inactivity. Especially after spending 12 months in a completely different mindset, Ken had correctly surmised that I would need to go on several training courses to learn these new languages' intricate semantics. So he asked me to 'try to be patient', while he found a role for me 'during this exciting period of change for the department' – and while I waited to attend the next available courses.

This period of sitting on the edge of my seat would apparently last a few weeks. And privately this suited me at first, because the prospect of suddenly reimmersing myself in line after line of computer code, day after day, did not actually fill me with quite the sense of 'excitement' Ken obviously thought he had imbued me with.

But this only allowed my mind hours to wander again. Rather than 'keeping busy' or 'distracting myself with work', using those hackneyed remedies for stress and relationship loss, I was simply afforded more time to contemplate the past – and my impending future.

In hindsight, now we were apart, it probably did not help me that Cecilia now sat thousands of miles closer to me than when we were together. Myself, her and the man I had been supplanted with all sat under the same roof now, separated only by lifts, glass-fronted doors and, from my perspective, betrayal. But hindsight is not always 'a wonderful thing'; with its easy perspective it can be a terrible, torturous thing.

At that time, in my mind, I felt I needed to sit things out and face down her and my demons by not running. Because even if I had run, I would not have been able to escape a small boy's smiling face when I closed my eyes. There was nowhere I could run to where the slam of any door would not return me to a small besieged rooftop or the shattered peace of a riverside at a time when I thought of nothing but her.

A clichéd Army maxim dictates that: 'The mind rules the body.' But now I was on civvy street, I found I was not in overall rule of my mind.

And a clichéd civilian saying states that: 'In the Army, you are only a number.' But from where I sat now, this was simply untrue. I had always felt more of an individual when I was an integral part of a fraternal team, in uniform and on a mission, than when I was just wearing the same dark suit as everyone else, sitting devoid of ultimate purpose at just another desk in a building full of identical thousands.

I did not have this view before going on tour, which was why I had joined the Territorial, and not Regular, Army. I held the view that I could do all the sexy stuff the Army offered but at times of my choosing – and living on a higher civilian wage.

As a younger man, in so many ways, before I went to Iraq, I had lapped up the Canary Wharf and investment-banking lifestyle. I laughed with my colleagues over how we were 'corporate whores' and how our salaries and bonuses were officially labelled as 'compensation packages' in perverted corporate parlance. I spent my money on TVR cars and 'TVR' cocktails. I managed to keep my relationships with the women I met in this environment monogamous, but I soon lost count of how many I had slept with. I gym'd it profusely. And in what spare time I had left after all this, I played part-time at being a supposedly semi-elite soldier.

But going to Iraq had changed my perspective. What had been an insidious, creeping sense of spiritual emptiness in my life was suddenly rammed home with a crash as earth-shaking as the Scud missile that landed close by on my very first day of wartime service.

And as you know too well now, it was throughout this drawn-out epiphany that Cecilia's light had appeared on my horizon. And I had wanted to believe she was something that revelations dictated she was not.

My Army ID card had been the passport to these strange and lethally vibrant other worlds. And my Army ID card was a sign of this new identity I had now – *my* identity. Underneath the words 'BRITISH ARMY IDENTITY CARD' was printed my number, but with it my rank, date of birth and height – and my name. Alongside these personal identifying details was my photo. And electronically superimposed over one corner of me was the Royal Crown – under which I had the honour to serve.

My Bank ID card, on the other hand, just showed my photo with an eight-digit employee number underneath. And this was only ever used to press against sensors that silently decided whether to grant you access to the innards of the Bank – or not, if the Bank suddenly decided one morning to dispense with your services.

I carried both ID cards with me, but, though I could not admit it, in truth I now only needed the Bank's. And this reflected the underlying tension in my life: I could not let go of my soldier's identity now, because I had been somebody as a soldier, and I did not feel like anybody as an employee of the Bank. And I did not feel anything in common with anyone else there any more.

But with as much crushing realisation as I'd had to face with the reality of Cecilia, I knew that the more I held onto my soldier's identity, the less chance I would have of ever readjusting back to my civilian life.

This scared me witless. From being someone and doing something, even if it was in a fucked-up situation in a fucked-up foreign country, I now felt the grey jaws of anonymity yawning open around me again. I did not want to let go of the defining identity I had forged for myself in the desert sun. I raged against the dying of its light. I did not see how I could go quietly back to my dark old life with newly opened eyes. I saw the inherent, clinical avarice; I saw the accompanying ultimate emptiness. In short, I was a soldier suddenly among civilians. And I had issues.

My stolen smoking breaks out of the office were my islands of tranquillity within the stretching expanse of each 'working' day. I could suck down smoky calmness in the fresh air outside before wading back into the tower in front of me. I didn't care if the cigarettes were killing me; I felt more life being sucked out of me by the sterile vacuum towering above, steam pouring from its tip into the cold sky, like some giant, bloody cancer stick.

As a soldier among civilians, I realised I was not readjusting from a country where men asserted themselves by trying to kill one another. The necessary pool of aggression I had to nurture out there, ready to release at the flick of a switch, had been brought home with me. For I defy anyone to claim they can just kill these feelings off at will, without so much as a trace, on their return home.

But after training and self-preserving necessity had first encouraged and then embedded this aggression within me, it had been unrequited. It was as unspent as the unfired rounds I had handed in with my unfired rifle.

And I felt my impotent frustration as a soldier in turn compounded by my impotent frustration as a lover. In what had felt like every waking minute of all my last months in Iraq, there had only been the insidious drip-drip of powerless rage and grief muddying and swelling the already darkened waters inside me.

Now I was a suddenly isolated ex-soldier and a predictably humiliated ex-lover, I felt the final black tempest of resulting emotions threatening to engulf me.

There was no sunny stream of life waiting for me, after the cocktail of her, him and Iraq. There was no escape from this square one I found myself at again. Because without this banking job, I would be nothing but a TA soldier on 'dole patrol', with absolutely nothing else filling the opening void in my life.

Each morning, I lifted myself out of bed feeling drained empty.

Towards the end of a cold lunchtime outside the office, I was sucking down the last half of a cigarette in the cold shadow of the Bank. And across the road, I saw the two of them leaving the building together, through its ever-revolving doors. I forced myself to remain still and stare straight ahead, gritting my teeth while my chest wound tighter and tighter. I did not want to give them the satisfaction of seeing me flee.

But I do not think they saw me; all their attention appeared focussed on each other. So when they disappeared into the crowd together, I thought I could safely turn away, walking the few paces to a nearby door that led to underground car parks. The glass door swung smoothly shut behind me. It was quiet inside the marble vestibule. And in the sudden hush, I felt the anger that had condemned me here unwinding from around my body.

I took my first steps down the winding stairwell. The first flight was lined with white granite, marking the limbo between the avaricious realm above and the underworld waiting below. My footsteps echoed sharply in the silence.

Circling round to the second flight, the marble and granite suddenly stopped. My footfalls came slower and quieter, as the very sun itself began to fall silent.

But I still kept heading down, circling past dimmer and darker levels – until at the fifth circle I could retreat no further from the world above.

And now, safely alone in empty silence, submerged in sullen shadow, I curled up into a tight ball. And I cried.

*

I guess I could have carried on wading through the mire on my own. But I was tired of doing so. And I was just tired; I wanted it all to end. In fact, by now, the only way I was eventually getting to sleep was by smoking myself to intoxication and then imagining I was not slipping light-headedly into sleep but sinking gently into the abyss of death. But my recurring dreams within the oblivion of each night were no escape.

I knew that I needed to talk, in an attempt to release everything inside. Maybe by airing everything, I could rationalise – even to the point of acceptance – all that had passed, and what was now.

I could not burden my friends any more; I wanted them to enjoy their times with me as much as I could with them. And I could not worry my family any more than I had already.

So there was really only one avenue left open to me.

I sought help.

*

I hadn't known what to expect from a psychologist – and a Harley Street one at that. But the indications I dared to entertain were that Ashley might, perhaps, prove everything I hoped one could be.

He had asked if I could run through a short history of why I now sat in front of him, if I was able.

I complied. But initially I had stumbled, as my mind struggled to condense all that had led to me being here. My vocal cords fought to express the memories that leaked out; I felt the weight of it all pressing down on me.

I began at the beginning, right back on the eve of invasion. I began with the memory of Cecilia's shining eyes taking their place among the desert stars above me. Though I remembered the fires already burning menacingly along the skyline in Iraq, I remembered all the idealistic purpose I had felt. I remembered the promise that had come with a letter at that war's end – and how hope had been fired in me as I looked up into another night sky, as it glowed in ethereal beauty over the Garden of Eden.

But, of course, I had been naive.

Under the scrutiny of Ashley's professional gaze, I felt the shame of my blind faith. And my shame dictated that I recounted the beginning of my tale staring at the floor, for I could not bear to see any hint of censure on his face as I stammered through the beginning of events that ultimately, deep down, I believed I had brought upon myself.

I was all of halfway through this first attempt to unfetter the clutter of past and present from my mind when I first stole a glance up to Ashley's face.

I was taken aback by how his eyes looked kindly in at me.

While I had begun the tale hunched forward in the armchair and stuttering, I suddenly felt the tautened muscles in my back beginning to uncoil, and my vocal cords releasing, as I realised I could, perhaps, be safe in telling him of everything – free from the judgement and condemnation I piled on myself.

Now we had eye contact, I noticed how he sat quietly and patiently through my increasingly lucid overview of why I now sat in front of him. He looked at me thoughtfully, nodding gently and encouragingly to me as he listened, taking written and mental notes of points he thought pertinent.

Occasionally I threw in self-conscious barbs of self-deprecating humour to try to punctuate the monologue. He smiled warmly at these efforts – but I noticed him make written and mental notes when I said them.

With every deep breath preceding each leap-of-faith admission to him, I was finding that even just through this initial but comprehensive act of catharsis, I was beginning to feel the glimmering possibility of release. Every spoken memory was a lifted burden, with each cleansing exhalation spiriting another ghost from me, borne forth on increasingly flowing words to pile like corpses around the two of us.

The heavy oak door to his room was closed to the rest of the world. And, secure within the peace inside, I felt the city outside slipping away far below me . . . forgotten . . . as the world narrowed to just me, Ashley, and the fount of my past gushing forth into the air between us.

When I finally finished, my body sank back into the deep leather of the armchair.

'Thank you, Jake,' he said contemplatively – and sincerely, I thought. Then he paused, before adding: 'The first thing to say is that we're all human. And with what you've been through, Jake, you have no need to be so hard on yourself.'

And following my baring of my soul to him, just that one opening observation, incisively cutting through all the self-criticism nurtured from my stammering childhood, positively reinforcing who I was now and where I was now, won him my trust. And considering my ability to trust had been shattered into splinters, its fragmented shards slicing through every darkened recess of my mind, his absolution won me over all the more.

Ashley explained how every individual had differing levels of mental resilience, but no matter who you were and how 'strong' you perceived yourself to be, we were all human and therefore emotional beings. So, unless you were a sociopath and therefore devoid of emotion and conscience, it was impossible for one to experience something abnormal and not be affected by it in some way.

'Or in other words,' he said, smiling warmly at me, 'if you experience something mad and it doesn't send you a little bit mad, then you were probably a little bit mad to begin with.'

I laughed in surprise and he winked good-naturedly at me.

'What you are experiencing,' Ashley continued, 'is a completely normal, wholly natural and totally understandable psychological reaction to the combination of abnormal events you have experienced.

But the good news is that I'm confident you will be OK, Jake. Despite how you currently see yourself, I can see a lot of strength inside of you.'

My eyes flicked to the floor under the praise; it was good to hear, but in equal measure it made me squirm with discomfort inside.

'Thank you, Ashley . . . But . . . I don't know . . . I will admit to feeling weak coming here. I never killed anyone out there – and my team never lost anyone either. There are soldiers who'll have been through far more than what I have.'

'OK . . . If you look at things objectively then yes, maybe other soldiers have been through more. But by that same measure, I'll guarantee there are soldiers who have been through less than you – by your measure – and who would still benefit from the treatment you've had the courage to admit you need.'

Fuck it, that 'praise' thing again.

'But stress is not an objective thing,' he continued. 'It is entirely subjective to the individual experiencing it. Therefore the true measure of how stressful a life experience is is how it is *perceived* by the individual.'

I creased my brow in thought.

'Most people I see here are going through divorces, bereavements or have lost their careers. All these experiences are completely valid in terms of stress. But the thing to remember is that when stressful events happen simultaneously, the accumulating stress is multiplied in the mind.'

'Right . . .'

'A good analogy is that of water being poured into a container. Each stressful event pours more water in, increasing the burden and pushing the mind closer to the limit of what it can handle without an adverse reaction. Too much, and the mind simply overflows.'

It made sense; I gave him a quiet nod.

'In your case, you suffered the breakdown of a relationship with a girl you loved while you were living in a hostile environment for months. And now you've been suddenly shoved back into a world where – I completely agree with you, by the way – a lot of the public is far more interested in vacuous things like *Big Brother*, it is absolutely no surprise that you are sitting here in front of me now.'

'OK . . .'

'I'm just trying to counter the punishment you're meting out to yourself for being here, Jake. Are you OK for me to drill down a little deeper?'

'Yes – please do, Ashley. Honestly, all this is helping me. I'm probably too analytical for my own good – but in view of that, I need to understand, so I can move on. Does that make sense?'

'Completely. But you're putting yourself down again – stop it; there's nothing wrong with having some intelligence.'

'Right – OK, sorry,' I said, smiling bashfully.

'Right then. Well, so you understand more – and hopefully don't punish yourself any more for being here – I think the nature of the threat you faced in Iraq reflected the nature of the threat you perceived from home.'

I looked at him quizzically.

'The reason I say that – and what was underlined to me the more I listened to you – is that as a soldier, ultimately, there is very little you can do to counter an IED, or a rocket, or a mortar. You can't shoot back – and therefore you have little to no control over your own destiny. Is this accurate?'

'Well, in the final analysis, I suppose, yeah . . . There's ECM and stuff, but in the end you just have to hope an IED doesn't get you. And with the mortars and rockets . . . Yes . . . When they're coming in, all you can ultimately do is hunker down and hope they don't land on you.'

Ashley nodded before continuing. 'And in your relationship with Cecilia, you did not have any control over what she may, or may not, have been doing behind your back while you were away. It was impossible for you to know what she was doing while you were in Iraq. And as a result, you felt you had no control over the destiny of your relationship with her. Is that fair?'

I took a deep breath and nodded, staring back down at the floor.

'OK. So, just to help you understand, it's exactly these feelings of lack of control – of helplessness – that can be the psychological killer . . . And you underwent that for months, Jake – the drawn-out loss of your girlfriend combined with the prolonged and constant threat of being killed or maimed . . . So if there's one thing I can ask you to take away from our first session, it is the knowledge that you are not "weak" but that you are instead just as human as everyone else.'

I lifted my eyes up to his.

'OK?' he asked.

'OK,' I nodded.

'You have to understand, though, that unless we had Cecilia here in front of us, we'll never fully understand what was in her mind.'

Fuck.

I needed to understand *why*.

'But from everything you've said, I have no doubt that one day you personally will find another relationship that does work.'

Ashley's words hung in the air. I wanted to believe them.

'Maybe . . .' I ventured. 'I hope so. But I've never felt that way about anyone before. And it scares me that I'll never feel that depth of emotion for someone ever again.'

Ashley paused to look at me. His eyes narrowed for a quick second behind his glasses, as he chose his next words carefully. 'Maybe you won't feel the same way about someone else again, Jake . . . But rather than thinking about it in terms of more or less, consider that it may instead just be . . . different.'

'Woah . . . OK . . .' I said quietly in contemplation.

Ashley's kind eyes looked at me again. 'Give yourself a break, Jake – you're all right. And don't worry; it may take a little bit of time, but I'm very confident that you're going to get through this.'

*

Ken had no issues with me taking 'time off' to see Ashley. There wasn't any work for me to take time off from, after all. And before all those training courses started, these sessions could be seen as a 'developmental investment' in one of his employees.

So every Wednesday afternoon, I made the journey from my Canary Wharf office to Ashley's Harley Street practice. For one hour every week, the rest of the world and all its distractions were shut away. The heavy oak door to Ashley's room swung smoothly closed behind me. Safely secluded under Ashley's supervision, I began to unravel the tangle of the past and its repercussive tendrils creeping into the present.

It was not long before I began to see that Ashley's confidence in me was as well placed as the trust I placed in him. I saw I was safe in his hands, as each successive session with him began to steadily loosen the grip my inner demons had on me. One at a time, I drew them from within me out into the open air, exposing them in all their vulnerability in front of Ashley. Held nakedly up for analysis, I learned to view these creatures in a different light.

But this enlightenment also brought a wave of sadness washing around me. Because, in the one best hope of analysis of Cecilia I had,

I was beginning to see our relationship for what it was. I was beginning to see that I had fallen in love with an unreal ideal, as for all I knew she herself may have done.

'I remember my phone call with her just before I went out on the ground with the Americans,' I said quietly. She told me that things ought to be "magical" between us. She said it in a little singing voice: "mag-ical . . ." A couple of hours after that I was seconds away from killing an insurgent . . . Jesus . . .' I finished tiredly, rubbing my hands on my temples.

Ashley had correctly ascertained that the bulk of my mental baggage was associated with Cecilia, so it was the demon of her within me that received the most attention. But as the disintegration of our relationship had apparently exacerbated the stress I felt out in Iraq, Ashley also felt that some light had to be shined on the 'valid in themselves' experiences I had had out there, as he put it.

I told him the one that came foremost to my mind was the Iraqi boy pointing the pistol at me.

Ashley nodded.

'I just didn't expect that from a child,' I said. 'He couldn't have been any more than eight. And this kid just happened to do this at the one point in the tour when . . . I don't know . . . I wasn't myself. I didn't react how I'd been trained. Instead I just looked at him – and half hoped he'd just get on with it and pull the trigger. Sorry, Ashley, I feel ashamed admitting this to you. I wasn't professional; I really feel I was just . . . weak.'

'What is the Army training for a child pointing a pistol at your face?'

'Well . . . Fuck . . . I don't know. I guess I could have been justified in just slotting him.'

'But you didn't, though, did you?'

'No.'

'And I know you say that you wanted him to shoot you, but do you think there may have been more to your thinking than that?'

'I suppose . . . Though there wasn't much time to think at the time.'

'OK . . . Well, you were fully prepared to shoot the armed insurgent who was threatening you and the two Americans, weren't you?'

'Fuck yeah.'

'Right . . . So if we take the stress of your relationship with Cecilia as a constant through this period, what is different about that night with the armed insurgent and that day with the armed child?'

'He was only a boy. I didn't want to kill a little boy.'

I felt a lump suddenly come to my throat and I swallowed it down angrily. There was no way I was going to blub in front of Ashley.

'OK. So by inference, you would rather die than kill a child . . . What is weak about that, Jake?'

'Nothing . . . I guess.'

'Absolutely right – nothing. It was anything but weak, Jake. And judging by the boy's shaken reaction to you just staring him out, it sounds like you actually afforded him a massive wake-up call – for him to realise what a monumentally stupid thing it was that he was doing.'

'I hope so.'

'I hope so for his sake too. But thanks to your restraint, there's one more kid running around out there supporting Manchester United . . . and not West Ham, the little bugger.'

I laughed in surprise. And his kind eyes smiled at me again.

'Thank you, Ashley.'

*

I still remember the colonel's words before we invaded. I cannot forget them.

But I also remember that the 'light of liberation' was not in that child's eyes as he looked up into mine.

Today, I am thankful that I did not stain my soul with the 'mark of Cain' by killing him, but I think my 'restraint' went deeper still than that.

I think that, like the colonel, I just wanted it all to have meant something.

*

Each session with Ashley was purely at my pace. Throughout their course, we sometimes went over old ground, but this could only be realistically expected with the more stubborn of my demons. And my most stubborn demon, of course, had a real-life name.

But every week Ashley and I went to work, chipping away at Cecilia and every other demon's handhold within me. Through what analysis we could conduct of her, I gradually learned not to demonise her. And the furious grief I felt inside, which was only hurting me, began to wane as a result.

It was only once the darkness had lifted away and taken the

demons' possessions of me with it that I saw Ashley's treatment for the exorcism it truly was. With his help, I had learned to view their diabolic malignance through different eyes. By confronting them and then learning to attach different meaning to them, I learned first to tame them – and then, through renaming them, to finally put them to death.

By the end of my final session, their corpses were quietly laid to rest back in my head. But now they were interred in new mental compartments. And marked on their headstones was what they only were now:

Memories.

*

The sessions with Ashley had kick-started new energy, purpose and direction within me.

Back at the Bank, this was manifested in a newly acquired job title. No longer was I just another System Analyst; I had become just another Business Analyst instead. But this supplanting of a single word in my job title had brought a wave of positivity washing around me in the office.

Outside the office, the sea change of positivism I was beginning to feel was reflected in other areas of my life. In the TA, I was now part of a small team of instructors on the HAC's six-month Patrol Selection Course, training and selecting hopeful recruits for the most challenging role within the regiment: the patrol squadrons. And in my personal life I would even meet someone new, in time.

The process was of progress perpetuating progress, with each reinforcing and compounding the other. The tangible life progress that had been enabled by my sessions with Ashley in turn enabled the rapidly snowballing success of my psychological recovery with him.

I had tentatively reached out my hand and Ashley had thrust his down to where I sat submerged in my darkness, pulling me to my feet. Then, just like I had seen the fires twinkling across the horizon in Iraq, right back at the beginning, I had been able to see the flickers of a life after Iraq and Cecilia glowing on my horizon.

But this almost hadn't happened. Before I had resolved to face my demons head on at the Bank and then with Ashley, when I only felt the loss of her and was unable to make sense of the world I found myself back in, I came close to completely losing my way. I had compiled a military CV. Although I hardly recognised the soldier on paper, it was all undeniably true. Even I could not deny that this soldier was me. Then I posted it off to an employment agency specialising in recruiting appropriately skilled individuals into the Private Military Contractor industry.

I didn't look upon it as being a bodyguard or a 'mercenary'. I only looked upon it as an escape, with a return to a country whose terrible certainties were now more appealing than the muddle of ambiguities I found myself in now I was back 'home'.

Three days later, I got a phone call from a man with a suspiciously Sandhurst-sounding polished authority to his voice. He told me that my CV was a 'strong match' for one of the positions he was recruiting for in Iraq. It had a six-figure and non-domiciled tax-free salary. Was I interested?

Yes.

But rather than the two weeks' notice I'd asked for, would I be available to fly to Iraq in ten days' time?

And, Christ, I came very close to taking the job.

But, looking inside myself with the offer on the table that evening, I knew I would no longer be serving a fading higher purpose. Now, I would be doing nothing but just selling my soldiering skills to a private company.

As tempting as the pile of money was, I weighed it against the realisation that if anything went very badly wrong on the streets of Fallujah, Baghdad or wherever else I was sent then I would be completely on my own – or with only whoever else was left alive in the vehicle with me – and with no British Army QRF to back me up.

What price to place on your life? The answer to that question lies in how desperate your life circumstances are, or what you perceive your options within that life to be. Having been to Iraq, twice, I realised instead how staggeringly blessed my life was back home in contrast – even with Cecilia in the background.

So I decided not to throw all of that away, along with, possibly, my life. I realised I had to stop running. Rather than take another and potentially fatal wrong turn in life, I resolved to face down my demons at home instead. And when I found I no longer had to do this, I began to look around me with new eyes for the next direction in my life.

*

At another crossroads ten years before, when I'd graduated from university, my decision to join neither the Regular Army nor the RAF, but to remain in the TA while pursuing a more lucrative civilian career, had presented me with a world of vocation options.

The issue was deciding which one to pursue. After reading any number of glossy recruitment brochures, which made 'realising your potential' as a chartered accountant sound as fulfilling as being the first man on Mars, I realised I needed to speak to people actually within each industry – just to try to cut through all the marketing crap.

Being a recent graduate, who therefore thought he knew quite a lot by virtue of having a degree, but by virtue of studious youth knowing the square root of fuck all about the real world outside the books he'd read, I thought a graduate careers fair in London might be just the thing.

Pushing through the crowd of other wide-eyed wannabes, however, up and down aisle after polished aisle of 'blue chip' companies and conglomerates peddling their party lines with air-hostess smiles, I might as well have been flicking through a brochure. They all began to merge into one corporate blur. Even the process of elimination was proving hard; my degree in Politics and International Relations was generically vague enough a subject to 'qualify' me for any number of graduate training programmes being promoted there. About the one thing I couldn't do with it was train to be an astronaut.

So, wandering, it has to be said, increasingly bored and directionless past stalls of organisations selling their wares with the inducement of free pens and other crap, it could well be argued that the IT industry picked me.

Or, equally, it may be that I was just suckered by another pretty face.

Underneath the banner of an American IT services giant, I noticed a strikingly elegant woman in her sexual prime and a close-fitting suit coolly watching the milling of post-adolescence floating by with detached poise. Back then, when I was only of graduate age and life experience – and, more to the point, recently split from a similarly young girlfriend – the most sophisticated word that suddenly shouted through my mind was: 'MILF'.

I found myself loitering to read her company's billboards of 'mission statements' and God knows what other blurbs, my mind distractingly enlivened by other things.

When my eyes just happened to drift back to her, she was looking straight at me. As she took the few steps to close the distance between us, she just smiled this alluringly assured half-smile. She knew.

'Interested?' she asked – with just the imperceptible flick of one eyebrow.

Oh yes.

And that's how I got into IT.

Well, it wasn't *just* that I fancied my recruiter, of course; that would have been insane. But she undeniably piqued my interest in what she had to say. And when I went away and did my own research in addition, I did decide to go for the graduate programme she was offering.

As a non-geek being trained up for a so-called geek's job, I did have some trepidation about my future colleagues. However, I hadn't been one that had bullied outsiders when I was young; with my stammer, I had been an outsider. I found that the few stereotypical 'geeks' I did come across, with their number increasingly diluted in the stream of mainstream-subject graduates like me coming on board, were nearly to an individual just harmless, decent people. This was despite – or maybe because – some of them must have been hounded to retreat to their bedrooms and ZX81s by bullies who probably ended up being the more boorish of bankers.

I did not hold this view of some bankers before working for a bank, because I had no experience of them and therefore no reason to do so. After training placements with the American IT company in the States and on the Continent, before being placed on a 'flagship' contract that happened to be in a deathly quiet part of the British Midlands, I was only too happy when I was headhunted by an employment agency in London to work for an investment bank in 'the City'.

Though the bright city lights of London had initially been very bright, and despite an almost doubled wage to ruin myself on in bars once out of the office, I knew that something was amiss. Throughout it all, I had always known I was naturally better at dealing with people and words rather than computers and code.

I could apply my mind to the hard, labyrinthine logic required of programming, and I gladly took the 'compensation' of all the pay and bonuses thrown at me. But the further my career penetrated down this path and the more 'successful' I became in it, the more I realised that it was just not *me*.

Where the TA had initially been just a moneymaking diversion on weekends when I was at university, it gradually began to morph in meaning into something of very different stature every time I escaped into its tests or training on Wednesday evenings or weekends.

It was the foil to my civilian existence. But by early 2003, when I received a phone call telling me I was a 'go' for the invasion of Iraq, it had become nothing short of a parallel life – and a personally mandatory means of defining *who I was* through the medium of *what I did*.

So Iraq could only have been a seismic experience in my life. With the power of tectonic plates crashing together inside me, my core was finally shaken awake – brutally exposing the seam of underlying tension that had been building inside.

Seminally entwined with the impact of this shatteringly real other world had been Cecilia. And from my very epicentre, I wanted to believe that she and this other world's shining promise of higher and magnified meaning could be true.

But of course it was all just a lie. And you will already know this.

I stood on steadier ground after the aftermath, though. The aftershocks dissipated, and then the last tremors of shock within me disappeared. I looked around me with eyes that did not see only what they wished to see; I listened with ears that did not hear only what they wanted to hear.

I could have heeded part of my nature, finally running away to join the Regular Army. As I was actually at the maximum age the Regs accepted new recruits – a decrepit 32 – it would have to be now or never.

But I decided on never. The prospect of all my years of TA service suddenly counting for nothing and starting right down at the bottom rank of a Green Army pile did not appeal. In fact, with the foresight allowed by these years of service, combined with the elevated perspective afforded from my ivory tower in Canary Wharf, the thought of suddenly going back to being addressed as a 'cunt' on basic training by an instructor years younger and quite probably less experienced than me, and with suddenly no say over my life and on less than a quarter of the pay I was on now, was even less appealing than remaining as a System Analyst.

Ironically, because of my awakening experiences with the Army, though, I couldn't be a professional pilot or even a police officer now. The tinnitus in my left ear from one too many loud bangs had put paid to that. But I learned to accept this in turn – and not only through the force of necessity.

I could still remain in the TA, doing the things that I now recognised were an inescapable part of who I was. And after my last tour, I could do these things among like-minded friends with whom I now had nearly everything in common.

However, my perspective within the TA was also now balanced by the realisation that it could not be a surrogate means of defining myself. It could only be part of a greater whole. Though this part was a necessary one in my life – satiating my need for its adrenalin and self-confirming challenges – I saw that it could not solely define me.

And by remaining in the TA I could even choose to do another tour again – should I again feel the primitive, inescapable yearning to. But as a TA volunteer, as opposed to a Reg, I could choose when and with whom I might serve again.

This new state of mind enabled me to subtly change the direction of my civilian career. In hindsight, I found that a subtle change was in fact all that had been needed. I suddenly found myself quite happy to be just another Business Analyst.

Admittedly, a Business Analyst sounds suspiciously similar to a System Analyst, especially when you still find yourself working for the same bank. But the clue to the difference between them is indeed in the name.

As a Business Analyst, I analysed business methods and wrote the Plain English documents that told the System Analysts what to do. I spent my days engaged in dialogue with the actual business users of the IT systems within the Bank. I questioned them on how they wanted to conduct their business differently. I documented their answers. And then, acting as the lynchpin between them and the System Analysts, I ensured they were delivered what could be provided.

In short, where I had dealt with computers and code, I now dealt with people and words. Whereas I had been able to do the former, I found I was far better suited to doing the latter.

I actually got to speak to people. And, God, as a human and therefore social animal, I felt better for it. The Bank was a gilded cage no longer. Instead of feeling its glass walls stifling me and tormenting me with the blue yonder beyond as they closed in on me, the view they afforded just became an ordinary, breathtaking panoramic backdrop to each working day. I mean, it reached the point where I actually began to *enjoy* parts of the working day. And these days only lasted eight hours or so, five days a week. And then every time I walked out of the Bank I was *free*! No longer did I have to be on call for a plethora of Back Office trade gateways and messaging systems that just constantly fucked up – and usually at about two in the morning, or when you were mid-coitus, or just actually beginning to unwind before facing it all again the next day.

Carpe diem'ing to reach this point had been just a case of seizing the day – though, admittedly, only when I was mentally ready to do so.

I had creatively persuaded Ken to put me on Business Analysis courses. And afterwards I used my newly acquired BA lingo to subtly adjust my CV, creatively highlighting what little experience I actually had in 'client liaison and requirements gathering', 'SWOT analysis', 'JAD', 'RAD', 'JRP', 'defining functional specifications', 'process mapping' and 'user interface prototyping'. I even thought I knew what I was talking about. So I confidently began applying for Business Analyst positions within the Bank.

A little knowledge can be a dangerous thing, though. The niggling worry I did harbour was that my near non-existent work experience in business analysis would be shown up over the course of an extended interview.

So I did have some nerves when I was invited to one for another department, five floors higher up in the Bank. The two women interviewing me had clearly taken the time to read my CV beforehand. They asked a few confirmatory questions just to ensure I was actually the person on paper – and that I actually knew what 'JAD' stood for, for example, and what 'Joint Application Design' actually entailed. But this phase of the interview didn't seem to last long – no more than 15 or 20 minutes it seemed. And what would turn out to be the majority of the remainder of my time in front of them was instead spent answering questions about what only took up two lines on the 'Career Summary' part of my CV:

Feb 2003–July 2003: Compulsory TA Mobilisation: Iraq.

Jan 2004–Dec 2004: Compulsory TA Mobilisation: Iraq.

They did ask a lot of stupid questions, but I was happy to deferentially field them, as each minute I did so was another used up within the hour we had, foreshortening the window of risk I had of exposing the gaps in my BA acumen – and looking stupid in front of them.

The soldier got the job.

I did become just another 'Business Analyst', working for just another bank. But I got to actually interact with people as part of my job, and I dealt with the richness, certitudes and nuances of words rather than the sterile, syntactic vagaries of code.

I was paid more to do this more enjoyable work, too, though I knew my pursuit of happiness was of only incidental concern to the Bank, which in the final analysis was only concerned with the pursuit of profit. But in lieu of any other calling in life now, I resolved to use the Bank as it used me. I accepted my 'increased compensation package' with the full knowledge that I was only whoring myself to a very old Beast.

I could plead my excuses here, citing how working for a bank indoctrinates you to the single-minded pursuit of money. But I won't. I knew what I was doing.

However, the one thing I will say is that in my supporting role as a BA I did not realise the true nature of the Beast at this time. I would not wake up to the real depths of its avarice until the rest of the world did.

In late 2005 I only felt lucky, with Fortune smiling down upon my efforts and granting me success in them. But 'Fortune favours the audacious', and the very act of resolve in itself was enabling – as anger can be, when it is channelled into a force that can be perceived to be constructive instead of self-destructive.

The anger-driven origins of this resurrection were nothing but an outright refusal to be beaten down by what had happening between her and me. But the Furies did not rise up from beneath the earth to punish any of her words or any of her actions. And Ashley showed me how such thoughts were ultimately only most harmful to myself. He showed me how holding onto the hurt and anger only hurt me, by perpetuating the self-destructive anger within. With his help, I had learned to redirect my fury from a depressive malignance turned in on myself to an outlook that was instead outwardly bloody-minded in its determination to effect positive change in my life.

The best 'revenge' I could ever hope for would be to pick myself up and endeavour to live my life in happiness, forever free of her.

It became only about me – and my future.

Sometimes I would still think of her, though, because I would still sometimes see her at the Bank. As my old work mates Carl and Andy still occasionally worked with James's team, I would hear gossip that would hurt at first but ultimately only cement the healing process in the longer term.

Come the new year of 2006, when I was firmly ensconced in my new role within the Bank and no longer dreaded the communal areas in case I should have to see him or her, I heard that they had split up.

But as much as I greeted this news without any surprise, I also found that I met it with ambivalence. Maybe this was because I had written her a letter. Though Ashley had endorsed the cathartic contents and commended their lack of anger, he cautioned me on actually sending it, as there was no telling the reaction I might receive. But I was sure she would be unable to respond – and I had indeed received no reply from her.

It was this final act, of telling her my truths, that finally enabled me to truly expel her ghost from deep within me. With the act of sending this handwritten, unanswered letter, I could finally say goodbye to her. With this act of returning what I felt belonged to her, I could finally let go of that fleeting promise of all that was and all that could have been, with all its broken hope born of broken promises – which were all now nothing but air.

I turned my back fully on the memory of her and all that she had promised. And my steps out of the darkness suddenly became lighter as the last vestiges of hurt finally fell away. My journey upwards hit critical mass. Everything became easier. The light sped towards me with exponentially gathering velocity.

And then it all just stopped.

Suddenly transfigured, I took a moment to look around me and within me. And I saw that it was good.

And then, when I wasn't looking, I met a woman called Kate.

*

A clichéd train of thought dictates that when you are complete in yourself, when you feel you do not need someone to complete your life, then that is perversely when someone invariably appears who can complement your life. But this was exactly how I met Kate. So in my experience I can only bow to this cliché being *ben trovato*, and born of truth.

I met her on a night out with Moxy and Charlie, on Saturday, 1 October 2005.

Leading up to this date, and as the three singletons from our Iraq patrol, Moxy, Charlie and I had formed another clique within the now very tightly knit clique that our 'Sierra One Two Delta' team had become after its Iraq tour. This is not to say that our team refused to have anything to do with anyone else in the HAC, though, or anyone else that had been to Iraq with us – far from it.

However, possibly because we had the fortune to have such a good, laid-back yet professional PC in Alex, we had gelled as a unit far more than the two other teams out there with us, who now didn't appear to meet up post tour at all. In fact, individual soldiers from these teams wanted to meet up with us instead, just as these same soldiers had voiced increasing desires to transfer into our team during the tour.

Back at the HAC after Iraq, elements of the now officially defunct 'S12D' team infiltrated themselves into a position where S12D could have a deceptively high influence over the future of the very regiment itself. This was enabled after Alex's commissioning as a lieutenant and his immediate appointment as the officer commanding the Patrol Selection Course.

If recruits to the HAC passed the six-month basic training of the HAC's Recruits' Course, PSC was the final six-month course these soldiers then had to pass in order to qualify as Special Observers and finally become part of the HAC's very *raison d'être*.

Standards on PSC were significantly and necessarily higher than the Recruits' Course. As a guide, when I passed my PSC in 2002 after receiving a waiver from the Recruits' Course due to prior experience, the estimated pass rate from walking off the street to final qualification a year later stood at 25 per cent, after only half of each course's intake passed.

Freshly back from Iraq, Alex was a natural choice for overseeing PSC, where it was not only the importance of imparting operational knowledge that was vital. Students also learned that taking on board this knowledge was vital to not only safeguarding their own lives but, more importantly, those of their teammates.

Tim and I quickly transferred onto PSC as instructors under Alex. The three of us had the help of a Regular Army sergeant, who was another good-natured Tim, and a couple of other HAC instructors. But for a year and a half it was effectively three soldiers from S12D who trained and selected hopeful Special Observers into the HAC, because, aside from the other Tim, we were the only three TA soldiers who were there without fail on every training night, weekend and exercise. But this was OK; we were our own little S12D mafia.

At first we were a law unto ourselves. We conducted our training and selection quietly but ruthlessly. We never shouted at any of our students because we didn't have to – they were all volunteers and it was up to them to reach the required standard we set. If they reached it, we took genuine pride in having nurtured them to this point. But if they didn't, we failed them without hesitation, though we took no pleasure in doing so.

There were never any complaints about the standard of our instruction, but after only a handful of students passed PSC in the summer of 2005, followed by only two on our second PSC in the winter of that year, we began to hear rumblings of disquiet from the HAC headshed above.

It was Max who was evidently chosen to 'have a word' with us directly. And if he was chosen he was a good choice by the headshed, as apart from the other Tim, who had also been to Iraq, and another SAS soldier on loan to the HAC, we probably wouldn't have listened to anyone else.

'Listen,' Max said. 'This isn't Telic 4. We're not sending these fuckers straight off to Iraq.' Though his choice of words may have seemed simple and unloaded, in reality this was rarely the case with Max.

The distinction he was making was that the HAC soldiers who had been chosen for our 'Telic 4' tour had been first selected as those of a higher calibre – at least on paper. Then we had been trained to within an inch of our lives by him and Rab, so that in the HAC's first deployment as an independent unit since the Second World War, we didn't just make complete arses of ourselves and by extension the regiment as a whole.

The impression I gleaned was that we were effectively being told to wind down the standards to where they had been pre-Iraq. From a headshed point of view I could understand this, because if only two people passed the biannual PSC course each year, the HAC would soon be a rather elite, but a rather frighteningly small, entity for a commanding officer (CO) who no doubt wanted to be in charge of a regiment as opposed to a troop.

Maybe the recruits on PSC could be afforded more leeway to grow as soldiers once they had passed into the patrol squadrons. But Charlie, for one, had come straight off PSC and onto our tour of Iraq. And having just come back from Iraq and knowing the HAC was only going to carry on sending soldiers on operations, we were now selecting soldiers for doing the job for real – not for some fucking adventure holiday hobby with an attached drinking club with which they could just liven up the odd weekend, as I thought some of the HAC 'old and bold' seemed to regard it.

But these 'old and bold' would never deploy on the ground as we had done or might do so again. They invariably outranked our little mafia. By the end of our third course in the summer of 2006, I couldn't shake the feeling that Alex and the other Tim had been leaned on from above.

Considerably more than two students passed that course. It was news to me that being caught sunbathing and cracking jokes outside your supposedly covert OP no longer constituted a fail. I think Alex was as frustrated about this as me and Tim, though.

I did not regard myself as some kind of standard-fascist; I took the personal view that if we wanted to fail someone then it was for very good reasons. With the unforgiving reality of another theatre of war appearing on our television screens in the summer of 2006, among the highest of these reasons was that we could well be saving their lives. In late 2005, no one had heard of Helmand, though. At this time, our creeping elitism was only informed by our memories from Iraq.

In another of his moments of clarity, Charlie had labelled our time in Iraq as 'a blessing and a curse'. In other words, our lives had indeed been enriched by our larger-than-civilian-life experiences on tour, but this also ensured that we began to feel separate from those we walked among afterwards.

This could especially feel the case after five too many beers on a night out together with the masses swirling carefree around us. But it could also be applied to how we felt on our return to the HAC, where Iraq veterans still only constituted a very small minority within its ranks.

But the blessing of our experiences abroad, followed by our shared fish-out-of-water experiences on returning home, was that first deep, then profoundly unshakeable bonds of friendship formed as a result.

Admittedly, this was also helped by the fact that no one in our team was a complete knob.

And no one was less of a knob than Tim, who with a marriage date set halfway through 2005, was suddenly facing being let down at the last moment by his supposed best man.

Feeling that if anyone had been a complete knob on our tour in Iraq, it had been me, with my unwilling but steady withdrawal from my friends, I leapt at the chance to redeem myself by organising a surprise stag weekend for Tim.

It was a complete surprise; he thought he was just meeting some of the Telic 4 crew for a couple of routine beers after work that Friday evening. But after a couple of pints we presented him with a daysack his beloved and sworn-to-secrecy Liv had packed for him – complete with passport inside. Three hours later he found himself being shepherded onto a plane to Bratislava by ten of his closest soldier-friends.

Though it was of secondary concern, I found that to help such a close friend, who had so gently acquiesced to the prospect of never ever having a stag do, helped me in turn. There was a mutual, silent glow of warmth inside me as I watched the wide-eyed shock on Tim's face just transform into this wonderfully broad, quiet grin of realisation as he sipped his can of beer close among us on the train to Heathrow. But he deserved it.

Quite whether his body deserved the liquid punishment imbibed into it over the next 48 hours, though, was another matter.

We 'got on it' as soon as we landed – and no one more so than the groom, who after a slap-up meal of takeaway fried tripe (in lieu of any chip shops to be found), finished the night regurgitating said tripe (plus a modicum of lager) into a hedge he then needed to be persuaded was perhaps not that suitable a place to spend the night. The two pretty, young Slovakian tour guides assigned to us probably got a feel for how the rest of the weekend would go at this point.

Beer and weapons do not mix, though. So we were all sober by the Saturday afternoon, when we were minibussed out to a weapons range deep in the Slovakian countryside.

The range itself was enclosed within the high rock walls of an old quarry. This was a wise location, judging by the look of the stag party preceding us, who literally had to be handheld as they fired these strange 'machine guns' roughly in the direction of a variety of targets only 30 or so metres away.

We quietly watched these other British lads as we waited for them to finish. For us this was just going to be a laugh, but for some of them this was clearly a very big deal; I guessed they'd never seen a real-life assault rifle before, let alone fired one. We didn't laugh at them, though; they were just another reminder of how far removed from our civilian peers we had become.

'Fucking hell . . .' Charlie said quietly, with a shake of his head, before stating just this thought.

With them out of the way, we lined up in front of the guy running the range, who one of the girls had told us was 'ex-special police' – though I may have misheard that.

I thought I was seeing things when, just behind him, his colleague took this opportunity to release what could only be described as a wolf from the back of a van.

'What . . . ?' I said incredulously, pointing at the animal now jumping excitedly up at its owner.

'Ah, Czechoslovakian Wolfdog,' the man said proudly.

No, that's just a wolf, mate.

I smiled and nodded politely. If it was 'ex-special police' as well, they must have used it to eat rioters or something.

One of the girls then said something in Slovakian to him. I winced as I thought I heard the word 'Iraq' mentioned.

But he beamed at us all instead, suddenly throwing his hands up into the air and exclaiming: 'You are all soldiers! Thank God!' Teaching hungover stag parties how to use automatic weapons was evidently a stressful business.

Immediately he took us over to two long wooden tables at the firing point. They were festooned with a variety of firearms whose histories spanned decades. There was the ubiquitous fare of various Kalashnikovs, obviously, but mixed in with them were weapons that must have been left over from the Nazi occupation here: MP40 submachine guns and Luger pistols. Then there were the tommy-gun-type weapons that the Soviets had used to kick the Nazis out before they occupied the country instead. They even had some more recent, completely crazy-arsed Skorpion automatic machine pistols lying around for good measure.

The drills for any weapon are pretty much the same once you know where all the relevant bits are. After watching us for a couple of minutes – probably just to ensure we were in fact British Army and weren't going to blow each other's heads off – he dumped a whole extra pile of ammunition behind us and pretty much just let us get on with it.

When we finished, he asked us if we want to fire the 'big gun'. It sounded intriguing; the group before us hadn't been offered this.

He stepped towards a tarpaulin stretched out on the ground beside one of the tables. The lump of something long was concealed beneath it. But we were none the wiser as to what this something was when he lifted the tarp away, though. I mean, we knew what manner of object it was – it looked like a Czechoslovakian version of our British Army GPMG. But we were damned if we could put a name to it. The veil of mystery was only partially lifted as we crowded round to have him talk us through its operation. We knew how to operate it then – but if he hadn't explained that the pistol grip was bizarrely also the cocking handle, for instance, we probably would have been there all day trying to make the thing go 'bang'.

A long belt of 250 rounds was lying invitingly on the ground beside the weapon. We unanimously agreed that the weapon had Tim's name written all over it.

'Tim!' we all suddenly called out in discordant cacophony.

'Nah – I'm all right . . . Jake should take it, I think; he organised all of this.'

'Jake!' came the new call.

Not being one to refuse a good offer, I said a thankful 'thanks' to Tim and allowed them all to retreat back to a seated area behind, while I knelt down with the guy to load the weapon.

I asked him if I could fire it from the hip, standing. 'Like so?' I said as I stood up, miming the stance and action to him.

'Sure,' he said with a nonchalant shrug of his shoulders.

I pulled my ear defenders back onto my ears. Picking up the heavy weapon in the sudden muffled silence, alone on the range, the whole world narrowed to me, the weapon in my hands and everything I was now going to obliterate in front of me.

He probably thought I was going to walk aimed bursts from target to target.

'Fuck it,' I thought.

And I hosed down the entire range in one single left-to-right 250-round burst of automatic fire instead. The weapon bucked and reared in my hands, alive as I walked its furious, dancing destruction into everything to my front. Dust and crap flew everywhere – *and Jesus Christ, it felt good!*

I even slammed a couple of rounds through the woodwork of a tiny wooden shed rather stupidly situated slap-bang beside the furthest right of the targets.

Rounds suddenly spent, I quickly knelt down to show the guy 'empty' before making the weapon safe. However, in the sudden quiet – even through my ear defenders – I could hear the sound of hysterical laughter crying out behind me.

I turned round to hand the weapon back to the guy with a satisfied grin; it had been gloriously therapeutic – though it could have been more so if Cecilia and James had actually been on the receiving end. Just then, I noticed the guy's colleague fast-walking past us before beginning a slow jog in the direction of the little shed beside the targets. Then he gave up the poor pretence of nonchalant haste and just ran. I looked quizzically back at everyone; some of them looked like they were going to be sick laughing.

'You shoot a duck,' the guy said matter of factly.

Duck? I didn't remember seeing a duck . . . Hey ho, though.

'Bit of lunch then,' I grinned at him.

'No, his dock,' he said, pointing at his colleague, who was now flinging open the shed door. 'You shoot his dock.'

His . . . dock?

'Oh shit . . . his *dog*.'

'Yes, you shoot his dock.'

Oh, for fuck's sake.

I closed my eyes in horror as I turned to look up-range again. He must have put it in that shed when he thought our shoot was over, nicely out of the way so they could clear up – and just in time for me sawing the range in half.

But, forcing myself to rip my eyes open again . . . there, unscathed on a lead, was the quietest, the most docile and the most suddenly cowed wolf you could ever see.

The poor little fucker – I didn't think it was *that* funny. I thought watching Tim swallow his own vomit back down in a plush restaurant later that night was far funnier – especially considering he was now wearing the present of an official Slovakian police T-shirt. Drinking champagne out of a fairly clean ashtray earlier that evening may or may not have been to blame.

Tim's T-shirt would at first cause much confusion among the locals in the bars, who found themselves edging away from him and thereby fortuitously clearing a good passage straight up to the bar in each establishment we visited before being kicked out.

Confusion was quickly followed by consternation, though, as the local people saw at first hand how their police officers appeared to spend their off-duty time. In fact, a good portion of it appeared to be spent pouring Sambuca into each other's mouths and then setting fire to it. They probably weren't used to their police officers doing press-ups on the dance floors of strip clubs, either, or telling them very earnestly that they 'had a tight ass' when ordering drinks, after Charlie had provided a slightly misleading Slovakian phrase card for us all.

They probably realised we were English at this point. It is safe to say that we probably did not do much to boost international relations between the two countries that weekend – though one of the pretty tour guides and I did end up offsetting some of the damage together at the end of the night. That weekend was as good for me as I hoped the uncharacteristically debauched weekend was for Tim, in one of his last ever as an unmarried man.

Even at the airport in the morning, we let England down. At the check-in desk beside us, of all the people checking onto the same EasyJet flight, straight out of the '90s rave scene, was the Prodigy.

Tim appeared from out of the nearby toilets, wandering glassy-eyed back to us from yet another post-stag episode of opening up the sluices at both ends. He had only just got back to us when the cleaning lady emerged from the toilets after him, mop in hand and iridescent with rage.

'Fucking Inglish!' she screeched after us.

The Prodigy looked positively affronted.

The reputation of the Slovakian police probably needed some repairing after we left, too.

But it was through bonding experiences such as this that the ties between the soldiers of a little team called S12D only deepened further.

As the three single blokes within this tight crew, Moxy, Charlie and I soon began to go hunting for compatible body parts on a weekly basis. We went though an extended tourist-trapping phase, within which our hunting ground invariably became the gritty, late-licence delights of the multistorey O'Neill's in Leicester Square. When I'd first moved to London I'd actually met a girlfriend in there, but in the months just after Iraq none of us were particularly looking for girlfriend material. We just wanted to have a drink, have a laugh and have sex. Sometimes we met girls who wanted the same thing as us – though sometimes, of course, we didn't.

Charlie will still swear to this day that he pulled a Muslim virgin there. But as much as he swears 'to Allah' that this is true, there is no way to corroborate this claim; Moxy and I were otherwise engaged with other, less exotic Christian girls at the time – and whose religious denominations couldn't be any further from our minds at that particular point.

We did meet the two Catholic girls, though, who after hearing our reason for knowing each other then proceeded to tell us, in suddenly noticeable Irish accents over the din, how their dads were 'in the IRA' – and one of their uncles – and one of their brothers. This transpired to be a positive attraction for Charlie, but, off to one side, I tried to explain to him how either they really weren't that interested, or, on the off-chance that they were, how they really weren't *that* fit to risk getting even a little knee-capping for.

Most girls there were as half-drunkenly straightforward as us, though.

And all this was fun, but fun was all it could be.

Where the months of one-night stands had been an escapist and ego-repairing necessity post-Cecilia, by late 2005 I was reaching an old, familiar place once again, as I slowly returned to who I had been pre-Cecilia.

Deep down, I just wanted something more.

And I found this, deep inside a dimmed Soho bar.

Or maybe more accurately, she found me.

But in that first heartbeat when I saw her, I thought she was Cecilia. My heart froze as my eyes locked on her, standing rooted to the spot as a cold rush of conflicting emotions surged through my veins.

She was walking away from the bar, crossing my vision from right to left. Just before she passed behind Charlie and Moxy in front of me, her eyes met mine: the same sky-blue eyes, with the same light-chestnut hair flowing to her shoulders, the same svelte body, the same petite height and very nearly the same beautifully delicate face . . . With an exhalation of relief I could see she was not Cecilia, though the initial resemblance had been terrifying.

Through the space between my friends, I watched her walk away. But then she stopped dead, standing still for a second, before turning about to retrace her steps . . . past the backs of Moxy and Charlie – and straight up to my side.

Months later she would tell me that she almost bottled approaching me, but instead turned herself around with the thought: 'Oh, sod it, what have I got to lose?'

By this time, I would know that she loved me. But what her brave, open and heartbreakingly good heart did not know when we first met was that I would ultimately only bring her hurt – when she lost me.

I will only ever carry deserved guilt for inflicting this pain on her, because in this story she is one who never, ever deserved any hurt.

Despite what you may think, her physical similarity to another was not an attraction, at least consciously. I had to look past it to see the physical beauty she carried in her own right. And what made this all the easier was the beauty that Kate carried inside her.

She accepted my past, and she understood that to make myself vulnerable again by implicitly trusting another would take time.

Repairing myself as an independent individual had been one thing; rehabilitating myself as a partner for someone else was another. But she never once took my emotional caution personally.

Over the months we spent together into the spring of 2006, she showed me that I could trust again. I relearned that I could be nothing other than myself with another and still be accepted and wanted, as I accepted and wanted them.

Without any airs of pretension or hidden feelings of insecurity, we were no one but ourselves with each other, with mutual respect for one another.

We never argued, because we never had any cause to.

She healed the remaining wounds left by another.

And the sex was always good.

For a time, with things at this blissful level, Kate was all I could ever want. We spent more and more time together. We met each other's friends – and then we met each other's families.

'She's a sweetie, Jake,' my mum had said to me. This was high praise indeed, in contrast to her tersely measured consideration of Cecilia after Iraq.

Mums get some things right.

Apparently Kate's mum thought very highly of me too. But I think she may not have got this right.

A week before Christmas in 2005, we took the Eurostar to spend what could only be described as an archetypal romantic weekend in Bruges. For two days we escaped into the fairy-tale setting of snow-sprinkled medieval streets, fairy-light-twinkling Christmas markets, candlelit dinners and midnight ice-skating. Steaming cups of hot *glühwein* warmed us before we retreated for lovemaking in the five-star hotel, in either our bedroom or the steam room.

But there was a but. And that was that I did not look at Kate the same way I had looked at Cecilia in Copenhagen.

As there was nothing wrong with Kate, this either meant there was something wrong with me or, worse, because nothing could rectify this, there just was not that level of clichéd 'chemistry' – for me at least.

Back home and into the new year of 2006, I was aware that I was not progressing healthily along the deepening-emotions route.

She must have realised. I liked her, a lot. And I cared for her, very much. But, if only for me, that intangible, elusive something was not there.

215

I decided to stay with her and keep with it, though; I thought maybe my feelings for her could grow with time.

But this was a fallacy.

As spring turned into summer, I knew that our relationship had reached a terminal point of no return.

I wasn't going to say those three words if I did not feel this love; I had learned at my personal cost what responsibility lies behind saying those words to another, when you know that they love you.

As frustrated as I was with myself, I knew I could not force myself to feel something I did not.

I knew that I had to end things with Kate – as gently as possible – but ultimately for her own sake, because I could not lead her any further down this garden path.

But it was at precisely this time, during the summer of 2006, that I saw things on television that would not only seal my withdrawal from Kate but from everything in my new, old life back home.

*

The images were blurred and pixelated. The sound was indistinct and distorted. But there was no mistaking what was being filmed.

My eyes were transfixed to the screen; my heart thumped with the soldiers' on it.

But I was not there; nor had I ever done what they were doing.

They were on a besieged rooftop: I'd done that. But they were being engaged with small-arms fire – and, dressed in no more than shorts and body armour, they were giving everything back in kind to their would-be killers.

The Afghan dusk was lit up with incoming and outgoing tracer fire. Its air was filled with the thump and crackle of automatic gunfire and the deep crumps of distant explosions. Hitting your ears with the same force as the roar of the weapons were the calls, and the shouts, and the screams.

It was the sound of methodical, directed anger and quelled, redirected fear.

It was the sound of battle.

And I wanted to be there.

I needed to be there.

*

Against the backdrop of this war suddenly breaking out in some

Afghan province called Helmand, I talked over volunteering for it with a number of people.

There were my friends, obviously, who were split into two uneven camps, with those few civilian ones thinking I had 'already done my bit' outnumbered by my older and firmer civilian and Army friends, who knew me better than that.

My oldest and closest Army friend, who I had known for over ten years, but who had by now left to raise a family and no longer had the option of doing such things, simply whispered, 'You fucking prick,' in envy. He knew I had already made up my mind.

I did not mention my 'interest' in doing another tour to Kate, at least not yet. I did not want to upset her until I had to. But I drove up to Oxfordshire and floated the idea with my dad. However, in the twilight years of his life and living alone with thoughts I could only guess at, I don't think he fully understood what I was saying to him. As always, I could only hug his frail, failing body goodbye at the end of the visit. But this time he did hold onto me for a bit longer, before saying, 'Take care of yourself.'

Then I went to see my brother. We went for a pint in town to talk it over and then we got gratifyingly drunk. He said he couldn't say he wanted me to go, but he would always support me. 'It's in your blood, Jake,' he said. But 'Have you told Ma?' he asked, with loaded consideration.

So the following day, I talked to my mother.

She knew as soon as I mentioned the idea to her that I was going to do it. But she asked where I would be going.

'Afghanistan,' I said quietly, watching her carefully.

I will never be a mother watching her son go off to war, so I will never understand the depth and dimensions of feeling I saw written across her face at that instant.

'Oh, Jesus,' was all she could say, before she closed her eyes and fell quiet.

'Sorry, Ma.'

Then she took a deep breath and looked back to me, before exclaiming: 'Well, here we go again!'

We both laughed, but I saw the tears she had fought back.

I am sorry, Ma.

I sat beside her to hold her hand. And yes, I felt like shit. But I had to go, and she knew it. She knew me as well as I knew myself.

'It's just in your blood, Jake,' she said. 'You've got too much of your grandfather in you – the old warmonger,' she said proudly. 'Just get one of those bastards for me, OK?' She laughed again.

'OK – deal,' I replied gently.

But she still had those tears in her eyes when I hugged her goodbye.

How long had mothers been preparing their final goodbyes to their soldier sons like this? How many millions of times had conversations like this been played out, in how many thousands of tongues?

'*Bella detesta matribus,*' Horace wrote 2,000 years ago: 'Wars are the dread of mothers.'

But what did he really know? He wasn't a mother.

*

Everyone who knew me well knew I was going to go.

These are the reasons I had to go.

If you do not agree with them, that is your prerogative. You are your own person who has walked your own individual path in life and thereby formed your own neural pathways.

Some of you will recognise some of them, though.

And these were my reasons, born from who I was and the path I personally trod to reach them.

I needed to soldier for real.

My family knew it was 'in my blood' as much as I did. I could deny my nature no longer now, after it had been nurtured in such a military family as mine – and then self-denied for so long in adult life afterwards.

Iraq had been real in itself. But I had never experienced the pure, unadulterated *war* that now screamed out of the television into me. It invaded my being with its debased calling. It assaulted my senses with its consummate Siren song. I felt it dragging me away from everything at home.

In more cerebral justification after Iraq, there was also the fact that Afghanistan as a campaign had some legitimacy in international law. However, to say this was a reason for volunteering to go there would be risible. It only contributed to the overall attraction.

Iraq had taught me that there were many shades of grey, depending on your perspective. Peacemongers might well label me a warmonger, but aside from the fact that there are some things in this world that *have* to be fought for, they would never understand that feeling you have on the ground, deep down in the dust and the weeds with your mates, which *nothing* back home can compare to.

For me, truly, Iraq had become akin to *coitus interruptus* without the ejaculation. It had become my very own *Jarhead* experience of being fucked over by a girl, taking incoming and not ever firing a single fucking shot in return.

I was done with the taking now.

And this fed into the other reason I had to go.

In lieu of finding the love of my life, getting married or seeing the birth of my hypothetical children, my tours in Iraq had been by far the most overarching experiences of my life. Their elevated meaning fed straight into the values that had been nurtured in me since I was a child.

But if I never did another tour, in recalling the greatest experiences of my life in all those long years to come, I would always have to remember a girl who, for me, did not deserve to be remembered.

I felt the memory of her had indelibly contaminated my tours. And I felt this memory forever casting a shadow over these highest of life experiences.

I did not want to have to always remember her, along with the pain of losing an ideal someone who had never really existed. So I could see no other option but to do one last, real war tour, or else I could never be truly at peace.

I knew this would not expunge the past, but in doing this final tour I would be able to remember it only for whatever savage purity it held, without the contamination of any other influences bleeding into it while I was there.

With my mind's eye on this one last foreign horizon, I split up with Kate. I tried to do it as painlessly as I could. But naturally it was anything but painless.

After all she had done to heal me, I hated myself for the pain I had ultimately brought her.

But for her sake this had to stop. And I had to go.

So I gave the HAC the nod that I was willing to be 'intelligently mobilised' for 'Operation Herrick 6'.

They gave me the nod that I would be going.

And now with my volunteering officially becoming a 'compulsory mobilisation', the Bank would never be any the wiser that I had volunteered, again.

*

At home, there is nothing like the funeral of a friend to force your own mortality upon you.

219

Even into his 50s, John had been such a strong and vital soldier. But now he was suddenly dead from leukaemia. It made me angry; he didn't deserve to die so young.

I hadn't expected Max to be there, though. I hadn't realised he'd known John too.

At the bar afterwards, he asked what I was up to. I told him my name was down for the next tour of Afghanistan. Frail mortality must have been on both of our minds. He took a moment to look at me, before speaking in the quietest tone I'd ever heard him use.

'Good chance of getting whacked out there, Jakey.'

At first there was nothing I could say to that truth; I could only nod slowly in acceptance of it.

But I remembered the final contentment John had voiced about his life, because he had lived.

And whether the following is considered a cliché, truism or even an aphorism, I do not care. Because, coming from a dying man's lips, these words carried a wisdom only the dying would know about.

He said the regret over the few things he had not done pained him far more than the many things he had done.

Though I knew I could be hastening my own death by doing so, I fully subscribed to this point of view.

But then, of course, John and I had walked very similar paths in life.

*

The last time I ever saw Cecilia was on a bright autumn day in Canary Wharf.

It was some time after I had sent her my final letter, but it was very soon before I would leave the Bank once again, prior to my five months of pre-deployment training.

My mum had taken the train into London to share an al fresco lunch with me. She said on the phone that this could be her 'last chance to meet her suited son like this', with the unspoken suffix: 'before you put me through hell trying to get yourself killed all over again'.

I was looking for my mum among the rows of tables outside one of the bars. But there, sitting down at one of them only a few metres away, and facing me, was Cecilia.

There was a man sitting opposite her with his back to me. But I didn't recognise him and my interest in him stopped there.

In that moment I looked briefly back into her eyes, I felt nothing. And I have no doubt that my face looked as blank as all the dispassion I felt.

I walked past her to carry on looking for my mum. But then, after walking ten or fifteen metres away, at a push like Orpheus walking out of the Underworld, up into the light, I suddenly could not help but look back.

And like his dead lover, she was suddenly lost to me. She stared down in silence at the lengthening ground between us.

But I turned away. And I would never see her again.

*

You may read these next words. But they are only meant for you, Kate, if you are reading this.

I am sorry.

7

ASCENT

Nobody is driven in to war by ignorance. And no one who thinks he will gain anything from it is deterred by fear.

Hermocrates

War is sweet to those who have no experience of it.

Pindar

It was rare that I came across a soldier who expressed fear at the thought of Afghanistan. And it was rare that I felt fear.

I was consumed by my preparation for the tour, but to say there was simply no time to feel any trepidation during the five months of build-up training from late October 2006 to early March 2007 would be simply untrue. There was just that old, overpowering sense of purpose burgeoning within me once again, which overshadowed all other subordinate emotions I might have.

Indubitably this was a psychological defence mechanism, keeping my young, single mind focussed on its now sole *raison d'être*, by not focussing on how its very being could very soon be ended. During my waking hours, emotional states born from 'fear', 'love' or even alcohol-induced maudlin reflection were surplus, superfluous and surfeit – as I knew they would be in Afghanistan.

I did not regard them as weaknesses, but I knew the impending and lethally unforgiving reality of Afghanistan rendered them redundant. I could not afford to feel such things, just as Afghanistan would be no place to feel such things. They would only drag me down.

The world narrowed to my day-to-day training, the mates who

immersed themselves in it with me, and the tour, ticking closer to us with each passing day.

Thus was my conscious mind. But with the glimpses I had of my subconscious, I knew I could be no automaton. Sometimes I woke from my dreams smiling in my sleeping bag, complete in my new existence. However, sometimes also I caught glimpses of all the other aspects that made me human and whole but that had been pushed to the peripheries of my mind, fighting to be acknowledged.

Sometimes I found myself in love with Cecilia all over again, only to be betrayed all over again. When I woke from these nightmares, drained from horror and fitful sleep, I found them worlds more disturbing than any upcoming deployment – because she was meant to be *history*.

I could not work out why I was now dreaming of her all over again – at these of all times – now I was finally free of her. Other than my mind now associating going on tour with an escape from her, I began to suspect that it was the finality of everything that was finally coming home to me as I prepared to leave home once again, one final time.

I knew that there could never be any reconciliation with her, despite the traces of residual, terrifying feeling still stubbornly haunting my dreams. I knew now all the meaning I had attached to her had been madness and waste.

I accepted with deadened fear the fact that I could very soon die, though in truth the danger of Afghanistan was only part of the allure – just as it had been with Cecilia. But now my life could soon end, it was only the history of it all that scared me. It was the feeling that maybe I could have done things differently that haunted me. 'You always regret the things you did not do,' John had said to me. And on waking I sometimes caught myself feeling that if only I had done things differently, I would not have lost her.

But, as much as I had been unable to escape my attraction to her, there was no escaping my reality now.

Nothing felt so real as the new life I was now throwing myself into. The tension between the yawning-open prospect of 'holding my manhood cheap' at home, as Shakespeare put it, happy enough with Kate, and the lethal lure of *living*, for however long, in a calling every repressed fibre of my being was being drawn to, was gone.

And *awake* and feeling so *alive* after the brutal morning run, or whatever else we had to do first thing, my conscious was grounded in the here and now once more; it was consumed with consummate purpose all over again.

The training and bonding with my future comrades in arms only further elevated my self-confidence and my confidence in those I now served among. This collective state of mind was reflected in the soldiers around me. We knew what we were doing. And this knowledge not only increasingly applied to the minutiae required of our respective roles but also to the complete embrace of where we would soon be employing our skills for real.

To a man, we all wanted to go – and none more so than the nine TA soldiers from the HAC who had all volunteered to be 'compulsorily mobilised'. Eight of this little band, including myself, had been posted to our Regular Army counterpart – 4/73 ('Special OP') Battery – while the ninth of our group, a medic, was posted to some 'normal' artillery unit called 19 Regiment.

The eight of us at 4/73 were a mixed bag of youth and experience in terms of HAC patrol soldiers. But we were all HAC patrol soldiers; we had all passed the PSC course to wear the same coveted Special Observer green triangle on our left shoulders as those in 4/73. One of our eight, James, had even passed PSC while I was an instructor – and before the stage when I felt quantity had to count more than quality.

Of the other soldiers, only two, Charlie and Ollie, had been on tour before. Charlie had been with me in Iraq, while Ollie had been to the Balkans before going on the Iraq tour after ours. In fact, by now, Ollie was the only other soldier in the HAC who could match the number of tours I had been mobilised for. Back in late 2006, three tours in five years was more than many Regular soldiers would undertake.

I knew the other HAC soldiers, Tom, John, Mark and Kris, well enough too. Though the eight of us soon dispersed among different teams within 4/73, for a while we would form a non-exclusive clique within its ranks – grinning broadly as soon as we caught sight of one another. This was a special, chosen escape for all of us. To a man, we could hardly wait to conduct all manner of fighting reconnaissance and Surveillance and Target Acquisition patrols in Afghanistan – in the most sublime manifestation of our Special Observer roles.

As physically uncomfortable and exhausting as the training may have been at times, as foreplay went before a tour it was a soldier's wet dream – though often a windswept, pissed-wet-through one.

There was the usual incongruity of half freezing to death in wintry England while training for a Middle Eastern summer tour. But any shaking you had when you paused for rest or thought was only the cold. Any fleeting fears you might have were channelled into the valleys and marshes you drove and ran through, calmly screaming orders and acknowledgements in faster, louder and ever more fluid practice engagements, firing SA80s with under-slung grenades, Light Machine Guns, General Purpose Machine Guns, Heavy Machine Guns and Grenade Machine Guns.

By mid-December, the process of assimilating those of us from the HAC into 4/73 was complete. Everyone knew what they were doing within their teams, and every tight, cohesive team knew how to act as one within the tight, collective whole.

God, it felt good.

But then, just before Christmas 2006, and with absolutely no warning, 4/73 was suddenly taken off the ORBAT.

Rumour Control took a couple of days to get its act together, but its whisperings soon informed us that our deletion from the upcoming tour's 'Order of Battle' had something to do with Donald Rumsfeld resigning as US Secretary of Defense. Apparently, this had made the British government question whether it would send the recently announced uplift of 2,000 soldiers to Afghanistan, of which 4/73 formed a part.

Down at ground level we knew fuck all about what the gods were thinking – if, in fact, they were doing much thinking at all. But what the eight of us from the HAC definitely did know was that we were damned if we were going to spend the next twelve months of our mobilisation moping around some barracks in Catterick, as one scare story now suggested. The 4/73 Regs who suggested this clearly hadn't the slightest inkling of what we had sacrificed in our civilian lives to be in Afghanistan – and absolutely nowhere else.

Though we did not know it, an officer outside of 4/73 would come to our rescue. Considering how much we wanted to be literally staring down the barrel at the Taliban, as opposed to staring down its metaphorical opposite end in a godforsaken barracks in Catterick for a year, he truly was our knight in shining armour.

He suddenly appeared, all gift-wrapped in pressed-clean Army fatigues, during what had increasingly felt like a depressingly pointless live-firing contact lane through a semi-frozen swamp.

I had just been through. Huddled in the relative warmth of a semi-derelict 'range hut' with everyone else who had covered themselves with iced mud and were now cleaning their weapons instead, I heard the door open and the words 'Lance Sergeant Wood?' tentatively called through it.

There would have been catcalls of 'What you done now?' – but no one recognised him, including me. At that point, morale wasn't high enough for catcalls anyway.

'Sir?' I said, stepping outside into the freezing, still air with him. It would have been deathly quiet in this part of the middle of nowhere, but the shoot was only halfway through, so our conversation took place against the staccato background of semi-automatic gunfire punctuated with screamed orders.

'Jake, isn't it?'

'Yes, Sir . . .'

He proffered a clean hand for me to shake. I was impressed; he couldn't have failed to notice the layers of dirt, cordite and oil smeared all over mine.

'Call me Jim – I'm the new HAC training major.'

Jim was the brand-new training major more like; we'd only been away at 4/73 for a couple of months, but I'd never seen him before. He must have been posted into the HAC in that time.

Jim said he was there to find new homes for us now that 4/73 was off the ORBAT.

I am fairly sure my next words were, 'Thank fucking God,' because I remember him smiling at me.

But then he shut me up momentarily with praise, saying he'd heard that during the training so far I had 'impressed the most' out of the eight HAC soldiers – and as one of its two highest-ranked soldiers there (all of a stratospheric lance sergeant), he wanted to give me first choice of where I went, before asking my opinions of where the other, even lower-ranked HAC lance corporals and troopers should go.

Naturally the praise thing was as uncomfortable as it was welcome, but the rest of it made sense to me: being so new to the HAC, he personally wouldn't know these soldiers from Adam.

'The choice' he had engineered for us turned out to be either going with the Grenadier Guards in the Brigade Reconnaissance Force (BRF) or deploying with an artillery regiment, 19 Regiment, in one of their Fire Support Teams (FST).

I would have just automatically plumped for the Gren Guards and the BRF as the natural recce choice, but in weighing my options I asked him out of curiosity what exactly it was that Fire Support Teams did.

Suddenly he was more animated. Grabbing my chance to light a cigarette, I watched his eyes light up as he described commanding an

FST in Helmand with 7 (Para) RHA, only months ago. He had been *there* when I had been watching at home. And just like the pixellated, distorted images had drawn me in, sucking me away from everyone and everything at home, now he, one of those soldiers, was standing in front of me, in the flesh. He had my complete attention.

He said the FSTs were specifically attached to the infantry, who in turn were there specifically to fight. 'So every member of the FST needs to be able to fight. We were throwing hand grenades back at the Taliban, just the other side of the wall to us. Make no mistake; it was fucking full-on. Halfway through the tour, the FSTs were at half strength from deaths and injuries . . . We had to have emergency reinforcements flown in from the UK.'

He paused mid-flow. At this time I could not fully appreciate why, so I filled the silence by offering him one of my cigarettes. I lit it for him and he inhaled a deep, long drag.

'Thanks,' he said, a little quieter, before adding emphatically: 'That's why every member of an FST needs to be proficient with calling in "danger close" missions – as a matter of routine.'

'You were routinely calling in artillery that close to you?'

'You'd better believe it. But don't worry, if you go into an FST as a lance sergeant, 19 Reg'll crash-train you up to OP Ack level. You'll know what you're doing.'

The butterflies were beginning to stampede around my stomach; this was beginning to sound very, very attractive. But I only nodded calmly to him, taking another deep drag on my cigarette, watching him intently, before asking my next and deciding question.

'Did you get many rounds off as well?'

I knew this could well have been a very stupid question, but at this crucial moment of decision I wasn't taking any chances.

'Hell, yes!' he laughed. 'My oppo spent half his time on the Fifty Cal! Look . . . Now you lot are available, that's precisely why the CO of 19 Reg wants you in his FSTs. His blokes are going to be great at calling in fire missions, but he's concerned they're taking over from paras and marines, in Helmand, in the summer fighting season. So the more soldiers he has who can handle themselves in a firefight, the better. That's where you lot come in – now you've been primed for that here.'

He gesticulated at the pair of 4/73 soldiers who had just finished the contact lane, smiling and walking towards us covered in shit.

'Seen,' I said, nodding slowly again.

'The Gren Guards want all of you, but they'll only get two. 19 Reg needs you more, so five of you'll be going there.'

'OK . . . But that only makes seven; who's getting left behind?'

Jim told me that, having chosen Full Time Reserve Service rather than being mobilised, Ollie wouldn't be going. He'd be staying with 4/73 regardless.

Christ; poor fucking Ollie.

But 'Right' was all I could say to that, before taking a deep breath.

'So . . .' Jim said, taking another drag down of his cigarette with a wry smile spreading across his face, 'Where do you want to go, Lance Sergeant Wood?'

God, from where I had been looking at pointlessly kicking around Catterick or demobilising empty-handed, it all sounded too good to be true.

Even allowing for exaggeration, being in an FST attached to the infantry sounded like a guarantee of a good, busy tour – regardless of whether I received all this suspiciously sudden, sexy extra training.

The BRF might be sexy in interesting ways. But aside from the ultra-anal boot-bulling bullshit I thought I might come across in a Guards barracks, I had no telling what their remit for 'reconnaissance' in Afghan would be. It might be a promising case of 'looking for trouble', but then, for all I knew, it might not be; I didn't want to be sitting in an OP somewhere while everyone else was having all the fun getting rounds down. I had done all my taking in Iraq already; now I only wanted to give all that love back.

I had heard enough. I only wanted to be in the thick of things. And if the FSTs were a surefire way to get there, then I would take this man's word for it – because he had been in an FST in Helmand, so he would know.

'OK, you're on, Sir. I'll go with 19 Regiment.'

'Good man,' he beamed, clapping his hand into mine to shake it again. 'You won't regret it.'

*

My suggestions for the others' postings became posting fact. Charlie, recently promoted to lance corporal and a proven quantity in Iraq, would take Tom with him to the BRF. And the other troopers, James, John, Kris and Mark, would come with me to 19 Regiment.

I kept my role in their futures quiet from all of them, though, along with my reasons. I couldn't see any good coming of advertising this information, should they ever feel aggrieved over their new homes.

And for those who came with me to 19 Regiment in January, there would be grievances. These grievances were at first only to do with questioning why we had to be split up as a group, but they soon also encompassed why they should have come to this unit at all. It was not just the sudden culture change of being thrust into this Green Army unit that caused rancour; it was the nature of its training regime.

And, as much as I did not want to, I would agree with them.

*

Why 19 Regiment was called 'the Highland Gunners' I did not know. They even used the Scottish flag as a background for their Royal Artillery flag. No doubt there were depths of history lurking behind this nomenclature, but the regiment was based in deepest Wiltshire, southern England. I must have met all of half a dozen Scots in the whole time I was there.

This was only an observation and not a criticism, though. It was neither here nor there in contrast to the rising alarm I soon felt, when I got the impression that some in 19 Reg just did not grasp the reality of where we were going in a matter of weeks. Maybe this was because the five of us from the HAC had been spoiled with the comparative intensity of training at 4/73. But when we were in barracks at 19 Reg, there just seemed to be a few too many tea breaks and aimless, endless periods of waiting around after thrice daily 'parades' with too little training in between, compared to what we had grown used to.

The average day at 4/73 had begun with a brutal run or tab in the darkness, before spending the day on the ranges fine-honing our team tactics and weapon skills. In the dark of the evenings we carried on in the light of classrooms: learning and practising Emergency Close Air Support, signals and more and more advanced first aid. It was exhausting, but we were in our element, training for war, and the weekends we had off to recuperate were *earned*.

By 1 February 2007, though, after some weeks of somewhat less demanding training at 19 Reg, I was beginning to feel our extended tea breaks were considerably less earned.

Instead of going for a run that morning, I had to spend it preparing my room for a routine pre-breakfast room inspection by the battery sergeant major, which he then didn't even turn up for.

Mark, John and I would go on our own run together that night instead. But to use the operative Army term, it was the examples of time-wasting 'bullshit' like this at 19 Reg that pissed us off something chronic. Would an unnaturally well-presented room make us better soldiers in the face of the Taliban? Perhaps not. For all I knew, though, maybe the Taliban would flee to the hills in the face of such merciless tidying.

Could the time have been better used with training relevant to counter-insurgency operations? I thought so, even if it should just have been a lung-bursting phys session at that hour. It didn't take much imagination to know that should a brother fall beside you in Afghan, you would need all your strength and stamina to carry and drag him to safety – with all his kit, armour and weapons dragging you down as well as your own – through all the pestilential shit, heat and incoming fire magnified in your head as inherent to an Afghan summer.

There were some phys sessions at 19 Reg – sometimes even in the mornings – but they were nothing like we had known at 4/73 or the HAC. The hardest run we ever did was tremulously hyped for days beforehand as some kind of savagely paced 11-mile tab, run as a squad. But on the day we didn't carry bergans or even weapons; we only carried daysacks on our backs. And 'running' frustratingly slowly beside the Patrol Training Instructor at the front of the pack, the fittest had lifetimes to look over their shoulders and see 19 Reg soldier after 19 Reg soldier falling off the back of the squad.

Mark and I measured the route that evening: it was barely five miles. I could not work out whether I felt pride or shock that the average HAC patrol soldier was literally miles fitter than the lowest common denominator at 19 Reg, whom we would now be going to war with.

The captain commanding my FST had actually turned up to this tab, unlike the other phys sessions that had been run. He explained that the 'fruit-only diet' he was currently on was the reason for his slow pace, although I suspected the real reason was the reason he was on the diet in the first place.

Captain Featherstone was fat: there is no other way to put it. On civvy street this would not matter so much, but the prospect of having to carry his six-foot-plus bulk in the event of it being ballistically punctured in Afghan only provided me with more impetus to do my own extra phys prior to deploying.

After watching his 'fruit-only diet' descend into the comfort of a 'crisps and chocolate diet' on exercise, I considered the hernia-inducing possibility that it could well require all four of his subordinate FST members to carry him in the event of his body becoming a dead weight.

As the team's forward observation officer (FOO), he had his talents, though. Watching him controlling artillery-fire missions on Salisbury Plain, I could only hold the highest opinion of him going about this aspect of his job. He was quick, slick and ultra-confident on the radio to the guns. And watching the fall of shot of his directed artillery rounds, his adjustments to fire looked bang on to me.

By this time, I knew enough of the basics of calling in artillery missions to appreciate his work. But, despite everything the HAC training major had promised me, I still had not fired one myself – and my knowledge never would stretch beyond the basic level I had, because I never would be trained as an OP Ack (a FOO's assistant) at 19 Reg.

Initially, this was disappointing, to put it mildly. But I could not take it personally, because this had been explained to me as soon as I had arrived at 19 Reg. The reason given was that in the time it had taken us to get from the HAC to 19 Reg, they had managed to recruit already qualified OP Acks from other units.

The OP Ack in my team was a Hampshire lad my rank, height, build, complexion and even eye colour – but he was called Martin and was from 1RHA. Watching him directing fire missions just as superlatively as Captain Featherstone, I could only respect his already confirmed appointment within the team.

There was no way I was going to be trained up as the joint tactical air controller (JTAC) in our team either – or, to put it in layman's terms, the guy controlling the airstrikes. The HAC training major had also hinted that this could be a possibility for me, but after finding out exactly how long the training for that vocation was, the prospect of me completing all those courses in time for Afghanistan in March was risibly impossible. And, of course, the team had a JTAC in training already, though by virtue of the various courses' length, this other Alex would not link up with us until we were about to go.

So in the FST of five that I found myself in, that left me and an indefatigably upbeat nineteen-year-old Scottish lad called Gilly as the drivers/gunners cum radio mules/general dogsbodies. It was a far cry from the training I had been promised. But I was only in the same position as the other four HAC soldiers in the FSTs. Now we were here, we had no option but to make the best of our situation.

With a mental shrug of my shoulders I would soon come to terms with my lowly position, because in truth the situation did not really matter. The Army was not my career. And on this last tour to end all tours, I only wanted to walk the same earth as the Taliban and shoot them as they shot at me. That said, if I had a choice between being the team driver and doing top cover as the team's gunner, I wanted gunner.

At 4/73, everyone had made it their business to know the Fifty Cal Heavy Machine Gun and its associated drills inside out, because *everyone* had wanted to fire this five-and-a-half-foot-long monster at the Taliban in so-called 'anger'. But whether you were firing it from the turret of a vehicle or planted in the ground on a tripod, anger couldn't come into it. The feel of it angrily juddering into life in your hands and the deafening, stuttering noise of it spitting bullets the size of your hands filled your senses. But as its operator you needed to be as mechanically detached from the reality of the destruction it wreaked as it was. Sometimes it demanded almost ham-fisted strength to cock the weapon, but firing at ranges over a kilometre away, it always required precise aiming through its optical sight to delicately lay the three- to five-round bursts on target.

It was a cold, murderous beast. And I wanted it to be mine in Afghan.

There was a solitary Fifty Cal 'familiarisation shoot' laid on one afternoon at 19 Reg. Again, in contrast to the depth of training at 4/73, it was a shallow affair in terms of instruction. Each soldier waited their turn to walk up to the one Fifty Cal. Then, finally behind it, there was only enough time and ammunition to fire three rounds in single-shot mode before squeezing off two bursts of automatic fire. And that was it. There wasn't even any aiming required; the Fifty was locked on a fixed point of aim. What basic drills were taught were incomplete; they didn't even include how to clear a stoppage.

But luckily I got a stoppage on one of my bursts, which I cleared with the 4/73-taught four-point check before the instructor trying to mollycoddle me could even try telling me what to do. 'Er . . . yeah . . . That's it, well done,' was all he could say after I had quickly loosed off my second, and final, burst.

It was lucky because Captain Featherstone was watching just behind me. And it was lucky that he was watching, because it was directly after this that he appointed me as the team's gunner.

'Slick,' he nodded to me in appreciation as I walked past him afterwards.

So I kept quiet about my 'slick' drills being, in actual fact, just well-practised, 'correct' drills. I couldn't see any point in souring the atmosphere now that I had got what I had been gunning for.

What was harder to accept with good grace was the situation facing some of the other HAC soldiers at 19 Reg. Some of them were looking at being their teams' drivers. In this role, it was very clear to me that, in addition to their SA80s, they should be armed with pistols.

I remembered the streets in Iraq when I had been a driver, when every HAC driver had an issued pistol strapped to their chest as their only realistic means of self-defence while in that seat. Inching through cluttered streets, asking a suicide bomber suddenly running up to your door to just 'wait a moment' while you reached round to unclip the superfluous 'world-class' rifle behind your head had not been seen as a viable survival option.

And I remembered a young boy pointing a pistol at my face, and smiling.

I had been on top cover when I saw him, but I could just as easily have come face to face with him as a driver. While the top covers on the back of Snatches in Iraq could easily pick off such a close target with their handheld weapons if they so chose, in Afghanistan we would be in weapons mount installation kits (WMIKs). And on these cut-down Land Rovers, the heavy-calibre turret-mounted weapons carried for top cover were devastatingly effective for mid- and long-range engagements. But at spitting distance they were useless, because aside from taking time to wheel the weapon round to bear, they also only pointed earthwards so far. So for a WMIK driver to suddenly be presented with such a close-in and immediate threat, the only person who could defend him would be himself. And the only weapon a driver could immediately bring to bear and actually wield sitting behind a steering wheel would be a pistol.

I had already arranged with the stores department at 19 Reg for our personal weapons to be delivered to us from the HAC. The 19 Reg SA80s that had initially been assigned to us looked like they'd been sat at the wrong end of a range, and some of them didn't even have SUSAT optical sights mounted on them.

Asking for pistols to be issued to the drivers proved more problematic, though. Seeking to garner support and speaking to Mark's FST commander about the need to issue him one, I was only met with a blank stare and the words: 'Pistols are for officers.'

Maybe this officer also wanted a parade stick along with a First

World War service revolver to face the Taliban with – though I didn't ask. But I did bite, saying that weapons should be role dependent and not rank dependent. I didn't give a fuck if I made a name for myself by speaking out of turn.

I phoned the HAC quartermaster again, thinking I could at least ensure the five of us from the HAC would be suitably armed as drivers. But the phone conversation was over within a minute.

'You don't carry a pistol and a rifle on tour,' he replied.

'We did on Telic 4, Sir.'

'Well, I need them for training.'

And the conversation was over.

The next person I phoned was Jim, the HAC training major. I thought he would surely know what I was going on about – and, sure enough, he agreed that carrying a pistol was more appropriate in certain circumstances, before telling me he would have a word with the HAC quartermaster. Finally having someone of rank actually listening to me now, I also found myself voicing my frustrations over the training at 19 Reg. But he only sought to manage my expectations, saying, 'Look, you're in a hat unit now. It's going to feel frustrating compared to 4/73 and the HAC.'

He was right about that. But at this time I had to content myself with this, as my FST was imminently due to depart for our final training exercise in Kenya. However, I did mention my frustration on the pistol issue in passing to my mother. And as an ex-Army officer herself, I promptly heard her go ballistic over the phone, before promising me she would raise the issue at the Families' Briefing Day being run at the HAC while I was in Kenya.

The thought of that made me grin wryly. I almost felt sorry for whoever would be on the receiving end of her wrath. She'd come close to scaring the life out of me a few times when I was little, though I had sometimes deserved it. Out of fear, I had learned not to lie, or cheat, or steal. And I learned to think of others before myself.

So I was hopeful Jim could sort things out while I was in Kenya – with some gentle, pointed motivation provided by my mother.

*

Kenya was more like it.

With a profound sense of relief, I found the training at last begin to pick up to levels I had grown used to. It was here also that my now broken-record badgering of Captain Featherstone for more extracurricular training looked as if it was finally paying off.

Maybe a factor that had finally concentrated his mind was my relaying to him the reported 50 per cent casualty rate in FSTs during the Herrick 4 tour, as Jim had relayed to me. If our FST was split in two, as was entirely possible, with him and Martin in different parts, it would only take one of them to be hit before Gilly or I would be responsible for controlling the artillery while Alex controlled the aircraft. I made no apologies about talking about his hypothetical death in coldly objective terms. I think it was when he stopped taking this personally that he finally understood where I was coming from.

So, to Captain Featherstone's absolute credit, Gilly and I sat on a Kenyan hilltop one afternoon with all the FOOs and OP Acks. Ignoring catty comments behind us from some officers whose noses I guessed had been put out of joint, we both fired a live artillery mission each.

Prior to this, the two of us had only had one day in the Invertron simulator at 19 Reg, where the focus had been on training us. Our live-fire missions weren't 'danger close' or anything whizzy, but at least Gilly and I had controlled the guns for real now. In Afghanistan, where things could not be any more real, we would now have the extra confidence to call artillery down on the Taliban – and not down on some completely random grid square, or on our own sides' heads.

Our fire missions went very well in terms of accuracy. But, naturally, they set fire to what looked like most of Kenya. So the rest of our day was spent beating out the resulting bush fire, though we did get some help from a couple of itinerant tribesmen who just materialised rather worryingly beside us in the smoke-engulfed 'beaten zone' we had only stopped firing at minutes before. We didn't want to start killing people with our artillery just yet.

Whether Captain Featherstone had finally got fed up with my constant harping for more training and just wanted some peace before going to war, I didn't know. But whether it was a case of him just giving in or actually recognising the impending reality of where we were going very, very soon, I really didn't care.

During some spare hours the next day, Captain Featherstone allowed me to teach our FST contact drills, should we really get in the proverbial shit. As much as it hadn't occurred to me how some Army units just didn't know this stuff, they all appeared to take it on board at least as much as I had been incessantly seeking to master their black art of controlling artillery.

For the final week of the exercise, our FST slotted in with the infantry company we would be attached to for the whole tour: C Company of the 1st Battalion, Royal Anglian Regiment. With only weeks to go to deployment, after we as a team had done absolutely zero training in first aid, Captain Featherstone called us over one evening after orders so we could actually sit in on two first-aid lessons the Anglians happened to be running. It was something, at least.

It was as we were revising the procedures for treating open chest wounds, catastrophic arterial bleeding, blast injuries and battle shock that I had my first real look at the young infantry soldiers we would be going to war with. They looked terrifyingly young. As unfazed as Gilly looked beside me, at his all of 19 years, as the growing litany of life-ending gore was delved into deeper and deeper, I saw some too, too young eyes growing wider as they contemplated what fate could await them.

I saw a boy who looked like my little brother when he was still only a teenager. He had the same fair hair, blue eyes and slight, boyish build that made him look like he was still growing. I had to look away momentarily then, before hardening my mind back to the task in hand.

God knew how their mothers felt.

My mother had so far been brave in not voicing the depth of fear she felt for me, but I knew her well enough to be more than aware of it. Even I thought I might be now pushing my luck with my third tour in five years. In the times I had gone to Iraq, I had epitomised the mentality of so many soldiers in thinking that these horrific wounds or deaths might happen to others but never to me, whereas now I thought a little differently.

Iraq helped in making this Afghan tour not such a big, bad unknown. But Iraq had also taught me that my mortality was ultimately ruled by chance. I knew very well that I could be killed, maimed, emasculated or turned into a paraplegic in Afghanistan. And I knew that every bit of training I had ever received would only mitigate the chance of such things happening so far.

So a little fear would be only natural. The problem was that I just could not feel it during my waking hours. And going where I was going, I was aware that maybe this was unnatural. With the glimpses of terror that I did catch in my dreams, the only fleeting conclusion I could reach was that it was as if a whole section of my brain that dealt with particular emotions had just been switched off. In focussing only on my training and the tour ahead, with all its unknowns, I could only guess that my mind had locked all the terror into a tucked-away compartment, storing it so it could be dealt with later when all was done and I was back home again – if I lived.

But I understood the fear that the young lads who had never been on tour before might be feeling. They were the ones showing true courage in going to Afghan, because courage can only be present when fear is present. Courage is when you overcome your fear by continuing on a path *in spite* of the fear it brings you.

I saw this courage embodied in a boy who came into the tent I was doing radio stag in one evening. One ear on the radio, I had been whiling away the time before Martin took over by chatting with the C Company signallers, while they kept one bored ear in turn on their radios. Seb and Joe were some years older than the average age of 19 in the platoons, so they had both been on tour before, unlike all the teenagers outside.

The three of us had just reached the conclusion that after the realities of a tour, one simply could not abide reality TV shows such as *Big Brother*, *Pop Idol* or *The X Factor*. Joe had been saying how when he last got back from Iraq, his girlfriend had been raving about how amazing *The X Factor* was. When all he could say was, 'What's *The X Factor*?' she had sat him down to watch it one evening, just so he could realise what all the fuss was about. But sitting through its glitz, shit and show, his inner monologue had only screamed: 'Get me back to Iraq.'

I was glad I wasn't on my own with this. But then the young private who looked like my little brother walked in. He barely looked 19.

He sat quietly down in the empty chair beside me. After he had exchanged a few words with Seb and Joe before falling silent, I decided to introduce myself – if only to make conversation by ensuring he was OK. He shook my hand. He told me his name was Tommy. And when I asked how he was doing, he just started talking.

He had only been with the Anglians a few weeks before this exercise. Before, he had been in his basic training – though he had been back-squadded six weeks of it after tearing ligaments in his ankle. But with more than a trace of pride, he recounted how his CO had said he was proud of him for sticking with it and doing much of the course all over again.

Then, without so much as a pause, Tommy started talking about his family. It was then that I began to realise how much this lad needed to talk to someone. So I just listened to him. And I only offered supportive comments when he needed them.

Seeing my three-quarters-read copy of Sebastian Faulks's *Birdsong* on the table beside me, he said his dad liked to read too. But he said his dad also spent a lot of time looking after his mum now. She had been ill for a while. Though Tommy did not say why she was ill, he said she had found religion recently. Now his dad went along with her to church. He said she was really worried about him. And he was desperately worried about her. I saw the pain this caused Tommy, because I saw the tears that he fought from his eyes when he said this.

So he changed the subject to his granddad, who had also been in the forces. Though not really with it any more, Tommy said he had seen a flash of recognition and pride in his granddad's eyes when he had seen his young grandson in uniform. He said making his granddad proud meant so much to him. And Tommy said he thought the Army had really helped him, because he thought he had been too lazy before joining. Now when he went home, he saw the 'dross' of people his age in the area he'd grown up in. He said most of them chose to be on the dole and contributed nothing with their lives apart from procreating and adding to the local crime figures.

I could only listen and learn from this; I had been packed off to the privileged isolation of a boarding school and so I knew nothing of growing up in such an area.

But a buried part of me knew the depths of emotion hidden behind his sudden, blurted confession that he was having 'some jitters' about going to Afghanistan. There was no reason for him to fall so guiltily silent then, after he had finally aired this fear to a stranger who would listen. I only saw a boy who didn't want to die just yet.

And I only saw a disarmingly honest, good young son who was now being thrust from his family into a distant war. So I told him, to gentle nods from Seb and Joe, that feeling some fear now was completely natural, and totally understandable.

I did not tell him that I wished I could feel as he felt.

Instead, I told him that my FST was attached to his company for the whole tour. And I said that whenever the company was in trouble, my FST would be there to call in mortars, artillery, attack helicopters and fast jets to help them out.

I told him he and his mates had been very well trained and that everyone would look after everyone else out there. And his family would be desperately worried about him, but they would cope because they had each other. And while he was away, he would always have them with him too, I said, tapping my head.

'They'll be so very proud of you too, Tommy.'

'Thanks, Jake . . . I'm glad you're going to be out there to talk to.'

'You can talk to me any time, Tommy – you're never on your own.'

'Cool,' he said, with a happier smile, shaking my hand gratefully.

Then he left. And I numbly stabbed the Menu buttons on the radio with a dull, muted anger, over how someone so young, brave and innocent should now be facing the end of his life.

*

You will get to know my teammates, Martin, Gilly, Alex and Captain Featherstone, better in Afghan, as I would. Because it was there, living in conditions pared down to almost a state of nature, and at times even struggling for our very survival, that we would truly get to know one another.

And it would be there, in turn, that I would learn more about myself. Though when holding a mirror up in the cosy and sheltered values of home afterwards, I would not like all that I saw.

*

The six final days of the exercise were unrelenting bursts and slogs through the Kenyan outback, putting in company attack after attack. Well over 20 soldiers had to be treated for injuries they had picked up, ranging from the predictable twisted ankles to the even more predictable heat injuries.

Gilly did his back in one morning, so Martin and I had to add his radio and spare batteries to our already heavier-than-average kit. This may perhaps explain why my reserve CamelBak water bladder burst later that night, when I and the weight of all my kit landed on it.

The company was putting in another attack in pitch darkness. With our FST merged with the Officer Commanding's Tactical Party (or OC's Tac) in the middle of its three platoons, I was trotting happily along right behind the OC when all of a sudden I found myself lying on my back and looking at a multitude of flashing stars spinning in front of the heavenly multitude above.

It turned out the OC in front of me had pushed through the lower limbs of a thorn tree, its branches encrusted with spikes as big as your thumb. Finally free, one of the boughs had just dutifully snapped back, straight into my face. It was hardly the OC's fault, though. After Martin helped me up, we just carried on – though I was aware I couldn't see out of my left eye any more, and I also suddenly had no more drinking water.

So by the time we laid up at dawn, I was fast approaching the physical state that soldiers define as 'in clip'.

But, in the first of the times that Martin and I would look after one another as brothers, he laid me down under a tree, pumped me full of Dioralyte and picked the last pieces of tree out of my face. When he used some of his own precious drinking water to wash the congealed blood out of my eye, I even got to see again.

The C Company OC knew my name after this, when he came over in the morning to make sure I was all right. I think he was impressed that I had just carried on the attack regardless, but I was impressed by how he cared for the men under his command. From all the orchestrated chaos of last night, it would have been all too easy to forget a lance sergeant falling over behind him.

Maybe under the leadership of such a man, I thought, soldiers like Tommy could be all right. With how refreshingly and vitally hardcore this final training was, I was relieved that the OC of C Company so very clearly realised the reality of where we would be, so very soon from now.

*

Our flight home was delayed by 48 hours. But after a 36-hour journey, hopping first to Oman and then to Jordan, where our aircraft managed to get hit by lightning, the Royal Air Force finally delivered us back to Britain.

After that we had a few days' leave to shake ourselves out before all the FSTs met up back at 19 Reg for the final days of admin prior to leaving for Afghanistan.

It was during those final days, among all the hours of document checks, issuing of dog tags and the plethora of other last-minute tasks, that I was told that I had a meeting with the CO.

I was not told what it was about. But I was pretty sure I knew, because on one of my days' leave I had visited my mum, who had given me the lowdown on what had been going on while we had been away.

She had gone along to the Families' Day at the HAC. After she had listened to and read every assurance that all her and the other family members' welfare needs would be met by the HAC while we were away, the HAC officers there had opened up the floor for questions.

It was at this point that my mother raised the pistol issue. But she told me the line they took with her was that we were correctly armed as per Army regulations, before emphasising how the SA80 rifle was far superior in firepower to anything a pistol could muster.

Both these assurances were indubitably true. But for a driver, of course, they were of absolutely no comfort.

'I'm sorry, Jake,' she said miserably. 'I did try.'

I could only thank her as much as I assured her that she had done everything and more that a mother could possibly do.

But judging by the cosy images printed in the HAC's glossy welfare booklet she had been given, we wouldn't need much arming at all. By the look of the two full pages of them, we'd be spending our six-month tour followed by crowds of smiling and adoring Afghan children, playing football and strolling peaceably through breathtakingly panoramic open plains.

So when I was invited for 'an interview without coffee' with the 19 Reg CO, it didn't take much intelligence to guess what it would be about.

In contrast to the complete chewing-out I expected, however, I actually got to sit down for it. And the CO turned out to be polish personified, as he calmly set out to me how we were all correctly armed as per Army regulations – and how much more effective the SA80 was than a 9-mm pistol.

In turn, I could only politely try to put across the realities of drivers needing pistols as their only credible form of self-defence from the driver's seat. I could only say my piece. But I don't know how much he agreed with me.

The subject was changed to asking me if I had any other concerns. So I told him of the concerns I had over our training too.

But he told me this was my fault, because as a lance sergeant I should have raised them through the chain of command (CoC) earlier.

I would have bitten at this, telling him I had long tried raising my concerns through my 'chain of command', but I felt there really wasn't any point in doing so now. My only impression was that he was done listening to me, and that our chat without coffee was over.

*

Just before we all flew to Afghanistan, there was a regimental photo taken at 19 Reg. We slowly sized off, then slowly filed onto the raised stand before the CO stood in front of us and told us how we were all ready for Afghanistan. He told us, 'You have received the best training possible.'

Stood high up in the rows of other gunners, lance corporals, bombardiers and sergeants, I was suddenly surrounded by barely suppressed, bitter laughter – which the CO must have heard, in spite of being so far removed from us. But I could not laugh; his words made me too angry.

I cannot remember the padre's exact words afterwards. But I know the effect his words had, in contrast to the CO's. I fell as respectfully silent as everyone else around me, who I can only imagine also had to suddenly fight a betraying lump back from their throat. Eloquently and simply, he told us to remember all the training we had ever received in the Army. And he told us, packed into the stand as we were, to just now be aware of the other soldiers' shoulders touching ours. Yes, we could feel aroused about it later . . . But for now, he asked us to just quietly be aware of the soldier next to us.

I felt the warmth and closeness of the other soldiers' shoulders on mine. And I felt Afghanistan, only days away now. I hadn't heard a silence like it. In the sudden hush of togetherness, he told us to always remember this feeling, to always look after one another, because none of us were in this alone. It would be by us all looking out for the soldier next to us that we all stood the best chance of coming back home safe to our families and loved ones.

Then he said a prayer for us all.

*

There were many things I had wanted to do before I died: get my pilot's licence, conquer my stammer, qualify as a paratrooper, own a sports car, have a threesome, find love, go to war, travel the world – though this is to name but a few.

As I grew older, this list expanded and contracted as I discovered new worlds and mentally collated their possibilities before finally ticking off their associated life experiences. Some experiences had been positively life-affirming; others had proved anything but.

But I could not regret any of them, as this list was all about living before dying. Now, going to Afghanistan, I was reaching the point where death did not scare me like it once had done, because by the terms I had defined for my life at that time, I felt that I had lived my life fully thus far.

If I did live through Afghanistan, though, if one day I did happen to find that elusive and so-called 'One', then I hoped I could bring new lives into the world.

But before I could do that, I wanted to kill.

I did not think this desire was born from any raging psychotic urge any more than it had its roots in the emotional deadness inherent to a psychopath. I did not pull the wings off flies when I was little; I cried when my pets died.

But now I was a soldier. And this latest and, for all I knew, last manifestation of my being was born from personal choice in my adult years, just as much from any nature that had been nurtured in my childhood ones.

I could try to excuse myself by saying I was indoctrinated through my training as a soldier. But this could only hope to explain my psychology in part once I had became a soldier – and not why I volunteered in the first place.

I did not join the Regular Army, as young soldiers like Tommy may have done, as an escape from a deprived area or in order to make something of my life. And where as a TA volunteer, the Army had provided a Yang foil to my Yin civilian life, my Iraq tours had suddenly injected the full reality of what it could mean to be a soldier into my mind.

Now as a fully-fledged though unblooded soldier, I was aware getting a 'kill' was a defining life experience – albeit a very private one, I guessed. Because, despite everything politicians and generals might say about stability and security, counter-insurgency or whatever other phrase they use to dress up the life-and-death reality at ground level, when they call upon soldiers to go to a foreign field where people explicitly want to kill them, it is these soldiers who must kill in their stead.

So there will not be a soldier alive today, after all those times shooting all those wooden and metal 'fall when hit' targets in practice, who has not considered what it would be like to line another flesh-and-blood human being up in his weapon's sights . . . and gently squeeze that trigger.

But as much as this is a soldier's most basic *raison d'être*, it is not often that you will hear a soldier explicitly talking of 'killing'. The K-word as a verb is instead often disguised and supplanted by any number of other euphemisms. In precise and technical military parlance, reflecting the ever more precise and technically removed means of killing, the 'enemy' becomes the 'target'. But for the soldiers who personally 'engage' these 'targets', these objects are colloquially 'slotted', 'dropped', 'hit', 'fragged', 'sawn in half', 'smashed' or just plain 'shot'.

Then the soldier will have achieved the noun of a 'kill'.

The author's supposition is that such words are used by the soldier in combat as an attempt to mentally disassociate himself from the reality of his actions, so he can continue to operate as a soldier – and perhaps, when all is finally said and done, as a human being back home.

But I had no relevant life experience with which to form such a supposition before I went to Afghanistan.

I wanted to know what it felt like to get a 'kill', though I already suspected that I might not feel anything at all – at least while I was immersed in the normality of Afghanistan.

Or, to be as honest with you now as I have to be with myself, without dressing it up as the notched life experience in soldier's terminology that it was, I wanted to kill someone.

*

Killing would be easier in Afghanistan than it would have been in Iraq.

In Iraq, our 'rules of engagement' had been those labelled as 'Card Alpha', which by their most basic definition meant you could only open fire if you ascertained that there was a direct and imminent threat to yourself or others around you.

But according to our lengthy Operational Training and Advisory Group (OPTAG) briefings on Afghanistan, we would be operating under 429A rules of engagement. Under these war-fighting rules, you did not have to wait for an imminent threat to yourself or others; as soon as you saw the enemy you could engage him, even if he was sunning himself under a tree. And you could carry on engaging 'Terry Taliban' as he fled to the hills, with you not having to stop until he was dead, injured, surrendering or, alternatively, if you anticipated collateral damage to 'Johnny Afghan'.

The catch, however, would be in trying to differentiate 'Terry Taliban' from 'Johnny Afghan' – who could well be one and the same. But considering that one of our 'combat indicators' to watch out for was an otherwise uncharacteristic lack of civilian populace, and that probably the first indication we would have of the Taliban's location was when we were being opened up on, we were told this identification issue would probably not be so much of a problem.

We were told these attacks on us would be largely 'spray and pray' and 'shoot and scoot' affairs. But after being told that we would not be above the law when it came to measuring our response to them, we were also reassured that it would be 'better to be judged by twelve than carried by six'.

This was of some comfort, considering the latest estimate of Anti-Coalition Militia strength in Afghanistan, which had been put at 446,000 individuals. Of these, it was estimated that a minimum of 200,000 were 'Tier One', full-time, fight-to-the-death hardcore fighters.

There was an estimated breakdown of the different factions within this hardcore, but I thought that perhaps from a soldier's point of view down in the dirt it really didn't matter that much whether the man trying to kill you was Taliban, al-Qaeda, Hezb-e-Islami Gulbuddin or part of the Haqqani Network. But I did learn that 'the Taliban' translated as 'the Scholars', so at least our foe might be well read.

Beyond this 200,000 were the 'Ten Dollar Taliban': part-timers who earned their nickname from the wage that the Taliban paid them. But, with their poorer military skills, we were told that they weren't fully trusted by the Tier One Taliban. That, I thought, made them sound akin to how an admittedly dwindling number of Regs still looked upon the TA as STABs. But if there was one thing you could say about us STABs, it was that as a general rule we tended not to drug ourselves up on opium or marijuana before battle, unlike our poorer Taliban cousins.

That titbit about our enemy's recreational drug usage brought us on to how the Taliban derived much of its income. Ninety per cent of the world's heroin was derived from Afghan opium poppies. And of all the Afghan provinces, British-occupied Helmand was the biggest-yielding province. And the area around the town of Sangin was the biggest-yielding area in Helmand.

Apparently it wasn't so much a case of undermining the West from within; it was just good business. A farmer could earn $50 a year growing wheat or $200 growing opium. However, it was the Taliban as middleman who, of course, made the real money exporting the stuff to us.

Though President Karzai in his faraway capital of Kabul had

ambitiously pledged to get Afghanistan off the top five opium-producing list by 2010, we were expressly told that we were not there to start razing the poppy fields. We were told we were there to provide security for the Afghan people.

By not burning their poppy fields to the ground but instead maintaining a security umbrella that international development agencies could safely work under as they improved these ordinary people's lives, we would win their 'hearts and minds' in the classic manifestation of a successful counter-insurgency operation.

It was a good pitch; it really sounded quite good indeed. But judging from the reported dearth of development outside of Kabul, plus every ground-level account and piece of helmet-cam footage I had seen coming out of Helmand, the 'continued consolidation of stability and security' while the nascent Afghan security forces trained to take over from us just looked more like a plain old-fashioned war to me.

Maybe our Western values would somehow be instilled in these people. But in a country where the average life expectancy was 42 and with the price of that life coming in contrastingly cheap at $10 plus the bonus of martyrdom, our alien values might just as equally not be snapped up.

With the low literacy rates and stories still reportedly being orally passed down the generations of how the British only came to Afghanistan to take what they wanted before then just fucking off without giving anything, the 10,000 British troops stationed in Helmand might just have their work cut out.

But we were told that we should learn from history. We were told of the Russians in the 1980s who had 'just lost the plot' and started bombing everything before realising too late that they could not win against the mujahideen's guerrilla tactics.

So we were directed to read detailed analyses of battles and ambushes waged in this conflict in 'The Bear Went Over the Mountain', written from the Soviet side, and 'The Other Side of the Mountain', written from the mujahideen perspective.

We were not told how Alexander the Great was the last person in history to successfully 'pacify' what would become Afghanistan, over 2,000 years ago. But some of us listening knew this. Maybe, some months later, this would be why I would see a WMIK in Helmand on whose bonnet the driver had painted the name of the Macedonian king's beloved warhorse: 'Bucephalas'.

Instead, for the battle of 'hearts and minds' ahead we were reminded of the many social customs that the Islamic Pashtun people indigenous to Helmand held. We were told to show respect to this proud people, whose tribe's foremost traits were summarised to us as 'loyalty, hospitality and revenge'.

Before a short war-pornography movie that everyone appeared to wake up for, comprised of various clips of contact footage with the Taliban and filled with shouts, screams, airstrikes and automatic gunfire, we were told: 'Be careful what you wish for.'

*

From the RAF's super-base at Brize Norton in my home county of Oxfordshire in southern England, we flew by RAF TriStar to the multinational super-base in Kandahar, southern Afghanistan.

The lush green of a bright English morning in springtime was left far behind. With a sudden thump in the dead of the night, in a blacked-out cabin and wearing helmet and body armour along with everyone else as its cargo, we landed in Afghanistan.

Our aircraft taxied past rows of sleeping military hardware in their hardened air shelters: F-15s, F-16s, F-18s, Harriers and Apaches. But it was the drones that really fired the imagination. I had not realised how huge those 'Reapers' really were, how beautifully and elegantly evil their lines looked up close – in the flesh.

I nudged Martin to peer past me at them.

'Nice . . .' He nodded appreciatively in the darkness. But I saw how his tight grin mirrored my own.

Then our aircraft stopped. Its captain wished us a 'safe tour' over the intercom. And its door opened to allow us to file outside.

There was no blast of desert-heated air hitting our faces as we walked out of the aircraft; a spring night in Afghanistan turned out to be only slightly warmer than one in England.

Mounting our awaiting coaches, we would now be whisked past the last tantalising reminders of the luxuries of home. Neon-lit through our coach windows, we saw how the other half would live in this former Alexandria while we squatted in our mud huts, with their super-gyms, mega-shops, vast food halls, air-conditioned coffee and juice bars, cinemas and hamburger joints.

Instead, we were deposited in a dimly lit, cavernous aircraft hanger filled with bunk beds, so we could grab what few hours of sleep we could before catching our Hercules flight to Camp Bastion in the morning.

After some quiet cigarettes that I had to smoke on my own outside to unwind, I did manage to get some sleep alongside Martin, Gilly, Alex and Captain Featherstone.

But there was no chance of any sleep on the Herc the next morning as the promise of 'living the dream' as a soldier beckoned us ever closer with one bony finger. With the smell of kerosene and nerves filling our noses, we fastened our body armour and helmets to ourselves once again before strapping ourselves in turn into the aircraft's hull. But before the roar of the four turboprops firing into life drowned out all other noise and earplugs had to be stuffed in to hear anything afterwards, I heard a heavenly, simple, ethereal sound.

Rising out of the high-pitched whine of electrics, piped straight into us over the aircraft's intercom, was the serene, lifting levity of a cathedral's pipe organ. And then drifting into this mounting tranquillity came the most beautiful of guitar riffs, just tinkling at first, before elevating in volume and intensity to complete the most uplifting and sublime song intro that you could ever hope to introduce you to this foreign and incoming other world.

Every ascending lyric chimed with my senses, as I sat shoulder to shoulder with those others being lifted to 'Where The Streets Have No Name'. I looked first to Martin and then Gilly beside me. We shared the same silent smile.

The RAF crew on that Herc had clearly put thought into what song they could play the freightloads of young, nervously waiting soldiers they transported. And I will always be thankful for this lifting flourish they provided at the beginning of our journey. Because as much as we didn't expect it, it only took little touches like this to make our morale soar as high as the short flight we had with them.

*

In contrast to the sprawling metropolis we had glimpsed at Kandahar, there was considerably less to wax lyrical about at Camp Bastion.

It had a medium-sized Navy, Army and Air Force Institutes (NAAFI) shop, which was the only shop. If you fancied pushing the boat out one evening and not eating in the inflatable mess hall, there was a van parked outside the NAAFI selling four different kinds of pizzas, with slightly differing variations of the same four ingredients on them. Gilly said it reminded him of the bar on base at Kenya, whose menu board offered toasted sandwiches with a choice of four fillings: 'ham', 'cheese', 'ham and cheese' or 'cheese and ham'. But to its credit, this bar had actually served real-life beer. Here, it was a foregone conclusion that we would soon fantasise about such ice-cold lagers with almost the same lust as we remembered the women who sometimes came with them.

Now just a few frustratingly long days away from 'living the dream' with the Taliban, the tedium of life on base at Bastion fast became wearing. Once you had squared away your kit for deploying into the field, there was precious little else to do outside of eating, sleeping, gym'ing it or expending the last vestiges of nervous tension wanking yourself into oblivion.

The time outside these tasks was largely taken up congregating in the camouflage-net-shaded smoking areas, regurgitating rumours while sitting on the edge of your wooden seat as you waited and waited to find out just *when* your team would be finally deploying into the field.

In retrospect, my team did not have to wait long for this, though the five days it did transpire we had to wait felt like a limbo-esque eternity at the time. And the pain of this was not eased by reports of the one FST already in place in Sangin, of which my former PSC student James was a member. Barely hours in Afghanistan and all of five minutes into his Army career, he was loosing off a Fifty Cal *already*, if all the rumours were to be believed. I was happy for him, though my envy and pent-up need to fire 'in anger' pained me just as much.

But, in retrospect, I would not have to wait very long for this need to be sated either.

*

Captain Featherstone called us into the smoking area. And though he would not word it as such, he had good news and bad news.

Tomorrow morning, we as an FST would be choppered into Kajaki. And there we would link up with C Company, who were already taking over from the marines at the forward operating base named FOB Zeebrugge.

But our FST would be split in two. And out of the five of us, he announced that only he and Alex would be going out on the ground with C Company's fighting patrols. By the look of Alex's impassive reaction to this news, I could only guess that Alex already knew this.

'But you three . . .' he said to Martin, Gilly and me, stuffing his cigarette into his mouth while unfolding a large map, 'you three, I need up on the most forward OP there.'

There wasn't a word from the three of us while we absorbed this. I didn't know what to think, so I kept my face as dispassionate as Alex's. 'The most forward OP' had good connotations of being exposed to the Taliban and therefore 'busy' in a fighting sense. Then again, the last thing in the world I had wanted was to be just observing in an OP while others were getting stuck in elsewhere.

'Right . . .' said Martin finally, scowling slightly. 'So what's that going to involve?'

The map was now spread out on the table in front of us. With the nib of his biro, Captain Featherstone pointed to where our new home would be for the foreseeable future. 'The OP on that hilltop's called Sparrowhawk West. The marines only kicked the Taliban off there a couple of months ago. And you can see – situated at the end of that spur of high ground as it is – how perfect it is for observing and dominating the ground below it.'

My mind clung to the word 'dominating' as we all peered down at the map. As he talked us through the ground in more detail, we did see what he meant about the OP's location.

Sparrowhawk West sat on the westernmost tip of a thin, finger-shaped, two-kilometre-long ridgeline. Tightly packed contours plummeted sharply away from the narrow apex of this high ground. And it looked as skyscraping as it was steep: suddenly soaring 650 feet from out of the plains below, Sparrowhawk West stood as high as some of the towers in Canary Wharf. Just climbing up there would be good phys – especially carrying all our kit for an unknown number of months' stay.

Captain Featherstone's biro directed our eyes from west to east along the ridgeline. Dotted at five hundred-metre intervals were three other OPs: Sparrowhawk East, Normandy and then Athens. These three would be manned by one of C Company's three platoons, with all of them taking their turn to rotate through while the other two platoons ventured out on patrols from the FOB.

And there was the FOB: nestled just north of Athens and right underneath this most easterly OP.

Then the biro moved a couple of hundred metres to the east of Athens and the FOB – and to the reason for us all being there in the first place.

Even on the map, the earthen dam looked huge. But then it did have to hold back the waters of a massive 12-kilometre-long lake that stretched out to the east and almost off the map.

From this edge of our map, we saw how the River Helmand fed straight into this lake before being finally spewed through the dam. And this force of nature would have powered the hydroelectric plant we also saw marked beside the FOB, but Captain Featherstone explained how just before we had captured it from the Taliban, they had sabotaged the plant out of spite. Or maybe in their minds it had been a very clever scorched-earth policy. But whatever their reasons, the Taliban had only succeeded in plunging a large section of Helmand back to the Stone Age – which from our point of view was what they seemed to fanatically want anyway.

As Captain Featherstone then explained it, our and C Company's mission was to clear a six-kilometre radius around the dam so that civilian contractors could come in and get the power station up and running again without fear of insurgent mortars and rockets landing on their heads. This in turn would win us the hearts and minds of all the locals, who would see how we had literally brought that 'light of liberation' to their lives.

But even as we looked at a map round a table, the prospect of just one infantry company cleansing such a vast swathe of country looked like a tall order. Even at the maximum fighting strength of 24 men per platoon, there was no way on earth – and especially Helmand, I guessed – that 48 soldiers plus a handful tagging along with the OC could ever hope to clear such a radius of enemy and then, crucially, *hold* that ground. It didn't matter how omnipotent our blokes might be as soldiers; they couldn't be omnipresent.

But I kept this thought to myself, along with a quote from one of Napoleon's generals suddenly springing from my memory banks, which I was pretty sure went as so, as he saw 'the Thin Red Line' advancing on him:

The British Infantry is the finest in the world –
Thank God there is so little of it.

But then, of course, the United States Air Force (USAF) hadn't played much of a part in the Napoleonic Wars. So I kept my trap shut and carried on listening to our brief.

The River Helmand flowed directly west from out of the dam, hugging the northern edge of the high ground the OPs occupied. Running parallel just between the two was a road running out of the FOB.

The river snaked south as it wound round the foot of Sparrowhawk West, along with the road. This road, nicknamed the A38, then led straight into the small river-hugging town of Kajaki Olya before curving like an artery into the immediately adjacent and more densely populated Kajaki Sofla.

I noticed how Kajaki Olya basically began at the southern foot of Sparrowhawk West. And this caught my interest because Captain Featherstone told us that everything south of our OP was currently in the hands of the Taliban.

In fact, everything just across the river to the west of our OP was Taliban too. Bar some disputed territory that the marines had recently cleared round a village called Chinah and a recently deserted ghost town named Tangye just across the river from the FOB, everything to the north of our OP was also Taliban.

East of our OP was fine, though. The ridgeline, the FOB and the dam belonged to us. And if the Taliban wanted to occupy the 12-kilometre lake beyond, then they were of course welcome to try.

So sitting up on Sparrowhawk West, we would in effect be surrounded on three sides by Taliban territory. But we would also have a ridiculous height advantage, allowing us to see everything from just under our nose to kilometres away into the distance. And with this 270-degree arc of fire, Captain Featherstone sought to allay fears I felt nagging not only at myself but also Martin and Gilly.

'C Company have got their mortars set up at the FOB – so don't worry, you *will* get to fire them! And you'll be sharing West with some of the boys from the Company's fire support group – so there'll be plenty of opportunities to get on their Fifty Cals . . . Jake.'

It was like he had read my mind.

But our primary role on the hill would be surveillance . . . of course.

8

ZENITH

Those that I fight I do not hate,
Those that I guard I do not love.

W.B. Yeats

A para was asked what he felt when he shot a member
of the Taliban.
'Recoil.'
Text message circulating among soldiers, pre-Herrick 6

I wondered how much we would end up like the Royal Marines we took over the hill from. To a man, the eight of them were tired, dirty and wore beards the Taliban would be proud of. And the ones I spoke to hated their officers – about as much as I guessed the Taliban hated them.

Captain Featherstone had joined me, Martin and Gilly in climbing up the near-vertical 'goat track' that branched from the road out of the FOB all the way up to Sparrowhawk East. Sitting on our heavy bergans for a minute to rest at the summit, we took in our first sight of Sparrowhawk West, now sitting just slightly below us.

It was a mound of rocky, light-brown-coloured earth protruding like a wart from the last bit of high ground the ridgeline could offer before it fell away into the river valley far below. A single roll of waist-high razor wire circled the base of the mound, the diameter of which looked no more than 50 metres across. Beyond this wire, I saw how the ground plummeted away in a sharply convex slope. And in turn, I saw how we would indeed be able to see far, far away into the distance – but also how we would be blind to any attempt to overrun us until the enemy were literally at our wire.

Inside the perimeter and dug into the rise of the mound were a handful of small mud huts, exactly the same shade of brown as the dirt around them. I didn't see a single one of their walls that hadn't had a huge chunk blown out of it. There was no telling whether this damage had come in the marines' fight to acquire this real estate from the Taliban or whether it was from years earlier when it had been a Russian OP overlooking the mujahideen.

I counted five huts where the marines had first built up the damaged walls with sandbags before laying a wooden roof on top, lining it with blue plastic sheeting and then adding more sandbags on top of that for good measure.

One of them was going to be our home – though it could never, of course, be Home.

The glimpses of bright-blue plastic sheeting were the only bit of colour within all that pale brown. Standing out as incongruously as they did, they were also the only sign of any life.

But maybe the marines were only hidden on the western slope – for this would provide the best eyes on everything to the west of Sparrowhawk West, as well as taking in everything to the south and north.

This was a truly alien landscape to my eyes, holding life signs unlike anything I had seen before. To the north stretched a vast, flat, arid brown plain. Pale scars of dried-up wadis, or riverbeds, knifed through the earth below us. Scattered like pockmarks between them were pockets of far-flung mud-walled hamlets, and sitting solitarily between them, isolated in the expanses of dust, tiny mud-walled compounds. Out of the mists of the distance beyond, shooting abruptly up from the lowland, were the jagged brown peaks of mountain ranges.

To the west, I saw how the banks of the river widened considerably as it curled around our ridgeline. It was looking here, over the top of Sparrowhawk West, that I caught my first glimpse of the 'Green Zone'.

I had heard about this riverside area in news reports and briefings. Now I finally saw it. Months later, in another part of Helmand Province, I would be immersed in it. And there its biblical beauty would be overshadowed by terror, numbness and death.

But not yet.

At this point I only saw a verdant Eden. I saw a sliver of green clinging for life to the arterial lifeblood of the River Helmand as it slithered its snaking way through the dust-filled wasteland beyond.

The nomenclature was accurate. The Green Zone was indeed green, but it was also a sharply defined zone. There were no mudflats on the river's western bank; the lush green began right there. This green of crops and natural vegetation stretched for some hundreds of metres before suddenly just stopping, to be immediately replaced again by barren brown mountains.

The sharp division between irrigated life and bleak, parched peaks was even more accentuated looking to the south. The dividing line was the road running parallel to the river and into the towns, if you could call them that, of Kajaki Olya and Kajaki Sofla. Immediately to the right-hand side of the dirt road was the emerald green of riverside pastures, while immediately to its left were the dry lines of steep, rocky hills, rippling away from our ridgeline until, way off to the south, the ground once more ascended steeply into mountains. Huddled along the right-hand side of the road and merging into the greenery were mud-walled compounds, huts and houses. These grew in number as the road led away from us, from just a handful of dotted huts at the bottom of our hill to intricate complexes of compounds all the way into Kajaki Sofla.

For all the people who lived down there, I was sure this landscape was nothing more than a backdrop to their everyday lives. But now there were infidels occupying parts of it, I was also sure that some of them wanted nothing more than to see us dead. So at that time, sitting on that bergan and sweating at the top of that goat track, I could only cursorily think of the words 'savage beauty' to describe the panorama around us before I turned all my focus to that waiting brown mound.

'Look at the view!' Captain Featherstone said enthusiastically.

'Yeah . . . What a shithole,' Martin retorted. For Captain Featherstone, after all, would not be living up here.

Gilly and I smiled at each other in agreement with Martin. But with the moment of first impressions now over, we hauled ourselves back to our feet before reburdening our backs with overloaded bergans for the last push over to Sparrowhawk West.

It was here, dropping our bergans down beside what looked like an improvised open-air living area, that we met the bearded hill men we would be taking over from – and some considerably fresher-faced ones from C Company's Fire Support Group (FSG), with whom we would be sharing the OP.

Captain Featherstone immediately started talking to a man who would turn out to be the OC of C Company's FSG. It transpired that he too would not be staying up here. But he had also at least taken the time to come up and help settle his boys in.

It was as these two were talking about the rotation of the FSG boys between the hill and patrols below that I noticed a gaunt, sidelined marine staring with depths of blackness at Captain Featherstone's ample back. I thought this might have been due to some people just rocking up and dumping a load of kit in what was still his front room, and now he was just being ignored in a space he had literally fought to acquire – which I guessed would make anyone angry.

I went up to him and cautiously offered my hand. We introduced ourselves with mutually respectful nods: me absorbing his bearded, wizened features and sun-faded Commando dagger badge on his arm, with him in turn clocking the shiny, clean para wings and stripes stitched to mine.

'That wanker's not staying up here with you, is he?' he said, returning his glower back to Captain Featherstone.

'No . . . No, he's going out with the OC's Tac.'

'Yeah, thought as much . . . But good . . .' He spat on the ground only a metre behind Captain Featherstone. 'You're better off without him.'

I could only nod mutely before he looked me hard in the eye, adding, 'You'll see officers for what they really are out here. Just wait, mate . . . You'll see.' Then his eyes reinserted their daggers into the back of the captain he had never seen before, shaking his head in disgust.

I hoped I wouldn't see what he was on about. But I knew sure as hell I wasn't in any position to argue with him. So, erring on the side of changing the subject, I asked him if he could show me, Martin and Gilly around instead. His jaded eyes seemed to brighten at the opportunity to look after the new lads. For myself, any questions over why he felt so let down by his leaders were soon replaced by quiet contemplation of the realities of our new home.

We were standing in the kitchen and living area – or, to be more accurate, we were standing in a dugout consisting of a pile of ration boxes, some stacked wooden pallets for a table, and a deeper hole in the ground in which to burn wood.

On either side of this ten-metre-wide depression were two small mud huts. The three of us would be housed in the smaller of these, whose outer wall faced south, while the five FSG boys on rotation from below would sleep in the already claimed other, whose outer wall faced west.

In between the huts, and shielding the communal area from the south, was a chest-high wall of sandbags, with two GPMGs and a Grenade Machine Gun (GMG) mounted on it for defence.

The corrugated-tin-roofed observation post had been built up with sandbags against the western wall of the FSG hut. Captain Featherstone and the OC of the FSG were now inside it talking to the marines on stag, so we would have to look inside it later. However, we could see how it had a full 270-degree field of view – all the way from the south-east, through the west, to the north-east.

It was the view just down the slope in front of the OP that quickened my heart. Behind the parapets of a low, U-shaped sandbag wall, with their long black barrels pointing south and north-west into the river valley stretched out far below, were two tripod-mounted Fifty Cals.

It was a sight as alluring as Cecilia. I stood transfixed to the spot.

I felt a gentle pat on my shoulder before Martin's Hampshire twang rang equally as gently beside me. 'Come on, old man – you'll get your chance on them later.'

I had to drag my eyes away to his face. He was smirking at how I hadn't noticed the guided tour moving on.

I gave him a guilty grin as we about-faced to catch up with the marine and Gilly. They had stopped beside a tarp-covered pit behind the OP. Here, the marine explained, was where all the drinking water was kept. Because these plastic bottles were the only water we had on the hill, they were only for drinking.

'You'll be reliant on heli resupply for everything here – food, water and ammunition,' the marine said, before a trace of bitterness returned to his voice. 'But no doubt you've heard there's fuck all Chinooks in theatre, so you'll need a crystal ball to work out when you actually get resupplied. So this stuff's only for drinking – meaning there's no washing and no shaving up here – but you'll get used to that too, don't worry.'

I guessed we would have to.

'Even the little 'un might get some bum fluff by the end!' he said, jauntily cocking his head to Gilly while winking at Martin and I.

Gilly shrugged his shoulders, smiling magnanimously while muttering something in Scottish.

We followed the marine up the stone's throw to the top of the mound. Here was the Light Electronic Warfare Team (LEWT) hut, where a couple of signallers surfed the airwaves with a couple of interpreters, listening to intercepted Taliban radio calls. They slept in a mud hut we could see dug into the eastern slope of the mound, nestled safely between the watchful eyes of Sparrowhawk West and Sparrowhawk East.

There were two other mud huts on this eastern slope. One was the roofless 'gym', with metal picket posts and dirt-filled ammunition tins acting as barbells and dumbbells. The other was introduced as: 'The Gentleman's Pit of Self-Contemplation'. The 'Vacant/Engaged' sign hanging outside its hessian door gave away its purpose. But as it was his first tour, Gilly could be excused for giving the marine a quizzical look.

'The wank booth, mate,' the marine explained flatly.

'Cool . . . !' Gilly grinned with wide, surprised eyes, making me and Martin laugh.

So there would be some privacy for such essential destressing – and far more than was allowed by the toilet facilities.

Shitting took place on the north slope of the hill, in a cut-off oil barrel with an improvised wooden seat precariously perched on top for comfort. In a vague attempt to preserve modesty, a hessian-lined frame had been placed round three of its sides. In truth, though, it had been a correspondingly half-arsed attempt to hide something that really didn't need to be hidden. I didn't think about the prospect of people being able to see something we all did. I thought about the view. I mean Jesus, how often could you have a crap on a mountaintop with the Hindu Kush stretching out before you?

'One of you is going to have to burn the shit at the end of each day,' the marine added. 'But you get all of five pounds extra a day for doing it, I think – so whichever lunatic wants the job at least gets paid for it.'

'Mine!' Martin interjected straight away, before smiling at how he'd beaten me and Gilly to the job.

'Fucking hell, Martin,' I laughed. 'You're welcome to it, mate!'

'Don't worry, boys, pizzas are on me when we get back to Bastion!' he grinned graciously. 'Even buy you an Irn-Bru to wash it down with, Gilly!'

'Ah, well, you've sold it then,' Gilly replied, rolling his eyes, as we looked to where the marine's finger was now pointing.

'That's our desert rose . . . Our 70,000-pound urinal,' he said proudly.

Sticking waist high out of the ground was the now empty sleeve for an expended Javelin missile. Again, you had to give the marines full marks for ingenuity, for how often could you get to piss down a surface-to-surface missile tube while standing on top of the world?

But this piss tube marked the end of our guided tour of Sparrowhawk West, because there was nothing more of our new home to see than this.

The marine pointed along the path leading up to Sparrowhawk East.

'That path leads straight along the ridgeline, linking all the OPs,' he said. 'You're going to have to yomp along it from time to time because, like I said, the resupplies here are a fucking joke – you'll die of thirst before the fucking RAF comes. But there's a bigger supply of drinking water at Athens – water bottles get driven up to them from the FOB. You'll just need to get yourselves across the hilltops and fill your jerrycans from there.

'Keep to the path, though,' he added pointedly. 'The Russians mined everything to fuck on the slopes here. But you'll see white-painted stones dotted along the path's edge, and on either side of the goat track you came up. They mark the limits of where it's been cleared. Stick to inside them and you'll be fine – unlike the poor fuckers who got hit down from East.'

'What happened there, mate?' Martin asked.

'Sniper team pushed down the hill to bag some Terry. You can still see some of the kit they left – helmet, a daysack – that kind of thing. Just don't go down there.'

'Understood – thanks, mate,' I nodded.

'You've gotta know your boundaries, but, lads, don't ever ease up on the Taliban. They only respect strength and they'll fucking punish you if they catch even a whiff of you letting up on them. Fucking smash them – they fucking deserve it. When you're on stag, you'll see a reference point down in Kajaki Sofla called "French Doors". And you'll hear plenty of gory rumours of what happened, but what's a cert is that the Taliban killed some French soldiers round there about a year ago – badly – and then to commemorate the occasion, they painted the French tricolour on the compound's doors.'

He paused for a breath, but there was only silence from me, Martin and Gilly. The three of us were now hanging on his every word.

'Just smash them – they're fucking animals. You'll hear plenty of rumours of what happened to the Russians who used to be on this hill too – they ended up being holed up in that building you'll have walked past coming out of the FOB. You can see the craters from the RPGs on the outside of it – and the bullet holes where they were trying to hold them off on the stairs . . . until their ammunition ran out . . . None of them lived.'

He breathed again. I had to remember to breathe.

'We killed a load of Taliban to get this hill, and they want it back just as much as they want their revenge. They fucking died here – right where we are here – and you've got to kill them now they're down there.'

The wind was picking up as the sun set on Sparrowhawk West. The figure of the marine suddenly seemed to shrink in the twilight. Suddenly, he seemed utterly spent.

'Understood, mate,' Martin said quietly.

'Absolutely,' I agreed gently.

Gilly nodded silently.

But the marine's last words only seemed to peter out tiredly. 'Look . . . When you're on stag at night, just remember one of you needs to walk round sometimes and get eyes on this place's blind spots to the south . . . You don't want them creeping up on you while everyone's asleep.'

Roger . . . that.

*

The marines stayed up on the hill with us for a couple of days to help us settle in. In fact, they said one of the reasons they wanted to give us such a comprehensive handover was that the paras they had taken over from had given them 'fuck all' when it was their time to go home.

We could not have asked for a better handover. They doubled up with us on the shifts in the OP, talking us through all the reference points on the ground below, their ranges, the patterns of life the locals led and everything to watch out for that was indicative of 'Terry' being up to no good.

But then, late one afternoon, they were gone.

And as night descended, Martin, Gilly and I, plus five young Anglians named Robbo, Stu, Caz, Daz and Chads, suddenly found ourselves alone on a hilltop in Afghanistan.

*

My eyes snap open to the sound.

Daylight.

Wooden beams and a corrugated-iron roof sharpen lazily into focus above me. I feel like crap. It was still dark when I got in from the graveyard shift, but it feels like I've only just closed my eyes.

The sound comes again.

'*Definitely* a dicker!'

That's Robbo.

'You sure?' comes another voice.

'Yeah, he's a fucking dicker – he's got eyes on the patrol and he's talking into something!'

Right, this sounds interesting.

I unzip my mossie net and pull on the pair of shorts folded ready on my bedside bergan before stuffing my feet into the Army-issue sandals lying ready on the dirt floor. Fastening their Velcro, I see Martin's pit is unzipped and empty. But there is some groggy movement through the mesh of Gilly's mossie net.

I pull a T-shirt over my head and walk to the door, pulling its hessian material aside to emerge, blinking, into the bright morning sunshine outside.

Standing a couple of metres in front of me, and looking over the sandbag wall with a pair of binoculars, is Robbo. Just beyond him on one of the GPMGs is Captain Taylor, the FSG OC. I'm surprised to see him up here, but any other thought is immediately drowned out by the *bang-bang-bang-bang* of his Jimpy loosing off a four-round burst. He fires another two bursts before turning round to Robbo and asking, 'Was that close?'

'Yeah . . . Yeah, about five metres to the right of him,' Robbo replies, still looking through the binos. Then he turns his face to his boss, laughing. 'Think he shat himself – he just put his arms up and legged it down an alleyway!'

'Yeah . . . I aimed off to the right,' Captain Taylor says as he makes the Jimpy safe, before pointing its barrel up to rest in the upper V of its X-shaped picket-post mounting.

'Oh, right . . .' says Robbo. 'Warning shots, then?'

'Yeah.'

I don't believe him either: three bursts on a GPMG landing only five metres away from a target before asking: 'Was that close?' do not sound anything like warning shots. I reckon he just plain missed and tried to cover it up. Standing in the OP half an hour later with Caz and Martin, Caz comes out with exactly the same theory. But to his boss's credit, we reckon there had at least been the intention to drop the guy.

This conversation provides the verbal backdrop in the OP as we watch for C Company's first patrol out on the ground, inching its way south into Kajaki Olya. Gradually, we see their small beige figures begin to emerge from out of the dead ground at the foot of our hill.

Through telescopes and telescopic laser rangefinders, we watch the ground ahead of them. Our eyes sift through the chest-high green stalks of the riverside opium fields, with the pink of their budding yields just beginning to flower. Our eyes scroll and zoom into the myriad of dark hedgerows, the scattered complexes of small mud-walled compounds and the leafy, tree-lined alleyways.

We search for black-clad figures hiding with black intent.

But it is quiet. A small handful of locals are tending the fields. Crackling over the radio come only the reports of the odd individual wandering up to the two platoons, exchanging pleasantries with the interpreters.

Then it becomes quieter.

The radio is silent; there are no more reports of locals approaching the patrol.

Through the laser rangefinder, I scan metre by metre down 'Tally Alley', as the marines have named it. Our patrol is beginning to slowly clear its length from the northern end at the foot of our hill. There is no sign of any Tally along the dirt track, or among any of its small mud buildings.

Too quiet?

Suddenly, while we had been scouring the ground looking for hidden figures with weapons, we now instead notice that the poppy fields have been completely deserted.

'What the fuck . . . ?' Martin says slowly, echoing my thoughts as he peers through the telescope.

Panning quickly over the surrounding fields, there is now absolutely *no one* to be seen in front of our patrol.

Boom!

Then the shockwave and even louder boom of another explosion – coming just down the slope from our OP.

'Fucking Jesus!' blurts Martin, as the three of us look as one over our sights to locate the splash of the explosions below.

'Contact!' comes yelling over the radio.

The dust now billowing up the slope into the OP can only have been from an RPG. Without any screams of 'Man down!' over the radio, I guess the other boom must have been another RPG fired at the patrol, and not an IED ripping into them. However, as the rippling cracks of small-arms fire begins ringing out below, we can see no telltale puffs of smoke on the ground betraying the RPG firing points.

I stuff my eye back into the eyepiece of the rangefinder, peering once more into every conceivable bit of cover around Tally Alley.

Then we see them.

Just a flash of movement at the edge of your scope at first – catching your eye and making you centre your optic on it.

There! Four dark figures running – into that compound!

Martin's voice shrills, 'Did you see them?'

'Yes, mate!' I reply, as Caz calls out, 'Yeah, going to the Fifty!' before sprinting out the door.

Through the cross hair of my laser rangefinder, I can now see clouds of dust kicking up all around the little compound as the platoons hammer its walls with small-arms fire.

Everyone's seen them.

'Lasing!' I call in standard warning to Martin beside me, on the off-chance the laser bouncing back from the target might burn out his retina while he stares through a telescope at the same target.

'OK, mate,' he says, lifting his eyes.

I press the rubber button and the range flashes up alongside the target. 'Nine hundred metres!' I call down to Caz while he's banging the top cover of Gun Number One secure after loading its belt of ammunition.

'Fucking smash it, mate!' Martin adds for good measure.

Caz grins at us both, holding a thumb up in acknowledgement as he sits on the sandbag seat behind the gun. I watch him check the range on his gun sight, cock the weapon ready and then suddenly sit very still as he carefully aims, minutely aligning sight and target and preparing to fire the very first rounds in his life 'in anger', ever.

I am watching a seminal moment in a young soldier's life as it unfolds before my eyes, building second by second to that final climax.

And I covet it.

Now comes the release. And this sweetest of sounds comes with a rhythm more slow and deliberate than a GPMG. But it smacks your eardrums with such deeper pitch and volume, belying all the power cannoning every half-inch-calibre bullet through the Fifty's long, dark, smoking barrel.

A red tracer round from his burst zips through the air and – there is no other word for it – *smacks* into the target below.

'That's on, Caz!' I call out.

My eyes return to the rangefinder for a better view of his fall of shot. Along the front wall of the compound, small puffs of dust dissipate as quickly as they blossom from the impacts of the patrol's smaller-calibre rounds. But there is no mistaking the heavy-calibre bursts from Caz, kicking up billowing clouds of dust on the wall as his rounds tear into it.

'You're hitting dead centre of the front wall, mate!' I call down again.

His left thumb comes up again in acknowledgement. But now Robbo is setting himself down beside Caz to spot his rounds for him. And, not to be left out, Chads and Daz are manhandling the north-facing Fifty alongside Caz's.

They quickly set it down on its tripod, letting the sheer weight of the weapon bed itself into the ground. Daz takes a sandbag from the wall as a seat, dropping it and his butt down at the firer's position, as Chads loads the Fifty with a belt before sitting alongside with a telescope to spot Daz's rounds.

Now the target is being hit by the cacophonous barrage of two Fifties along with two platoons' worth of rifles.

In truth, even the Fifties' rounds will have a job punching through the thick mud walls of that compound. All this fire is nominally only suppressing fire, pinning the enemy in place, before they can be finished off with something bigger.

To this end, over the radio from the patrol's mortar fire controller (MFC) comes a mortar mission. But this is quickly cancelled with the words 'check fire', in readiness for what will soon rain down on the target instead.

Our Fifties are check-fired in turn. In the sudden lull, I notice Stu standing behind me in the OP.

'All right?' I smile at him.

'Yeah! Kicking off big-time styley, ain't it?' he grins back.

Then it occurs to me that if you don't ask, you don't get.

As the same 'full screw' rank as Martin and Robbo, I outrank Stu's more junior lance corporal. But I am in the FST. And the Fifties are officially his and the rest of the FSG lads' bag. So as much as I would never feel comfortable doing so anyway, I do not start throwing rank around like some jumped-up asshole. I diplomatically ask the question instead.

'OK if I jump on one of those Fifties, Stu?'

'All up for you having a go, mate!' he beams at me. 'In fact – brilliant idea . . . Caz, Daz! . . . Standby, me and Jake are coming down!'

But it is just then, as Stu and I are about to make our way down to the Fifties, that the first of the 'fast air' rolls in for its strafing run.

It is just a dark speck in the clear blue out to the west at first, hanging only slightly higher in the sky than we are on the hill. Our eyes are drawn to it by a steadily growing sound, like the winds of a gathering typhoon. And this sound suddenly increases in pitch and volume as the speck suddenly takes the form of a twin tail-finned American F-15 accelerating in a shallow dive straight at the target in front of us.

Just as suddenly, there doesn't seem to be any sound, as a long grey sliver of smoke trails from the aircraft into its slipstream.

But this is only a trick played on us by the speed of sound. The target in front of us erupts in dust as the supersonic cannon rounds hit it. And then the crackling roar of the F-15 firing them hits our ears – barely a second before we see its shadow shooting over the surrounding poppy fields.

Against the throaty roar of the pilot throttling forward to climb away, with incandescent counter heat-seeking missile flares falling in his wake, we whoop and laugh in triumph and awe.

Stu and I canter down to the Fifties as the wingman follows his leader's example. Together with Caz, Daz and Chads, we marvel with grins and 'fucking hells' at the pure and lethal spectacle of it all.

Then there is a moment of quiet. But this is not filled with any moments of quiet reflection any more than it is filled with sympathy for the four men being hammered from above. It is for a quick BDA to be conducted. And as it comes over the radio, Martin relays the result of this Battle Damage Assessment down to us.

'They're going to drop bombs!' he shouts excitedly. 'And . . . Wait a minute . . .' he says, holding the radio's handset to his ear, before calling down again. 'Captain Taylor says get those Fifties going again! . . . Keep the fuckers in there till the bombs drop!'

Daz and Caz immediately jump up from behind their Fifties to allow me and Stu to take their places.

I sit behind my gun and check the SUSA optical sight's range. I unclip the T-bar to 'go rogue' in free aiming, feeling the weight of the weapon press comfortably down on me through the diagonal shoulder bar. Now I search for my target through the sight; I find the river running to the right before panning left to find Tally Alley. Then I follow this dirt track down towards me until, right there in the middle of the 'T' of my sight, is the targeted compound.

It doesn't look any more than 30 metres wide. This width almost fills the SUSA, which I am now focussing all my attention through, to the detriment of anything else.

I can see into this compound from my raised vantage point up here on the hill. It is only ten metres or so in length. Within its seven-foot-high mud-brick walls I see a low, flat-roofed mud building built against the front wall. On the left-hand corner of this front wall, I can see the only exit point for the four men trapped inside: a single small gateway beyond which I can see a tiny mud hut built into the left-hand wall, with a dark and gaping open window which is only welcoming fire inside it.

As a communal weapon, this Fifty's SUSA is not zeroed to me. So to get my aim in, I decide to aim my first burst at the dead centre of the target, straight into the roof of its main building.

I click the safety catch off and my fingers rest over the handlebar trigger on the weapon's soft mount.

The 'T' within my SUSA is now centred on its target.

There is no last moment of reflection or thought or feeling in this final moment.

My fingers gently squeeze the trigger for a five-round burst. And suddenly the gun comes alive, juddering with ferocity in my hands and pummelling my ears with noise as it blasts each round with a supersonic crash out of its barrel.

With a second of shock, before that surprise freezes into cold satisfaction, I see the puffs of dust that show the rounds are landing exactly where I want them.

I bring my aim down a notch to the centre of the front wall.

WHUMPWHUMPWHUMP.

On.

Now I have zeroed my eyes to the weapon in my hands, I swing its aim just slightly left to the only viable exit point from which those men can hope to escape the compound: its small gateway.

And I shut this escape off from them, as I deliberately fire one carefully aimed burst after another through its small opening.

Stu and I then begin to fire in turn. One burst immediately follows the other's in a relay of suppressing fire, as we close the door shut on any hope the men trapped below might have of being able to flee.

Every fifth round in our ammunition belts is a tracer, and I see these burning, red phosphorous-tipped bullets cutting through the dust clouds of dirt being kicked up. Some of them zip down to disappear into the darkness hiding beyond that large gaping window in the small gate-side hut. I am happy with this, because this means that anyone still alive and hiding within that small darkness is now being ripped apart.

I walk my bursts around the gateway and into that window, probing with each burst, as I reach down into the compound – searching – feeling – for those 'kills'.

Sometimes, in between our deafening bursts, we hear the high-pitched whizzes and sonic snaps of incoming small-arms fire over our heads. These bullets can only be specifically aimed at us, sitting right here. But the chances of me or Stu being hit by any of these rounds fired up the hill to us is very small, fortified as we are behind a protective sandbag wall – and with the added metal bulk of a Fifty Cal sitting between our legs and in front of our torsos.

So we just ignore whichever Taliban are trying to save their brothers holed up in the compound below – wherever they may be. We carry on our allotted task of suppressing fire on the appointed compound.

Sometimes, though, and for variety, I walk the occasional burst along the top of the compound's front wall. The first rounds of these bursts kick up pulverised dirt along its edge before the remaining bullets smack straight through the middle space of the compound and into the centreline of its rear wall. I do this in case, out of desperation, the men trapped below are thinking of climbing the walls to escape.

But I am just settling my aim back on the gateway after one of these bursts when my entire gun sight is suddenly filled with a huge, millisecond's flash of brilliant orange – before a massive, violent eruption of black dirt.

The shockwave of the bomb rushes over our bodies just moments before the sudden, awe-inspiring clap of its detonation reports sharply in our ears.

'Woah!' Robbo shouts beside me, as an involuntary 'Fuck!' escapes my lips.

Stu yells, 'Fucking hell!' before adding, 'Lick me *out*,' for emphasis.

With boyish hoots of delight, we whoop and laugh and cheer against the background of the 'crump' echoing away through the valley below us, like the last, dying rolls of a thunderclap.

'I do *not* want to be on the end of that . . . I'm scared to be here,' Stu says, just a little quieter.

We all quieten as a towering pillar of dust rises out of the stricken compound, before this is gently blown towards the river, dissipating into the wind.

But before any of us can formulate any further words, the wingman's bomb suddenly hits.

Now, with our eyes out of our gun sights, we can see the terrible majesty as it unfolds: the silent orange flash and the silent, unfeasibly violent upheaval of the very earth, the silent, concussive blast hitting our faces just before the thunderclap of hundreds of pounds of high explosive finally punches our ears, and then nothing but the silent, billowing crown of dust floating away in the thin air before that too fades into nothingness.

Where there was once life, there is now nothing but rubble – and silence.

'My God . . .' Robbo says quietly, in shock.

Our hill falls silent in turn.

The patrol walks back to their FOB.

What other Taliban there are melt back to wherever they came from.

And with our part in that day's events now also concluded, there is nothing left for us to do but unload our guns and make our way back to our own mud huts.

*

After a post-contact fag I decided to make lunch for everyone. I cooked up a cauldron of beef noodles with Oxo cubes and bolognese sauce, with corned beef thrown in for good measure. It tasted fucking great.

In the afternoon, Chads came across the hilltops to Athens with me, so we could fill up two jerrycans of water and not die of thirst up on our hill.

It was a lick out tabbing up and down the steep peaks across the ridgeline, especially on the way back when griping legs also had to contend with a bergan full of water in addition to helmet, body armour and personal weapon – which in my case was a Minimi 'light' machine gun. It was light at least compared to a Jimpy, and certainly a Fifty – though it did seem to get heavier.

As a phys session, the tab was fantastic, though. The last thing I wanted was to get 'skinny fat' sitting on top of the hill. Actually having some water to drink at the end of it, even to cook with, made it extra worthwhile.

I had also wanted to apologise to Chads. During my post-contact fag it had occurred to me that he would have been next in the queue to fire the Fifty I'd jumped on – though I had admittedly done so with Stu's blessing.

He just smiled and told me not to worry about it. 'Wait till the Javelins get delivered to us,' he said. 'You can have all the time on the Fifties you want as I shove those babies up the Taliban's arse!'

So that was all sorted then.

Another great thing about doing all that phys was that Chads and I could justifiably pig out on the spag bol Robbo cooked everyone for tea.

The twilight period just after the evening meal would always turn out to be the best part of the day. You could kick back around the pallet table with a warm bellyful of food, smoking a cigarette to unwind and to keep the mossies at bay. Against the tinkling musical wallpaper provided by Martin's battery-powered iPod speakers, you could chat and banter and laugh with everyone else stuck up here with you.

This evening was especially good, because with the impending arrival of Chads's and Stu's Javelin missiles and my 'guru performance' on the Fifty, as Martin worded it, I was officially welcomed into the FSG Fifty Cal club, with my name being written onto the white board in the OP as one of their gunners.

So my smile was all the broader. And when Gilly came back from 'having a shite', commenting in his broad Glaswegian accent how 'more flies went up my arse than shite came out', I laughed all the harder.

As we were finally forcing ourselves to wash out our cooking pot with rationed teaspoons of water, though, one of the LEWT guys appeared out of the murk beside us. He thought we might be interested in a Taliban radio conversation they had intercepted, not long after the second bomb had hit.

'Come and have a look if you want,' he said.

I wondered if he might have been feeling left out of our little get-together. So curiosity did get the better of me; I did take the short walk to the other side of our mound to read what he had logged.

With all the fuck-all use that hindsight is, I still do not know whether I should have done this.

By now it was pitch dark. And I read the scrawled words in the LEWT hut by the flickering of candlelight:

Musafer: Can you hear me Rahbarmal?
Rahbarmal: Yes I can hear you. What's happened?

269

[Musafer is crying, poss injured.]

Mus: You got eyes, you saw everything, what's going on?

Rah: Tell me what's up.

Mus: The aircraft dropped bombs on us and destroyed us. Please come and help us.

Rah: I can't promise I will help you now. Probably I'll help you later.

The logbook detailed further calls from Musafer to Rahbarmal before they trailed off to nothing. None of them had been answered.

The adrenalin of pouring rounds into that compound had by now long subsided. Whether I was now in some type of chemical low following it, I do not know. But I felt subdued as I put the logbook down, thanking the LEWT guy before walking out into the blackness outside.

I sat down alone on the hillside up from my hut, shielding the orange glow of my cigarette in cupped hands as I looked down to the south.

The river gleamed like a vein of silver in the moonlight. But the land beside it was only an infinitely deep expanse of black. It was into this void that I now stared.

Just down there, and all alone in the dark, was a terrified and bleeding man called Musafer. For all I knew, he was bleeding out.

Sitting up here in the quiet, and with tendrils of smoke curling out of my mouth, I contemplated the long, dark, lonely night ahead of him.

I felt more than a moment of empathy for him. And mixed up in that moment, somewhere, was probably a trace of guilt.

But, sitting all alone there in that dark peace, I had to kill this moment – for sanity's sake.

After taking one long, final drag of my cigarette, I extinguished its light on the rock below me before flicking its spent butt away, off into the darkness down the slope.

Sleep well, Musafer.

*

In the morning we saw four prayer mats suspended across the compound's open gateway. Someone said this was a sign for four people having just died there. This theory would seem to fit the events, but I still do not know if this is an actual custom.

Later that day, though, and from sources I can only imagine were locals returning to the surrounding fields, news filtered up to us from the FOB that four men had been killed in that compound. Three had reportedly died from 'blast injuries', while the fourth had apparently died from 'bullet wounds'.

When I take over OP stag from Martin late that afternoon, I mull over this information as I cast my telescope over the ground below. Inescapably, my eyes sometimes linger over the bomb-damaged compound.

Four of them had been uninjured enough to run in there. Though the mud walls would have sheltered them from the patrol's small-arms fire at ground level, they would not have had such protection from our Fifties and the F-15s, which were both firing into the compound from above. Considering that a hit from an F-15E's 20-mm Gatling cannon would quite literally tear a man apart, it began to sound more than feasible to me that it had been one of us on the Fifties who had killed this man.

Maybe this man had been Musafer.

But I cannot think about this any more.

Not now.

Not here.

*

As time passes, when you are on your own for hours each day doing OP stag, with your eyes traversing over all that deceptive peace below, there will be nothing for your mind to do but think.

And in between these OP stags, and the gratifyingly eventful firing of weaponry into the Taliban, there will also often be little else to do but think.

Eating and subsequently evacuating your innards of that intake only takes so long. Masturbating in a designated area, where everyone knows what you are doing and where someone indeed might be waiting for you to finish, certainly takes only so long.

Talking will be a diversion, as will reading books or writing letters home. But you cannot do all of these, all day long, for all the days you are up here. There is no library on Sparrowhawk West. Opportunities for deeper conversation will usually be limited by fatigue. Shallow small talk will be quickly shunned by virtue of its meaningless inanity in the environment you find yourself in. A drought will quickly be reached of things to say in letters to your family back home. Between the military details you cannot tell them about and the military actions you do not want to tell them about, there soon comes precious little else to talk about.

I ask my mother to send wet wipes and books. Wet wipes are the only means of washing we have. Books, on the other hand, provide something to escape into, by distracting the mind from the cabin-fever-inducing prospect of all the innumerable impoverished days up here stretching out before us, surrounded on three sides by people who would gladly skin us alive, with only our thoughts and each other for company.

Many of our thoughts will soon revolve around women. We will miss them all the more because of their absence. In our hut, Martin will always have his wife as a fallback to keep him company in his head. But for me and Gilly, both single, our thoughts can only return to the ghosts of girlfriends past.

So while Martin was on stag one afternoon, Gilly and I sat on our camp beds smoking endless cigarettes as we swapped rose-tinted reminiscences and correspondingly coloured conclusions of women who were now either dead to us, or we to them.

This particular vein of conversation had been kicked off by Blink 182's song 'I Miss You', strumming over Martin's iPod speakers, the supply of batteries for which was beginning to run alarmingly low. With wistful memory, we both found ourselves articulating how we had been remembering those girls in particular who had felt more for us than we had for them. Now these girls had long paid the emotional price for their ultimately unrequited feelings, we both found ourselves regretting how badly we had treated them, lied to them and even cheated on them. And we both found ourselves wanting to be with these girls now, because, to the very end, they had wanted to be with us. We only remembered why we had got with them in the first place – and not why we had then lied to them, cheated on them or spurned them to be in this bitch of a place called Afghanistan.

After this conversation, it should have been Kate, of all people, who invaded my dreams.

But she did not. My succubus was Cecilia. I felt the torture of her coming back to haunt my mind on this hill, because it had been the lethal combination of my mind and her that had led me to be here.

In my quickly festering pit in my isolated mud hut, I probably could have slept better, or got to sleep faster. But in truth a lack of sleep affected everyone. Everyone had broken sleep from, without fail, having been woken up at some point of the night to do OP stag, every single night.

There is a certain lethargy that invades your being as this routine becomes a rotating, mechanical blur of day to night to day to night.

Trying to catch up on sleep during the day is one way to combat this growing feeling of listlessness, but this is impossible if you then have to scramble to the guns and try to kill people. As the days unwind from spring into summer, the mud huts will actually absorb the heat of the day, providing shaded ovens for you to try to sleep in.

But you have to try to sleep, if only as something else to do to pass the time. So you lie naked bar your pants in your pit in your mud-brick oven, blocking your ears with quiet tunes from your solar-charged iPod. And when you then close your eyes, you feel the only real privacy you can ever feel up here in that close, infinite darkness behind your eyelids.

Soon it will become too hot to sleep during the day. You will feel dripping, restless sweat congealing on sticky, salted layers of older sweat as your baking brain meanders through the past.

As time goes on, there is more than a danger of becoming lost in these wanderings, because your only frame of reference will be what you remember. And your only anchors to sanity will be the other men experiencing their own cabin fevers on top of this hill, and the insane environment you are now immersed in, where firing heavy weaponry into other men below will become an emotional outlet to be seized upon.

*

I didn't get to fire on our next engagement. I had only just got to bed after spending four hours on the pre-dawn graveyard shift in the OP with Gilly. Again, it felt like I had only just closed my eyes before I was suddenly startled awake by the sound of our Fifties opening up.

I stumbled out of bed as fast as I could to get to the guns, but they were both already manned at the firers' and number two positions by Stu, Chads, Caz and Oli – the latest FSG addition to our hill.

I would have been completely within my rights to just go back to bed, but with all the racket this would have been pointless. I thought I could at least make myself useful by providing an extra pair of eyes in the OP alongside Martin and Robbo.

I found the role of observer up on our hill informative. By listening to all the chatter on the net, as well as being able to observe everything that was going on around and below, I was afforded an eagle-eyed change of perspective from the tunnel vision of a gun sight.

The FSG WMIKs had driven out of the FOB ahead of the foot patrol and up onto a flat-topped mound to the north-west of us, referenced as 'Shrine Hill' (so called because there was an ancient mud-brick shrine to an unknown god on one of its slopes). They had put this foot on the ground in order to cover the patrol's subsequent advance past them. This tactic was completely sound, but it had also promptly resulted in the FSG coming under small-arms fire from the closely neighbouring village of Chinah.

Chinah had been cleared by the marines just before we got here. But, of course, there hadn't been enough of them to occupy this village – alone among all the others dotted around – *and* their FOB. So, with the evidence unfolding quite clearly in front of our eyes now, there had been absolutely nothing to stop the Taliban just quietly filtering back into the ground they had been pushed out of.

It wasn't like there were any more of C Company than there had been marines, either. And Chinah was just a few little dots on a map dwarfed within the whole, gargantuan six-kilometre radius that C Company had been tasked with clearing.

The few young British soldiers here would be living the soldier's dream of being in contact central. But what the pitifully few of us could ever hope to actually achieve in strategic terms, short of just holding onto the non-operative dam, or in terms of this actually being worth the risks taken by young Essex boys, was fucking beyond me.

The reason this pissed me off so much was that just down there on Shrine Hill, the point had been driven home through the medium of a Kalashnikov bullet straight into the leg of a young Fifty gunner named Lee.

In a variety of ways, and from a variety of perspectives, he was both incredibly unlucky and incredibly lucky. Two weeks into his first tour with the TA and it was over for him already. But with the millimetres of chance thrown in at the Taliban firing point, he was lucky that the bullet hadn't killed or castrated him.

The Taliban firing point is quietly pinged by us – a small walled compound with a dome-topped building inside, right on the northern edge of Chinah. And our two Fifties pour suppressing fire into the target as Martin begins directing a mortar fire mission onto it for good measure.

He fine-tunes the fall of shot from the mortar boys down in the FOB: 'Left 100, repeat . . . Left 50, repeat . . .' until the compound is engulfed by the dust clouds of explosions.

Into all this dust spits tracer fire from our Fifties, as we hear over the radio how the single dedicated MedEvac Chinook for the whole of Helmand is now inbound to pick up Lee. Hopefully, no one else will be shot in the rest of Helmand while it is on its way to us.

But also hopefully, the Taliban who shot Lee are being nicely holed up in that pounded compound so something big can finally finish them off.

That something big comes not in the form of a multi-million-dollar fast jet but in the diminutive figure of a 20-year-old Essex lad called Chads – and a 70,000-pound Javelin missile.

The RAF had finally delivered them to the FOB yesterday morning. The signallers at the FOB had driven them up to Athens. And for us, the full afternoon of tabbing across the ridgeline with five-foot-long missiles strapped to bergans already full of drinking water is now going to pay off.

Robbo gets on the net to ask 'Zero Alpha', the C Company OC, for permission to fire a Javelin.

And, 'Permission granted, with a happy smile!' comes the answer.

Chads has already set up a missile on its tripod. Now he crouches down underneath it, peering through its thermal-imaging command launch unit (CLU) sight as he first acquires the target, and then locks the missile's own sight onto its destination.

He is going to be the first Royal Anglian to fire a Javelin in Afghanistan. And as a strange, high-pitched whine comes from the missile, whinnying as it strains to be released, everyone on the hill stops what they are doing to watch.

Suddenly there is a loud *click* – and half a second later a sheet of flame shoots out of the Javelin tube's exhaust, launching the silver missile with a roar into the air before its main motor fires into life, punching it off into the blue yonder at a velocity you can only gawp at open-mouthed.

The glow of the rocket engine disappears off into the sky, leaving only the faintest smudges of smoke in its wake. Then everyone's eyes swing back as one to their telescopic optics, looking for the missile hit.

Ten seconds later, there is a quick flash of light as the fire-and-forget Javelin punches a hole straight through the target's domed roof.

In that moment, Chads basks in total respect from everyone on the hill. Though for reasons of standard squaddie piss-taking, this admiration can only last for a few seconds, obviously.

Now the air assets are on station: two F-15s, plus the Immediate Response Team (IRT) Chinook and its Apache escort to extract Lee back to Bastion.

One of the LEWT guys appears beside us in the OP, gulping in breaths as he hurriedly blurts the latest radio intercept from the Taliban below:

'Aircraft are here – be careful . . . Fetch the professional to shoot at the aircraft.'

Too late.

Down below, Alex is already talking the F-15s onto the target. To complement Chads's work, a 500-pound bomb duly drops slap bang onto the domed roof of the target.

The dust clears. The domed building has ceased to exist. And the LEWT guy doesn't come back to us with any more radio intercepts.

The IRT Chinook lifts Lee away on the first step of his journey home.

I watch the two platoons go back to their FOB. Otherwise, and even with only two platoons and three FSG WMIKs out on the ground, there is quite literally next to no one left in the FOB to defend it.

In turn, there is absolutely nothing to stop the Taliban filtering back into the part of the village that has just been cleared through the medium of high explosive.

But this will become the routine. C Company cannot do any more than this, because there is only C Company here. And C Company cannot hold any ground they clear, because there are only enough of them to occupy one small space at any time in the massive six-kilometre radius they have been tasked to clear.

Considering every time they leave the FOB how nakedly vulnerable to being overrun it is, they sure as fucking hell are always going to come back to reoccupy this home from home.

And you know that sooner or later, the Taliban will just reoccupy the land C Company have cleared them from – which is the same ground that the marines cleared them from before.

But what the fuck am I going to do about it, sitting on this hill?

I go back to my mud hut to get some breakfast.

Gilly was still in bed when I stepped inside. I was dumbfounded if he was still asleep after all that. Still, I was quiet as I reached under my camp bed for my mother's parcel. Like me, Gilly had had no sleep – and I also remembered reading some supposedly scientific research in a newspaper saying that teenagers needed more sleep in the morning than their venerable elders.

Silently, I took my mother's first parcel outside, sitting down at our pallet dining table to rummage through its contents while waiting for everyone else to sit down beside me.

There was no bread for toast, so I squeezed Marmite onto sesame crackers, munching them down while staring with a glazed early morning gaze at the GMG sitting forlornly at the wall between our two Jimpies.

It looked forlorn and forgotten, because it wasn't going to get fired now, or at any time in the foreseeable future. The reason for this was that we didn't have any ammunition for it – period – and this was because apparently there was a theatre-wide shortage of the stuff. But the fact that the ammunition-less weapon was indeed just sitting there, silent and useless, appeared to indicate that someone, somewhere along the logistical chain, had completely fucked up.

Munching down another sodium-laden Marmite biscuit to help raise my blood pressure even higher, I considered that if there was indeed a theatre-wide shortage of GMG ammunition, then this would appear to indicate that someone back in Britain hadn't had the foresight, or basic fucking nous, to allocate enough of this resource to us lot sitting out here, surrounded by Taliban.

This person was probably a different individual to the one who decided that fifty-odd Royal Anglians were somehow sufficient enough of a resource to clear and hold a six-kilometre radius round Kajaki Dam of Taliban. I could only guess at who had decided that just one dedicated IRT Chinook for the entire province of Helmand was sufficient to MedEvac all its casualties.

What if someone else had been shot in Nowzad, Sangin, Garmsir or any of the other places British troops were operating in, as the one solitary IRT Chinook made its way to us in Kajaki? Would one of the five other Chinooks the RAF had in theatre step up to the mark? I had to wonder, because these five were plainly already overstretched servicing troops spread out over an area half the size of Britain – and everyone in the FOBs were completely reliant on heli resupply for the basics of food and drinking water – and ammunition, supposedly.

Yet again, the scheduled water drop on our hill had been cancelled. If we didn't want to die of thirst, we yet again had to spend the afternoon tabbing four kilometres over a ridgeline, in plain view of the Taliban, just so we could fill up jerrycans from Athens.

Already I felt myself getting as embittered as the marines from whom we had taken over the hill. But what really riled me was that very young men – and I mean 19 years old fucking young – were being needlessly exposed to extra risk, just because some middle-aged twerp back in London hadn't done their sums properly.

Whether it was 'lions led by donkeys' I didn't know. But it sure as hell looked like boys being led by blinkered bureaucrats to me. And in between them – and again back in Britain – could only be some senior-ranking careerist officers who were either hamstrung by what they were given or should just have known better.

Though it will always be the soldier's prerogative to complain over his lot because of things like this, there was no point in voicing any of this to Martin, Robbo, Stu or any of the others who sat down beside me. We all knew the situation we were in. And we all knew there was nothing we could do to change it.

Martin fishes his iPod speakers out of our hut, so we can have a background soundtrack to our Afghan sunbathing.

Gilly stumbles bleary-eyed into the brightness after him – and straight into the jaws of overly bright and chirpy cries of 'good morning!' from Stu and Robbo. He slumps down beside me and, without a word needing to be passed between us, I give him one of my cigarettes, lighting it in turn for him so he can feel human again.

Martin has put on a Norah Jones album. I listen to the forgotten chirruping of birdsong on one of its tracks, as we listen to Stu and Chads affectionately ragging Gilly about not getting any post yet.

Stu offers to write a Gilly a letter. And I see Gilly's eyes light up briefly as Chads says he will get his missus to send out a parcel with a two-litre bottle of Irn-Bru in. Of course, Chads then says that he will call Gilly over – and pour it all out on the ground 20 metres from him.

Gilly takes all this with good grace, though, laughing along with the rest of us, because there is no intended malice behind any of this. On the contrary, this is just squaddies buoying each other up in the only way they can over things they cannot control – with sadistically caring black humour.

But then it is time to traipse over to Athens to get our drinking water, before the day becomes too hot, and we each sweat out a jerrycan's worth of water as we lug a full jerrycan of water back each.

When we get back, beat, we eat our rations of lunch out of their sealed aluminium bags. Then, as the sun rises to its zenith, and its hottest, the FSG boys retire to the shade of their mud-brick oven to play on their PSPs, as Gilly retires to his own shaded oven to attempt sleep once more.

Martin begins his stag in the OP. With no PSP to play on (though my mother, God bless her, has told me that she will send me one – together with another solar charger), I occupy myself by baking bread for everyone in our improvised mud-brick oven outside.

It was easy once you knew how. When I was little, I used to watch my mum making the greatest homemade bread, which only your mother can make, in our cosy, Aga-warmed family kitchen.

Now, up on this hill, for baking tins I use two of the rapidly rising number of empty ammunition tins. The bread mix has only to be stirred up with water, kneaded and then plopped straight into them. Then all I have to do is get a good fire stoked up on the floor of the oven before sliding the tins in on top of a metal grate, which the marines had somehow acquired from somewhere.

Once this is done, I close up the oven door with more bricks and just let the stuff cook, for however long it chooses to take. With the absence of any olive oil with which to lightly drizzle the tins and no reliable temperature control other than just re-stoking the fire, it isn't like it's an exact science.

I smoke in the OP with Martin to pass some of the cooking time. But as the loaves are getting close to the ready/smoked-to-a-cinder mark, I occupy myself with a copy of *FHM* lying on our pallet table.

'Special Edition! 85 Man Skills!' screams the front cover. As a man, you cannot help but look inside, to see if you can be judged as a man.

'85: Enjoy a weird holiday!'

'84: Make a fire from scratch!'

I stop reading the special edition of *FHM*.

*

The next day, four men of fighting age were seen moving around a field about two kilometres to our west. It looked like they were digging.

Martin radioed it down to Zero in the FOB below. And I got the nod to fire warning shots.

I punched a couple of bursts into the ground just to the right of them. We watched their small, dark forms scattering in all directions, like fleeing ants.

We thought they could have been Taliban digging a trench system. In our siege mentality on the hill, this was reason enough to fuck them off.

But now, in my mind, they could just as easily have been farmers tilling their land. Maybe they were just trying to dig an irrigation ditch to the adjoining river. And if they were just trying to scrape a living in this earth, then I can hazard a guess as to how they felt about my Fifty Cal rounds slapping into it beside them.

Gilly tried out his latest joke on me later that night:

'Why are the Afghans so pissed off?'

'Tell me.'

'Because there's a telly ban.'

It worked with a Scottish accent anyway.

*

Next morning, I volunteered to go over to Athens on my tod. The pretext for the trip was to pick up another Javelin missile, in addition to the sack of post that Zero had said was waiting for us. These ostensible reasons formed part of my reasoning, but I also just wanted to do a burst of hard phys along the ridgeline, at my own pace, and to just get off our claustrophobic hilltop for a short while – to breathe – for the sake of my body and my mind.

I wore my body armour and carried my Minimi obviously, but I fucked my helmet off and only carried a single water bottle in my otherwise empty bergan.

Then I could just run, free, across all the hilltops. As I approached Athens, the brilliant, sun-sparkling turquoise of the lake beside the dam looked all the more breathtaking against the brown, rolling mountains and the cloudless, shining-blue expanse above. You could almost pretend you were somewhere else, somewhere that was just sunny, beautiful and peaceful.

But, of course, you are not somewhere else.

And the lightness that had borne me across the hilltops to Athens quickly evaporated as I discovered that there was neither a Javelin missile nor a sack of post ready for me to pick up.

I asked the bored Anglian on stag there if I could use his radio to request that these items be driven up. After I got an affirmative response from Zero, I spent the next 20 minutes smoking with the bored Anglian in the OP.

And he was really bored. They never saw any Taliban. Consequently, they never fired a shot at anything. But this wasn't so surprising, because the majority of their arc of fire was comprised of a 12-kilometre-long lake, and the Taliban weren't especially renowned for launching amphibious assaults.

'We got the beach, though,' he grinned, before winking and patting the grenade pouch on his webbing. 'Even get a spot of ballistic fishing from time to time . . . Yummy . . .'

It turned out they could climb down to the water's edge any time they wanted – there was even a white-painted stone, mine-cleared path down there. They could wash their clothes, wash themselves, 'fish', sunbathe, swim – and just escape from everything for a few hours every day. They basically got to go to their own private beach while the guy on stag, high above them here in the OP, kept an eye out for Taliban.

After 20 minutes, the Javelin and post still hadn't turned up. So I got back on the radio to Zero only to find a new signaller on shift, who claimed he didn't know anything about me waiting up here.

I put the same request in again, to which I got the same affirmative response.

And after a further 20 minutes, in which I realised just how truly boring life on Athens could be, a Pinzgauer suddenly appeared beside us with a small bag of batteries for me to carry over to Normandy – but no Javelin – and no post.

By now, I only had 20 minutes in which to leg it back to West before C Company put in another patrol on the ground. So there wasn't any time to beat the Pinz driver to death with the bag of batteries. As I sprinted and slogged up and down the hilltops back – dumping the batteries at Normandy as I passed through – I could only curse Zero as being a bunch of fucking morons, no matter which part of the planet you had the misfortune to talk to them on.

The guys on Sparrowhawk East had heard me politely banging my head against the wall that was Zero, though – and as I appeared, pouring with sweat, on their hill before the final push to West, they gave me a present of one of their Javelins. Which was nice of them.

The truth was that it was going to get fired on West, though, thrust out into Taliban territory as we were. But we still weren't half as exposed as the young lads on the ground – and I needed to get back to West to do my bit covering them from above.

Up the final incline of our mound . . . Lungs bursting past our razor wire . . . Then the LEWT hut . . . Over the apex . . . And finally back home with – I looked at my watch – a minute to spare.

'Jake!' Stu called out, smiling broadly with outstretched arms in our dining area, as my run slowed to a jog, then to an exhausted walk in the final paces, before I proffered the sweaty missile into his hands. 'Oh, you shouldn't have!' he beamed. 'Thank you! . . . I'll fire this one specially all for you this morning!'

For it was Stu's turn to fire this time – and Chads's to watch.

'Jake, you pimp!' Robbo grinned welcomingly, appearing from behind the OP with a radio strapped to his back.

'Yeah, nice of me to make it – I know!' I said, discarding my empty bergan to the ground. 'Jesus fucking Christ – whoever the fuck's down at Zero needs their fucking head examined – after all that there's no post, sorry, guys.'

'Woah, easy there, boy!' Robbo said in a calming tone. 'Heard you on the blower – our boss'll get on it, don't worry, he's good like that.'

'OK . . . Still think they need fucking shooting, though.'

'Tell me about it. You can shoot some Taliban now, though – less paperwork!'

'The patrol left?'

'Nah, you've got a few minutes. Chill – get some water down you.'

That sounded good. As Robbo listened to a squall of traffic over his headset before transmitting a curt acknowledgement, I glugged gulps of warm water from the bottle out of my bergan.

Gilly was waving playfully at me from the OP. He was grinning more than usual – I didn't know why. I waved hello back as Martin appeared in the darkness beside him, giving me a thumbs up and another grin.

Stu was setting up the Javelin in the centre of our southern, sandbagged wall. Immediately to his right was our very latest addition to the hill, Frank, on one of the Jimpies. To his right, leaning against the wall with his sniper rifle, was Caz.

Oli was sat down behind the GMG to the left of Stu, which was curious, because I didn't think we had any rounds for it.

So with Daz now down in the FSG WMIKs, that meant that Chads had to be on his own on one of the Fifties in front of the OP – which meant, I guessed, that the GPMG mounted to the wall to the left of Oli was all mine.

'That Jimpy mine, Robbo?'

'Yes, mate, all yours – hope that's all right. One of the Fifties bust and Chads jumped on the other one as you were away.'

'Fair one.'

'Glad you're here actually, mate,' he muttered. 'I think that chick was angling after a go on it.'

'What chick?' came my muffled reply, as I pulled my heavy, sweat-soaked body armour off over my head – just to feel a few cooling wisps of air on my naked torso before having to don it again.

'Urrggh . . . The lads are fucking drooling over her – but I'm telling you, I'm not going to roll over and let her fire just because she's batting her pretty little eyelids.'

Oh my fucking God . . . *that* chick . . .

Standing outside the entrance to the OP, and now staring up at the two of us, was the most impossibly foxy, elfin female.

Yeah, we'd only been on the hill a few weeks. But we'd been on this hill for *weeks*, without so much as a sniff of female company. And to torture our sexual starvation even more, this girl looked like something straight off the front covers of the *Nuts* and *Zoo* lad mags strewn around our huts.

'I mean, what does she think this is?' Robbo vented. 'A fucking shooting holiday? End of her tour and she thinks she can just swan up here from doing whatever REMF shit in the FOB and jump on a Fifty Cal – just so she can tell whoever back home that she hosed down some Taliban. I don't know her from fucking Adam – for all I know, she'd brass up our blokes. I mean, fuck, if she was a bloke I'd just tell her to fuck off.'

'Well, she's definitely not a bloke, mate.'

And, fuck, you knew a girl's arse was good if it looked good in combats – which were tailored with anything but attracting the opposite sex in mind. She had tucked a tight singlet top into the waist of her trousers. The thin material clung to the narrow of her waist before suddenly curving around the outline of her ample, pert breasts.

I was half-naked and she was still staring. And along with the impending contact with the Taliban, I could feel some base part of me beginning to growl with lust.

And, fucking damnit, she was smiling now.

'Oh, *God* – you as well,' Robbo said, shaking his head in resignation.

'No . . . No, I'm back in the room, mate,' I said smiling – tearing my eyes back to his.

That smile from her was going to last me weeks.

But now I have to forget all about her, because a General Purpose Machine Gun is demanding my attention.

Seeing that everyone else along the wall is bare-chested in the heat, I too dispense with my body armour, and only wear my helmet, for it is only our heads that will be visible to the Taliban below. There is no one here to inanely tell us off.

I detach the SUSAT from my Minimi and set it down beside my Jimpy; I set its iron sights to eight hundred metres; with its trigger depressed, I vigorously pull the working parts back and forth a few times to ensure they have been oiled sufficiently; I crack open one of the boxes of link on the ground at my feet; I load the weapon.

Like Oli, Stu, Frank and Caz on their own weapons beside me, Martin and Gilly ready to lay down mortars from the OP, Chads on our one remaining Fifty, and Robbo poised behind us to oversee it all – I wait.

But beside me, I cannot fail to notice that Oli has mysteriously loaded the GMG with a belt of grenades.

'Where the hell did you get them from, mate?'

'Special present from Captain Taylor,' he says. 'We've got a box for up here and a box for the GMG below. But that's it. After that – that's that.'

'Make every round count then.'

'Oh yes . . .' He smiles up at me, with a wink.

'Patrol's mobile – standby!' Robbo calls out.

I hold the SUSAT up to my right eye and search the ground below. The two platoons will be clearing Tally Alley again and my 4x magnified view traverses up and down its length, hunting for hints of threats.

It is deserted. But we know now that the absence of any civilian population is in itself a combat indicator.

The three FSG WMIKs will be shadowing the platoons as they edge forward, trundling slowly down the A38 road running parallel to Tally Alley and ready to lay down suppressing fire from their turret-mounted Fifty Cals as soon as the Taliban are contacted.

My SUSAT searches the length of this road as it leads into the too, too quiet town of Kajaki Olya. My eye lingers over compounds, alleyways and tree lines. As my eye takes in the myriad of spitting-distance ambush spots in all this clutter, I can only hope that everyone in the front seats of those vehicles has a pistol strapped to their chest.

Now I see the beige figures of our boys moving out of the dead ground at the bottom of our hill. They move and go firm, move and go firm, as they step ever closer to Tally Alley. And there on the A38 now is the lead WMIK – edging slowly forward in tandem.

One of the LEWT guys is suddenly behind us. Intercepted radio conversations have the Taliban 'ready' and 'waiting to hit the first vehicle when it comes through'.

Our eyes scour the ground ahead of the WMIKs with new earnestness.

The platoons clear Compound 1.

It is the compound Musafer and his three friends died in.

But there is only quietness.

And as the second compound on Tally Alley is cleared – and then the third – and the fourth – there is still nothing but silence.

But now I can hear some words being exchanged between Robbo, Martin and Gilly down at the OP. And now Robbo is calling up to Caz: 'Caz! Get eyes on that dicker directly west across the river! He's in that field with sheep in it – all on his tod!'

Out of the corner of my eye, I see Caz swing his sniper rifle west as Robbo strides up to him to help him get eyes on the dicker.

They have it covered. Along with everyone else on the wall, I carry on searching the ground to the south, ahead of our advancing ground callsigns.

Martin's voice comes up from the OP. 'Definitely a dicker, Caz! He's got eyes on our blokes and he's talking into something!'

Silence from Caz.

'You got him, Caz?' Robbo asks.

'No.'

'Your rifle's pointing right at him mate. Field directly west of the river – it's the only one with livestock in it – right there bang in the middle of it – bloke looking this way and talking into something.'

'Right.'

'Yeah . . . Yeah, I got him,' comes Frank's voice.

'Yep,' Stu also confirms, before adding sunnily: 'Hello, mate, we can see you!'

'Seen?' Robbo's voice is beginning to sound impatient.

'No . . . Not seen,' Caz says quietly.

'I'm going to sack you soon, Caz! Why is it everyone has eyes on this cunt apart from you?'

'I *can't* see him, *all right*?'

But now this conversation is finished – because, with a stuttering crackle down below in Tally Alley, the first, inevitable, shots are ringing out.

High up on this hill, you feel your chest suddenly tighten with anticipation and empathy for the young lads below, who are now suddenly locked into a fire fight for their lives.

But this is as far removed as you will feel from what is unfolding below, as the first Taliban rounds zip and whizz over your head, specifically aimed at you, standing on this hill.

But this does not scare you.

It makes you angry.

And you find that this anger is channelled through the machine gun that you quickly cock, aim and fire into the Taliban firing points you can see below, dotted along a woodline 200 metres to the east of Compound 1.

The Taliban betray their hiding places in the tree line with the puffs of smoke from their firing weapons. With clinical, directed anger you fire carefully aimed five-round bursts into these puffs of smoke.

You find there is nothing you want more than to kill these people, who want nothing more than to kill you and your friends.

After each five-round burst you steady the weapon and bring your point of aim back to the target. Then you fire again.

In between the deafening blasts of yours and all the other weapons lined along this wall firing, you sometimes hear the strange, high-pitched wasp's buzz of incoming rounds zipping past you.

Off in the far, far removed distance of your peripheral vision, you are dimly aware of the LEWT boys who came out of their hut to watch the show, and the girl who came up here to watch some killing before she went home, diving to the ground for cover.

But you do not move from the weapon that you continue to fire, because you only want to kill those bastards trying to kill you and those boys below. And in that moment, you know that everyone else lined along your wall is the same.

A Javelin missile clunks out into the air just beside you. The roar of its rocket firing into life just in front of you fires your soul with black adrenalin and joyous hate. You find yourself screaming over the top of your weapon, 'Fuck, yeah! Get in you *fucker*!' before stonily drilling more rounds into that tree line.

And when you see a whole section of that tree line disappear in a flash of light; when you feel the thunderclap of the explosion in your ears and you know without any doubt that men have died – you roar and cheer with the rest of your friends along your thin, sandbagged wall.

When it is all done; when hundreds of spent cartridge cases litter the pale, hard dirt at your feet; when an American F-15 screams past your hill in a show of force that only the United States Air Force can put on; when the ground below is almost completely obscured with the smoke fired from mortars to cover the platoons' safe withdrawal back to the FOB – you hear the quiet voice of a LEWT guy behind you, relaying how the remaining Taliban are radioing their commanders to report how they have killed 20 of us.

And with the last, dying embers of adrenalin, you laugh along with everyone else at how pitiful their lies are.

As I look behind me, my eyes remember the girl. But now I see how hard-as-bullets her erect nipples are.

With this new information, I can only form the crotch-tightening judgement that for some women at least, watching half-naked men killing other men is a turn-on.

After she had walked back down to the safety of the FOB, what was also undeniable was the steady stream of young men walking over to the hill's wank hut, of which I was one. Sanity and suddenly full balls dictated it.

Later that night, when I was sated from the firing and masturbating, I found myself able to reflect on why Caz had not shot the suspected dicker. He could not have failed to see the man. And the irony of Caz not shooting this man, after he had previously reckoned his boss had missed a dicker and then lied to cover up the fact, did not escape me.

But where everyone else on the hill had convinced themselves that this man was a dicker, the final act of killing had been delegated to Caz. And it was Caz alone who would have to line this man up in his sniper scope . . . and gently squeeze that trigger.

Up on that hill, I tell myself that I would have taken the shot.

But much, much later, and with all the time in the world to think back home, I will do anything but condemn Caz in my mind. Instead, I will come to envy the particular peace of mind he afforded himself – though, for all I know, he may now torture himself about it from another, impotent perspective.

But he never did take that shot. And by choosing not to squeeze that trigger, he ensured that this man's death – be he Taliban dicker or more than possibly just innocent shepherd – would never be on his conscience.

*

The FSG boys come and go on our hill. But Martin, Gilly and I remain *in situ*.

The FSG boss comes up to visit all of us from time to time. He brings post from our families and a satellite phone to talk to them on. He brings morale and we respect him for it.

But, with bitterness, we choose to forget who Captain Featherstone is, because as our boss he has forgotten about us.

Daz comes back up the hill. When I ask him, he confirms to me that every time the FSG WMIKs go out on the ground, the drivers have to sign out a pistol for self-protection along with their vehicle keys.

I am profoundly glad that the 1st Battalion Royal Anglian Regiment recognises this real-life operational need. But it also only makes me curse the attitudes of other commanding officers of other regiments.

I receive a parcel from the other HAC boys in theatre. For just a short window of time, all of them bar me were in Camp Bastion. It is good to hear from them all. But in the letter that they have all scrawled on, Mark tells me that his and Kris's FST have been loaned to the BRF. And Mark tells me that he and Kris are the only two drivers in the whole of the BRF not to have pistols.

When I write back to them, I urge them to press for pistols through their 19 Regiment 'chain of command'. But once I have done this, I have to stop thinking about it, because I have done all I can do sitting on this hill. The anger I feel over this stops me from sleeping.

And we need our sleep, whenever we can get it.

Each Groundhog Day begins in darkness with the whispered words, 'You're on stag, mate.'

If your daily and nightly stags in the OP coincide with the almost daily and nightly Fifty Cals and Javelin missiles being fired from the hill, then you have lucked out. Because this means that your downtime will be just that.

Often, though, you spend four hours seeing in the dawn of just another day in the OP before spending the next four hours firing a Fifty Cal. Then in the afternoon, when it is too hot to sleep, you try to sleep. Often, you can only lie on your camp bed sweating new sweat into festering, salt-encrusted shorts, with the tortuous half-dreams swimming through your head that only a cooking, cabin-fevered brain in a war zone can conjure up.

Then you go on stag in the OP again. And then you go back to your mud hut. And only now, as the day cools into night, are you able to grab some snatched hours of sleep – in a mud hut that has absorbed all the heat of the day, to the point where it actually glows when viewed through thermal imaging.

The alternative is sleeping outside with the rats, flies, mosquitoes and camel spiders. But no one wants their face chewed off by a camel spider as they sleep, so no one does this.

Then, when it feels you have only just closed your eyes, you feel a hand shaking you awake again. And you hear the words, 'You're on stag, mate.'

And then it begins all over again.

You repeat this routine every day and every night, for weeks, and then months, until you feel as if you are going mad. And then you just keep repeating it.

I store up my madness to unleash on the Taliban through the medium of Heavy Machine Gun rounds.

After three months of this, Martin says to me that I now only seem myself in the half hour immediately after I have fired the Fifty Cal. But in truth, this only mirrors the change I see in him and Gilly in the half hour immediately after they have controlled the mortars.

My ears scream at me after these engagements. But as the piercing whistle dies away, so does the sense of release.

Like the junkies addicted to the heroin we see flowering in poppy fields below us, I always need just one more hit. I chase the dragon. And with the fire I exhale in purging breaths onto the ground below, I create only destruction, as I bank more and more ravages for my mind back in that long-lost place called Home.

I had used to keep a count of the rounds I had fired, by counting the empty ammunition boxes beside me at the end of each engagement. After the impotence of never firing a single shot in Iraq, I felt a quiet satisfaction when I hit the 500 mark here in Afghanistan. But then I reached the 1,000 mark – and then the 2,000. And past the 2,500 mark I no longer keep count, because by their sheer weight of numbers, the numbers of rounds I have fired has become as meaningless as the reason I am firing them in the first place. They are no longer the mark of a man. Where firing was at first a rush, and then a release, it has now become just another everyday function, like evacuating your bowels, to be carried out as part of your daily routine.

At the end of his daily routine, Martin incinerates our shit with flame. And at the end of your day, you may see a black mark added to your name up on one of the wooden beams in the OP – on the 'Sparrowhawk West Confirmed Kills' board.

Sitting in your mud hut afterwards, you may try to pinpoint the exact moment that you took another's life. But the chances are that you would have been firing onto a distant point of aim your Number Two talked you onto, so you cannot. He will have seen the target die, not you. And so it is he that adds the mark of Cain beside your name.

The only memory your mind's eye can recall of the event will be of a sandy or green adjusted point of aim through your gun sight. And the only sounds you can remember between the thumps of your Fifty Cal firing are the words: 'Up 100 . . . Right 50 . . . On . . . On . . . On . . . OK, mate, that'll do.'

And then there would have been one less person in the world.

Sitting in your mud hut afterwards, you may try to attach some meaning to this thing you have done.

You may try to feel something.

But there is nothing to feel.

*

We distract ourselves in a number of ways from the killer monotony and the monotony of killing.

We read letters. We write letters. We read books. We look at the pseudo softcore porn of lad mags sent out to us. We play on PSPs for the hour and a half that our small solar chargers can charge them up for each day. We think. We talk. We think more after there is nothing left to talk about. We kill. And we think nothing of killing, because it is no longer something remarkable to talk about.

We masturbate in the wank hut. It reeks of rotting sperm in the heat.

We wash ourselves using the wet wipes sent from our families at home. For those of us who are old enough, we grow beards, because there is not enough water to shave – and by extension, the conditions are too unsanitary to risk scraping a razor over your face everyday.

We share the heat of the day with a plague of flies. But in our FST hut we are fortunate enough to have a pet lizard called Larry who chomps his way through bellyfuls of them.

Rats scurry past your hut in the twilight. But as the sun falls at the end of just another day, more sinister wildlife comes out to feed.

I had seen camel spiders in Iraq, but here on the hill they are larger in size and sheer numbers than anything I have seen before. They are barely spiders: they make a furry tarantula look cuddly cute. These things look like severed hands; the skin stretched across their large, fleshy torsos is the waxen shade of a corpse's. With their fangs and stalking, bony legs, they scuttle and jump in the peripheries of your vision like the walking, leaping nightmares that they are.

Their reputation as flesh eaters of the sleeping precedes them. As they emerge out of their holes to hunt, just the glimpse of one near your bare leg is enough to set off a wave of excited panic through everyone nearby, each leaping to their bare, sandalled feet in alarm and shouting, 'Where? Where?'

Killing them becomes blood sport.

When you have religiously checked your bed space before zipping yourself safely behind its mosquito net, it is as entertaining as it is comforting to hear this killing as you drift off to sleep. No one embraces this with more fervour and fear than the latest addition to our hill from the FSG: Bungle.

Sometimes you hear a shriek of panicked laughter, making you giggle yourself. Then you hear Bungle screaming, 'Die, fucker!' to the background of what sounds like everything in their hut being thrown in one specific direction.

The methods of killing soon escalate, if only to liven things up. Before the FSG boys go to sleep, their hut is often lit up by the momentary *whump* of improvised flamethrowers, as insect repellent is sprayed past a naked flame to incinerate the predators-turned-prey.

But the sound of shots suddenly fired in the LEWT hut puts all this in the shade.

Your first thought as your heart leaps to the noise is that the hill is being overrun in a sneak attack.

The second is that someone has snapped and is now going postal with cabin fever.

And the final, horrible conclusion you come to, with more time to think as your heart still thumps in reaction to the noise, is that someone has simply put a bullet through his brain to finish everything.

But, of course, someone had only taken his pistol out and shot a camel spider. With this, the only logical escalation this particular killing can now take is to begin using hand grenades.

This does not happen, perhaps fortunately. And it is Bungle with his flamethrower who mounts the most impressive tally of incinerated, mangled camel spider kills.

But with his Javelin missiles, Bungle incinerates and mangles far more people.

Now that Stu is down the bottom, our only other Javelin firer on the hill is Chads. With his goatee beard, he now looks like a very young version of Robert De Niro in the film *Heat*.

Imagine this stern face atop a body strutting for laughs, completely naked save for a neon green *Borat* mankini. The Afghan interpreters camped in with the LEWT guys loved him that day – and it wasn't even 'Man Love Thursday', of which we had heard so many lurid rumours about before coming to this country.

Another emotional outlet is watching the cut-off metal barrel we shit into having its contents being burned each day. This is especially entertaining if Martin tries to pour diesel straight onto the burning shit. He does this once, but never again. But this does not stop Bungle from following in his footsteps only a week later, making his sudden, excited shrieks all the funnier.

Burning our rubbish in its big metal cage is enjoyable as well. It is calming and good to set a small fire burning and watch it die to embers at the end of the day. But we will be told by Zero to discontinue doing this near dusk, as they say the flames will give away our position to the Taliban.

I think perhaps the Taliban know exactly where we are, though. In fact, we now know that they know exactly how many of us there are up on that sandbagged, skylined OP on top of that big hill they were booted off, with aerials poking out of it and really loud weapons that keep on firing things at them.

Now the radio intercepts by the LEWT guys not only have the Taliban counting our pitiful numbers up here on the hill, with unnerving accuracy, but talking openly of overrunning us.

So we burn the rubbish during the day instead, as instructed. And rather than staring quietly into the glowering embers of a fire with a cigarette as darkness comes, we watch the dark plumes of smoke rising straight as an arrow from our overt OP into the windless, bright-blue sky over the Kajaki Valley instead.

Late one night, when all the trip flares beyond the single roll of razor wire separating us from the Taliban begin going off, we detonate all our Claymore mines and fire our personal weapons into the darkness.

But there is no incoming fire. And we are not overrun.

In the light of morning, there are no blood trails or bodies littering the slopes away from our hilltop. After we set up new trip flares and new Claymores, it is as if the previous night had only been a bad dream.

But after this night, and now the '300 plus' Taliban below know that there are only ten of us on this hilltop, there is a quiet feeling of unease that invades your mind as you try to sleep in the coolest recesses of the night. As you lie in your festering pit, fantasising of showers and pizza in Bastion, you know that the thin wall of your mud hut and a single roll of razor wire are all that separate you from being skinned alive by the horde of nightmarish creatures you know are hidden down in the topography below . . . watching you . . . as you watch for them.

This sense of vulnerability is underlined in our minds when we have to traipse across the hilltops to pick up drinking water. There is no disguising when we do this, because for fear of being blown up by mines we have to keep to the single mine-cleared path along the ridgeline, skylining us to all the Taliban watching below. We have to leave a skeleton crew behind at the OP, and we know the Taliban will see this.

Soon there is a Taliban sniper. Firing up the hill, he will have to be lucky to kill one of us. Though he only has to be lucky once, he has not been lucky yet. As his largely daily potshots lobbed up the hill to us have never yet hit anything, we largely ignore him until Gilly thinks he spots the firing point. Then, after a few bored bursts from our Fifty Cals, we never hear from him again.

The air strikes that Alex controls onto Taliban positions provide cabaret, though we admittedly watch them with increasing detachedness due to their regularity. Alex brings this death down from above to preserve the lives of the C Company boys who patrol in front of him. In our isolation up on the hill, it never once occurs to us that we would feel as vulnerable as the Taliban who fearfully watch the skies. 'Friendly fire' was just something that happened to other people – like maiming, or death.

Sometimes, we watch as an entire section of a village is destroyed, though the bombed compounds have always been positively identified as bona fide Taliban firing points and should therefore have been deserted by the civilians who will now own nothing but rubble.

The entire western edge of a village called Bagar Kheyl disappears in one such strike. A B1-B bomber drops a clutch of two thousand-pound bombs, and after the shock and awe of their detonations hit us three kilometres away, the entire village is obscured from our view by a colossal, lingering brown and black dust cloud towering hundreds of feet into the air.

In the hours afterwards, we watch with disinterest as ant-like figures crawl over the rubble left behind, digging out what is left of the human beings buried underneath so they can be reburied within the magical 24-hour window that will see them delivered to Allah and Paradise.

By the end of our time in Kajaki, Alex will have controlled the dropping of the combined weight of over 70,000 pounds of bombs. But this figure discounts all the strafing and rocket attacks by the Harriers, Apaches and A-10s. We do not know the poundage of all those fired projectiles any more than we know theirs and the bombs' long-term cost to the land that they hit – or, indeed, the cost of all the destruction that all of us bring to this corner of the world.

Alex saves British lives by taking Afghan ones, as compounds are 'denied' to the Taliban by also denying them to the civilians who have long fled from them. But Alex also saves our lives on this hill not by calling air power in but by calling it off.

Early one morning, we were shaken awake by the deafening thunderclap of an explosion. The bang was so close and the shockwave so violent that it made the walls of our huts quake, loosening clouds of dust down onto the quivering material of our mosquito nets.

We stumbled, blinking, into the daylight. By the sheer power of the blast, it could only have been a bomb. But no one knew what the hell was going on. There wasn't a patrol out on the ground – and so it couldn't have been 'us', via Alex, who had dropped it.

But there, just down the hill from us, was the undeniable sight of dust settling over a bombed compound. And up in the early morning haze, we could hear the roar of a jet circling overhead somewhere.

It didn't make any sense. The Taliban had long given up the compound, as it was far too easily within swatting range of our Fifties.

The sound of the jet engine roared louder and closer.

Everyone was trying to get eyes on it – but no one could see it.

The roar drifted off into a distant rumble . . . followed only by silence. And everything went quietly back to normal again.

Until I went down to the FOB a few days later to drive for the FSG, and just happened to raise the incident with Alex, we were none the wiser as to how close our hilltop had come. They had felt the bomb down in the FOB too. Alex had switched on his radio and found the right frequency at the exact moment that an American voice was talking the aircraft onto a bombing run of a 'Taliban gun emplacement' at the 'western end of a large hill feature running east/west, just south of the river'.

Or, in other words: our hill.

Thinking that it might be best to interrupt this conversation before it was carried through to its lethal conclusion, Alex said he had politely but firmly interjected using his 'Widow' callsign and waved the aircraft off.

That would have been the point we heard the sound of the jet engine drifting away to nothing before, none the wiser, we sat down outside to have breakfast, and smoke, and stare absently into space.

And along with sparing our young, ignorant lives, Alex no doubt also spared the International Security Assistance Force in Afghanistan and the USAF in America some embarrassing press coverage – though admittedly in just another faraway story about death that people back home in Britain might, or equally might not, pay even a shred of attention to in their newspapers.

*

When I went down to drive for the FSG, another thing I found out was that these independently controlled air strikes were part of the build-up to a big American operation. The US 82nd Airborne – part of 'Task Force Fury' – were going to cleanse Kajaki Olya and Sofla of Taliban.

They would not be going in for another week. And for one week – or two – or maybe even three or more – I would now be driving one of the FSG WMIKs laying down fire support for C Company's patrols.

Another thing I quickly became aware of was that Captain Featherstone did not like this, at all, because I guessed he wasn't involved in my move down the hill, at all.

The FSG needed a driver; I fitted the bill. Martin had graciously released me from the grind of the hill with the smiling words: 'You lucky bastard.'

Though our captain had become aware of this arrangement afterwards, I could sense in his demeanour more than a sniff of a sniffy sense of being sidelined.

I put my hairy head around the FST's door to say hello, though; Alex was pleased to see me at least. I gave him my digital camera with its footage of air strikes to download and purr over. But when Captain Featherstone appeared to run out of strained platitudes as I cast my eyes over the FST quarters' actual, *real-life* mattressed beds, air-conditioning unit, fridge and working shower – I couldn't be bothered to stay any longer.

Where on the hill I had effectively been part of the FSG as a Fifty gunner anyway, I was immediately made to feel welcome in the FSG quarters in the FOB. With a warm smile, Captain Taylor introduced me as 'Jesus', by virtue of my appearance, to the few lads who hadn't been up the hill. For the first time in I couldn't remember, I suddenly felt relaxed – and at ease.

I smoked and smiled and laughed outside the FSG rooms with old and new faces. We sat on benches made from missile cases around a square wooden table lined with carpet. On this table was an empty ammo box, which was used as the communal ashtray. Leaning against this box and naming the area in which we all sat was a small, wooden sign with sun-faded letters penned on it.

This was 'The Priory'.

A gentle-mannered lad called Si said he had put the sign there. He said that this place was somewhere that the lads could talk about anything and everything. In the purest form of group therapy, where everyone breathed the same dusty air and lived exactly the same lives together, I would see that he was right.

Now the FSG had me driving, they could take three WMIKs out on the ground. Together, we drove up ahead of the C Company patrols to cover their daily forays.

Everything looked so much more cluttered and closer together down on the ground. In the complete opposite of what I had imagined up on the hill, everything looked so much smaller once you were among it all. From up on Sparrowhawk West, Shrine Hill looked like a hill. But now, as we drove up it, it seemed barely bigger than a mound.

Of course, a number of my perspectives may have been skewed from my time on the hill that rose darkly above us, casting a long, foreboding shadow across the entire valley.

The deafening crashes of Bungle's or Caz's Fifty firing just above my head were all too familiar, along with the ever so occasional, whistling buzzes of subsonic Taliban fire zipping past us.

As a driver, your ears were presented with two choices. You could stuff earplugs in and thereby preserve your hearing – or you could not. This would appear to be a no-brainer of a decision, but, of course, the counter-intuitive realities on the ground dictate otherwise.

As a driver, you can also be a signaller. As much as monitoring a radio net is fairly difficult when you have plugged out all sound, you also want to know when those whistling buzzes come too close, so you can belatedly duck and share the same, alive laughs along with everyone else.

So you just stuff a finger intermittently into one ear as the teenager on the back of your vehicle wordlessly kills people. Though you feel yourself being permanently deafened, the situational awareness you have afforded yourself also allows you to hear things you never thought you would hear. You hear the sound your own Fifty Cal bullets would have made as they cut through the air towards the Taliban.

At first you only see a muzzle flash high up on that hilltop you left behind. And then (when Bungle isn't drowning out all sound in the space just behind your head), you hear the unmistakable *snap-snap-snap* of the hill's rounds breaking the sound barrier as they shoot through the air above your vehicle.

But no matter where they are fired from, everyone's rounds converge on the same point.

Through graticuled binos you see a stricken compound erupting with flowers of dust. Then it just disappears in a flash of orange and black dirt. And after the final word of that thunderclap gently pummels your face with its shockwave, you turn your vehicle around. Hoping to sweet and holy God that you do not drive over a mine, you drive back through the wadis to the ghost town of Tangye. And, trundling along its eerie length, you feel the reassurance of the pistol strapped to your chest, before all your vehicles have to stop and take it in turns over the bottleneck of the rickety wooden bridge back into the FOB.

Then you step out of your vehicle, taking off your helmet to savour the hot air cooling your head as you amble back to the Priory, and sleep, before waking up to do it all over again.

After a week of this freedom, I felt human again.

But it was then that Captain Featherstone told me he wanted me back up the hill.

And though I had a selfish, vested interest in maintaining my sanity by continuing to go out on patrols, I did not understand the logic of this decision.

The FSG boss and his right-hand man, Shane, both say that I am achieving far more down here with them than being 'just another pair of eyes up on the hill'.

I agree with them. But Captain Featherstone only tells me that he wants me back on the hill.

When I say in frustration, 'But that means the FSG will only be able to take out two WMIKs . . . ! Sir,' he only says, 'Well . . . That's their problem,' before walking off.

Much later – when I am safely back home – I will have pause to reconsider that the hill was short of men, too.

But as I pack my kit to go back up the hill, my mouth only utters expletives.

Captain Taylor says he will speak to Captain Featherstone to try to get me back down again. I thank him for this, because he can tell that the FSG has been helping me out as much as I have them. But I do not hold out any hope, because it is my boss who will have the final say – which I feel means this hope can only be dashed.

I like Captain Taylor, very much, because he not only cares for his boys, but also for Captain Featherstone's. But my respect for the FSG boss is ironically just another reason why I am not endeared to my leader as he tags along after me, back up the goat track to the hill.

'You can't pick and choose,' he said breathlessly behind me, as he took the opportunity for a night away from the FOB to watch the first night of the American op going in up on the grandstand vantage of Sparrowhawk West.

I said nothing to him. I decided I needed all my breath for the climb instead.

'Look, you've got to understand, the FST has to fit around the Company . . .'

I thought that was exactly what I was doing when I was driving for the company.

'I'd get in the shit if anything happened to you out on the ground, too.'

And with this comment, and just the exertion of dragging my sorry, bergan-laden ass up the near-vertical climb, I had to stop listening. Mercifully, he shut up.

I mellowed when I saw the guys again, though. Oli and Stu waved their hands in the air excitedly, shouting 'Jake!', and Gilly almost bowled me over, hugging me tight as soon as I put my bergan down with the words, 'God, it's good to see you, man!'

I mirror all of their happy grins back to them. But I am only happy about seeing them again.

Now, as the second-oldest man on the hill, Martin grips my hand with the warmest of handshakes to welcome me back home.

Back . . . fucking . . . home . . .

*

If you had viewed our hilltop through night vision when the American op went in that night, you would have seen it lit up like a Christmas tree.

Festively flashing, infrared 'Firefly' beacons festoon the roofs of our huts. And should Santa and his jet-powered reindeer decide to conduct another blue-on-blue bombing run on us in the coming daylight, we decorate the inside of the OP with a collection of coloured smoke grenades to fuck him off with.

Gilly writes, 'Do we look like Taliban, you daft cunts?' on one of the smoke grenades. Everyone concurs with this opinion, though if you were to dress our dark, bearded features in dish-dashs now, we would indeed look every inch like Afghans.

Captain Featherstone stands in the dark OP with me and Martin as we wait for the American air assault to begin. He talks to Martin as I pointedly keep watch on the ground below through thermal imaging.

He talks of how frustrating it is down on the ground and back in the FOB.

He says that he hasn't even come close to cocking his rifle yet.

Martin acknowledges this with a bored, 'Oh, right?', while the deep, heavy drone of an AC-130 Spectre Gunship circles over Kajaki Sofla.

Then our boss changes the subject to his frustrations with the power supply in the FOB. 'Sometimes it cuts out for an hour – almost every day, without fail – it really annoys me!'

I have to take a deep breath and take my eyes away from the SOPHIE thermal-imaging sight for a moment. I know exactly what Martin is thinking in the silence he greets this with, as we don't even know what electricity *is* up on this hill.

From then on, no one talks to Captain Featherstone unless he talks to them. Once he has seen all the spectacle that he thinks the night can offer, he leaves us to carry on stagging on through the night while he snores on the camp bed he has set up for himself outside our hut.

Martin had refused to let him bed down with us. He said there wasn't enough space.

Even the camel spiders will reject him.

While Captain Featherstone is sleeping, Martin sees the American Chinook being shot down.

It was the last bird to drop off troops. He says that it had just lifted away when it seemed to hang in mid-air before suddenly lurching over to plummet nose first into the ground, exploding on impact.

It burns all night.

And in the morning, Captain Featherstone packs up his kit and goes back down to the FOB.

*

When I went back into the OP, I found that our captain had added his name to the 'SPHK WEST FST 4' triangle we had penned artfully on one of the OP's wooden beams.

This needled me; this would be the one mark we would ever leave on this hill. In no way did I feel that he was part of our crew up here on Sparrowhawk West. To illustrate the point, he hadn't even added Alex's name.

This small piece of artwork was the one creative thing we had been able to do in a sea of destruction, where the only sign of us ever having been there on the ground would be rubble, fresh graves and a still inoperative hydroelectric dam still in 'government' hands.

When we hear of 10,000 free cigarettes being dished out in the FOB below, but our captain sending none up the hill to me or Gilly, the penned letters of his name beside ours will rankle further. It was Captain Taylor – God bless him – who sent 200 up for us each, along with the extra, morale-boosting present of Bungle. Whether Bungle had his morale boosted by reaching this particular point again in the FSG's rotation of manpower, however, was a moot point.

And when, a few days later, apparently without even a hint of shame, Captain Featherstone will tell Martin over the radio that he has opened one of Martin's morale parcels from his family, helping himself to its contents, I will be as speechless at this news as Martin.

In the ensuing, incandescent fit of rage, I finally take a knife to the offending part of the wooden beam where he has written his name beside ours, gouging it free of him.

Now I am as tanned, bearded, gaunt and tired as the marine who introduced us to the hill.

And now I hate my officer, as much as the marine hated his.

*

Kajaki is dead while the Americans are there. The Taliban just melt away and keep their heads down.

But then the might of Task Force Fury is needed elsewhere. And when they go, it is just C Company and the Taliban again.

Now the coast is clear, an emboldened Taliban take the opportunity to contact our OP – right from the very foot of our hill.

We fire our Fifties and Javelins back into them in turn.

And everything goes back to exactly how it was before – as if the Americans had never been there at all.

*

After the American Chinook was shot down, the next, belated water drop by the RAF was just that. The pilot quickly flared to a hover over Sparrowhawk East as usual, lowering the under-slung pallet-load to the ground, dust flying everywhere. But with over ten feet still to go, the load was suddenly cut loose. As the dust cleared in the wake of the pilot just getting *the fuck out of Kajaki*, we saw that half of the plastic bottles had burst from the impact of hitting the ground.

The precious, useless liquid bled darkly into the pale, dry earth.

Just a week later, when we have drunk the last drops of the rationed remainder, we will again leave our hilltop defended by only a handful of men as we walk over the ridgeline to fill our empty jerrycans, dry-mouthed, tunnel-visioned and dizzy-headed from dehydration in the searing heat of the Afghan summer.

We will repeat this routine every other day until we leave Kajaki, because the RAF resupplies will dry up to the point that even the guys in the FOB will be on rationed food, water, diesel fuel and mortar ammunition.

This does impair operational effectiveness. From a bureaucratic overseer's point of view, this just means that the number of patrols have to be cut back, allowing the Taliban yet more time and space to filter back into areas they have been cleared from.

According to the official voices we read in our newspapers, there are 'enough' support helicopters in theatre to service all the troops in Helmand.

But the troops in Kajaki disagree with this official line, as we hear rumours that though there are 'enough' support helicopters in theatre, their 'flying hours' have had to be reduced. Though I have no idea whether these reduced flying hours are to rest the aircrew, or safeguard the equally overworked airframes, I deduce that with either or both being the case, there is either or both a shortage of aircrew and airframes in theatre.

We will also hear that after the American Chinook was shot down, Kajaki is now considered as a 'hot' area by the RAF. But this is of no comfort to us while living on the receiving end of Taliban fire and living on the non-receiving end of resupplies.

Rumour Control then filters news up the hill to us that the RAF's

301

Chinooks have in actual fact been temporarily grounded. And when Dan, another young soldier from the FSG, returns belatedly to us from his two weeks' R & R, we are provided with a first-hand insight into why this may be the case.

He tells us that the first Chinook he boarded to lift him from Bastion to Kajaki had developed some kind of problem as it hovered a few feet up, making the pilots land in caution before shutting down the engines. And just as the rotors were coming to a stop, one of the blades had snapped from its axis.

It didn't bear thinking what the result would have been had this happened mid-air, en route to Kajaki. Luck had everything to do with it. So it wasn't that surprising when Dan said he felt 'safer being on a hill surrounded by Taliban' than being 'up in one of those fucking death traps'.

In truth, this and the resulting, unintentional, inattention from the RAF are probably only two of the factors that lead someone to write on one of the beams of our OP – in parody of the Army's recruiting slogan of 'Army: Be the Best' – the words: 'Army: Be Depressed'.

When Stu rotates back up to our hill from his two weeks' R & R, he says that Martin, Gilly and I have become, 'I dunno, more subdued . . . More withdrawn.'

But his first reaction on seeing me again had actually been: 'Jesus Christ!'

Our hair is long. With greasy, matted sweat, it sticks up in styles metrosexuals back home would swoon over as uber-sexy. Our beards are full. And with our black hair, dark eyes and deep tans, one of the Afghan interpreters living with the LEWT guys tells us with a smile how we now look like Afghans.

But to the freshly shaved FSG boys who rotate back up to the hill, we look like hill men – for that is exactly what we are. And as the eldest of the three 'hill rats', as Martin has christened us, my hairiest appearance is apparently the closest to Jesus Christ's.

Jesus did not feel the need to shoot people with a Fifty Cal, though, which is probably why the nickname sticks.

And I do not know if Jesus was visited by such demons in his dreams.

Martin does not talk about his dreams, but from the sounds I sometimes hear from his bed, I know they cannot be good.

In Gilly's latest nightmare, an Afghan man is sobbing as he takes his infant son up to our hill. His infant son is wearing a suicide bomber's vest. And when everyone on our hill sees this, everyone on our hill apart from Gilly wants to kill this child. Gilly is screaming 'No!' as we level our weapons. The father is crying; the child is crying; Gilly is screaming. But no one listens.

And from out of my own abyss, I still remember the girl I came here to put behind me.

Gilly, Martin and I sit in our candlelit mud hut with easy listening music in the background. We drink from hip flasks and we smoke and we talk and we listen and we laugh and we pretend that everything, really, is all right.

But then there comes the time when we have to try to sleep.

Gilly: 'What do you call a vagina with teeth?'

'Tell me.'

'A vicious cunt.'

*

To cow the rebuoyed Taliban, the OC of C Company has decided that, along with his platoons' aggressive patrols, a night-time 'show of force' is needed from all the hilltop OPs along the ridgeline. At a given signal, all of our Fifty Cals and GPMGs will fire their tracer fire simultaneously for a given time.

I can see the psychological logic to this. But as much as I respect the OC, I am concerned that this show of force will also enable the Taliban to 'count our guns', as the Zulu horde did before descending en masse onto the isolated British outpost of Rorke's Drift.

But who am I to pass up another opportunity for the release of firing? Along with everyone else who takes their places behind their allotted weapons, I wait in the darkness for the radioed signal.

Instead of firing into a specific target, I will be firing across the river into a deserted hillside, because we are, after all, only doing this for show. And as I sit and wait, all the resentment that I have ever felt about anything on this hill begins running again through my cabin-fevered brain.

I see all my demons sitting on that hillside – just there – in the darkness that sits right in front of my eyes.

When the signal comes, when everyone opens up as one with blinding muzzle flashes, deafening, mechanical roars and angry-red, hot-spitting tracer fire, it is initially difficult to force my fingers to fire any more than the restrained, disciplined, three- to five-round bursts that have proved so effective at killing people.

But then Martin's voice calls down to us from the OP: 'Up the rate of fire!'

Suddenly I am not looking through the tunnel vision of a SUSA sight. Suddenly I am not firing those regimented, controlled, three- to five-round bursts. Now I am letting rip with twenty- to thirty-round bursts, screaming silently in release as I channel every shred of pent-up rage I have through every round that cannons from the vengefully alive beast in my hands, drilling them straight into the face of every demon that has had the fucking gall to come and torment me on this hill.

When everyone must suddenly fall quiet as one again, I would sob in thankful, pure release. But I find that this final, tail-end emotion is not available to me.

And from this point on in Afghanistan, I will find that I sleep as peacefully, and as deeply, as the dead.

*

As my *Cast Away* beard grows longer, Captain Taylor will playfully observe on one of his morale visits to the hill, where he brings post and a phone, that I need a ball called 'Wilson'. But like the C Company 2IC, Captain Hicks, who now also takes a benevolent interest in the three FST guys going stir crazy up on that hill, he can always only stay for so long.

Tempers shorten as beards grow. But our fallings out, over things as irritably minor as who feels they have been doing all the cooking recently, or who didn't help out with the post-meal cleaning up as the rats and camel spiders scurried past you in the twilight, are also short.

Martin, Gilly and I may feel stuck with each other from time to time, but as the three-man permanent fixture on this hill, we also know that we have to carry one another through our time here. This bonds us ever closer to one another.

We share everything we have with one another. And when one, or even two of us, are facing a collapse of morale, there is always one of us at least who has enough shreds of morale banked to buoy the others.

We live by the motto: 'Share the love; share the pain.'

The biggest thing I can do, especially now I have had a week's holiday down the bottom, is continue to share all the contents of my mother's steadfast morale parcels with everyone.

I had told her how Martin had reached the stage of fantasising about Snickers bars. And sure enough, just a few parcels later, there was a Snickers bar for Martin. His eyes almost popped out of his head when I gave it to him. But, of course, he broke the chocolate bar into three. And all three of us indulged in a foreign taste of Home in our mud-hut home, high up on a hill in Afghanistan.

Now, though, we can look forward to a taste of Home for real. Now we know our team's R & R date: 4 July. The date is burned into our brains, but as each passing day is ticked from the calendar in these final weeks, this only seems to make this last stretch all the longer.

But we know that when we return to Afghan two weeks later, we will have a change of scenery and routine to look forward to. C Company is going to be replaced by B Company at Kajaki while we are on R & R. And as our team goes everywhere C Company goes, we too will then be moving down the river to another part of Helmand, to conduct foot patrols in the Green Zone near Sangin.

This final stretch of waiting was far worse for Martin and Gilly than me, though, because, true to his word, Captain Taylor had managed to negotiate another stint for me driving one of his WMIKs.

I will enjoy the fact that Captain Featherstone appears to hate me doing this. But another thing I will notice during my second stint driving for the FSG will be a photo fixed to the wall in the building housing the FSG and one of the platoons.

The photo is of 10 Platoon, fresh faced and just in theatre. Above it is an inscription:

'They came out boys, they went back as men.'

The reason this 'before' photo struck me was that I had just seen this change in the young sentry who had let me into the back gate of the FOB.

I hadn't recognised him at first. And until he recognised me, the glare of the sun made his features seem far harsher than I remembered.

He was the baby-faced, blond-haired soldier who was the spitting image of my little brother when he was a boy.

But the boy I'd seen on exercise in England no longer existed. It was in his eyes, his face, the way he spoke and the way he carried himself. 'Confidence' would be too glib a term to describe what now emanated from him. The hard-edged, detached gaze to his eyes, his whole demeanour and posture, now carried a weight beyond his years.

Tommy walked up to me with a smile of recognition, and we

crouched down outside the back gate for a crafty fag. I was in no particular rush; I wanted to see how he was doing. It turned out he had been back off R & R no more than a week; now he only had the end of tour to look forward to.

'How long is it now?' I asked.

'One hundred and three days,' he answered, with a sardonically sunny, resigned disposition.

One hundred and three long days to live in discomfort and boredom, isolated from everyone and everything back home, while facing the Taliban directly through firefights, or indirectly through their mines and IEDs.

'How was your R & R?'

'Good – but not long enough.'

Days that may drag by out here correspondingly skip by too quickly at home.

'Any stupid questions?'

'A few – I found I didn't want to talk about it, though.'

I nodded my head in recognition.

These young men have already experienced more than most will in a lifetime. And at this time, there is a quiet resentment among many, myself and Tommy included, that our efforts and sacrifices in places like Afghanistan and Iraq are not recognised back home.

'There's no respect for squaddies any more' he said flatly. 'Chelsea Pensioners are the only soldiers who get any regard now. That's no disrespect to them, they went through hell, but where's the respect for us?'

When I go back up the hill, I will see this thought echoed in Stu's face that night as we watched the end of *Jarhead* on his portable DVD player. We were watching the joyous, flag-waving homecoming that the US Marines returned to. Beside me, I saw Stu's face suddenly fall. I had never seen him look so sad.

'We won't get anything like that,' was all he said.

And we wouldn't.

Out here, we have to read old copies of the same newspapers everyone else reads back home. And there is a growing perception among us that many civilians live in a bubble, where obsession with *The X Factor*, or *Big Brother*, or Paris Hilton, or Ashley and Cheryl Cole, or Paris Hilton Dancing on Fucking Ice with Overpaid Footballers, outweighs the real-life, life-and-death struggles being played out for them by young soldiers who then have to come home and live among them.

There is utter contempt for Paris Hilton, who we feel could not face up to her actions by doing the mere 30 days in prison for her drink-driving. She did three. Three days away from her pampered, insular bubble, before psychologists assessed her as being a suicide risk.

Yet in the celebrity-obsessed culture back home, for many this rich heiress is held up as a role model, with details of her life pored over in tabloid newspapers, with front pages devoted to the latest mundane chapter in it, in all its vacuous detail.

And a soldier's death for his country is relegated to the back pages – while maimings are no news at all.

I pick up a week-old tabloid paper on the hill. The front page leads with the latest on Paris Hilton and the latest on *Big Brother*. Altogether, there are three pages on the former and six on the latter, including a 'special' four-page *Big Brother* pull-out.

The 150th soldier to die in Iraq and a lance corporal shot dead on the same day in Afghanistan get half a page, on page 19, under the small header: 'We Are Proud of Them All'.

On page three, however, is an article on a soldier arrested for groping women in Germany, headed by a picture of his regiment's cap badge and the word 'Shame!'.

There is no such picture or header to shame the Fire Service in the back pages, though, as a fireman is reportedly sacked for viewing Internet porn with the pyjama-clad daughter of a colleague.

We have to read this shit, because aside from the letters from our families and partners, who may or may not be remaining faithful, these newspapers are our only link back to 'Home'.

Does the press pander to sections of society that are banal and valueless? Or is society itself influenced by the tabloid glare on such mediocrity?

I read that the Channel 4 boss was 'not proud' of *Big Brother*, 'a celebration of mediocrity' he, or someone else in the paper, called it.

But it obviously made money, because a large section of the population lapped it up. Maybe it is a distraction from the real world, where Sunday Blues foreshadow a nine to five, Monday to Friday grind; where obsession with the superficial overrides nourishment of the soul; where entertainment with the irrelevant distracts from the mundane and meaningless.

Some recognition for those who give themselves, regardless of politics, to keep this bubble safe and intact, would be appreciated.

I think this up on the hill – and I hear it when I speak to Tommy, Martin, Gilly, Easty, Eddie and every single other soldier who echoes these thoughts in carbon copy back to me.

Maybe it is not the public's fault, though. They know nothing about war. Some play computerised war games where inflicting 'death' accrues points and suffering it only means that your avatar respawns a few seconds later. Others play at airsoft or paintball at the weekends, thinking they are something they are not, before reading tabloid newspapers about celebrity gossip on the tube to work the next day – flicking over the back pages where one of their soldiers died for them. Books are even less exciting, while films and actual war footage, should they even be viewed, are often presented as just another exciting titbit of opium to distract the masses from tedium in the bubble.

So when you, the soldier, are asked out-of-the-blue questions such as, 'Did you kill anyone?' maybe you can forgive the questioner, because they have no relevant frame of reference in which to truly know what it is that they ask.

But being on the receiving end of such questions such as 'Did you kill anyone?' is not to be on the receiving end of any kind of recognition.

So the soldier will not want to discuss the reality of such things with such people. He will not want to whore and cheapen what he has done just for the passing, ghoulish interest of someone who was not there. Too often this most personal of questions will be asked with a childlike frisson, thinking that they could possibly have a glance into the depths of an actual, real-life killer's mind.

And as polarised and isolated as I am up on this hill, I will want to rub the faces of these ghouls into the guts of dead Taliban, just so they could know how it feels to be on the receiving end of such a question.

But sometimes, here, I will also wish to see those guts, just to trigger some feeling over what I have done.

I know there is a dull ache growing somewhere in my head, but my mind cannot let it out.

*

Chads came with me when I went back up the hill for my last stint before R & R. But before we started up the slog of the goat track, we stopped to look round the 'Russian Building'.

Lying just outside the FOB's back gate, the rectangular, flat-roofed and stone-walled two-storey Russian Building is pointedly not part of the FOB.

It is abandoned, empty and silent.

We can only guess what the Russians used it for: housing troops, or workers on the dam maybe.

But what is not in any doubt is what it ended up being used as. The battle scars it carries bear quiet witness to the horror stories we have heard.

The Russians had soldiers up on our hill too. But these ghosts of ourselves had apparently been abandoned by their officers in the rush to withdraw in '89. The story goes that these boys fled down the hill to the FOB, chased by mujahideen, only to find themselves alone and surrounded by their pursuers.

We hear they holed up in the building in front of us now. But however those Russian boys got there, we can see how they died.

On the upper storey of the building, the windows of the left-hand corner room have been completely blown in. There are gaping chunks in the walls around these windows from multiple RPG hits. Where there are not whole chunks of wall missing, there are the pockmarks from hundreds of bullets.

This, Chads and I guess, is the 'Last Room on the Left' the boys ended up in, before their ammunition ran out.

We go inside, leaving the heat and brightness of the day with its twittering of birds behind us.

It is dark, cool and unnaturally quiet inside.

As we walk deeper into the empty corridor along the ground floor, we not only find ourselves not talking but also consciously breathing quieter as we try not to make any sound with our footsteps. Just the slightest sound we make seems to disturb the peace here, echoing harshly in our ears through the emptiness.

The corridor opens up into a large space. But it is too dark to see much other than the grey, blank walls we gravitate towards, so we turn back on ourselves to the concrete staircase we had passed by the front door.

Chads walks in front of me along the corridor. I have to force myself not to look over my shoulder into the darkness we leave behind.

It is brighter as we take the first flight of steps up. But now we can see what happened on this staircase, our minds are plunged into dark, horrific imaginings.

As the staircase turns back on itself to the first floor, we can see how they tried to hold them off coming up the stairs.

The wall facing the landing has been cratered from all the rounds hitting it. And the wall up the stairs to the landing has been scoured by multiple ricochets and scorched black by flame.

Now on the landing, looking down the staircase as the Russian boys did, we see how some of the bullet holes can only have been made by a larger calibre weapon – maybe even a Dushka, akin to one of our Fifty Cals. They must have set it up where we stand now, blasting every demon that came up those stairs for them – before the ammunition ran out.

And as you walk down the corridor, now they are running past you – into that Last Room on the Left.

You do not mean to, but you disturb the peace of this tomb as you walk into it.

A flurry of screaming birds suddenly bursts through the air in front of you – straight through the blown-in windows into the clear blue outside.

And in the second that your heart leaps, you do not understand where they came from.

But then you see the bullet holes.

These are not dotted sparingly around the walls of this room. No. In this room, there is barely a square foot of wall that has not had a bullet through it.

This is where the last of them died – where they could not fly any further from their killers.

And if you stop and hold your breath – if you listen very carefully – you can hear them screaming their final screams.

But I do not know what the Russian for 'mother' is, so I cannot listen for it.

And now, 20 years on, even their mothers might not be left alive to remember them.

You feel this place needs some kind of memorial. But as long as it stands, one has only to walk inside it to feel the full horror of the young soldiers' final minutes. And this is more powerful and more moving than any plaque with forgotten names etched onto it can be, on a forgotten memorial in a home city that the inhabitants scurry past with far more important things on their minds than who died in their name.

The full tragedy is that only we, as soldiers, will see this building – because we, as soldiers, already appreciate the plight of the common soldier, no matter what language he speaks or when he fought.

Even if this building could be packed up and set down again in Red Square, or Trafalgar Square, it would only be an attraction for the kinds of ghouls who rubberneck at road-traffic accidents. And should a politician with blood on his hands be forced to walk into it, you know that his power-driven brain would just not 'get it'.

As for the silent majority, all those years on from whichever war . . . I mean, who the hell in London ever remembers why Trafalgar Square is called Trafalgar Square, as they breeze through it to just another bar?

*

After my second holiday of going out on patrol, I go back to the different reality of the hill – where killing is done with clean, clinical detachment while living in foetid squalor.

An A-10 screams low over our hill after doing the business. And, inverted, the pilot waggles his wings to wave at us. We cheer and wave back at him. And for as long as we remember him for the rest of the day, he is 'the Pimp Daddy'. But then we imagine him going back to a swimming pool, pints of iced tea and girls on tap after he lands in his Kandahar super-base, so we forget him.

Later, our senses will be momentarily fired by the sight of an RPG exploding in an airburst over our hill. But we will only look up at it like one would at an unspectacular firework, before this too is blanked from our memories.

*

Before our team got away for R & R, my mother sent me another parcel. But this one was different to the others, because, enclosed with the aisle's worth of treats from a supermarket, she had also enclosed a postcard, with a painting of the Wittenham Clumps on its front.

I look at the postcard from a foreign country and I remember the largest of these hills, snow clad in winter with a large clump of trees at its top. And I remember sledging – laughing with joy – down its slope with my brother.

It all seems so far away now as I look out across the Hindu Kush, as if it happened to someone else, or never at all.

Now I remember before my brother was even born, burrowing – alive with joy – through huge piles of autumn leaves in another English wood.

Maybe my mother had been right when she said the Army was in my blood. But now that the Army is all that is in my blood and the blood of one-time little boys is on my hands, I do not know how to find my way back home to the happiness of that little boy I remember, when everything in life was possible.

As requested, my mother also sends me the life of Julius Caesar to read.

Where I am, this provides pure escapism for me – when the antiquated word 'honour' actually meant something, or was at least held up as something to aspire to; when in battle you could fix your enemy right in the eye, as close as lovers, and, *gladius* in hand, stab the life from their groins and throats.

I do not think that the long-range bullets I fire provide the mark of a man; I am only dimly aware that they are dehumanising me.

They are my opium to see me through my time here. But with each hit they give, they only provide a fleeting respite from the past I cannot escape from and the present I have chosen to mire myself in. And, grounded as I am in the reality of this hill, I do not yet fully appreciate how this addiction is infecting my future with malediction.

With this clinical, psychopathically detached behaviour considered as normal, proper and expected on this hill, I cannot yet stop to think – because I cannot allow myself to here – of how these respites may be blackening my soul in all the time I will have left on my own back Home – should I even live through the remainder of my months here, in some other corner of this Hell of a country.

As much as I choose not to remember Musafer, and as much as the thousands of bullets I have fired into 'positively identified' Taliban positions just blur into one noise, I do not know which is the better or worse for the mind: being divorced from the terrible reality of your actions, or by knowing them, maybe one day being able to confront them.

The Romans often used to settle their soldiers in the lands they had conquered – for the soldiers' own sake as much as for the populations' back home. It was considered that their dehumanised killers might best be kept separate from civilians who would never truly know what had been done in their name.

Not so in our time. And with the comparative deprivations of this country, we now cannot wait to get back to the foreign luxuries of Home, even though our R & R will only be, at most, two weeks long.

*

The RAF airlifted a temporary replacement for our team into Kajaki. But after we had handed over to them, flight after flight to pick us up was cancelled.

With only three days remaining before we missed the flight home from Kandahar, our half jokes that we would all need to shoot ourselves in the foot to get out of here dried to a bitter resignation that we would only be spending our two weeks' R & R in Bastion, or worse, Kajaki.

As things turned out, the only way we did get out of Kajaki was by someone being shot.

But it wasn't as a result of one of us finally going postal; the victim was a soldier on patrol with the Afghan National Army (ANA), who luckily did not die.

So we jumped onto the back of the Chinook that came to pick him up. And with all irony, it was the one, solitary IRT Chinook for the whole of Helmand that took us back to Camp Bastion.

We didn't stay very long at Bastion. But we stayed long enough to understand why this sprawling bastion of bullshit had earned the nickname 'Camp Bullshit'.

Wearing regulation T-shirts and sun hats while showing high-ranking, non-commissioned rear-echelon motherfuckers (REMFs) 'some fucking respect' by 'putting some fucking Sirs at the end of your sentences' was apparently quite a big deal. I thought taking lives and being shot at was quite a big deal, but neither of these things ever happened at Camp Bastion, so perhaps I was wrong.

I saw, too, how many hundreds of the base rats at Bastion had pistols strapped to their legs, saving them having to carry the sheer weight of a rifle back and forth to the cookhouse.

We were still at the 19 Regiment lines when news came in of its first combat fatality on this tour.

I did not know Sergeant Wilkinson, but Alex said he was his friend.

He had been driving a WMIK at the time. Then a suicide bomber blew himself up beside his vehicle.

We listened to the padre's heartfelt words in the communal smoking area.

We bowed our heads for a minute's silence.

And while everyone was quiet, I read the words on one of the prayer cards he had laid out:

> *Holy God, in this troubled land, though I know you not, you know me.*
> *Preserve my soul to everlasting life.*

But then it was time to catch our Hercules to Kandahar.

And before we knew it, we were suddenly sitting in a sterile metal tube filled with recycled air, winging through the stratosphere towards Home.

9

DESCENT

If you could hear, at every jolt, the blood
Come gargling from the froth-corrupted lungs . . .
My friend, you would not tell with such high zest
To children ardent for some desperate glory,
The old Lie: Dulce et decorum est
Pro patria mori.
                    Wilfred Owen (killed in action one week before
                                                    Armistice Day)

That field has eyes, and the wood has ears.
                    Geoffrey Chaucer, 'The Knight's Tale'

I had been born and raised in Oxfordshire. So in later years, while I sat embroiled in the deserts of other countries, my mind would remember this England as nothing other than God's Country.

Now as I stared through Perspex, past a wing with hydraulically lowering flaps and through white wisps of cloud, I saw its fertile patchwork of fields and leafy, sleepy villages stretched out below me once more.

Jerusalem herself lay waiting, reaching up for me for this last of fleeting embraces.

But I did not recognise her lush, verdant fields stretched out far below. And I did not recognise her old, familiar huddles of gently rolling hills and clusters of deep, dark-green woodlands.

This strange and forgotten otherworld looked so impossibly and unnaturally green. She looked so impossibly and unnaturally peaceful.

And my eyes looked down at her coldly, because I knew that in only nine days I would have to leave her once more, perhaps for the most final of times.

I was not descending in a plane, coming Home.

I was watching an alien world as it ascended towards me – and one that I could never begin the process of readjusting to, because I knew that I would just as soon be returning to another world, whose normality was as alien to this home as I now was.

The foreign, moisture-laden clouds that greyed out my view of Home were of some numbing comfort. They wrapped up the aircraft in a limbo of cotton wool, cushioning the sudden bump of my return – before I was suddenly flung forward in my seat as engines screamed in reverse thrust, tyres rumbling on tarmac, before all was smooth once more, wheels gliding silkily along a taxiway before finally nodding to a gentle, sickening stop.

Nothing has changed at Home. The grandfather clock in my mother's living room still ticks the same tock, over and over, chiming down the dwindling hours before Home becomes just a distant memory once again.

My family says they are proud of me. Of course, I would rather hear this than the contrary, but I cannot say that I am proud of myself, so I find that I cannot 'talk about it'.

My mother describes me as 'a real hero ... just like your grandfather'. But I do not know what to do with this accolade for her son, other than to let her have her moment, if it helps her back here.

In Oxfordshire and in London, I go through the motions of recalled, learned and expected behaviours. My body language, facial expressions and monotone answers react politely and demurely, and with restraint, to all the strange, old social stimuli.

I find that I cannot be in the here and now.

I find instead that this transient interlude of luxury and sterility, countryside and city, with concerns that are not concerns, is just something that happens in my background.

I sleep with a girl I had been seeing on a casual basis after Kate. And when the next day, in tears, she says the words 'I hate you' and 'I love you' within a minute of each other, I find that I feel absolutely nothing.

My mother, too, cries when it is time for me to go back. And though I remember this is the most natural reaction a mother can have to an occasion that might be the very last time she ever sees her firstborn son alive, her tears jar me. I feel the rawness of her emotion stirring something inside of me that I do not want to see. The feel of her arms around me is too close and too warm.

My body goes through the motions of holding her reassuringly in return. My face smiles confidently. I hear my words telling her not to worry, promising her that I will come back.

But I feel no emotional connection to these outwardly human gestures.

I am not there, because I never left Afghanistan.

*

The man I did not kill is lying in one of the little veins of water that channel the river's lifeblood into the dust, and he is only just dead.

His features are peaceful but already drained to a shade of ashen wax against the dark, shallow water he floats in face-up, arms flung slightly to his sides, with pale palms, dark eyes and still mouth all open and skyward in a tranquil picture of finality.

Long, lush grass flourishes up the banks from the water's edges, framing the scene. And in the future, with all perversity, I will remember it looking like an oil painting of the death of Ophelia.

His face is turned up to where I look down on him from the bank, and he holds a serene expression of pure release: all life, all pain, all gone. His gaze passes straight through me and up, through and beyond the canopy of branches arching over us, where light filters through into our private, shady grove.

Eyes earthward, I notice how his dark hair flows and blends into the thick, cloudy water. It is the same colour as the black shirt and trousers he wears. I see that he is barefoot, like most of the locals here. I might have wondered if he was a farmer killed by mistake, but I know he was not. Not today, not on his final day. Farmers do not wear olive-green chest rigs with pouches for AK-47 magazines strapped to their fronts. He was Taliban, and he was trying to outflank us, and he was killed by 10 Platoon.

*

Before I first went to Afghanistan, a text was doing the rounds of the HAC soldiers getting ready to go, sent from one soldier's phone to another in an air of anticipatory excitement as our individual flight dates drew nearer. We were, after all, flying in for the first full season of summer fighting since the paras went into Helmand a year ago.

It went so:

317

> A para was asked what he felt when he shot a member of the
>   Taliban:
> 'Recoil.'

It did not occur to me then that in addition to the physical kickback of the weapon in my hands, the recoil I might just be lucky enough to feel might also be felt in my soul.

Because the truth is that in the darkest and most naive recesses of my soldier's soul, I wanted a 'kill'. And I wasn't alone, very far from it. Because to cut through the smoke screen of regiments, trades, nationalities, even religion, what is the base purpose of a soldier?

We licked up the bravado of a sensation we knew nothing about as we prepared to go. Maybe it would be a thrill, a defining moment in my life: the omnipotent act of taking another's life, and another life-experience box ticked.

Or maybe it would just be as straightforward and impersonal as aligning sight and target, squeezing an index finger, or thumb, and then feeling my ears ring.

Which was how it was. The weapon recoiled. The man died. And my soul did not recoil in horror. I tried to feel something, anything, in my hilltop mud hut afterwards, but there was nothing.

Acts that would be considered cataclysmic and horrific back home were just normal and expected in the life we immersed ourselves in here. These Taliban were trying to kill us as much as we them.

So the most I came to feel was just some kind of numb, distant, disinterested hatred of dehumanised objects in scopes and rangefinders. We were just enemies.

I divorced myself from my humanity, just like my companion soldiers. I sat on my hill, a prisoner to my past, and watched the monster being made of me as I killed: love drowned and pity dead.

Many months later, though, when Afghanistan becomes memory and the cosy values of life at home become normal once again, the image of a little mud-walled compound sitting in a flowering poppy field will keep me awake at night.

I will see into nearly all of it because it lay at the bottom of our hill. And superimposed over the picture will be the black 'T' of my Fifty Cal SUSA gun sight, because I was shooting at four men inside. I will forever be pinning them down so an F-15 can drop a 500-pound bomb on them.

I will remember the tearful words of a terrified dying man.

And much later, safely back home, feeling will sometimes ambush me when I am on my own, and I will shake and break down. Sometimes this will happen when I am in the shower, naked and vulnerable, and if it has to happen then here will be best, because the water will hide the tears, and it will wash them away. As always, I will have to remind myself of what reality is here – of what they would have done to me, or my friends.

Of what they will do.

But it will not take away the memory of methodically firing bursts of heavy machine-gun fire into every dark corner and hiding place within that compound. Carefully and exactly walking the rounds into any refuge: detached, cold, pathological – searching – feeling – for those 'kills'.

I will scream and wither as my soul screams and withers, as my mind's eye brings the gun sight to the fore – and I remember the bleeding, terrified man's words.

He was dead by the next morning. They didn't come to help him, and he bled out in the compound we had holed him up in.

*

This is no glassy stream or weeping brook. There is no single red poppy floating neatly beside this man I did not kill, representing sleep and death in a Victorian artist's language of flowers.

He was not pulled gently under and away while chanting snatches of old lauds to ease his passing. He was shot and stuck just like his friend twisted in the sludge near us, or another, open-mouthed and wide-eyed too, but lying among opium poppies with the back half of his head missing, his brains feeding the Taliban's cash crop standing ready to collapse London veins.

God knows what brought him to die at this spot. But I am the one incapable of my own distress here, edging nearer the precipice in this escape from a lover's rejection, staring down with dead eyes at a dead man's heavenward gaze.

I am alone with the corpse of an enemy draining into an irrigation ditch. So I turn my back on it and walk back to the rest of the OC's Tac, where I lower myself back down to rejoin them sitting in the brown water seeping downstream from the muddy death, like the dark blood that oozes from a dead man's wound.

*

Apart from the death of one of our own, it had been quiet at FOB Inkerman for the first fortnight.

Martin did not fly in to rejoin C Company with the rest of our team; he was on loan to another FST and, fatefully, would not be with us for another two weeks.

So it was only Captain Featherstone, Alex, Gilly and I who shared the Chinook ride to our new home, along with the last members of C Company to be flown in.

And of all the flights I have been on – whether I was piloting or not – this was one I would take with me to my grave.

Laden down with kit, we lumbered up the Chinook's back ramp, the searing-hot downwash and deafening roar of the rotors suddenly replaced by the ear-splitting scream of their turboshaft engines as we hauled ourselves into the dark inside.

No one strapped themselves into the cargo benches running down either side of the fuselage. There wasn't any point, as the sheer volume of kit hanging off each of us, and how tightly we wedged ourselves up against each other in our seats, rendered this health and safety gimmick utterly superfluous. And no one wanted to be feverishly fiddling around with some release latch hidden away under some layer of equipment if the helicopter was in the process of being turned into a colander on a hot DZ (drop zone).

But the tail gunner lashed himself to the wide-open back ramp, crouching for stability behind his GPMG as the crescendo of noise went up a notch – with the deep, unmistakably-Chinook, *whump-whump-whump* of the twin rotors pulling us into the air.

We flew high at first. The tail gunner was silhouetted by clear, pale blue, with just a beige hint of ground in the haze touching the ramp.

Just off in the distance we could see our escorts taking position behind us: two Apache Longbow helicopter gunships, the distinguishing radomes atop their rotor blades just visible past our tail gunner's head.

Then there was the sensation of speed picking up, with lightness in our stomachs telling us our altitude was now plummeting, and the roar of the slipstream buffeting through the open back growing even louder.

Suddenly we are low, shooting through mountain ranges as our Chinook's pilots fly her as fast and low as she can possibly go.

I crane my neck over the constriction of my body armour and helmet to glance through the porthole beside my head. There is just a blur of brown rock. I feel myself beginning to grin.

The g-forces of the steep turns press me back into my seat. Now I remember the first aerobatics I ever flew solo. I remember this! *This is fucking flying!*

The tail gunner is pressed down into the ramp every time the horizon twists this way and that – to near vertical angles. The mountainsides zip past us – you can almost reach out and touch them. We are so far below their peaks that these aren't even visible – half our view out the back is taken up by the valley floor that flashes by only feet underneath us; the other half is swivelling flashes of blue mingling with brown.

And just there – *right fucking there* – and somehow keeping close station either side of our back ramp, are the two Apaches. They are so close you can see the black visors of the pilots' helmets, the chain gun that points everywhere the visors do and all the Hellfire missiles carried on their stub-wings.

The horizon twists up and down, left and right, as the ground skims by underneath us – but there they always are: two beautifully evil birds of prey, mothering the precious, lumbering beast leading the way in front of them.

The heady, all-pervading smell of burning kerosene is in my nose as the wall of noise fills my ears. I look across to Gilly and Alex sitting opposite me. Three achingly wide grins all meet as one, as Gilly punches a thumbs up to me.

This is what it feels like to be alive.

Then we burst out of the brown into the green of the Sangin Valley, and all smiles are suddenly wiped from our faces as the dark interior we sit in is lit up with flashes of light.

We remember the American Chinook being shot down.

But from out of the leaping of your heart and the spasms in your bowels come twinges of measured relief. The flashes of light are just counter surface-to-air missile, incandescently burning flares shooting away from your aircraft.

This is either a good, preventative thing, or it is in reaction to something very, very bad, which is going to smash into us and bring us burning and screaming into the ground at any second. As cargo, we have no way of knowing – any more than we know why the Apaches are now keeping more of a distance from us.

But sudden death does not come, and our bird continues screaming over rooftops and skimming treetops.

The pilot banks us into a steep turn, before suddenly, heavily, flaring us to a shuddering stop. There is a flash of beige mud walls and the feel of wheels hitting ground, travelling up our spines. Then all view out of the back disappears in a whirlwind of whipped-up sand, and we are running, one man followed by another and another, out into the blinding maelstrom.

We crouch down in a semicircle within the sandstorm, goggles pulled down from our helmets onto our eyes – waiting. With a deep, thudding scream the Chinook lifts once more into the air, its rotor wash blasting every millimetre of exposed flesh with flying, stinging dirt.

Then you discover quiet again – past the ringing in your ears. And as the dust dissipates with the last of your adrenalin, you lift yourself up from the powdery earth suddenly beneath your feet, and you also find that you can see . . . your new home.

Camp Bastion or even FOB Zeebrugge it wasn't, but our descent had at least got us off that hill.

*

Forward Operating Base Inkerman lay ten kilometres north-east of a town called Sangin, in Helmand Province. To the rear of its mud walls was mile upon mile of dust-filled wasteland, before the horizon suddenly rose up into those jagged brown mountain ranges you flew through.

Immediately in front of the FOB was a dirt road. And if you were to turn right out of the FOB's gate and drive north-east along the road's bumpy, potholed length for many miles, you would find yourself driving into a town called Kajaki Sofla, with a hill occupied by homicidal young men overlooking you.

But you would not do this, because you would only be minutes out of the FOB and not even a mile along the road before you were blown up by an IED.

Just as in Kajaki, though, this road separates the barren wilderness from Eden. The side that the FOB inhabits is pale dust, dirt and rock. But stretching for two kilometres immediately the other side, all the way to the fat, winding artery of the River Helmand, is the lush emerald of the Green Zone.

Even from up in the FOB, you can see how the veined maze of irrigation ditches channel the river's lifeblood into what would otherwise only be dust. It is a pure sea of green hiding a labyrinth of bushy tree lines, dense, head-high cornfields, chest-high poppy and marijuana fields, streams, ditches, grass banks, scattered hamlets and meandering, winding paths to lose your way down.

Birds chirrup in the peace. And it all looks so biblically beautiful, should you find yourself forgetting how Eden can also be Hell.

Your new home in this normality is a rectangular compound some hundred and fifty metres long by a hundred metres wide, with perimeter walls made out of pale mud about ten feet high. It is very similar to all the other mud-walled compounds nestled beside it, in fact, but these now lie empty – because their neighbour is now occupied by two platoons of British infantry, a mortar detachment, an FSG, an FST and a platoon of the ANA.

Perhaps through experience, the locals have learned to give the no-man's-land between the Taliban and us a wide berth.

But there are fewer of us now. C Company's 9 Platoon has gone to Nowzad, taking the FSG guys with whom we had shared the hill. Only Robbo and Dan remain, who are now snipers shared between 10 and 11 Platoon. And in each of these remaining platoons, their three sections of eight men have now been reduced through injuries to five or six men apiece.

At the back of the FOB is a large, open area where the choppers come in to resupply us – and, indeed, where you found yourself resupplied to the FOB. Along its rear wall are the toilets, or, to be more accurate, the holes in the ground with wooden seats that you hover your arse over clouds of flies to shit into. Beside these, equally out of the way, should the Taliban decide to blow it up, is a diesel tanker full of flammable fuel.

Push this out of your mind, though, as you will always have to when straining constipation-causing rations for lifetimes of minutes out of your rear end.

Come forward a hundred metres, across the wide-open helicopter landing site (HLS) and to an internal dividing wall. The infantry boys sleep against this mud wall. Just the other side of it is the thirty-metre-long, hundred-metre-wide area where your FST will sleep and wait and think with the mortar boys, huddled together out in the open on the sharp, stony ground with thin parachute canvas stretched over you for shade.

There is no room for anyone bar the FOB's two medics to sleep in the small one-storey main building to your left here. This mud-walled building is the communications and medical centre, with a sandbagged sanger on top of its flat roof. It is this sanger that is the main observation post into the Green Zone in front of us. There is a single Javelin missile set up beside it, as there is no hilltop here for the different FSG to set their Fifties and Javelins on.

To the right of where you will sleep is the burn pit, where all rubbish is burnt. It smoulders all day and night. In time, you will always stand over this acrid pit to take a piss, because, along with everyone else here, you will develop the same siege mentality that is unwilling to risk walking across all that open ground to the back of the FOB just to answer a call of nature from the litres of water you have to drink to ward off dehydration.

In front of your open-air sleeping space are three pits pickaxed into the ground, hiding three mortar tubes.

Just a few metres in front of them is the last internal dividing wall of the compound. There is a large opening off to its left, in front of the main building. You will walk through this every time you go out on patrol, down to the rickety metal gate that opens out onto the road.

Towards the right of this dividing wall, though, beside the burn pit, is another, smaller hole. Squeeze yourself through this and suddenly you find yourself at the top of an earthen bank, with another internal dividing wall running to your left.

The last, front wall of the FOB is 20 metres below and in front of you. As you walk down its bank, the whole Green Zone is stretched out in front of you, before you descend to cover and safety behind the final, front wall.

Here, littered all around you across the baked earth, are desiccated, sun-drying turds – for this corner of the FOB is the ANA's open-air toilet. And when you walk through another hole in the dividing wall to your left, you find yourself in the little area where they sleep and wait and think.

The reason you will come here is to get all the drinking water you need to stay alive in the blistering, soaring Asian heat.

You draw the water out of the well with a bucket on a rope. There is no point wondering what causes it to have such a jaundiced colour and foul taste as you pour it into your water bottles, because the alternative is not drinking and simply dying of thirst.

Your bowel's suspicions will be confirmed when the well water is soon condemned as unfit to drink. But then you are reliant on heli resupply for drinking water, which you will know through experience is not the best state of affairs to be in.

On the plus side, though, the well's water is considered safe enough to wash with. Without any sarcasm it is now absolutely *fantastic* to be able to sprinkle your stinking body with water from a solar shower bag at the end of each day.

The only thing offsetting this simple pleasure is the lingering sense of vulnerability in your mind. The Green Zone, with its myriad of hiding places for the native Taliban, is just metres away from your naked body.

The ANA have their front wall. Just above them, we have ours. But both are equally visible from the multitude of hiding places in the Green Zone that the multitudinous Taliban will fire from.

And the biggest, most visible and inviting target of all is our main eyes and ears into this leafy lair, the main sanger, which as a rule cannot usually see the dark, hidden eyes that can always see us.

The main sanger on top of the main building juts out above us all. On top of its wooden roof is the big metal ball of a mortar-locating radar. But this is not working – and never will be working for all the time you are here – when all those incoming mortars will explode all around you.

So the sun-glinting, inoperative mortar-locating radar ball sitting on the sanger's roof will just act as a beacon for the Taliban homing in on us. In the complete antithesis of its role, it will instead be another aiming aid for the Taliban mortar crews, acting as nothing more than a big, stupid hand waving in the air for us to be attacked, pinpointing our position.

Maybe this is why the sanger's sentries share their sandbag walls with cardboard cut-outs of themselves. These will give the Taliban something else to shoot at, while also giving the impression that there are more people in the FOB than there really are. You laugh when you first see these cut-outs. But on the occasions the two platoons and the ANA go out on the ground, when you will find yourself part of the skeleton crew of twenty left behind to defend the FOB from being overrun by the 'one hundred and fifty plus' Taliban now trying to kill you, it suddenly becomes less funny.

In short, FOB Inkerman is a self-contained, stinking dust bowl with a recent, secondary but apparently important, role as a bullet magnet.

We are told that the FOB was established to take the Taliban's attention off the nearby town of Sangin. After a period of peace at our FOB, this plan will work.

What they had not thought ahead to do when establishing Inkerman, however, was to fortify it. So we will lie down on the same ground to sleep or die, beneath the same sky that bursts with stars or incoming fire.

And though I do not know this yet, in this peaceful little river valley I have begun the process of descending from a position of killing with impunity on a hill, to being on the receiving end of every bit of horror I meted out.

*

Before we received the first intelligence of only '50 plus' Taliban moving into our area, things had been beautifully, boringly, deathly quiet.

Walking out of the gates on patrol, one footstep was crunching in sun-scorched dirt and then the next was suddenly soft and soundless as you stepped into fertile pasture. Dead wilderness and mountains lay behind you as an overgrown greenery of life opened up before you.

Streams and other little man-made waterways criss-crossed the land, nourishing the vegetation flourishing out of it. Vast fields of crops were interspersed with thick tree lines, hiding pretty hamlets of mud-walled homes. The men who lived in them and worked the fields were always friendly with us when we talked to them. Their children were fascinated by us. The boys would gather round us as we walked slowly past, laughing excitedly and jabbering away unintelligibly as they pointed at the heavy, evil-looking equipment we carried in the baking sun. But the girls would only peer round thresholds at us until we caught their shy stares with smiles, whereupon they would scurry inside, presumably to their unseen mothers – also obediently hidden within.

We gave the boys sweets with our clean right hands. And we smiled at them and their smiling fathers as we greeted them with 'salaam' ('peace') and 'tsungye?' ('how are you?').

We smiled because all the while they were around us, this meant that the Taliban were nowhere near any of us. They knew when the Taliban were in their area. Quite understandably, they did not want to be anywhere where we and the Taliban shared the same space. In turn, this meant we could relax just a couple of percentiles as we lumbered our laden-down way through Eden, where death could otherwise come in an instant.

The local men we came across told us that they were doing their best to keep the Taliban out. But if they could not stop them, they said they accepted the fact that they might lose their homes and even their lives – '*Inshallah*' – in the resultant fighting with us.

I couldn't think of anyone back home who would be that fatalistic. But then again, no one back home had lived through years of warfare on their doorstep.

On another day, though, for all we knew, the locals might welcome the Taliban with open arms. For if you are a simple opium farmer just trying to get by and provide for your young family, defenceless and alone out in the middle of nowhere, which side would you voice support for? Right: just the dog with the biggest bark.

I walked past a wizened old gentleman with a white turban on his head, sitting cross-legged under a tree. I said a quiet and respectful, '*Salaam alaykum*.' But his black fissures for eyes merely looked at me. I could not tell if their depths hid resigned acquiescence or hostility. I looked to see if I could tell, but he only looked down slightly before averting his eyes – waiting for me to pass on by.

I'd never felt so much like just another foreign soldier in someone's homeland before.

Later on that patrol, we lay up for the hottest part of the day in the shade of an empty compound. While we drank water, watched arcs of fire and looked at maps, five young boys hung around us for presents and banter through one of our interpreters.

They asked if they could have our watches, pens and water bottles.

We gave them boiled sweets.

One boy was set apart from the others. He was about eight, dark-skinned and dressed in the usual dish-dash and cap like his friends. But while they clamoured like gannets for the sweets we gave them, he was quieter and hung back. I wondered if it was because he was boss-eyed. I remembered how I'd been isolated by a stammer at that age.

But then this boy replied to a question about his family.

He said that his father was head of the Taliban round here – and that the Taliban were ready to die.

Bomber, a corporal from one of the platoons, quickly retorted that, 'We too are ready to die. Fetch your father. Tell him to come here and we'll give him a good kicking.'

But the boy said, 'My father is already dead.'

Later, two of the other boys erupted in a distracting play brawl.

This was cabaret for a few of us not on sentry duty, who thronged around to cheer them on. But it didn't seem like their hearts were really in it until, fight apparently over, one of them turned away. With his opponent's guard now down, the other kid clouted him as hard as he could in the back of the head.

'Ooooh . . .' echoed with smiling disapproval round our ranks.

'Maybe he's the top dog,' someone said. 'He's a dirty, underhand little git.'

So we relax only a couple of percentiles when the locals are around us. And when they are not around us, though nothing has yet happened, we know we cannot afford to relax at all.

The opium fields are beginning to brown and die now. Their bulbous, heroin-laden heads crunch satisfyingly underfoot as we handrail their vast swathes.

But though their chest-high density to one side of you seems to provide cover, you also know that this cover can just as easily hide dark eyes and dark weapons – along with all the hedgerows, tree lines, ditches, streams, walls, compounds, hamlets, bushes, copses, woods, corn fields, maize fields and marijuana fields that you come across.

A bullet can come from 200 metres away across an opium field, or it can come at point-blank range straight into you as you lift yourself, straining, drenched and covered with mud, out of the next stagnant, stinking irrigation ditch.

A live electricity cable lying on the ground, buzzing with lethal current next to your feet, is not a threat. But the absence of any locals for a period of time your sixth sense flags up as 'too long', is.

So you always keep your spacing between the next man and you, so only one of you will need to be shredded by the RPG that may suddenly be fired from out of nowhere into your line.

And especially when it is quiet, your index finger always rests on the safety catch of your weapon, ready to fire in split-second reaction into any threat that may suddenly present itself, throughout each second, every stretching minute and even longer hours that you patrol, sweating pints of body fluids in the searing, claustrophobic heat into heavier and heavier body armour.

Along with this, your mind is also constantly weighing up *what you will do* as soon as the contact with your enemy finally happens.

Scanning for threats and scanning for cover are your constant, unconscious trains of thought. But with mental and physical fatigue, of course, they pervade your conscious – which is also tied up with monitoring the radio net hissing and clicking in one of your ears, with its curt sitreps and orders between the OC's Tac and the two platoons orchestrating all your movements through all the open fields, tree lines, hamlets and rank irrigation ditches – trying to mitigate any threat before it happens.

There is no point just scanning the ground for threats near and far ahead of you, because you know the Taliban will do everything in their power to outflank you. So you scan everything to your left, right and rear too, near and far, searching for any hints of hidden movement creeping up on you, so you might see the sudden death before it happens to you.

Against this backdrop, every man, sweating and breathing heavily beneath his own helmet, looks to where he will take cover if the rounds come down now . . . or now . . . or now . . . until after some hours he suddenly finds himself back in the FOB, in all its mirage of safety.

You look to the woodline immediately to your left as a potential threat, exactly as you do the woodline immediately to your right. If the bullets suddenly come zipping or cracking towards you from one, then it is the other that will afford you some cover to dive into, preserving your life to return fire in kind. One will be life and one will be death. But you will not know which is which until the contact finally happens.

You cannot switch off, ever, because in your mind you know this could be the death of you.

In the normality at home, this constant assessing for lethal threats would be seen as some kind of chronic paranoia. But in the normality you live by minute to minute here, this behaviour is normal to the point that it may be all that will keep you alive. You would be as much a fool as you would be a liability to everyone else around you, if you were not to permanently sear this ingrained behaviour deep into your psyche – if you ever want to make it back Home, where no one will ever truly understand just *how this feels*.

Or, rather, how it does not feel. You dull your nagging, pent-up terror. You bury it deep inside, because with its paralysis, this is an emotion that is of absolutely no use to where you find yourself now. You tell yourself that there will be plenty of time to laugh it all out when you get back home safe, if indeed you make it back home at all – and find yourself capable of laughing about any of this.

These patrols, too, provide the opportunity to view all the 'hearts and minds' reconstruction taking place, ensuring that everything we do here is not just a complete and utter fucking waste of time.

On one of our patrols, we tab several kilometres out through the Green Zone to check in with an irrigation project set up beside the river.

But there is no one there. And there is no sign of any work there even beginning. With this, we see that there is absolutely no 'hearts and minds' reconstruction taking place in this corner of Helmand, as we maintain the security umbrella that is meant to enable this.

Then one day in late July, we received intelligence that '50 plus' Taliban were crossing the river into our area.

*

I did not know Alex Hawkins. And I was not on the patrol in which he was killed.

With Martin still away, Gilly and I took it in turns to stay back at the FOB when the platoons went out. This was so someone out of the 20 left behind at the FOB would be able to call down artillery fire on any Taliban force attacking in their absence. With the increasing numbers of intercepted Taliban radio transmits talking of hitting our FOB, whoever was left at the FOB took my Minimi for extra, close-in firepower.

As it happened, it was Gilly's turn to go out of the gates with the platoons and ANA to investigate the truth of the latest intelligence report, and my turn to stay behind.

While they were out we got a 'Stand to!' with further intelligence that the FOB was going to be hit within ten minutes. But on this day, this did not happen. So while I sat in the main sanger, thanking Christ I had persuaded Captain Featherstone to let Gilly and I set fire to most of Kenya, I only heard the explosion.

The Vector vehicle Alex Hawkins was commanding had driven over a mine. The Taliban had relaid it on one of the few tracks you could get a vehicle down in the Green Zone, just six hundred metres away from the FOB and on the way to the reported 'Taliban river crossing point'.

The IRT Chinook flew in to take his body away along with the other soldiers injured in the blast. I watched one of the escorting Apaches fire two Hellfire missiles into the abandoned, stricken vehicle to deny it to the Taliban.

A blanket of grey smoke was creeping over the Green Zone as the patrol came back into the FOB. The remainder of the FSG drove back in, parking their vehicles just to the left of the main sanger, in the sub-compound where they all slept. They sat in numbed silence against a small wall. But when I overheard the new company sergeant major saying, 'We will remember him,' some of them began to break down in tears. I could not even spare them a glance after this, because even a glance felt like an intrusion into this most private of grief-stricken moments.

And I cannot console any of them, because I do not know any of them, any more than I knew their friend Alex.

When Dan comes up the wooden ladder to the sanger to pick up a sniper scope though, I say, 'How was it out there, Dan?'

And I hate myself for my *stupid fucking question* as soon as it leaves my lips.

Dan is pale, drawn and drained. He shakes his head slowly as he looks down at the ground. 'I was the first team medic on the scene . . . It was horrible,' is all he can say.

A few days later, Dan will come up to me and apologise 'for the other day', saying: 'I was just in a world of my own.'

But I will tell him he has absolutely nothing to be sorry for – because he had absolutely nothing to be sorry for.

This day too, Gilly will open up to me about what he saw. He said the whole area reeked of diesel and that he had never seen someone being given CPR for real before. He had never seen someone die before.

'And what did he die for?' he suddenly spat angrily. 'I still don't know why I'm really here! Your man just died for another patrol based on some fucked-up intelligence from Bastion. I'll be pissed off as fuck if I die out here! If we're here for the reconstruction of this place then why aren't those cunts in here working now – when the locals and us have forced the Taliban out? I guarantee every single day while no work's done, another farmer turns to the Taliban out there – just because we're here.'

Said it all. A 19-year-old gunner had a better grasp of the realities of Afghanistan than most of the government in Whitehall.

And that is no disrespect to you, Gilly. Quite the opposite, mate.

*

Now our rules of engagement have been changed. From far away in London, it has been deigned that for all British Forces in Afghanistan, the war-fighting rules of 429 Alpha should be replaced by the White Card rules of engagement under which we conducted peacekeeping in Iraq.

We wonder how long it will be until the Taliban work out that in effect, with the realities of the Green Zone, we can now only shoot at them after they first shoot at us – and after they have been afforded all the space and time in the world to get themselves into position to do so.

Now, with any 'response' we make to such actions required to be 'proportionate', we fear that the lack of any Taliban Air Force may mitigate the biggest factor in offsetting our numerical disadvantage against them: the application of US air power.

As our JTAC, Alex rages: 'It's just going to put boys in body bags!'

With a sick feeling we swallow down in our stomachs, sitting and smoking with scowls on the hard, stony ground in our unfortified FOB, no one disagrees with him.

There is no one here to tell the Taliban that they too should now be moving from war-fighting to peacekeeping.

*

For some days after Alex Hawkins was killed, quiet returned to our area.

Our patrols into the local area continued as usual. But this quiet was always underpinned by a constant quiet tension while we waited for the Taliban to make their next move.

Martin is flown in. It is so good to see my friend again. He brings the morale boost of post and a big, confident grin with him.

After doing his back in hauling himself out of one too many ditches, Captain Featherstone is flown out. I am ambivalent about him leaving.

And then it was 1 August. And as this day was 'Minden Day', it was also declared a 'no patrols day'.

Chads had told me about the Battle of Minden while I was up on the hill with him. It had happened long before the invention of radios. He told me the forefathers of his regiment had received a relayed order to 'attack' French forces that vastly outnumbered them when the order was meant to have been 'withdraw'.

The soldiers picked flowers from the ground before they attacked. They put them in their headgear – one red flower in front of one yellow. It was to be 'blood before dishonour'.

And in the kind of history that a regiment seizes on, these forefathers advanced straight into the jaws of cavalry, artillery and then infantry.

And they won the day, as they won themselves immortality in the annals of their regiment. Every one of C Company's soldiers had the red and yellow 'Minden Flash' sewn to his shirt arm.

Chads had it tattooed to his flesh.

Here in Afghanistan, we got a whole day off from patrolling to commemorate the event.

In the evening, and as a form of fireworks display, the C Company OC and its new company sergeant major got on our mortar tubes and fired six illum in tandem out into the Green Zone.

Eerie, lengthening shadows danced through the trees outside our FOB as the parachute flares descended. When they went out, everything was plunged back into darkness.

*

C Company had a new company sergeant major (CSM) after the last one blew himself up firing some dodgy ordnance. I did not know the last one, but I liked the new one. His name was Terry, and he made a point of finding out all our first names in the FST before our first patrol together.

'All squared, Jake?' he asked, as Martin did the last checks to the radio on my back.

'Yes, Sir.'

'Good,' he replied, with a friendly wink.

Among all the mental steeling and mental tunnel vision of a patrol preparing to go into the Green Zone, tiny, human touches like this from our leaders made all the difference.

Now C Company also had a new overall leader. After Minden Day, the OC had flown out for his two weeks' R & R, so for the next two weeks we would be led by the Company 2IC, Captain Dave Hicks, who had taken such a benevolent interest in our welfare while we were on top of the hill.

I respected the OC deeply, but I respect Dave Hicks even more. In the evenings, he sits and smokes and chats with the four of us from the FST as much as he does with his C Company boys. And with all the time he spends with everyone under him, I see that he clearly cares deeply for those for whom he is responsible.

I think he is a dying breed of officer.

And the depth of his concern for his men would resonate all the deeper with me, against the backdrop of what was now coming straight at us.

The latest intelligence reported that a further '100 plus' Taliban had crossed the river to join the 50 already in our area, armed with mortars, rockets, RPGs, PKMs, AKs – and SPG-9s.

The SPG-9 is a tripod-mounted 'recoilless rifle'. It fires rocket-propelled, armour-piercing projectiles designed to take out tanks.

But we do not have tanks. And as much as we know that an RPG will have a job penetrating the bizarrely resilient mud walls found on all compounds here, we know that an armour-piercing SPG-9 round will blast straight through them. And mud walls are, of course, no defence against mortars and rockets, which will just plummet from the sky above to land among us.

We have no Hesco (sand-filled, improvised fortifying walls) at FOB Inkerman. Out in the open and exposed, we sleep and wait and think up against the compound's mud walls, for these mud walls are our only cover and protection. And up in the main sanger, the only protection is a thin wall of sandbags.

Before you go to sleep on the sharp, stony ground, there is no point thinking how even these mud walls may now be useless against the threat gathering somewhere just beyond them. Because as you lie down to rest before tomorrow's patrol, there is nothing you can do about it at that moment, before this threat finally reveals itself to all of you.

There is no point dwelling on how the now 'one hundred and fifty plus' Taliban moving towards you will outnumber you all at least three to one out on the ground. Because, lying there on that sharp, stony ground in the FOB, there is nothing you can do about that, either.

Even with your day off, you are too tired to do anything other than slip away into sleep.

*

I wasn't sure whether to count the ANA in my calculations of hostiles' versus friendlies' strengths. The platoon of them was on our side, I was fairly sure, but their combat effectiveness was openly up for debate among us.

Martin said he didn't trust them as far as he could throw them; Gilly wanted to give them the benefit of the doubt. With a shrug of his shoulders and a shake of his head, Alex was as ambivalent about them as I was uncertain of them.

Their Grenadier Guard, Operational Mentor Liaison Team

(OMLT) handlers, however, appeared to be just plain 'threaders' with them.

The ANA were a friendly enough bunch; I even had a bit of rapport going with some of them, as they were often behind me on patrol, tagging along behind the OC's Tac. 'IED,' I would say to them, as every Brit soldier did his personal five- and twenty-metre check of the ground around himself on longer stops.

I always said it because as much as they smiled and nodded in complete understanding of the acronym for 'improvised explosive device', the concept of 'fives and twenties' seemed completely beyond them.

It didn't get much better when the Brit soldiers in front of them went down on one knee or lay down in cover for extended stops – observing alternate, interlocking arcs of fire in herringbone formation. While we watched and waited, now ever alert, they amused themselves by throwing stones at frogs, or taking mobile-phone calls, or sitting down to chat among themselves – or just lying down for a quick rest.

It was almost entertaining watching their OMLT handlers stifling heart attacks as they tried to control them. But when the ANA are all that stands between you and a rear attack by the Taliban, you find yourself smiling less often.

On one patrol, one of the ANA simply went missing, sparking alarm in the OMLT guys. But after ten minutes he was seen tagging along with one of the platoons up ahead. It turned out he just wanted to find a better crossing point over a stream, where he needn't get his feet wet.

The OMLT sergeant shouted across to him: 'Come here! . . . *Come the fuck here!*'

But the ANA soldier only smiled blissfully, sitting down on the ground as he waited for the rest of his buddies to catch up with him.

The OMLT sergeant looked like a broken man after this patrol. 'Thank God I'm out of here tomorrow,' he vented with an exasperated gush of air to me, as we all unloaded our weapons back at the FOB.

Lucky bastard, I thought.

But then I hadn't been dealing with soldiers who were 'almost constantly off their heads on weed'.

'What?'

'They told me it makes them fight better,' he said resignedly, before lighting another cigarette with yellow-stained fingers.

Probably as he did, I choose not to dwell on how, hand-in-hand with all the 'hearts and minds' reconstruction taking place here, it is the professionalism of these ANA soldiers that will dictate when all ISAF coalition soldiers will finally leave this country. Like the sergeant and everyone else here, I just look forward to the end of my tour.

You have to believe that you will make it.

*

The ANA had some use. They were useful for conferring some sense of legitimacy upon us in the locals' eyes.

But through the peace of this beautiful back end of paradise, we were seeing more and more huddles of black-clad men, openly staring at us with hate as we filed along the other side of gently babbling streams.

And this Eden is so painfully, idyllically beautiful. On a water stop, Alex remarks that one hamlet we had passed through – shaded by weeping trees, wreathed in delicate flowers and crowned with lamenting birdsong – would be a runner in his books for this year's 'Afghanistan in Bloom' award.

'Only because you haven't blown it up yet,' a C Company soldier quips back.

Alex does not laugh as much as everyone else at this. And I stop laughing when I see the look he hides in his eyes.

Even the ANA falls silent when we walk past yet another group of sullen, silent men of fighting age.

Our entourage of children have sidled away. All the workers in the fields have disappeared. And lounging on the opposite bank of the stream that our sand-coloured snake files silently along are seven dark-bearded men, all dressed in black.

They watch us intently and silently, with looks as black as the clothes they are uniformly dressed in. They look at us like we are the serpent in their Garden, cursed above all. We are the hated infidel in their Home.

You know in your gut they are Taliban, but there is nothing you can do. They are not armed, and they are doing nothing but innocently looking at you with hate.

You see if you can get a rise out of them with a smile and a cheeky 'salaam alaykum'. But they just keep on glaring at you in silence.

So all you can do is wait for when they do, finally, act.

We know how they terrorise men to fight for them, how they subjugate and stone women to death, how they beat children and torture their captives to death. Our intelligence has told us; the locals have told us.

And they want to kill us. So we want to fight them.

But I never would see a man I could point to and say without any doubt to any lawyer hovering in my subconscious, 'Taliban', until I looked down at three of them lying like waxworks in front of me.

I never saw the dark figures who hid themselves so well, in this ground they knew so well.

I never saw these unseen men who fired Kalashnikov rounds at us so close there were no buzzing zips in my ears, only the supersonic *crack-crack-crack* of bullets breaking the sound barrier beside my face.

Now Eden is Hell.

Now the chest-high poppy and marijuana fields hide the attacking Taliban as they creep nearer still to you.

Now the mud walls in the pretty hamlets are used as cover to fire back at your enemy as they crouch behind the next wall.

Birdsong is drowned out with gunfire and screams. Leaves fall down on you like confetti as incoming supersonic rounds crack into the branches above your head. In the streams that provide lifeblood to those crops collapsing the veins of London, you wade waist-deep through reddening water and mud to take cover – and outmanoeuvre – and kill.

But now the contact is finally happening – now you know from betraying puffs of smoke what tree line the Kalashnikovs are being fired from – now you know which bit of cover to take cover behind – it is just a relief. Now you are dealing with the known, as opposed to the ever-coming unknown.

And being so close to death – with those *cracks* coming so close to you – you suddenly find that you have never felt so *alive*.

You prostrate yourself behind the tiny dirt bank in front of you with Ian the medic, the top of it only centimetres above the rims of your helmets. And when a burst of incoming bullets sends clouds of dust into the air between the two of you – straight into the inches between your two minds, both your synapses firing in sensory overload – you cannot help but belly-laugh as you call across to him, 'Think you might want to get a bit lower, Ian!'

As alive in the pure *life* of the moment as you are, he laughs through all the snapping *cracks* and spatters of kicked-up dirt with a 'Fucking hell!' and a grin as wide as your own.

All this is fun while it happens, while it is no one but the enemy who dies. But when it is over, you find that your adrenalin dies along with the sheer thrill of this living *second by second*.

And in this numb afterwards, when you may or may not find yourself staring down at a Taliban corpse in a ditch, you suddenly find yourself going back to waiting for the unknown again, with all your deadened emotions and hyper-vigilant senses.

The adrenalin thrill that had fired life back into you drains away. There is nothing left behind in its wake. And when your dead eyes do look into those of a Taliban corpse – dead blood draining into muddy water – you find yourself feeling: absolutely nothing.

Nothing, other than a dim awareness that this life is now normal, in all its brutal, horrific simplicity – and an even dimmer understanding that no one will ever understand this back home, when the time comes to bring this normality back with you.

At that defining moment, you feel more in common with the corpse of this enemy than with anyone back home.

Your home here is now fulfilling its role as a bullet magnet.

C Company's routine now becomes a daily grind of: eat, sleep, walk out of the gates, get contacted, walk back in the gates, eat, sleep – and repeat.

But to liven up our downtimes back in the FOB, the Taliban fire RPGs, rockets and mortars into the space within our walls. And they fire anti-tank SPG-9s straight through them.

At first they do this every few days. But then these attacks come every other day, before increasing to every day – and then twice a day.

Adrenalin overtakes fear in all these moments. But in the body's chemical low afterwards, exhaustion and emotional walling-off always follow.

'I almost shat,' would be how Ian later described the contact that had he and I pressing all the dust of ourselves closer into the Afghan dust.

He just seemed very tired.

*

There is the picture of a Royal Signals sergeant in one of the week-old papers lying around the FOB. The article below this picture says he was killed by a rocket-propelled grenade. But there is nothing unusual about this, until Martin says that we knew him.

'Baz,' he asserts. 'He was the LEWT sergeant up on the hill for a while – when we took over from the marines. For the first few weeks

. . . Neither of you remember him, do you? . . . It's definitely Baz.'

Gilly and I sift our brains as the orange tips of our cigarettes flare and die in the darkness. But neither of us can remember Baz.

Martin shines a torch on the paper to show us the man's face again. But we still cannot remember him.

I mean, I can remember someone. But I cannot recall his name, or his face, or anything he said or did. I should remember him. I want to. But I just can't.

Later, as I turn over on the ground to sleep, I feel this gnawing at me. Of all the people who should remember him, it should be those he served with.

But my mind is an empty blank. My ears still ring from the contact earlier that day. And when I close my eyes, I see the dead Taliban looking inside me.

*

Why Gilly was flown out, I do not know. We were told he was needed to help stag on the radios at the Fire Planning Cell (FPC). But quite how these signallers, based back in the safety of Bastion, were in greater need of manpower than our fast-dwindling team at Inkerman was utterly beyond us. Gilly was pissed-off as fuck. And with his departure, there were now only two of our original FST of five left to go out on the ground.

Out of Alex, Martin and me, someone always has to stay behind at the FOB with my Minimi to defend it with artillery, should the now revised estimate of '200 plus' Taliban bypass the platoons out on the ground and seek to overrun the 20 of us left behind each time at the FOB. And this person should either be me or Martin, because only Alex is qualified to call in the game-changing airstrikes that can tip the balance in the platoons' favour out on the ground.

But now Alex can barely hobble metres, let alone strap all his equipment to himself and tab, run, crawl and wade through kilometres of Green Zone. His ankle is grotesquely swollen after going over on it during the last patrol. For all we know, it is broken. But what all of us definitely do know is that he is now going to be staying behind at the FOB while Martin and I go out on the ground.

In fact, with Alex now due to be MedEvac'd too, our FST is fast ceasing to exist. Now something only need happen to me or Martin to turn our formerly five-man FST into a one-man FST out on the ground. As Martin is far better qualified at calling in artillery than me, I am mindful that it will be best if this happens to me.

But before a replacement can be flown in for Alex – and indeed a full 'relief in place' for our skeleton crew – he will stay back at the FOB for defence and to relay and coordinate any airstrikes we call for.

We have to make do.

But on the night of 9 August, it was not just the lack of a JTAC on the ground that was concerning Dave Hicks.

He sat under our parachute canvas, sharing cigarettes and thoughts with us before the pre-dawn, long-range patrol in just a few hours' time. He didn't have to do this, but he did it all the same – as he did with everyone he trod the same earth with. It was the small, human touches like this that made me like the 2IC so much.

He made us laugh and feel at ease – as much as anyone could. And in this eased atmosphere, where you called him 'Sir' out of affection as much as all your respect, the three of you in the FST find yourselves discussing with him the convoluted way in which Martin or I will radio any requests for airstrikes back to Alex in the FOB, who will then relay them in turn to the attacking fast air.

But through your explanation of how this will 'work' out in the Green Zone – under fire – you also find yourself voicing tentative, unavoidable misgivings about this plan.

Of course, the 2IC already knew this.

In fact, he came straight out with it and told us that he had tried to get the patrol canned. He said that he had pointed out to Bastion the sheer distance we would have to go on foot the next day, with no JTAC and no FSG out on the ground, no doctor back at the unfortified, undermanned FOB and no credible medical evacuation plan – short, that is, of 'extracting' ourselves, along with our casualties, from the contact 'with minimum force' as directed by Bastion and then 'securing' a 'safe' area somewhere in the Green Zone for the IRT Chinook to land in. But above all, he said that he had pointed out the exhausted state of his men and their depleted numbers in comparison to the outnumbering Taliban.

'They just told me to get on with it,' he said quietly.

And God, I felt for him. As soldiers who were not from his regiment, I almost had the impression he was confiding in us.

We nodded quietly in turn, in much the same way that I imagined he had done on the radio to his superiors. There was no way he could be that honest with all those young lads in the platoons, though.

'How are the boys . . . mentally?' Alex asked him.

'OK,' he replied quietly. 'Some of them are a bit . . .'

Nothing more needed to be said.

With this, it was time for him to buoy their morale.

'We've got some very tired 19-year-olds here,' he said, before walking away into the darkness. I could hear the wan smile in his voice. But there was no mistaking the traces of fatigue and sadness he carried in it too.

There walked the finest of men, whose complete compassion for his soldiers, moral courage to stand up to his superiors and honour-bound commitment to duty made him stand out head and shoulders as an officer I would follow into the guts of hell – should he ask me to go there with him.

And that is exactly where we did go.

*

The ANA refused to go out with us in the morning. We did not know if they knew something we did not. Maybe they were just acting on the same sense of foreboding we all shared. I never would find out.

And so it was that 40 British soldiers walked out of the front gate of Forward Operating Base Inkerman in the dark, early hours of 10 August.

The patrol's objective was to check up on a riverside 'irrigation project' several kilometres away. But no one thought we would get that far – and not only because we had also been tasked with patrolling through a village called Regay en route.

The glimmering fingers of dawn were just reaching for us as we moved into the fields near the village outskirts. Tired, straining eyes that had grown accustomed to silhouettes were now beginning to see colours: the brown dirt and the green foliage, the dull metal grey of weapons held with sweating hands and the angry scarlet now spilling into the sky above the man you have been religiously keeping in eyeshot.

Sweating. Still sweating in the already rising heat. Always sweating into that close, heavy body armour, pulled tighter still to your body by the weight of all your litres of water and all your hundreds of rounds of ammunition and all the weight of the radio on your back. Your sweating hands hold the heavy rifle that is nothing other than life itself. Beneath the close, heavy helmet clamped to your head with the radio headset strapped to one of your ears, sweat rolls down to sting your eyes. If you do not wipe this sweat from your eyes with the sweat rag tied to your chest, it is like trying to see through tears.

And now – there – just off in the distance in Regay – two bursts of automatic gunfire.

You all go down on one knee. But through the ringing in your ears that will now never go away, there is only silence.

You do not know that these bursts are the Taliban's signal for 'Stand to'.

But as you slowly, silently, begin to filter into the village, there is no mistaking the combat indicators now screaming at your brain.

The village is completely deserted. Every single compound gate and door we pass has been padlocked shut from the outside. There isn't even any sign of livestock. Even the stream flowing to your right – shrouded in trees – is silent.

With hunched shoulders and sweaty fingertips rooted to the safety catches of your weapons, you gravitate as one towards the mud wall to your left – it seems to provide cover from that direction – until you realise someone only has to lob a grenade over the top of it. So now the only sound you can hear is you breathing – and the sound of everyone in your line now making absolutely no sound at all.

You know this is going to be bad.

Then, from out of all that dripping silence – with absolutely no warning and all the warning in the world – it happens.

A wall of noise suddenly hits you from your left. At first the only sound is of every assault rifle the Taliban have in their possession opening up on you. There are no high-pitched buzzes of bullets whizzing lazily past you. Against the background of their firing, there are only the *cracks* and *snaps* of the bullets breaking the sound barrier beside you.

But then the wall you take cover behind punches against your body as the first of the RPGs explodes against its other side. In the instant it hits, you feel the concussive shockwave of the high-explosive blast pummelling every fibre of your being, milliseconds before the thunderclap of its explosion pounds your eardrums. In that swirling instant knocking you out of this world, choking and blinding dust erupts from the wall to engulf you.

But with my radio tuned to the patrol net, I crawl to form up on Martin, whose radio is tuned to the mortar net back to the FOB, who is forming up on the 2IC, who in turn is desperately trying to wrest back control of the situation on the radio and find out exactly where the enemy is as the platoons begin frantically trying to get some rounds down in reply.

Some metres ahead of me, I hear a scream through the noise. I think it says '*fuckers*' or '*fire*', but I really cannot tell as it is like no scream I have ever heard before. It just sounds like some kind of rage-driven, grief-stricken bellow from the depths of someone's soul.

Which I think is exactly what it was.

The patrol net suddenly erupts with the call: 'Man down! Man down!'

And it is now that everyone's radios start to pack up.

I hear garbled half-transmissions – and then nothing at all. The 2IC has to get his signaller to switch his radio on and off to talk, as Martin tries to 'ber' the radio on my back, clearing its internal electronic buffer.

But Martin's attempts to get through to Alex at the FOB are at best intermittent too. And while all this is going on, the Taliban carries on firing everything they have at us – and just ahead of our wall, out in that open, is a casualty.

Then the 2IC's confident voice fires back into life in my ear. 'What's the status of that casualty, over?'

And, shouting over the incoming *cracks* into my radio headset, comes the simple, flat answer.

'He's dead.'

Just ahead of me, I see the 2IC's eyes close for a second.

'He's dead . . . He's dead, over,' repeats the platoon commander.

Beside me, the CSM immediately jumps down the net at him: 'All right, we got it! Just shut the fuck up, all right?'

As much as the platoon commander would have been understandably unsure that his first casualty status had been received – retransmitting to make sure – I have no doubt that the CSM was thinking of everyone's morale when he shut him up: because, for everyone listening on the patrol net, the news of our dead hits like a hammer blow.

'What's going on, Jake?' Martin shouts, turning to me with wide eyes.

'One dead, mate.'

'Fuck . . .'

Ian the medic immediately jumps into the cover of the stream to our right and begins wading off to see if he can somehow get to the casualty.

I stoop-run over to the 2IC to get an enemy grid we can begin firing mortars into.

But: 'I've just lost a man,' he says, looking up to me in the one fleeting and heartbreaking moment of human reaction any of us have any time for here. And I feel for him so much again, for it's now completely up to him – suddenly all on his own – to get the rest of us out of this mess.

'I'm sorry, Sir . . . What's the enemy grid – for the mortars?'

I scrawl it down on my notepad as I shout over the cracks and explosions to read it back to him. Then I crouch-run back to Del, the C Company MFC lying flat on his back against the wall, giving him the grid so the FOB's mortars can begin killing those bastards.

Scrambling along the ground as I am, he motions for me to get down even lower as he calls in the mortar-fire mission. As soon as he finishes, he tells me why.

'Something just came through that wall and missed your head by a foot, Jake!' he shouts over the din.

But then we both have to haul ourselves up to peer through these holes being steadily made in our wall, so we can spot where our mortars are landing.

There is so much dust being thrown up, though – hanging heavily all around us in the breezeless air – that we cannot see jack shit. And as soon as we hear the deafening *crump* . . . *crump-crump* of our mortars exploding as they land, we have to 'check fire' and stop them – because under our new White Card rules of engagement, we are forbidden to fire any ordnance if we can't see exactly where it is going.

The only thing I did see through all the swirling dust beyond that hole was an RPG exploding short of our wall.

Up ahead of us, some of 11 Platoon now detonate a bar mine to gain access to the cover of a compound – adding even more dust to swirl around us.

Now the net is filling with screaming reports of the Taliban outflanking us to the north, firing into us at right angles to the barrage that continues to pin us down from the other side of our west-facing wall.

They want to kill all of us.

But 11 Platoon is pinned down and completely embroiled in just trying to get any fire back down to the west. In fact, ahead of us, just past where our wall ends, many of them are completely pinned down in the open. Burning-red tracer fire zips and cracks all around them with puffs of dust, and for all these men in the midst of all this, returning any kind of fire is impossible. They can't even crawl into better cover, let alone poke their heads up to return fire. All they can do is try to make themselves as small as possible, behind what bumps and into what depressions they can find out in the open ground.

10 Platoon is in the north-flowing stream beside our wall. Now the 2IC pushes them up along its length, behind the pinned-down 11 Platoon, committing them to our northern flank to head off the Taliban trying to outflank us. They crouch for cover in the dark water as they wade past us, one by one. Among them I see Dan and his sniper rifle. But this isn't any time to exchange words. His face is sheet white.

Now every resource that C Company possesses has been committed. But the weight of the incoming, outnumbering Taliban fire is so heavy that we are barely holding our own, let alone 'winning the firefight' and so enabling us to extract our men pinned down in the open – and our dead.

'We need to get out of here, Dave,' Martin says urgently to the 2IC.

'I know,' he replies – while simultaneously listening to all the radio traffic I too can hear against all the background noise of the Taliban doing everything they possibly can to fuck all of us up.

We are only going to get out of here if the Taliban gun group to our west, pinning our boys down in the open, just fucks off. But, short of an act of God, there is no sign of this ever happening.

Another RPG hits our wall, sending more dust billowing over us. The 2IC lights a cigarette while listening to the latest from 10 Platoon.

His fingers do not shake.

Now, our peacekeeping rules of fucking engagement can take a running, fucking jump – because this is now just a fight for our lives.

'Call in the air,' he says to Martin.

'Yes, Sir!' Martin replies, with a spreading grin.

Martin confirms the grid of the Taliban position to our west – in the fuck-all visibility, it is all we have to go on. Then he relays this grid back to Alex at the FOB.

As Martin does this, I turn around and point my rifle back the way we came in. Because if the Taliban flanking manoeuvre to the north is just a feint to hide their real outflanking move – cutting off our 'cleared' route into Regay from the south – then it will now only be us few men in the OC's Tac who will be fighting it off.

We wait for eternities of short minutes for the fast air to come screaming in.

The RPGs keep exploding against our crumbling wall. We can

hardly see for the dust. And snapping over our heads is the constant *crack-crack-crack* of Taliban suppressing fire, in what I can only hope to look back on as a well-planned, well-executed Taliban ambush, using overwhelming force and overwhelming numbers.

While I listen to the shouts and calls of frightened, angry men in my ears, with shot-off leaves showering down on me from Kalashnikov rounds, I wait for the first Taliban to show himself round the edge of the wall I point my rifle down.

Then I'll blow that fucking cunt's head off.

But now the air is coming in. Martin shouts: 'It's two F-15s!'

For all I know, they are the same guys who swooped in for that first contact up on the hill all those long, distant months ago. But now we know what it feels like to be on the receiving end of their wrath.

The air that we choke through is so thick with dust that we cannot see them. But, oh God, we hear them – and we feel them.

The ground shakes beneath my feet as the force of the strafing cannon rounds hit. The crackling roar of their impacts merge as one into the thunderous roar of the F-15 firing this death from above. Within a second of all of this, the aircraft is shooting over our heads – the hot-spitting roar of its jets filling the dust around us with screaming, vibrating noise – which you feel in every fibre of your frail mortal body as nothing other than the Wrath of God.

And then for one sudden second, everything falls quiet.

You can hear the ringing in your ears.

But as soon as this moment happens, it passes. And in the next, you look down at the dirt in disbelief at what is now being screamed into the radio.

'Check fire on the air! Man down! Man down!'

*

The contact is over.

The Taliban melted silently away under the might of US air power.

After using this 'minimum force', we now only have to extract ourselves out of Regay to a 'safe place' elsewhere in the Green Zone so that the lone IRT Chinook can come in to pick up our casualties.

11 Platoon are first to slowly file past us on the wall, heading back out the way we came into the village. At the head of their procession are the solemn-faced men on point. And just behind them are the six carrying the field stretcher.

On it is the motionless figure of a young man. He wears the same desert boots and combat trousers as the rest of us, and his hands wear the same fingerless combat gloves.

But, unlike us, he has been stripped to the waist. His hands rest on top of the flawless skin of his naked chest. And the watch he still wears on his wrist rests beside a heart that no longer beats.

You cannot see his face. His whole head has been tenderly wrapped in the swaddling of many field dressings. They hide the bullet wound that ended his young life.

His name is Tony Rawson. He was an always friendly fair-haired private in 11 Platoon.

And now he is going Home.

Behind him is another casualty. But he is walking. He has a field dressing tied round one side of his face. This stops the bleeding from the shrapnel still lodged there from the F-15, after it opened fire to save the rest of us.

Ian the medic walks behind him. And while we wait for the last of 11 Platoon to silently file past, he slumps down against the wall beside me. He has done everything he can for the walking wounded, after being able to do nothing to save Tony Rawson. With his silence and downcast eyes, I see how this cuts him so deeply inside.

I light a cigarette in my mouth and pass it to him. He gives me a wan smile of thanks as his fingers take it, lifting it to his own lips for a long, shaking drag.

We sit there for a few moments until we see the first man from 10 Platoon. Then the OC's Tac plugs the gap again between the two platoons, as we all walk out as one into the fields.

We put about a kilometre between us and the village before setting up in all-round defence. And then we wait, watching our arcs in the quiet 15 minutes it takes the IRT Chinook to reach us.

When we hear it approaching, an orange smoke grenade is popped to show the pilot where to land. With the scream of turbines and *whump* of rotor blades, it flares to earth in the long grass within the middle of our circle.

High above it, two Apache gunships fuss over all of us.

And as Tony Rawson is being carried up the back ramp of the Chinook, the Taliban that have been following us all this time open fire.

Past the scream of the Chinook's turbines just behind you, you cannot hear the rounds that they fire. But you see the mortar round that explodes a hundred metres short of its now straining-to-leave target – just beyond the low mud wall you look over with the telescopic sight of your rifle.

But you cannot see the men that fire it. You cannot see any movement or any puffs of smoke in that myriad of tree lines you scour with your weapon's eye.

When the Chinook lifts off, blasting you with flying dirt in its wake, the two Apaches that stay behind to help you cannot see these men either.

But, of course, the Taliban can see these two Apaches, as plain as we can, up in that wide-open sky. And so, of course, the Taliban cease the firing that will betray their positions. And they just melt away once more – back off into the green.

They have only to wait until we are alone again.

*

When we get back to the FOB, the first man of the new FST being flown in piecemeal to replace us is there waiting.

It is only ten in the morning when we get back, but neither Martin nor I have any energy left to make Maggy feel properly at home.

We lay down our weapons. We take off our helmets. We undo the Velcro of our wringing-wet body armour and pull it off past our heads. And then we collapse into our pits, with leaden, spinning heads already slipping towards unconsciousness.

The numbing, peaceful ringing in my ears muffles the sounds of the others as they too lie down to leave this world. We all ignore the massive chunk now taken out of our front wall, with the Green Zone now overlooking all of us.

The only words I hear before I let go of the world belong to Del, lying in his pit.

'That was horrible.'

We'll talk to Maggy when it gets too hot to sleep. Then we'll lay to rest the grating, wide-eyed alarm with which he looks at us.

Not now.

Now I just need the world to go away.

*

When the sun rising to its zenith made sleeping impossible, Martin, Alex and I sat down with Maggy to eat lunch out of our aluminium bags.

We talk him through our routine.

Then the 2IC comes over to us to chat and smoke. He tells us he has just written a newspaper obituary for Tony Rawson, before emailing it over to Bastion. As our leader, he always has to be strong for us all, but we can all tell how deeply this hurt him. Just in terms of the number of fags he now smokes, his smoking habit has been increasing to on a par with mine.

He also tells us that the F-15 pilot had already sent an apology for the blue on blue. But from where we sit, there is no need for any apology from this gallant knight of the air. All he had to go on was a grid reference. Through all that dust obscuring the battlefield below, by committing himself to his charge he had done nothing other than save our young lives.

Godspeed, mate.

We discuss the morning's contact. And when this discussion is over, I share cigarettes with Maggy as I try to put him at ease about his new home. But I do not know why I do this, because I am not even fooling myself as I tell him that things 'aren't that bad'.

I do not know what the next day will bring.

And in the gathering twilight of this day, the Taliban attack our FOB again.

I poke my weapon through a hole in our wall. Before I fire, I see arcs of dancing, red tracer rounds zipping back and forth through the failing light. In between all these bursts of fire, I sometimes hear the *whoosh* of an RPG shooting over our heads before it explodes somewhere in the back of our FOB.

And there is no point thinking how an SPG-9 will cut straight through the mud wall directly to my front, shredding me into pulp.

There is nothing else I can do while I wait for this to happen but add my tracer rounds to everyone else's.

*

Later that night, I write down in my diary exactly what happened that day – as I always force myself to do at the end of every day.

I even write about the Javelin missile whose first-stage rocket motor had fired, propelling it into the air away from the main sanger.

Maggy said afterwards that he had never seen one fire before. But none of us had ever seen one like this before. The Javelin's second-stage rocket motor failed to fire. And without anything to propel it, the gleaming silver missile dropped like a stone onto the ground beside us, its warhead screaming and whining as it dutifully rolled in slow motion . . . straight into our mortars' 'misfire pit'.

'Fucking *RUN!*' echoed in screams down our wall. And after we had all sprinted away to jump like lemmings into the burn pit – and half of FOB Inkerman hadn't been blown apart by the resulting, mother of all chain-reaction explosions from one Javelin missile and thirty mortar bombs – we even got to see the breathless, giggling side to this running for our lives.

But when I finish recalling and writing about this, I rejoin everyone else in the blackness of sleep.

*

My eyelids are blinking open.

Sunlight.

'You all right, Jake? You were making some weird-arsed sounds in there.'

Martin's Hampshire accent brings the canvas hanging limply over our sleeping area into focus, and I turn my head to him.

He is sitting on his sleeping mat, looking quizzically at me through my mosquito net, spoon in one hand and a bag of what smells like sausage and beans open in the other.

'Probably just a bad dream, mate.'

I am still summoning the energy to get up.

Martin nods slowly in empathy while stirring his breakfast.

'Par for the course now, isn't it?'

'Aye . . . Good morning, anyway.'

'Good morning indeed, old man,' he replies, smiling. His eyes are dark ringed. They betray the strain and his own fitful night.

But, squaddie psychoanalytical conversation completed for the day, I unzip the mossie net, pull on some shorts, fix the Velcro across my sandals and pick myself up off the ground to face the day.

Scratching my beard, I wander over to the burn pit to have a piss. There is no way I am going to expose myself walking across all that wide open just to take a piss in that landing ground for RPGs. The fuel tanker beside our official toilet facilities now has a large hole in it from the attack last night. We think it was from an SPG-9. How the whole thing didn't blow up in some Hollywood-esque fireball, taking our shitters with it, is completely beyond us.

Along with absolutely everyone else who now takes the 25-metre walk to piss in the burn pit as opposed to the 150 metres to the urinal tubes, my reasoning is not only based on laziness. Considering the Taliban's now daily predilection for firing everything they have at us, whenever they feel like it, these distances out in the open are now measured in miles in our minds.

And one now instantly and automatically associates loud bangs with lethality.

I am standing over the burn pit, mid-stream, when a loud *pop!* sounds off right in front of me. In the instant it happens, my heart freezes over and I yelp out loud, twisting down and away from the sound, but too late.

Standing out in the open wearing just a pair of shorts with your dick hanging out is not the best way to face a Taliban mortar.

I can feel warm sticky liquid all down my front. I have to force myself to look down.

But the stuff I'm spattered with is brown. And it smells like treacle pudding.

I am spattered head to foot in charred treacle pudding. The smouldering heat must have set off a tin of someone's unwanted meal.

'You all right, Jake?' Martin calls out in alarm.

All I have to do is turn round. And then the wide-eyed, anticipatory silence of the mortar boys turns into cackles of laughter as I present my new look to them. Martin can't help but laugh too.

But I am not happy: a split second of primeval, bowel-liquidising fear – and now with my heart still trying to find a regular beat, I am being laughed at.

By reason of necessity and obvious nature, the Army tends to instil a fight, not flight, response in its soldiers. A sudden, terrifying threat to your person can instantly kick off corresponding levels of rage and aggression against what caused it. Of course, it is right and good to repress and control this aggression, though. Today's Army wants methodical killers, not berserkers.

So I cannot scream at them. And as Martin walks towards me, now quiet, I find my anger dissipating into gladness that they've been able to laugh at something this morning.

We need a bloody laugh.

Martin puts a hand gently on my shoulder. 'Come on, mate,' he says soothingly. 'Get yourself away and I'll put some food on for you.'

Shaking my head, then smiling and nodding in thanks to him, I start over to get my shower bag.

'You'll bring pudding, yeah?' he calls after me.

'Piss off.'

*

An Afghan soldier is helping me fill my shower bag from the well. I think he has taken pity on my appearance. After I haul up the bucket, I kneel on the ground and hold open the shower bag for him to begin pouring in a bucketful. I am wondering, again, just what the hell causes this water to be so *yellow*, when it happens.

The loud *whoosh* of a rocket-propelled grenade zooms over our heads, quickly followed by an explosion towards the rear of the FOB.

There are distant screams of 'Stand to!' – and I am sprinting back up to our admin area, shower bag long discarded. Beside my bed-space, I hear another explosion just forward of the ANA compound as I pull the heavy body armour over my head. Now, helmet on, I hear the cracks of incoming small-arms fire as I grab my weapon and run over to our 'stand to' position on the wall.

Well, that's just fan-fucking-tastic.

All the firing holes through the wall are now taken, and all that's left is a little viewing hole about head height. I'm looking at being a spare part in this.

Another RPG hits our wall. As usual, I feel the thump in every bone of my body before the thunderclap and dust engulf me.

Now our sangers are beginning to fire back, and the punctuations between their automatic-gunfire bursts are filled with Aidey screaming fire-mission details at our mortar boys in their mortar pits just behind me.

Mortars.

A Taliban mortar lands just beyond the wall we sleep against, slap bang in the middle of our FOB. Its explosion sends dust billowing over the wall into our empty bed-spaces.

Shouts of 'Incoming!' echo down our wall. Now the next mortar lands about 50 metres to our right, beyond our perimeter wall.

I cannot see fuck all through this bloody hole.

The next Taliban mortar lands no more than a couple of metres outside the wall to our right. We echo screams of '*Incoming!*' along our wall – and then there is silence.

It is now plain what the Taliban mortar crew are doing. They bracketed the distance to us with their first two bombs. And, satisfied with the results, they are now adjusting their mortars from left to right, walking their bombs in increments towards us until they have the direction spot on too. They now only have to do another 'Right 50'. And then they will begin killing us.

There is nowhere to run; we don't know where the mortar will land in the open area just behind our backs. There is nowhere to hide; all we have is the sharp, pale ground beneath us, and the mud wall to our front. So, all along the wall we roll into foetal balls against the dirt, making ourselves as low and as small as we possibly can.

That is all we can do.

There is quiet along the wall as we wait for the next mortar to come in. Every man on the wall is curled up like an unborn baby, readying himself to be sent back into oblivion. I am in my ball against the wall when it occurs to me that my genitals are poking out between my legs inside my shorts.

You're not fucking having them.

I quickly tuck them between my legs. Even if I'm maimed, I might still be able to have sex again.

For long, stretching seconds we wait. I imagine the Taliban mortar arcing thousands of feet high into the air above before tipping over, picking up speed in its terminal-velocity headlong plummet to explode among us.

I am scared, but I thought I would be more so. There is nothing I can do now but just accept what is going to happen.

Please, God, no . . .

My eyes are scrunched shut and I do not hear any more sound. This is just my last, quiet, private moment with my Maker.

That is all there is to do.

'*Medic!*'

The scream pierces through to me, bringing the sound of the battle crashing back into my ears.

Kelvin, two weeks back from R & R, is screaming the word down the wall to my right. It is echoed up the wall as soldiers break out of their foetal balls and look around them, confused at still being alive.

Kelvin is gesticulating down the hole in the wall, which leads to the ANA compound.

'Terry!' I shout to another of the mortar boys. Terry's face is just visible above the rim of his mortar pit, his eyes staring insanely wide at me. 'Terry, get the medic down here!'

Terry runs off to the main building and I run to the hole in the wall.

I'm in your hands now, God.

I stoop through it and scramble down the shit-littered slope to where Kelvin and Sammy are standing over an ANA soldier lying motionless on the ground.

The ANA soldier is on his back. He is conscious and breathing, but judging from all the blood splattered on the pale ground around him and soaking darkly into his trousers, his trousers appear to be all that is holding the pulverised lower half of his body together. He is bleeding everywhere from the waist down. And his legs are twisted grotesquely, his right swung over the left at a right angle halfway down his thigh.

We can't treat him here; we need to get him and ourselves out of the immediate danger first. I can see a hole the size of my fist in the front wall right beside us where the SPG-9 pierced straight through to blow him away. We will have to carry him up the slope to where the female medic, only flown in yesterday, is now gesticulating to us from the hole in our wall.

An Afghan soldier runs up to us, takes one horrified look at his comrade – and then runs off.

'It'll be all right, mate,' I say positively to the injured man. He smiles faintly up at me, flickering eyes trying to focus. He is going.

It won't be all right.

I grab the webbing strap on his right shoulder, Kelvin the one on his left. And Sammy, a big Fijian lad, grabs his belt as we begin to half carry, half drag the guy up the steep, shit-covered slope.

Now I know what the words 'dead weight' really mean. The air around us is searing hot, our heavy body armour constricts our breathing – and the man is so bizarrely heavy in his own heavy body armour. We struggle breathlessly to keep his ripped-apart, bleeding legs from dragging in all the shit as we haul him so, so slowly up the steep bank. And the further we get up this steep bank to the sanctuary of that hole, the more we are completely exposed to the whole Green Zone – hiding all those men doing everything they can to kill every one of us.

'Come on, come on . . . !' we breathe in desperate gasps to each other. There is no way the Taliban won't be able to see us now.

But the injured man is oblivious to all of this.

His face is young and clean-shaven. He stares peacefully up at me as I grunt and strain and sweat in exertion and fear above him.

Whenever I glance down to his blood-spattered face, he is looking up into mine. With all the blood I now see coming out of his ears, I know that he cannot hear anything. But his glazing eyes are locked onto mine. And, blown out of this world into the gathering peace of another, he just keeps smiling this faintest of smiles, straight at me. But the smile and flickers of life in his eyes come from so far away. And he slips further away on his journey from us, with each panting step as we drag him up the shit-covered bank.

Now his eyes are losing focus. Now he is murmuring soft snatches of song. There is no way of telling if he is doing this chanting for us, for him, for me – or if it is just another sign of the darkness coming to take him.

But Ian the medic is now at the hole – which is suddenly just ahead of us.

'Come on, lads! Well done, get him through!' he calls in encouragement from the other side.

But now at this hole, at the top of this bank, I can suddenly see the entire Green Zone set out before us from the corner of my eye. We are now completely exposed to Taliban fire. I feel my back cringe in terror as we drag him through the hole – just waiting through those last seconds again for the *cracks* of incoming supersonic rounds to start shredding through this inviting little group of us bunched together.

But they don't come. I cannot understand why they don't come, as the hole delivers us safely into the waiting arms of the medics.

Ian has a stretcher laid out on the ground. The sound of our sangers and mortars returning fire is now deafening. The four of us are lifting the soldier onto the stretcher when suddenly another Afghan appears behind us and tries to lift his friend's lower half by the boots.

The legs bend clean over the wrong way at the knees and we all scream and swear at him to stop. He backs away back down the hole, his face terrified, shaking his head in horror, with no comprehension of our words.

Ian is screaming at Aidey for our mortars to stop firing; we need to run straight past them to get the Afghan to the med centre in the main building – some 75 metres away.

I grab the front left handle of the stretcher – and it is as we all lift as one and look up that I see the dust cloud of where a Taliban mortar has just exploded slap bang in the middle of where we have to run. My senses are so overloaded and there is so much other noise that I never even heard its *bang*. There is no time to wonder how in hell the hot, sharp shrapnel that would have zipped through the air did not hit any of us.

We lumber with feet in time through the mortar's dust cloud towards the main building. Now past the dust, I catch a flash of figures skulking on top beside the main sanger: snipers, a Javelin crew, Alex and Dave Hicks.

In the final metres to the building, I am breathing so hard it feels like my chest is going to burst. But it is just as we reach the corner of this building that we feel the explosion above us.

Even with everything else going on, it comes straight out of the blue. And its cracking *thud* is so loud, deafening and powerful that the shockwave punches our bodies, thumping our eardrums and almost knocking the stretcher out of our hands, turning our coordinated strides into stumbling staggers as the air around us is suddenly filled with swirling, choking dirt.

'*Jesus Christ!*'

'*Fucking hell!*'

But we lumber the last few metres into the open doorway of the med centre. Ian suddenly sounds very tired:

'Get him in! Get him in . . . I'm too old for this shit.'

It is as we are placing the stretcher on the concrete floor that the screams for '*Medic!*' begin from up above us. Gasping and half-doubled over for breath, I run outside.

I can see someone's legs halfway up the ladder already.

'Roof! Roof!' a soldier is pointing upwards, calling out to me rapidly.

The pained cries for '*Medic!*' up above are as pitiful as they are blood-curdling.

Fuck this.

I cannot catch my breath, but I run into the med centre, telling Ian we'll bring the casualties in to him. Grabbing a stretcher, I have to push my way through congregating blokes to place it down at the foot of the ladder.

The first soldier comes bounding down the rungs, jumping from head height past the soldier standing on the rungs to land among us, where he doubles over on the ground, coughing for his life. Someone escorts him inside and all eyes turn back up to the roof.

The next soldier comes stumbling down the ladder, landing on the stretcher. I half catch him and he turns towards me, eyes staring madly, calling out for us to 'Get a stretcher!'

'It's all right, mate,' I shout over the noise to him. 'I've got one here – they're bringing them down now.'

He is staring wildly about him, and I have to put a hand on his shoulder to show him what is lying at our feet.

'It's OK, mate! I've got one here . . . Are you all right?'

His frantic movements suddenly stop. I look him over from head to toe for wounds as I lead him, now completely subdued, to the bench beside the med centre door. I help him to slowly sit down before his dusty body just crumples, closing up like a fan. But now the female medic is beside me, gripping his arm and releasing me back into the melee beside us.

Now the guys on top begin handing down the next casualty to the ever-growing mob below.

It is Dave Hicks.

He is being gently lowered to us feet first. His body armour has been taken off, leaving just shorts and trainers on him. I can see a deep red wound in the flesh of his left outer thigh, and high on his left chest is a small circular wound that has blood bubbling out of it. The blood from his chest froths, popping and winking in the sunlight with each laboured breath as he is manhandled down the ladder.

Someone says he has a head wound as well, but it must be on the back of his head – I can't see it. All I see is his face turned down towards us, his eyes half closed, with his head gently nodding and jerking like he is trying to stay awake.

He is tenderly laid down onto the stretcher. And as they lift him into the med centre, I call out after him, 'You're going to be OK, Sir – you're going to be OK!'

I have no idea if he is going to be OK.

Now the area round the med centre is milling with people, pressing in a massive crowd of legs, heads, breath, bodies, arms and sweat all round the bottom of the ladder. My head feels like it's going to explode in the middle of it; there are way too many people here to help now and *I have to get the fuck out of this.*

I back off a few metres.

I watch as another three casualties are brought down; they're more with it, crying out in pain.

Then I turn away along with the rest of the crowd.

I feel numb.

Through the screaming whistling I can now hear in my ears, it is now that I hear the quiet.

Our sangers and mortars have stopped firing. There is no more incoming fire. High in the air above us all is the reason: the distant rumble of a huge B1-B bomber circling overhead, waiting to be tasked for its bombing mission. The Taliban aren't stupid.

There is nothing left for me to do. I look around me. 'Stand down' hasn't yet been called, so the only place to go now is back against the wall. I see Martin sitting with Maggy over there, so I start to jog over to them – except I soon become aware that I am not.

I am stumbling, light-headed and detached, carrying some reeling, dumb aftershock along with me.

Martin and Maggy are silent, staring down at the ground as I slump beside them.

Martin raises his head tiredly to me. 'Good to see you, mate . . . I was praying there.'

'Me too,' seconds Maggy quietly.

'And me,' I third.

There isn't any more to say. My ears are whistling so loudly I had to strain to hear what they were saying. I don't want to think any more. I sit in the dirt, leaning against the wall beside the hole we dragged the Afghan soldier through. I can see his blood splashed over a pale stone. It is already drying in the late morning sun.

Smoke.

My fingers fumble for them in my thigh pocket. When I get the cigarette packet out, I see that it has 'Smoking seriously harms you and others around you' emblazoned across it. But I can only stare at the black and white letters of the warning as I sit beside the blood. The glimmer of sardonic, black humour dies as soon as it has flickered into life.

It is as my eyes shift from the packet to the lighter held in my other hand, that I see my knee.

It is shaking. But I don't know what is making it shake. I do not feel anything.

I watch it shaking with detached fascination. It is like it belongs to someone else.

But now I see that the hand holding the lighter is shaking too. And so is the hand holding the cigarettes.

I dig my heel into the dirt to stop the tremors and light the cigarette. I think I feel better for smoking it.

There is movement behind us. The CSM has his arm around a soldier's shoulders, gently leading him to sit down outside the main building. The soldier's body is shaking wildly and uncontrollably. The tears stream down his face and the sobs choke his breathing.

Battle shock.

I look at the soldier, diagnose him with it in my head, assess that he is being looked after – and then turn away to smoke. But I cannot feel anything; I feel dead.

Now there is the *whump-whump* sound of a Chinook helicopter in the distance, rapidly drawing close. And outside the main building is a sudden hive of activity, as stretchers are brought out of the med centre and carried towards the landing site at the rear of the FOB. The last stretcher has a dense gaggle of soldiers around it, one arm holding an IV fluid bag high above them all.

I can hear their voices going up in pitch and volume.

'Keep your eyes open!'

'Look at me, Dave! . . . Stay with me, Dave!'

Fuck.

*

'Stand down.' The command is echoed without energy or emotion down our wall.

I stand up and look around me. It occurs to me that I have not sweated all the treacle pudding off – and that I left a shower bag down beside a well.

I force myself through the hole in the wall, picking my way back down the bank through the shit and blood trails. Down where we found the Afghan soldier, one of his friends stands staring at the blood-soaked spot. He has a big, bushy beard that hides a friendly face. I recognise him as the ANA soldier I had seen looking lost in himself immediately after we had returned from a fighting patrol against the Taliban a few days ago. I wished I had said something to him then.

He looks sadly up at me as I approach him. I bring my right hand up and gently grip his upper arm.

'I'm sorry,' I hear myself saying. But these are two useless words in English that he cannot understand.

He smiles sadly and touches my arm gently back, saying two words in Pashtun or Farsi that I cannot understand.

I walk to the well and see that my discarded shower bag has already grown legs.

Let the poor fuckers have their one shower bag – I'll borrow Martin's. What the fuck does it matter?

*

That night, with everyone around me silent and numbed by the day, I lie on top of my sleeping bag and think of Dave Hicks. And I remember him sitting quietly with us in the dark only this time last night, only a few feet away from where I lie now.

I remember him saying, 'We've got some very tired 19-year-olds here,' before he walked away into the darkness.

I can't think any more.

*

I am being gently shaken.

Darkness.

I lift my head up to the silhouette above me. It's Martin.

'Bad news, mate. The 2IC didn't make it. Thought you might want to know.'

My head hits back against the ground. And I swear once to myself as I stare into the blackness.

That is all there is to do.

*

Much, much later, when I am back home and being treated for Post Traumatic Stress Disorder (PTSD), I will be enabled to see what was going on in my mind immediately after 11 August.

I am still capable of operating mechanically as a soldier in these following days. But operating mechanically as a soldier is now all I am capable of.

Martin says he is worried about me. He says I have the 'thousand-yard stare'.

Of course, I cannot see this stare. But by now we both have more than an idea what it means.

So, among all the soldiers here, this is nothing to be ashamed of. But as it really does just go with the territory we find ourselves in, it is just as equally not a badge of honour.

Martin is seasoned enough to never even think this, but I know of young men back home, sitting in front of war films and war games, who idolise this condition as some kind of mark of a true warrior. But from where I sit, if indeed I do have this stare, this pathetically naive thinking is a crock of shit. Because only some pathetically naive soul who had never felt this *nothingness* would say something so fucking dumb.

You are no longer human, with all those depths and highs and nuances of emotion that define you as a person. There is no feeling any more, because to feel any emotion would also be to beckon the overwhelming blackness from you. My mind has now locked all this down. And without any control of this self-defence mechanism my subconscious has operated, I do not feel any more.

But when I close my eyes, I see the dead Taliban looking into this blackness. And I see the Afghan soldier's face staring into it, singing gently as he slips into another world. And I see Dave Hicks's face, shaking gently as he tries to stay awake in this one.

With this, I lift myself up, sitting foetal and hugging my knees on my sleeping mat.

And I smoke in the silent, dead-of-night darkness that I find myself alone in.

*

Alex is flown out. But now a great many things descend on FOB Inkerman, only some of which is Taliban fire.

Along with another three members of the new FST slowly replacing me and Martin, a new interim OC for the platoons is also flown in. And, along with all of them, Bastion now also sees fit to fly us in a doctor, some Hesco with which to build fortifying walls and a thousand sandbags for good measure.

It only took a few deaths.

The new OC immediately instigates a policy of 'standing to' for a couple of hours in the first light and last light of every day. At first, this just feels like a completely needless fuck-around to me. The Taliban here rarely attack at these times, and I feel we are just re-enacting a Sandhurst-taught anachronism belonging to a bygone era of fighting.

But then it dawns on me that perhaps his reasoning is anything but to fuck us around. It dawns on me that in this aftermath that has left men staring blankly into space, he is just trying to instil some purpose and structure to our routine here. And with this, it dawns on me that perhaps he has only our best interests – and morale – at heart.

This more considered reflection is reinforced to me in the following days as the number of our patrols is cut right back. And these patrols venture such a tiny distance from the FOB that Martin and I have no need to go out on the ground with them. We watch over them from a rooftop at the FOB instead, which affords us far better eyes on the ground around the patrol than they have among it.

The reason that the platoons were now 'only' doing this was that a whole horde of reinforcements had driven into our gates, just to take some of the pressure off our beleaguered FOB.

The BRF was the first to turn up, though I did not initially know it.

The CSM poked his head under our parachute canvas and said: 'Jake . . . ? Jake, there's some HAC mates of yours just turned up.'

So I put on my body armour and helmet and picked up my weapon – as we now had to do walking anywhere in this place – and I risked the short walk into the HLS area where I was told they were.

James, Tom and Charlie were there waiting for me beside the BRF's WMIKs.

Tom will later say that when he was asking round for me, he was just met by the same expressionless blank stares that I apparently gave him at this moment of reunion. He will say it was like walking through a scene from *Hamburger Hill* – though, of course, I would just have to take his word for this.

But maybe this was why I felt them looking at me so much. There was no banter.

'You all right, man?' Charlie asked quietly.

'Yep.'

'Heard you've been hit pretty hard here,' said James.

'Yep.'

Tom is looking inside me.

And I am pleased to see them, I think, but I do not know what to say to them. So I give them what I think they want, with just the quickest overview of the past few days – but then I find just as quickly that I simply don't want to talk about it any more. So I light a cigarette instead.

I have to do this quickly so they don't see my fingers fucking shaking – *again*.

With this, I see that I have successfully killed what conversation there was.

But then everyone around us was screaming: 'Stand to!' again. And so that was that.

*

The 'Stand to' was set off by some intercepted Taliban radio transmits, which talked of hitting our FOB again in minutes.

But the attack did not come. And when 'Stand down' was called, I found that James, Tom, Charlie and the rest of the BRF had already driven out of our gates – pushing up north to see if they could find the Taliban.

They wouldn't find them, though.

In the coming days, we heard less and less of the Taliban as more and more heavy metal assets rolled into Inkerman in the shape of numerous heavily armoured and near-indestructible Mastiff vehicles.

In the face of all these reinforcements, the Taliban melted away.

They didn't outnumber us any more, so they didn't have the upper hand any more. So apart from the odd fleeting contact we heard of in the desert north of our FOB somewhere – which the Mastiffs literally shrugged off – the Taliban just backed off.

Until the morning of 16 August, that is – when a salvo of 107mm rockets was launched straight into the middle of our FOB.

I never heard them coming until that last half second before they hit. They shoot so fast through the air that it is impossible for you to hear them until they are on top of you.

There is a sudden screaming *zip* coming out of nowhere just behind my head. There is only time to close my eyes and begin to duck. And then the air behind me is being ripped apart by just another detonation.

It exploded in exactly the spot where all our open-air bed-spaces had been up until yesterday afternoon. A big digger had come in then, digging out a massive 'shell scrape' against our front wall for us to sleep in. It only involved us moving our kit a few metres that evening, but then we could sleep and wait and think below ground level – and below shrapnel level.

So of course this rocket landed exactly where we would all have been sitting up until a few hours ago. With all the laws of serendipity it was either going to land there or straight bang into the pit we had all just moved into.

But there was no serendipity for Martin on this, our penultimate day at FOB Inkerman before the two of us were officially 'relieved in place' by the new FST.

He had only walked up there to get some food. And we both think he only survived because he had been kneeling down, with most of the shrapnel going over his head.

But, of course, some of the shrapnel got him.

He didn't realise at first. He came running back into our shell scrape to put on his body armour and helmet and pick up his weapon. He didn't believe our shouts of, 'Martin, you've been hit!'

But then he saw the blood coming out of him – down his legs, on his arms and from his body – and his mouth hung open in incomprehension.

*

I do not 'Stand to!' like the shouts tell me to.

The new FST here can do whatever FST'ing is required.

I go after my friend in the med centre.

Inside, I see him lying on a stretcher and wrapped in bandages. I see the IV fluid bag held above his head, replacing the blood that is already darkening his bandages. And though I crouch for some time beside my friend, gripping his hand in mine, I see that he cannot focus on me or talk to me, because he is in so much pain that they have injected him with morphine.

I tell him that *he's going to be all right*.

It is all I can do.

I walk outside to light another cigarette. I find myself standing at the very spot where I saw Dave Hicks being lowered down the ladder.

And at this moment – at this spot – now my friend is in there and now I am the last fucking person from my FST left fucking standing here – *now I feel some fucking emotion* as I consider that *in no way is this fucking war worth dying for*.

Only our families back home even realise we're at war. The thought of any kind of hero's fucking welcome home in our country is just a fucking joke.

And I have absolutely zero fucking faith in how this war is being fought – with one fucking hand forever tied behind our fucking backs.

FUCK THIS.

*

The rockets and mortars came in again when we were taking Martin to the HLS. He was strapped onto a stretcher laid across the back of the CSM's quad bike. And I never was going to do anything else but lay myself across the top of his morphine-addled, bleeding body while we waited for the bombardment to finish.

I do this because Martin is my brother-in-arms. And I do this because he is as close to me now as my flesh-and-blood brother back home. But the parting shots of these rockets and mortars that send us both on our way do not hit us in this, the last moment we both have here.

When they stop, the Chinook comes into land. Past the scream of rotor blades and searing downwash, Martin is carried up the ramp into the helicopter on his stretcher, as I carry all his kit and mine behind him.

And then we leave Forward Operating Base Inkerman.

*

Martin was taken straight to the field hospital when we landed.

I went back to the 19 Reg lines. Here, the regimental sergeant major (RSM) asked me to hand my Minimi in to stores. I didn't know why. But everyone forgot about Martin's blood-spattered rifle, so I slung this around my body after lunch, when the time came to go to Tony Rawson's and Dave Hicks's repatriation parade.

I do not look at the other 19 Reg soldiers as the four-tonner drives us there. One of them will later tell me that I didn't seem my 'usual cheery self' on this journey.

Mine is the only brown HAC beret at this parade. As far as I can see, I am the only one wearing a field-grown beard. And as far as I know, I am the only one that had actually been there when these men died.

I gently but firmly push my way to the front rank as the hundreds of troops from a plethora of units line up in front of the airfield's apron.

I still have to tell a nurse forming up in front of me, 'I was there,' for her to move aside. But with this she makes space for me before looking up at me with wide, quiet eyes saying, 'This must be very hard for you.'

I thank her. But with this our conversation needs to end.

Thankfully, everyone now falls silent and still as the two military ambulances begin to roll slowly in front of us.

In reality, this parade ground is just another vast patch of sand beside the wide-open expanse of the runway. But for this last goodbye to our fallen, it is transformed into something altogether different.

The Hercules aircraft that will take them home is parked to our left. Its engines wait to start. Its back ramp is open, waiting for the coffins to be carried aboard.

The ambulances slowly drive past us to our right. They come to a halt where the coffin bearers and the buglers all stand silently to attention.

And now with oiled, slow proficiency, the coffin bearers pull the two coffins from the ambulances. The 2IC and Tony Rawson are already draped in the red, white and blue of our Union flag. They are carried in slow time to the middle of the parade ground, where they are gently rested on two platforms beside the padre.

The padre says his words. And I cannot register many of them, but I know that we all say: 'We will remember them.'

Then we all bow our heads. And I remember them in the silence that everyone else imagines them in.

But I cannot close my eyes when I do this. Their faces are already coming to me from out of the sand at my feet.

The Last Post sounds. But one of the buglers cracks. I do not know if it is the emotion or the pressure, but I have already seen a couple of soldiers fainting in the heat, slumping like dead men onto the hot sand.

Now the flag-draped coffins are carried in slow time up the back ramp of the waiting Hercules.

The coffin bearers withdraw to the ambulances as the aircraft's four turboprops fire into life. The drone of their engines drowns out the silence.

Then the Hercules pulls slowly away from us, taxiing to the runway threshold. And with a distant roar that washes over us all, it suddenly throttles forward, gathering speed, before rotating to leave the earth behind it.

It banks left after it has taken off, disappearing behind our heads.

But no one moves, because after only a few long seconds it comes from straight out of the air behind us – flying right over our heads.

It climbs slowly into the sky in front of us. And as it ascends higher into the blue, beginning its journey of taking our brothers back Home, it dips its wings slowly back and forth in salute – and in nod to the RAF Group motto it flies under in support of all the Army here on the ground:

'*Par Nobile Fratrum*' – 'A Noble Pair of Brothers'.

I know this because my dad used to fly these very same Hercules.

I keep my eyes on the sky while the troops disperse around me. I watch the aircraft shrinking to a distant smudge in the haze.

But then it is gone. And then there is only ringing silence, and empty sky.

I know the nurse is looking up at me. But I cannot look at her.

*

The RSM found me in the smoking area of the 19 Reg lines after the Repatriation Parade.

He sat down beside me and suggested that perhaps I should speak to a CPN in the morning.

'What's a CPN?'

'A psychiatric nurse.'

But he said this gently, without any traces of stigma in his voice, so I just nodded and said, 'OK.'

'Good lad – I'll tell them you're coming . . . Do you want to go over and see Martin after tea? The doctors told me he'll be out of the operating theatre by then – before he's flown back home . . . I can come with you if you like?'

'Yeah . . . Thank you, Sir, I'd like that.'

So we went to see Martin after tea. He was still off his head on morphine, but he recognised us at least – grinning at us from faraway as we stood at his bedside.

I remembered being on morphine after an operation years ago. It doesn't make the pain go away at all; it just moves it to another, faraway part of your mind. In this opiate-induced state, the pain just doesn't matter any more.

I also remembered speaking completely lucidly to the friends who came to see me – who told me afterwards that they hadn't understood a single sound coming out of my mouth.

So it is actually quite easy to smile and nod as Martin burbles away beside us. In fact, it is almost entertaining. Because, as much as he is completely out of it, covered in bandages and now due to be imminently flown home for further surgery, I am just glad to see my friend alive in front of me.

But when the time comes for us to say goodbye to Martin, I ask the RSM if it is all right if I meet him back at the lines.

He says, 'Sure' – though I think he says it cautiously. Regardless, that allows me to slip off elsewhere in the hospital, so I can find out what happened to the Afghan soldier I helped carry – and to find out about the final moments of my 2IC.

The wards I walk through are filled with physically injured soldiers. But, unlike the deaths that make it into the newspaper you will read with your morning coffee, you probably never will read of their numbers compiled into statistics, along with the numbers of all those injured on all the tours previous and subsequent to this particular one in 2007. You will certainly never read of the true numbers of psychological injuries, which by their inherent nature can lie dormant and repressed for any period of time before 'manifesting' and becoming unmanageable for the individual.

I find a nurse. After being pointed in the direction of the appropriate doctor, I feel I have to say the words 'I was there' again, as I try to explain why I need to know this information.

With this, the doctor gently explains to me how Dave Hicks was 'Dead on Arrival' – and how even if he had been hit right beside their operating theatre, they would still not have been able to save him.

Then, after a pause, he explains how they had had to amputate everything from the waist down on the Afghan soldier. And he had lived for a couple of days afterwards. But then he had died, without them ever being able to find out his name.

I say 'thank you' to the doctor. And I walk outside, where I find myself alone in the dark again. But its cocooning embrace soothes the *snaps* of my firing and dying senses. There is no one else around to disturb this quieter peace that I now find myself in.

I light another cigarette.

Then I slowly walk back to the 19 Reg lines.

But I have to wait alone in the quiet darkness beyond its Hesco walls for everyone else to go to bed, before joining them.

*

Maybe the CPN saw something in me the next day. Or maybe he just saw something that was no longer there.

He says that I have ASR.

He tells me that this acronym stands for Acute Stress Reaction.

Now that my FST no longer exists and there are only a few weeks to go before everyone's tour is over, he declares that my tour is now over. And he tells me that another reason he has decided this is that I have done three tours in five years – which, in his opinion, would be more than enough for a regular soldier – but unlike a Reg, I now have to go straight back into the alien world of civvy street.

'I think this should probably be your last tour, too, Jake,' he says. 'What do you think?'

'I think you're probably right.'

*

Some days later, I will learn that I am the fiftieth psychological casualty so far in this one particular six-month tour.

And some months later, I will sit in on a post-tour briefing about 'psychological issues', given by the Army to HAC soldiers' families, along with some of their recently deployed sons, boyfriends and husbands. It will begin by telling us all that '99.9 per cent of soldiers returning from Iraq and Afghanistan will not suffer from Post Traumatic Stress Disorder'.

And I would laugh in the lecturer's face when he tells us this – and bitterly, because such a statement will only increase my sense of mental isolation.

But I cannot laugh. And I can only listen to a few more sentences of this briefing before I have to interject and identify myself as one who now has Post Traumatic Stress Disorder.

The person giving this briefing will look shocked that I have interjected with such an interruption. But I will not care.

I will say that I refuse to be brushed under the carpet as some kind of statistical anomaly. But I will reinforce my refusal with the observation, without giving names, that if just the statistical cohort of all the HAC soldiers on this last Afghan tour is used, then only a few months after our return, the percentage of those diagnosed with PTSD is already running at over 30 per cent.

This will worry some of the parents in the audience. But if this was going to be a briefing on the reality of 'psychological issues' post tour, then I will feel that they need to know the reality.

I will also do this because I will feel fucking *damned* if I am going to sit quietly and be made to feel like some sort of freak for even a second longer, by someone who wouldn't know a front line if it physically assaulted him outside a lecture room.

The lecturer will appear to develop his own psychological issues throughout the rest of that briefing, stammering and casting furtive looks in my direction while also seeming to avoid any eye contact with me. He will remind me of me, aged 12.

But here at Camp Bastion, I do not yet have a four-letter acronym to describe my condition.

At this stage, the Army has only given me a three letter one.

I do not want to go home even just these few weeks early; if I cannot go out on the ground then I still want to be able to do something useful. So I work on the radios at 19 Regiment's FPC, tucked away in a corner of the Bastion Ops Room.

It is bizarre listening to 'Troops in Contact' reports coming across other radio nets while the officers around me drink warming cups of tea and write details on whiteboards, all to the cooling, sterilising background hum of air conditioning.

I thank Christ that my logistics-filled radio net never has anything so critical coming down it.

But I am still admonished by a high-ranking Ops Room God hovering behind my back – I don't know who – for not sounding 'enthusiastic enough' as I read back resupply requests from artillery positions. He demonstrates to me and everyone else there how I should sound. This appears to be some kind of shout into the microphone with random variations of pitch and intonation thrown in 'TO make it *INTER*esting!'

His words stab into my head as I stare down into the wooden grain of the desk in front of me. I had felt nothing but nothingness. But now suddenly the only thing I want to do is rifle-butt his soft, ignorant REMF face to bloody pulp, screaming the joyous black rage of pure release.

But I cannot do this. It would be inappropriate behaviour, and it would spill too many high-ranking officers' cups of tea.

And this sudden, blinding flash of rage terrifies me.

I hide my shaking, clenching fists under the desk.

Then I feel all the rage and all the terror and all the grief suddenly switching off. Now I am nothing but a safe, empty blank again, I can raise the eyes in my light-headed and distant head back up from the wood of the desk. And the snapping, impatient tuts and curses behind me only become background noise, as I continue the only way I can on the radio.

Back at the 19 Reg lines, though, I am aware that I am being handled with kid gloves. Maybe they can see that I am not completely there – I do not know. But I know that the CPN will have spoken with them.

The unfailingly likeable padre says, 'I heard you did really well out there.'

I thank him gratefully, but I do not know what I did do out there.

In my end-of-tour report, I do not recognise the 'bright, committed and professional' soldier that my battery commander praises as a 'consummate operator' of the Fifty Cal – and one who employed it 'against the Taliban with ruthless efficiency'.

Although I have to look away when I read them, I do understand the words 'savage close-quarter contacts'. But I cannot remember 'displaying tremendous courage'.

But at the end of our one-on-one, end-of-tour chat, in which he allows me to smoke as I read, I think I understand the heartfelt look in his eyes and the firmness with which he grips my hand to shake it, saying: 'Thank you for serving with my battery.'

And I will always – always – be thankful to him for saying this.

10

LACUNA

Do they matter? – those dreams from the pit? . . .
You can drink and forget and be glad,
And people won't say that you're mad;
For they'll know you've fought for your country,
And no one will worry a bit.
    Siegfried Sassoon (treated for shellshock alongside
                                        Wilfred Owen)

The thought of suicide is a powerful solace: by means
of it one gets through many a bad night.
                                      Friedrich Nietzsche

The RAF gives us a beer each on the TriStar home. And as I sit in the warm togetherness between John and Kris, we toast 'Home' and 'those no longer with us' as we drink down the cold, liquid headiness.

But in the warm and fuzzy afterwards, I cannot drift off to sleep as they can.

With clamped-shut eyes and sweaty fists, I sit with the religiously tightened seat belt pressing against my filling bladder, waiting for our window to blow out with explosive decompression – or for a section of roof to rip away, pulling people screaming into the sky – or for the hydraulics operating the control surfaces to fail – or for the engines to disintegrate and burn – or for a wing to just rip clean off its root to the fuselage, sending us plummeting and spiralling with sudden negative G through all those thousands of feet of nothingness – all before that final, body-shredding impact into the ground below.

I expect at least one of these things to happen at any second. But, inexplicably, not one of them happens. I am just as surprised when our aircraft does not suffer multiple, catastrophic birdstrikes in those hanging, vulnerably slow seconds before touchdown.

I used to be a paratrooper.

I used to be a pilot.

I did not think like this, when I used to be these other people.

As our aircraft taxies along the old ground of Home, I look down as John and Kris look up through the window. And I see those tiny, familiar tremors shaking through my hands again.

Unnaturally cool, moisture-laden air hits my face as I walk out of the aircraft. No one talks as we all file down the steps, finally facing the comfortable strangeness lying in front of us all, just before the soles of our worn-out desert boots kiss the rain-washed, rock-hard tarmac of Home.

There is no welcome waiting for us. There are no flags, or banners, or crowds of waiting loved ones. And we never will receive any 'welcome home' of this kind.

With bergans and bags picked up, we walk out of the military terminal and are directed to our relevant coaches. We load our kit into stowage holds. For those who were first in line to do this, there is just enough time to scratch the now screaming itch to smoke.

A civilian who will turn out to be my coach driver smokes beside me as I smoke. But he stares past me, blowing clouds into the cold air with surly disinterest as he waits for the last remnants of his cargo to finish loading themselves aboard.

When there are no more snatched seconds left to smoke, I climb aboard the coach after him. I see that John has saved a seat for me – waving with one upheld hand near the back.

I can see all the soldier's faces as I walk up the aisle. There are some quiet smiles, but there is no exuberance. There is no excited chattering filling the air. It should surprise me, but it does not, that many of the faces I pass stare out of the window with muted despondency.

My face probably mirrors theirs. And if their thoughts reflect mine, then they too will feel the quiet relief at having made it home. But this will also be tempered by the feelings of ordinariness and anonymity already closing in to crush them.

A US soldier is sat on the row of seats beside John's and mine. I guess he is attached to the British Army.

And as our coach begins to roll, with Lily Allen singing 'Don't Get Me Wrong' on the radio, I notice that absolutely no one has been talking. The US soldier's voice suddenly fills the void, saying, 'Well . . . it's not much of a homecoming, is it?'

But for all the British soldiers around him, this homecoming is anything but a surprise.

*

As a nation, maybe America has a guilt complex over how it treated its veterans returning from Vietnam. I was born when the last of them were coming home. By many accounts, the drafted soldiers who had just done their thankless duty in just another morally ambiguous war were spurned by their country.

So with the violence of in-theatre triggers and, equally crucial, alienation of post-theatre triggers now documented for PTSD, it is perhaps not surprising, now, that it was from this cohort of spat-on veterans that the condition now known as PTSD was eventually recognised in full diagnostic detail.

The suicides, alcoholism, homelessness and killing sprees of civilians in reaction probably helped focus the nation's mind too.

By 1991, American troops returned from the Gulf War to a heroes' welcome, though it probably helped that in the public's mind that this war had been cleanly won – as much as any war can be.

And when 9/11 struck in 2001 with a direct attack on American home soil – on a scale that Britain's public has not felt since the Second World War – it was only going to further galvanise American public support for their soldiers, as these soldiers waged their 'War on Terror' on behalf of their people.

It looks like the national debt to the common soldier has now been recognised – over there.

In this country, Falklands veterans were given a flag-waving welcome home in 1982. But when they returned to home life, slipping to the back of the nation's consciousness once more, it took years for the government to recognise the psychological wounds many of them carried. After speaking to some of these veterans myself, it is clear that all these years of non-recognition only twisted a knife deeper into these wounds.

And for me, now, there was only the feeling of being ignored as we returned from Iraq and Afghanistan.

With all thanks to the Vietnam and Falklands veterans, PTSD has now been recognised by our government. But there was no groundswell of public support for us, the common soldiers, when we returned.

And as much as there was never a whisper of any flag-waving parades through the streets, I just as equally was never spat on or called 'baby killer'. Instead, there was just the insidious, steadily corrosive feeling of simply being overlooked – and in favour of all the latest meaningless distractions inherent to our 'Celebrity Culture'.

The 'Military Covenant' between soldier and nation was just a piece of paper, filed away out of sight and out of mind.

Today, in 2013, there does finally seem to be an awakening of overt recognition from our public. I can only guess that recently formed charities such as Help for Heroes (born in the month I returned from Afghanistan) and morally courageous, outspoken public figures such as General Sir Richard Dannatt have helped galvanise this.

With caution, this makes me glad, for the sake of all the soldiers who come after me.

But for me, such recognition and appreciation is beyond the realm of any of my experiences, returning home at the times I did.

The psychological wounds of war and the reintegration of soldiers back into society are not new issues. They are obviously as old as war itself – with the Ancient Greeks and Romans recognising them thousands of years ago. Nascent science during the American Civil War talked of a condition called 'Soldier's Heart'. And when British soldiers were fighting just another faraway war in the late 1800s, their enemy recognised these issues too.

The Zulus employed spiritual healers to bless their warriors before combat, imbibing them with psychological strength as they prepared to face a technologically superior enemy. And when these warriors returned home – regardless of whether they had 'won' or 'lost' – these same healers went to work again.

Now he had become a killer of men, the warrior went back to the shaman to be purified of the violence within him. With the power of the 'placebo effect' (which our all-knowing scientists still do not fully understand but know well enough that it hinges on the power of total belief), the warrior then believed he could be a normal person again, allowing him to walk once more among all the other normal people. This could be viewed as a primitive shamanistic ritual belonging to the past. But you would be a fool to think this, as this ritual is more spiritually advanced than anything we have in today's society.

The catch, though, is that as products of today's scientific and materialistic society, we just would not believe in the spiritual power of these healers.

So we see 'psychiatrists', 'psychologists' and 'counsellors' instead, as science plays catch-up to thousands of years of spirituality and belief. And so, so slowly, within the impatient need for instant gratification in today's society, the stigma of seeing such science-based practitioners is being gradually eroded.

In lieu of seeing a shaman, today's British Army now stops its soldiers over in Cyprus for 36 hours on the way back from war. This is called 'Decompression', a term derived from the necessary hours of decompression deep-sea divers have to undergo immediately following their stay in the depths, as a safeguard against their return to the surface killing them.

The theory is that some beers on a private military beach with your comrades combined with some talks on psychological stress – and an apparent blind eye to any grief-stricken, ingrained violence needing to be vented among the soldiers – will provide a cathartic breathing space between the normality of the killing fields of Afghanistan and the normality of the blissfully ignorant bubble of Home.

But I say 'theory', because I have no personal experience of this, either.

Two casualties had been fastballed onto our TriStar at Kandahar, so we did not stop over for a day and a bit in Cyprus; we stopped over in Birmingham for the minutes required to offload these casualties on their journey towards hospital. There is no way I would begrudge the pressing need to evacuate these men – but the fact of the matter stands: that our psychological decompression was not conducted on a beach in Cyprus, with reflective, communal beers in hand but in uniform in classrooms at a windswept barracks in deepest Wiltshire. There was little sense of comradely togetherness, now we were already reimmersed in the drudgery of barracks life. Everyone was home now. And now we all just wanted to be done with everything and get Home.

The few, dragging days of roll calls and handing in kit were punctuated with briefings on Post Traumatic Stress and the warning signs to watch out for in ourselves and others. There was also a briefing from our PAX insurers, whom we had been paying hundreds of pounds to in case the Taliban blew bits off us or holed us in other ways. After all our briefings on psychological injuries, someone asked these insurers if our policies covered such injuries, should they materialise at a later point for any of us – or, in actual fact, right now.

There are no prizes for guessing what the answer was. But the answer we were given was at least couched with the word 'regretfully'.

The insurers told us that these psychological injuries were 'hard to prove', as obvious as they might be to the afflicted soldier – or his loved ones, who might well be now seeing a completely different person coming back to them.

Martin would later tell me that he received a daily allowance for the time he spent in hospital. But the single lump-sum payout for his physical injuries, which almost lost him his leg and which will affect him for the rest of his life, with some shrapnel proving impossible to remove, was nothing. The possibility that Martin's blast injuries might have been covered if he had been injured on a later tour will not be of any consolation. The money we had paid to these people during our tour now seemed nothing but waste – now we knew the true measure of how our injuries were valued.

The next morning, it was time for five HAC soldiers attached to 19 Regiment to demobilise back into civvy street.

And for four of them that took the drive up to the Reserves Mobilisation Centre at Chilwell, they would suddenly find themselves civilians again by the afternoon.

But, in view of my diagnosis of ASR in theatre, I was told to come back in a week to assess for possible PTSD.

In this sudden, bizarre, fish-out-of-water limbo, where I went back to my family but was still officially part of the Regular Army, I found that in my mind I was as clueless to whether I was coming or going as I was in physicality with the Army.

Every time I woke in my mother's house, be it in the cold light of morning or during the dead of night, I thought I was in Afghanistan. I did not know what to say about any of this in the numb daylight hours – to my mother, my brother or my aging and steadily slipping-away father. My brain drifted apart from these confusingly new, strange old moorings, detached, just as it had learned to switch off from the savage normality it was now supposed to have left behind.

But when I went back to Chilwell a week later, the psychiatric nurse there deemed me to be 'adjusting appropriately after a traumatic event'. So without any more ceremony, I was demobilised straight back to being a civilian.

I know now, without any shade of doubt, that a single solitary week – and one straight back from theatre – is in no way sufficient a period to assess for nascent PTSD. But I did not know this at the time, so I did not challenge my demobilisation at the time, because, aside from not being in any mental state to do so, it is also true to say that at this time I felt I just needed to get away from any reminders of the Army. In fact, I wanted to get as far away from it as humanly possible. I wanted to slip the fetters of my past that bit into my mind and escape this uniformed environment that only reminded me of things I did not want to remember.

So I had told the psychiatric nurse that I thought I was 'probably OK'.

I did this because, despite all my continued numbness and gathering, stabbing memories, I just wanted to get on with my life. I just wanted to leave the past where it belonged.

But this decision would come to cost me tens of thousands of pounds. And instead of escaping my past by driving through Chilwell's gates, I would instead find myself even more alone on the outside of them – where the ghost of Afghanistan walked with me in every footstep I took.

*

For those of us in the HAC who had just demobilised, we had six full weeks of post-tour leave to take before we had to return to our civilian careers.

Mark and I had planned a two-week road trip across America: from Atlanta in the east to Los Angeles in the west. From there, we would both fly to Brazil, where Tom and John would meet up with us in Rio de Janeiro for the start of a three-week country-hopping excursion round South America.

I think it was as far away from Afghanistan and home as we could get, short of spending five weeks staring at sheet ice and crowds of quacking penguins in the Antarctic.

But my plane ride from home was not any more bearable than my plane ride to home. After picking up my holdall, but with Mark still waiting for his, I told him I'd see him outside the terminal – because I needed a fag.

I do not care that the smoke will kill me, because with all the threats to my person that I now see lying everywhere around me, I expect to die soon anyway. And the nicotine is a drug that calms me as I wait for this death. All the carcinogens I inhale with it help speed me along this journey to the inevitable, waiting release.

I stand with my back against the wall in the designated smoking area outside. I ensure that I can see everyone coming in and out of the revolving terminal doors to my left. And I ensure that I have clear field of view into all of the parking lot in front of me.

Four US soldiers with small holdalls slung over their shoulders walk out of the terminal doors. Two of the men are in desert uniform, along with a woman. I know the fourth man dressed in civilian clothing is a soldier too, because as well as the fact that he is part of this group, it is easy to glean from the upright and quietly alert way that he carries himself. And his screamingly obvious, high and tight 'jarhead' haircut provides something of a clue, too.

I watch them for a few minutes as they all light up cigarettes and exchange quiet words within their huddle. But with silent stillness and peripheral vision, I am careful not to be noticed watching them.

A woman walks out of the terminal. For a second I think she must know the soldiers, because as soon as she sees them she claps her hands briefly in applause. But the soldiers only nod politely in thanks to her as she walks right by them and then away into the parking lot.

Then the soldiers go back to their quiet conversation, as if what had just happened was the most normal thing in the world.

I cannot get my head round this.

I wait for a lull in their conversation before approaching them, where I feel I have to validate my presence by introducing myself as a 'Brit soldier just back from Afghanistan'.

And with these words their faces ease as they realise that I am, to some extent, one of them, and not just some random bloke invading their personal space.

They tell me that they are on their R & R from Afghanistan. But I have never heard of the province they are taking a break from, any more than they have heard of the province I have just come back from.

I mention the lady clapping. I ask them if that is unusual.

'Oh no . . .' they say nonchalantly, shaking their heads.

I say that I have never seen or heard of such a thing in Britain. In fact, just before I had come here, I know that a Brit soldier in uniform had been refused service at a motorway service station – just for being a soldier.

Their jaws drop open in disbelief, saying: 'Really?' and 'Man!' and '*Damn* . . .' as they struggle to get their heads round this. They tell me that such a thing would never happen in their country. And, after they have judged our impending road trip across the States to be an 'awesome' idea, they tell me to show my military ID and say we have just come back from Afghanistan in every place we go to.

'You'll get discounts everywhere,' they say. And, 'We've walked into bars in some places and haven't had to pay for a single drink all night.'

'Home of the brave, man,' one of the soldiers adds, winking at me. 'Enjoy your stay.'

With this, I shake their hands, thanking them for their time and wishing them good luck for the rest of their tours.

But along with everything else that I had just seen and heard, what they had said about bars lodged in my head.

Just before I had flown out here with Mark, Martin had been released from hospital. And for the last time we would ever be together as a team, Captain Featherstone, Alex, Gilly and I met up with him for beers in his home city of Southampton.

The night was never going to end at 11 p.m. when the pubs closed. However, finding a late-night bar or club that would let us in was a mission that we completely failed. Martin hobbled along with us on his crutches; we knew he was in pain. But every club we found was apparently having a 'Student Night'. And if you didn't have a student ID, you weren't getting in. Our military IDs counted for jack.

At the very last club we were turned away from, Captain Featherstone went back to have a word with the bouncer. We were not abusive or overly drunk, by anyone's measure, but by now Martin and I had to keep our distance, because through gritted teeth we were ready to snap into violence.

I could hear our captain trying to explain to the bouncer that it was our last night together, after we had just got back from Afghanistan and before we all had to go our separate ways.

But the bouncer kept his arms crossed. And he only said: 'So what?'

*

Mark and I did get discounts all across America. In fact, we used our ID cards about as often as our debit cards, with the two usually used in conjunction.

In Arizona, we went to see an aircraft graveyard. In Britain, if such a thing even existed, it would no doubt be a visit to some rain-swept grassy plain, dotted with rotting metal hulks. But this was America. And stretched out in countless gleaming rows within the moistureless desert air were more mothballed jet aircraft than the RAF could ever dream of owning. There were even some suspiciously space-aged, wedge-shaped, unmanned drones lying around that the RAF would probably kill for.

I remembered looking through night vision high up into the sea of stars over eastern Iraq in 2003 and seeing something suddenly accelerating with impossible speed into Iranian airspace. For all I knew, five years later, whatever it was sat superseded on the sand in front of me now. The guy giving the talk on the bus certainly fell deathly silent as we were driven past them.

We had shown our military IDs before boarding the bus. The uncomfortably named 'Hero Discount' was even emblazoned on the price list beside the counter. And, as instructed by the American soldiers, we told the lady behind the desk that we had just come back from Afghanistan.

After everyone had boarded, the first thing the guide said after, 'Welcome aboard ladies and gentlemen,' was: 'I understand we have some personnel just returned from active service on board. Could you please raise your hands, sirs?'

With repressed, English sheepishness, Mark's hand and mine slowly crept up.

'Let's give these folks a round of applause, ladies and gentlemen.'

And, to a man and woman, they all fucking clapped us.

'Humbled' is not the word to describe the quiet, awkward gratification that Mark and I felt in that moment. Because we had not – and never would afterwards – experience such warmth and collective appreciation for the terrible things we had done.

Some days later, a girl prettier than my wildest dreams will kiss me in a Los Angeles bar. And, past the intoxication of her lips pressing tenderly on mine, I will explain this away to myself as her just being attracted to my accent. But regardless of attraction and the reasons behind it, she will say 'thank you' when she learns that I have just come back from Afghanistan. And I will know that she means it, because aside from her sudden, quiet earnestness, she and her friends will then insist on buying all the drinks for all the rest of the night.

Sometimes I will fantasise that I could be married to her now, if I lived over there.

But I knew I had to return to a country where such personal information would only elicit a blank look, and one where you were more likely to be refused entry to a bar because you were military than you ever were to politely accept any free beers inside.

And South America, John and Tom beckoned first.

Mark and I met up with them in Rio airport. Tom would later liken our foursome to that of four little goblins, jabbering unintelligibly and drunkenly away to each other in the code of English soldier lingo as we made our mad way around Latin America.

As much as we will laugh at this creature analogy, beers permanently in hand, we were indeed very different creatures to the peaceable and unsuspecting Latin Americans we walked among.

We go to a football match in Rio. And I find that I nearly shit myself in terror every time massive firecrackers are let off in the stands around us.

John and Mark sitting either side of me appear completely unaffected, though. They also appear completely unaffected by the weight of the thousands of shouting, chanting people pressing around us. The noise and the crowd and the random, thundering bangs that come with no warning overwhelm my senses. I feel myself beginning to snap – going clean berserk inside. My mind screams for escape as my eyes fix on the concrete floor at my feet.

Beer has spilled darkly onto the pale concrete.

But I know that my escape will just turn into a panic-driven, windmilling trail of violence through a completely innocent crowd.

And now I see the dark blood soaking into the pale sand at Inkerman. And now my mind shuts down just as it did then. And now suddenly I do not feel any more, as I shut off from everyone and everything around me.

The players on the pitch are just faraway, blurred, dancing objects, randomly stopping and starting with nauseating surges against a backdrop of green.

I cannot focus on the tiny bouncing ball that is everyone else's focus. And every time the crowd around me suddenly roars and rises to its feet, I slip further away into my shell.

From deep inside this shell, I want to be sick, or scream – or, from deeper still, scream in sobbing, purging release. But in my paralysis I can do none of these things.

So I just wait, cocooned in silence, for the noise around me to end.

In Peru, as we walk out of Cusco airport, fireworks are suddenly fired off into the morning air ahead of us. I have no idea why. But they bang with *cracks* and ripples that are nothing other than gunfire. Instinctively, I duck my head with wide-eyed adrenalin and alarm. But when this threat passes, with life carrying on around us as if nothing had happened, I find that my chest is so tight I can hardly breathe. And I feel my body shaking again in the hangover of adrenalin and fear.

In that second of blinding terror, I had seen Tom ducking with me. But John and Mark did not.

They looked back at us like we were mad.

*

Before we saw the new wonder of the world that is Machu Picchu, we spent some time getting high on alcohol and hypoxia in the 11,000-foot-high city of Cusco.

Two Ecuadorian girls latched onto our group there. They were on holiday too and would go everywhere we did in Peru. They would later tell us that they came up to us because we were 'different . . . *men*'.

I will remember Alejandra, as I remember that if I was the man I was before Afghanistan, I could have made so much more of her attraction to me – with all those lingering signs that I recognise from prior experience but no longer understand in all their most natural, human and tender nature.

But as much as the gentle frisson of her body against mine stirs something within me – and as much as I see how easy it could be to fall headlong into the depths of those big, dark eyes – I know that I am falling farther away into the dark depths of another abyss.

I feel the turbulent velocity of the fall buffeting against my head.

I cannot get to sleep. And my dreams seem to wake me as soon as I do finally slip deeper into the haze of nicotine and alcohol.

I am alone in these dreams. I run alone through streams and alleyways and thick green foliage from innumerable hordes that want nothing other than my blood. Sometimes I kill some of my pursuers. I shoot them dead. And if I do, I wake just as their waxen faces and blank, glassy eyes stare back into my own. But in other dreams there are too many of them, and they surround me, closing in on me from all sides. I wake just as I am about to be ripped apart.

There is nothing else to do when I wake in the darkness, sodden with sweat, but lift my heavy limbs out of bed and take them outside for another cigarette. And with the leaden exhaustion of just another night, I watch another city as it sleeps. Maybe this is why I feel so tired. But I think my fatigue runs deeper than the hours of sleep I lose each night.

I just want to stop, as I want everything to stop. I just want to crawl into a ball at Home. And I just need the world to go away, just for as long as it takes me to rest.

But this trip is meant to be all about having fun – with drinking and late nights and constant travelling.

But I am just so tired.

I know Tom killed in Afghanistan. One of his kills was a man he riddled head to foot with his GPMG. So he is the closest person that I can truly talk to out here; he says he understands the 'silent scream' rising inside me. So we talk as we drink late into the night, connecting as we disconnect from our disorientating, peaceful surroundings.

But alcohol only lubricates the coming of the demons.

And later still in the night, when everyone else is sleeping and I cannot, I still find myself smoking alone on balconies and outside front doors.

*

We almost ran out of fuel driving through the Atacama Desert down to Santiago, where there is no rain and no life, and where Mark almost made dying of thirst academic after almost losing control of our rented pick-up.

We shouted at Mark because we did not want the ignominy of dying on a road trip through Chile after making it all the way through Afghanistan. But even before there was any real possibility of dying, I could not relax when others were in control of the vehicle. I sat tight and quiet in the passenger seat as the driver drove and the others slept. Within me, I felt completely out of control when I was not in control.

But still alive in body, we flew from Chile to Buenos Aires, where we thought it diplomatic and prudent not to let slip to any of the Argentines that we were British soldiers.

On our final morning together in South America, sitting down for a late al fresco breakfast within the square of a crumbling piazza, I got a phone call from home.

It was from my HAC squadron commander. He told me one of the young students I had trained on PSC, Jack Sadler, had just been killed by a mine in Afghanistan. He said he thought I might want to know. He asked me if I could break the news to the others.

So our breakfasts went cold in front of us as we ordered another jug of sangria. And we drank as we remembered Jack and mortality and death.

It occurred to me that Jack could have been wearing some of my kit when he died, after I had donated my most Gucci of personally bought items to his HAC crew, which had replaced ours.

And though at first glance the death would not seem to affect Mark at all, with gentler reflection I think he took the news harder than any of us.

While we drank ourselves down with more and more sangria, he just took himself away on his own around the piazza, snapping last pictures of the crumbling buildings we now all had to leave behind, in these final moments we all had in escape from the realities of home.

*

Eight months after Jack Sadler was killed, the homepage of the BBC News website will feature an audio slideshow entitled 'Soldier and Son'. The website will say that the slideshow is of a father paying a 'moving tribute to his son'.

I will listen to Ian Sadler's words. But then I will find myself checking the top ten 'Most Popular' rankings shown on the homepage, subdivided into the categories of 'Shared', 'Read' and 'Video/Audio'.

The most popular Read story for that day will be: 'Katona arrested in attack enquiry'.

The most popular Video/Audio story will be: 'Britney lip sync routine put to the test'.

And 'Soldier and Son' will not appear anywhere in the rankings, for any of the categories.

*

Two thousand years ago, a Roman wrote that, 'He is best secure from dangers, who is on his guard even when he seems safe.'

These ancient words of wisdom will ring piercingly true to any combat-experienced soldier today. And I will learn that these words could also describe just one of the resulting symptoms of PTSD – with its constant 'hypervigilance' to dangers.

But by inadvertently describing this most natural of human reactions, I found that these words would also inadvertently describe the impotence of this hypervigilant reaction to some of the dangers within modern warfare.

Jack would have been as much on his guard as any of us, but as top cover on the back of a WMIK, he would never have seen the hidden mine that killed him any more than he personally, in those final, closing seconds, would have been able to do anything about it.

Warfare used to be a set-piece affair of looking your enemy square in the eye on the appointed day. But now you can be obliterated at any second, on any day and without any warning, clean out of the blue.

It is facing this modern threat, from which there is only so much you can personally do to protect yourself, that in its inherent helplessness is the psychological, as well as physical, killer.

Even hypervigilance would not have saved Jack. And, long after the rockets and mortars and RPGs and SPG-9s had finished exploding around me, I carried the baggage of this same lack of control over my destiny onto all my plane rides home.

The four of us were booked onto different planes back from South America. We just had to take whatever seats were available, on whichever flights, flying whatever routes to get us home before Christmas.

Not long after my plane had taken off, climbing steeply away into the pitch dark of night, there is a sudden *bang* from one of the wings as the whole of the passenger cabin is suddenly filled with a split second of light.

Then we are plunged back into darkness. And fear cries out from the throats of the passengers around me.

The engines stammer and struggle.

The aircraft's nose begins to pitch slowly downwards.

And with the captain's silence, the only conclusion I can come to is that he suddenly has his hands full with more urgent concerns than reassuring a planeload of terrified passengers.

But now this final moment has finally come, I find that I am not scared.

My worst fears are now going to be realised. And in these final moments, I find that I am suddenly relaxed, and calm. I accept what is going to happen, because I have always been expecting what is now going to happen. I have learned to make peace with death now, whenever I have no more control over my fate.

I just let go.

And all the passengers around me suddenly fall silent, as they too realise that there is absolutely nothing they can do.

There is only quiet filling those long seconds, as we all wait.

But then the engines recover their steady note, the cabin lights suddenly flick on and the captain's calm voice comes over the intercom to us, saying we had just been hit by lightning but that there is nothing to worry about. And we carry on slipping 'the surly bonds of Earth' high into the night sky – all the way back home.

I think I feel a twinge of relief. But long after our wheels eventually float back down to kiss the earth, I know that I am confused.

I had readied myself for death, all over again. But now I have to go back to waiting for it – all over again.

*

I was well known within the HAC. Whether I liked it or not, the para wings on my shoulder and the number of tours I had now done when many had done none at all set me apart. But for all of us who had just returned from Afghan, who now also found ourselves attending the Christmas ball at the HAC, we were the focus of some passing attention.

We were the latest returnees from the HAC's latest tour of duty. But the uncomfortable truth was that we had just returned from the HAC's first real combat tour since the end of the Second World War. And the death of its first soldier since the Second World War had brought home this truth to those HAC soldiers left behind at home.

So we were asked about 'contacts' and 'incoming' and 'getting rounds down'.

I kept my answers polite but short. And as much as these soldiers never asked me about such things, I never volunteered anything about 'death' – or 'terror'.

But at the end of another round of questions, a soldier's girlfriend who had been hitherto silent asked a question of her own.

'Did you kill anyone?'

These are the first words that she has ever uttered to me.

I stare back into her unblinking eyes. I don't even know her name. And the crowd that is engrossed in its own conversations around us continues to sip champagne and laugh and smile at any number of other things – of which none of the subjects could be 'killing'.

As she stares back at me, I see that she cannot read the look I give her any more than she can read its accompanying silence. I cannot tell her exactly what I think of her for asking this most personal of passing questions, as the very first words she has ever said to me.

'That's not something you should ask someone, when they come back.'

'Why not?' she replies tersely. I appear to have insulted her.

I can only guess I insult her even more when I turn my back on her, leaving her and the room she inhabited.

When the fireworks go off later that night, I have to find a dark corner all to myself and plug my fingers into my ears. But the *bangs* and the rippling *cracks* still crash into my eardrums. And the loudest *BANGS* still punch their shockwaves against my body.

And now the past is present and projected in front of my clamped-shut eyes all over again, I find myself rocking back and forth on my haunches as I try and fail to block out the *bangs* and the past and the scream that is rising ever silently within me.

But when the fireworks finish to muffled cheers and applause, I find that everything in my mind suddenly switches off. And, dislocated, numb and light-headed, I find myself walking back out to be among all the others, with nothing left to do but finish myself off with drink.

I drank with Charlie for a while. We leaned against a bar, and after a while, a girl came up to us to ask us about the medals we wore on our dinner jackets. She asked what each one meant. So I told her while Charlie *carpe diem*'d and bought her a drink. It appeared to be a revelation to her that the TA went to places like Iraq and Afghanistan. But she seemed polite, and she was definitely pretty, so we patiently explained how we returned to our civilian lives afterwards.

This was 'mad', apparently.

I nodded in agreement with her, though I completely misconstrued the context in which she applied the label 'mad'. Because after I said, 'Yeah, it's definitely harder coming back than it ever is going out,' she shook her head in incomprehension.

'But you just said that you go back to your normal lives when you get back.'

And what could I say to that?

Later, she asked Charlie and I why we were not in uniform 'like all these others'.

I said that they were in the Regular Army, while we were in the Territorial Army.

'Ooh, they're in the real Army then?'

I wish I had not, but I snapped then – though she still only heard a whisper of a raised voice and not the full brunt of all the repressed anger I was determined to not let out on anyone that did not deserve it.

'Listen . . . We walked the same ground as the Regs out there! And if the Taliban didn't discriminate then why should you?'

With this, I appeared to have insulted someone again.

'Who the fuck are we . . .' Charlie murmured again, watching her walk away.

In that bubbling moment I wanted to say, 'Who the fuck are they?' But then I saw the dismay in Charlie's face, and I could not bear having him feeling any more polarised than he already did.

I slept with a female Regular Army officer from another unit that night. And though she had not been to Afghanistan, she said she understood why I went quiet when it was mentioned. Just this simple understanding, with its simple depth of emotional connection, made me want to physically be with her that night.

But by virtue of my emotional walling-off, I could never allow this connection to last beyond the one night we shared together.

And this will be the last time I have sex for such a stretching, numb chunk of time that I will lose track of its length.

*

I sit beside just another stranger on the train. He is flicking through a newspaper dedicated to Paris Hilton, *Big Brother* and other important world events. Without a paper of my own to read, the corners of my eyes engage in the covert practice of reading someone else's paper.

But lost in the middle pages of this paper there suddenly appears a picture of Dave Hicks's face. I recognise this picture, because I was only yards from him when it was taken outside FOB Inkerman.

But I do not have time to read any of the attached article's words, because the stranger only glances at the unknown soldier's face for a second before flicking the page over to engross himself in 'Amy's Blake in Overdose Drama'.

This is not the Home I dreamt of in a distant, familiar land. I know it is now a ghost of myself that passes through these foreign throngs of the living.

I am a stranger in a strange land.

*

The sea of suits surges past me in the morning rush hour, and I want to gush vomit. But as I submerge back down into the depth of their ranks, drowning, my chest clamps tight at me, struggling for air – and I know there is more chance of my lungs bursting in panic than ever being able to purge the sickness from me.

I home in on my old life from the memory of countless past journeys – past the concrete and the steel, the sharp suits and towers of glass. But there are too many threats to watch out for, there are too many people darting and weaving and hurrying and pushing around me, within a too vulnerably exposed, wide-open space in which there is no available cover anywhere to dive into, all enclosed within an estate that I know is a prime target for people who would be Taliban.

Dressed in the uniform of my suit, I no doubt mirror the army of suits around me. But I feel anything but akin to any of them.

In immediate threat assessment, the first thing I do when I get back to my desk is to find out where in the building I will have to be extra vigilant for having to see either Cecilia or James Blake.

I enter their names into the Bank's intranet phone directory. And with a frozen shock that dissipates into relief – but which then just as quickly evaporates into nothingness – I see that he is now employed in a completely different building. And I see that there is no record of her even being an employee of the Bank any more.

So now I only have to deal with me being here.

Now I am alone in this sterile pressure- and profit-driven office, I find that I have to completely internalise the past that threatens to burst from inside me. And faint-headed with pumping blood pressure from having to do this through each of the thousands of seconds I sit here each day, I feel like at one moment I'm one heartbeat away from fainting and in the next having to clench my sweating fists under the desk to stop me exploding.

I get one morning off at my desk to find my feet within a pile of documentation. And then I am straight back into it – struggling and flailing to remember or even care what the hell the acronyms my project manager keeps spouting actually mean, let alone how they relate to whichever financial instruments and trade types being processed within the networked labyrinths of individual, interconnecting mazes of computer systems.

With over a year away from this environment, now I saw the constant drive for cost-effectiveness and efficiency at the Bank beginning to bite – and with no other purpose than to maximise the Bank's profits as it cut down on overheads like IT and Business Analysis.

'We need to do more with less.'

My project manager seems to chant this like some kind of mantra. And this is about the one thing I grammatically understand coming out of his mouth.

But only grammatically – the logic behind it seemed completely self-defeating to me. Even before he realised his one Business Analyst was in a world of his own, he seemed to be permanently on the precipice of a heart attack.

'So . . . every year, the business wants us to do more with less?' I ask him one lunchtime.

'Yes.'

'But . . . Logically . . . Surely it's clear that we can't just keep on doing "more with less". What happens next year?'

'More with less.'

'But ultimately that's impossible, isn't it? If we carry on doing more and more work with less and less resources, soon there aren't going to be enough resources, in time or manpower, to do what the business tells us they want done.'

And all just to squeeze even more savings into their fat end-of-year bonuses.

But I cannot say this, as to do this would be to call into question the very reason every banker walked through the door here.

'Well, that's what the business wants. More with less.'

Stop fucking saying that!

I didn't know if I now only saw this insanity because I'd been out of it for over a year and then dropped straight back into it. Or maybe it was just because I was the one here who was now insane.

And I did feel completely insane, which the pressure in the office was doing everything it could to compound.

My mind cannot focus on anything – anything – let alone the convoluted corporate-speak on my computer monitor, which though I stare at and read and reread all over again, I cannot even make sense of the first introductory sentence. The words seem to make sense as individual English words – mostly – but when I try to put them together as a coherent sentence, all the meaning falls away.

A grey bank of fog just seems to descend over my mind – which only gets thicker as I feel the pressurising, accusing eyes of my project manager boring into the side of my head, as I feel him noticing that I am not doing any typing, and therefore anything that constitutes productive work in the eyes of the Bank.

I suspect that this fog is nothing but my own fog of war, brought home with me. But my own frustration with wanting it to clear only seems to thicken it further still.

Any strange mass of unfamiliar, complex information leaves my mind flailing. I cannot memorise any of this new information, because I cannot process any of this new information. And as soon as any kind of external or self-induced pressure is added, my mind simply shuts down, shutting off in self-defence from the stress.

I wish my mind would not do this. But it is something over which I find I have absolutely no control. And, repressed deep inside of myself, I know that I am already dealing with enough stress as it is, as the past bubbles up from my subconscious to right in front of my eyes and into each of the dreams that keep me awake every single night.

What I now realise is that the only things I now *know* are the things always piercing my mind – bringing headaches that stab into my brain, as the most painful of memories appear in front of me.

This past that is my present is now *all I fucking know*.

And I can stay in that fucking ergonomic chair – exactly the same as everyone else's – and silently rooted to my desk like some automaton, as from out of the grey bank of fog stab the first screaming words of '*medic!*', or I can just go into the lifts that take an electronically pinging, hand-tapping-in-your-pocket fucking *lifetime* to descend – with *God, please*, no one I know walking into it.

But then I am walking through the grey foyer, out into the freedom outside – if only for a few minutes.

Only after I chain-smoke three or four cigarettes in quick succession, breathing gulps of city air down between drags, can I summon the wherewithal to go back in – all the way back to that silent desk, with all its silently building pressure.

Then repeat, ad nauseam.

Too soon, the stabbing headaches rise in intensity and frequency. They come with no warning, and at the moment they strike they half-blind me with pain, making me cringe down in my chair in agony, before ebbing away in waves in the seconds afterwards. But every red tide retreating from my mind's shore is only a harbinger for the next head-splitting tsunami.

And my guts: when I have to go, I have only seconds to go. Diarrhoea doesn't even begin to explain what fucking explodes from me.

But these symptoms are just what are going on in my body – and I know well enough that they are probably just physical symptoms of the root cause in my mind. Because, as everyone in the Army knows: the mind controls the body, not the body controls the mind.

But I am not in control of my mind.

Where the 'intrusive memories' start and the 'flashbacks' begin, to use terminology I would be subsequently educated in, I just cannot tell you.

There are snapshots of shouts and screams, snapping *cracks* and the sudden *BANG* of explosions.

When I am finally home alone, locked safely in long silence behind my bedroom door with the curtains pulled safely shut – then I can smoke in shaking, dark privacy, as I rub my temples to just try to make them all go away.

But they don't go away. They never go away. I always see that compound through my Fifty Cal sight. And I always see the dead Taliban looking inside me. And I always see Tony Rawson's bandaged head and the still-ticking watch on his dead chest. And I always see the ANA soldier's face with his eyes on mine as he drifts further away. And I always – always – see Dave Hicks's face, as the darkness takes him.

Now I am safely alone, I want to purge myself with the release of choking, purging sobs. But as soon as the grief threatens to come, so does the blinding, boiling, grief-driven rage.

Then suddenly everything switches off.

And I feel absolutely nothing as I look back at another man in the mirror, before watching him reach for another cigarette.

*

There is a monster inside every one of us.

Should you become a soldier, you will find that this monster is harnessed and nurtured in training for war. And should you become a soldier who goes to war, you will find that the monster becomes your symbiotic friend, as you give free rein to his primeval, growing blackness, enabling you to channel it at other men's monsters.

But the monster that is now you is redundant in peace. So within this peace you will feel the monster restlessly stir, because the person you used to be knows that the blackness must now be repressed, and under no account channelled into the strange confines of this peace.

So in the quiet of this afterwards, the shouts and the screams of the past seem all the louder.

When sleep comes late into the night now, the ghosts of the dead live on in my dreams. And when the spectral grey fingers of dawn reach through the windows, I feel demons born of the monster coming for me from within. They torment me with their rage against reality and my guilt for having survived.

It is now, if a door slams shut, that I feel the freezing, soul-numbing rush of paralysing terror I could never allow myself to feel in

Afghanistan. And then all feeling will fade again for the day, because if you could dare to feel the lightness of love or joy in your life, you would also beckon the overwhelming blackness back into your heart.

*

My work is put under 'performance management'.

Although it is never worded as such, I know that this is the first corporate step to excising deadwood from a corporation. But as a precaution, or possibly just to tick a box on a form somewhere, the Bank also sends me to a company-sanctioned doctor in the City.

Impatient, clinical eyes looked at me first. Maybe she expected just another corporate victim of desk-bound stress.

But when I looked up from my wringing hands and back into her eyes after half an hour of slowly softening questioning about what I had seen and done – and what I was now seeing and trying to do – the impatience was gone.

With tentative tenderness, she said, 'Look . . . You're a complete wreck, aren't you? . . . There's no way you should be at work.'

I have to say I only felt relief in that moment, because I knew if I spent much longer sitting at that desk, under all the pressure that came with it, I was going to completely lose my mind.

She signed me off work – 'sick' – on the spot.

And the doctor's suspicions, and mine, are confirmed when I am referred to a psychiatrist, who, after a blurred hour of detailed questioning but then without any hesitation, diagnoses me with Chronic Post Traumatic Stress Disorder.

This diagnosis comes as a relief too, because I think it is always a small, merciful relief to be able to know exactly what is wrong with you. I think this is because you always need to know your enemy before you can ever hope to defeat him.

But now the private healthcare company I had been paying into with every one of my monthly paycheques, for all the years I had been with the Bank, refuses to fund any treatment for me. The reason they give is that my condition was 'caused by war'.

So with nowhere else to turn, I now have no other option but to approach the Army for treatment – though I know this diagnosis will hang over whatever is left of my military career and, in all likelihood, end it.

*

It was when my mother told me she had been invited to a families' 'Post Operational Stress Briefing' at the HAC that I realised how much she had been let down.

She said that this was the first time she had heard from the HAC since the pre-deployment 'Families' Briefing Day' that had taken place there well over a year ago.

Along with all the other soldiers' family members, she had been led to expect very different treatment at the hands of the HAC. They had been told that as the soldiers' 'Parent Unit', the HAC would provide the first level of support for all their welfare needs while we were away. They were told that they would be contacted at bi-monthly intervals – or as often as required during our tour of duty. And they were told there would be various events planned, bringing together all our families and partners in a social setting.

But none of these things had happened.

My family had been abandoned. Through all those months in Afghanistan that I thought the Army would be comforting her natural, mother's apprehension, she had instead been in receipt of the square root of nothing.

When I spoke to other soldiers, though, the story only got worse.

Some of their family members had actually tried to contact the HAC while we were away. They had, after all, expressly been told to phone the HAC welfare officer with any welfare concerns they had. But instead of hearing a friendly voice at the other end of a telephone, they just had to listen to their phone calls ringing out.

While travelling in the Australian outback, Charlie's parents had heard of a massive shoot-out in the Garmsir region of Helmand, where they knew their son was based. The press reported that two British soldiers had been killed, with names to follow only once the next of kin had first been informed.

Over the course of a week, they drove for hours back and forth to the nearest town so they could phone the HAC welfare officer to ask him if it was their son that had been killed. But no one at the HAC ever picked up the phone. And Charlie's parents only found out that their son was alive when he happened to have the chance to phone them back home in Darwin, a full week later.

Charlie's parents, too, had never heard from the HAC for the entire tour.

And the same sorry story was repeated, speaking to soldier after soldier.

Before we went to Afghanistan, the HAC had given us all forms to fill in, listing magazines they could send us while we were out there. We never received any of them, though. And this had pissed us off, for a while. But such feelings of being forgotten by our 'Regimental Family' now paled into petty insignificance compared with the outrage we now felt over how our real families had been comprehensively ignored while their sons fought abroad.

Though we soldiers were not invited to the upcoming families' 'Post Operational Stress Briefing', those of us that could attend did. Because now we wanted answers as to why our families had been abandoned as much as they did.

*

The evening began with a briefing on PTSD, in which we were reassured that '99.9 per cent of soldiers returning from Iraq and Afghanistan will not suffer from Post Traumatic Stress Disorder'.

The brief did get something right, though. It said that the 'Regimental Family' here at the HAC would be absolutely vital in helping its soldiers readjust back to home life. The rationale given was that the HAC should be a place where soldiers could talk about where they had just come from with other soldiers who had either 'been there', or should at least have an inkling as to where these other soldiers were coming from.

But then the welfare officer stood up. And it was then that the evening turned into a bloodbath.

A single-sided printout listing why there had been no welfare was handed out. It said that that our operational receiving units, in our cases 19 Regiment and the Grenadier Guards, were responsible for welfare.

This was news to the families, who before the tour had been told that it would only be the HAC providing their welfare support. Indeed, over the resulting 12-month void of silence, they had never been told otherwise.

But the printout stated that the HAC had no formal welfare officer and as such was not resourced to provide any support.

Maybe this explained why the 'welfare officer' now introduced himself to us as the 'regimental operations support officer'. But this did not explain why, before the tour, he had been repeatedly introduced to the families as the 'welfare officer', and as such their primary point of contact for any welfare concerns. And it did not explain why the

HAC officer listed as the secondary welfare contact had also been as proactively communicative with the families as Lord Lucan had been for the past 12 months.

So maybe it was not that surprising that the printed statement, 'The HAC provides significantly more individual support to soldiers mobilised than is required and is provided by other TA units', caused such outrage in the gathered families. How a dearth of support was somehow 'significantly more' than that provided by other units was certainly beyond me.

After the onslaught of the first barrage of questions from angry parents, Lord Lucan went to fetch the CO.

But this did not help him any more than it helped the CO.

'I think the lesson I have learned is that we endeavoured to provide that which we're not resourced to provide,' the CO said. 'And I have to take on the chin the fact that we promised what we couldn't provide. It was put forward with the best of intentions and it wasn't delivered. And I have to put my hand up and say that's my responsibility.'

I respected him for saying this. I thought it took a degree of guts to be able to stand up and take personal responsibility in front of everyone here. But then a few minutes later he added that official responsibility for welfare actually lay with the Regular Unit we were attached to in theatre.

'Could you not then have informed the soldiers and families that responsibility for welfare was being passed to Regular Units?' a father asked. 'As it was, we were just left totally in limbo.'

'I can't disagree with you. Yes, I do think you should have been contacted.'

'Well, why didn't you?'

'I can only apologise . . . Short of doing it myself, I have no excuses whatsoever,' the CO answered, before adding, 'It has to be made absolutely clear that legal and moral responsibility for our soldiers are two different things. When they're on my strength prior to mobilisation and post-demobilisation, then I have the disciplinary, pay and every other responsibility for those soldiers. During the period when they're mobilised, I do not. I have no authority over them whatsoever and I have no command status over that. That transposes to the commanding officer of the unit they go to. I cannot influence them; I don't own them in any way. I clearly retain a moral cap-badge responsibility for them before they go and indeed when they come back – and that's part of why we're here this evening. But while they're away, I cannot influence that outcome. So communication to and from the soldiers is from us through the rear party of the unit they go to, to theatre and back again. We are not directly in the loop and therefore the communication . . .'

'Shouldn't we have had an introduction to their units?' a father interrupted. 'I mean, I can remember the last meeting we had here. My son was posted to the Grenadier Guards. And I asked the question should we relate to the Guards – who were very forthcoming about their welfare support – or yourselves. And you said no, there are only eight guys going out – stay with us.'

Another soldier's father added that after reading the HAC booklet promising that the HAC would be the key liaison for welfare, when it hadn't been, for the past five months he had been phoning the HAC on the numbers he had been given and not once had he ended up talking to the person he wanted to. He said he had left messages, but nobody had got back to him at any time. So he had given up using the phone and tried email instead. But the welfare officer had now told him he hadn't received any emails, as there was a 'problem with the system'.

And another father took issue with the moral responsibility, and recognition, shown to his son when he returned from Afghanistan. 'Every other unit that goes out there, they at least have a parade on the streets and get their welcome back with some degree of ceremony. But our fellows here seem to have just turned up, handed their kit in and off they go. It's pretty shabby, wouldn't you say?'

'I disagree, but I will take your comments on board,' the CO replied. 'But I disagree with that. And having done it several times myself, I know, and am entirely comfortable, that my soldiers have been treated significantly better than I've been, when I've been through this process myself.'

'I don't think that's the issue,' replied the father quietly.

Yet another father raised the point that he thought the HAC could just do better.

'What we could do better is tell you what we will deliver,' the CO replied. 'It may not be very much – and it probably won't be very much. But we will deliver what we can realistically do, 100 per cent of the time – and that's basically it. And that, actually, isn't very much. What I will clearly delineate is what we can deliver. That's the issue here. We promised what we can't deliver. In future, I'll promise what we can deliver. The criticism will be we're not doing enough, but I have to make the judgement as to what we have the resources to provide.'

The CO was then asked what had changed with the HAC welfare in the past couple of years, when soldiers had been extremely complimentary about it when they had gone to Iraq.

He pointed out that in welfare terms, there was a fundamental difference between the Herrick 6 and 7 tours in Afghanistan, where we were attached to Regular units, and the Telic 4 and 5 tours in Iraq, which were pure HAC deployments without receiving Regular units.

Now I could not keep quiet any more.

I interjected that the welfare on my second, Telic 4, tour of Iraq had indeed been good. But my first tour of Iraq had been Telic 1. And even though I had been attached to a Regular unit for this invasion – which, incidentally, had not provided my family with any welfare – the welfare from the HAC had been excellent. Contrary to the claims of the HAC not being resourced to provide welfare in such a situation, my mother had been written to and phoned by HAC officers at regular intervals, I had received mail from HAC officers saying how much they appreciated what I was doing, and we all had a slap-up dinner at the HAC to welcome me home and show all due appreciation to my family.

There was no time for the CO to reply to this, though, or even for me to finish talking, as my mother, who all the time had been sitting quietly beside me, leapt down the CO's throat to back me up.

I had not realised the depth of betrayal she felt until I heard her in that moment.

And her target was very clear, now standing solitary and momentarily lost for words in front of us all, but I felt my own measure of guilt for putting her through this purgatory.

My impression was that the evening never progressed any further than that. My impression was that of the families' questions and the CO's answers only going around in circles until the CO said, 'Can I . . . Can we just . . . Because time's running on . . . I've detected the underlying trend. I think we're sort of going over old ground with similar things coming out time and time again. I suggest we break now, have some further refreshment. Quite happy to take any one-to-one or group comments, or any of the other staff will do. And if you want to address any of the issues with me personally, you can make an appointment and I will do so. But I think we're sort of going over old ground now, time's running on and I'd like to cap the evening there, if I may. Thank you.'

Then he walked out.

And with his departure, I do not think that the irony of that evening's title – as a 'Post Operational Stress Briefing' – escaped any of the soldiers and families left sitting there.

*

One week later, I found myself in the regimental sergeant major's oak-panelled office, this time for my post-tour 'interview without coffee'.

But this time I felt completely severed from my surroundings. I felt like a head impaled on a stick.

I had enough pre-interview self-awareness to suspect I would be like this in the face of more stress, though. So, just as it had done a week ago, the electronic Dictaphone recording covertly in my suit pocket did all the remembering my mind could no longer do. But as the RSM specifically warned me not to repeat what was said and that our meeting was confidential, unfortunately I cannot tell you everything that he said. In any event, I merely watched the RSM's lips move. I heard sound coming out of them. But I only understood some of this sound washing over me as words, and still less as coherent sentences. I was given no opportunity to raise any welfare concerns. It was made very clear to me that this chat was nothing but a reprimand for speaking out as I had done to the CO.

When the RSM had finished, I was shown through another door to see the adjutant.

But now I was taking in even less of what was being said to me.

I think the adjutant was meant to be playing the role of the good cop in that evening's events. I know he talked about soldiers' and families' welfare, and I think he instilled some hope in me that lessons really had been learned at the HAC.

But my Dictaphone could not record any such flickers of feeling.

*

A Falklands veteran still fighting his own PTSD 26 years on told me about 'Post Operational Reports'.

He sounded angry when I told him that, apart from never having received these forms from the HAC, I had not been educated to even know what they were. He said that these forms were the only way to ensure that all lessons learned on tour were not lost when soldiers returned home.

So I sent an email to the HAC asking if I could be provided with a Post Operational Report form.

And in the emailed reply I was sent a POR form, as requested. But the 'advice' attached to it was to 'stick to matters relating to training/ preparation etc. and avoid welfare issues. The CO and the whole CoC are fully aware of the problems which resulted from welfare provision and have acknowledged them fully. A constructive POR commenting on how to better prepare HAC personnel for Ops will be very useful. However, commenting yet again on welfare could be viewed as unnecessary criticism and may well overshadow the other areas which have as yet not been commented on.'

Aside from the long-doomed cause of arming drivers with pistols, though, all the areas I wanted to cover were to do with welfare. The CO's words that welfare provided to subsequent families 'probably won't be very much' had set klaxons of alarm going off in my head.

But what was the point in now causing further strife with my 'Regimental Family' – in addition to my degenerating PTSD – by raising a POR about welfare, which sounded like it would not even be listened to?

I felt I had run out of options to be heard.

But I knew I could not let this go, if only for the sake of the soldiers and their families coming after ours. Frustration was now fuelling an already rising anger within me that concerns I saw as paramount were not being addressed.

Even after all that had been said by the families at that evening, we still had had no 'welcome home' of any description. And we still had no idea when our medals parade would be, which, in the absence of any 'welcome home', would now be the only recognition we ever received for our war service.

In the first weeks at home, I had watched other units from my tour getting homecoming parades through the streets on TV. I had watched them receiving their medals to applause and appreciation. I imagined how this recognition might enable them to begin to draw a line in the sand between what they had experienced in Afghanistan and finding a peace within the rest of their lives at home.

But all this had happened months ago. And with the absence of any recognition from my unit or country, I was now already in the domain of treatment.

*

Months later, the RSM's email announced that the medals parade would take place on 23 July – seven months after we had returned to our civilian lives. In the email, we were told the CO had 'agreed to three paid guests' per soldier for the presentation being held behind the HAC gates. We were also told that the parade would have a dual nature, in that long-service medals were going to be presented to other HAC soldiers.

I had been on one of these parades before, when I just happened to also qualify for a long-service medal after returning from my second tour of Iraq. Together with the other 'old and bold', I had taken regimental pride of place in front of my Iraq comrades. We were dressed to the nines in parade blues, while behind, my Iraq friends were in plain pressed combats.

We had long citations read out as our long-service medals were individually presented, honouring our long-service commitment to the TA, while behind, my comrades just had their names read out with the words 'Operation Telic 4' attached.

It had not felt right to me at the time. In fact, I felt it was just plain embarrassing, with many of the 'old and bold' basking in the limelight beside me not even having a single tour to their name over the whole stretching length of their long, distinguished TA service.

Now, in 2008, and considering that 23 July would be the only tangible prospect for recognition of the HAC's first group of war veterans since the Second World War, the prospect of that coming evening now felt even more wrong.

I did not think that war veterans and their long-suffering families should have to play second fiddle to old and bold, career TA soldiers who had never set foot in a war zone in their lives. And the fact that this 'recognition' was now taking place seven months after our return home only seemed like the final, denigrating insult.

So I sent an email back to the HAC.

Now that I had lost all patience with my 'Regimental Family', all the fight that I still carried with me from Afghanistan was channelled into this one email to my HAC commanding officer.

I spelled out the experiences of myself and my family, and all the other soldiers and their families who had had to endure the same treatment.

And I copied every HAC soldier into this email, because I felt they had a right to know what they and their families would be volunteering for, should they put their names forward to go on tour.

I knew I'd probably be pressing the self-destruct button on my HAC career as I clicked on 'Send'. But now I could think of no other way to get the HAC to listen, act and treat its soldiers and their families with the respect they deserved. Someone had to put his head over the parapet on this. I felt it might as well be me. Though some would subsequently tell me this was an act of moral courage overdue at the HAC, for me there was zero courage involved. Pressing the self-destruct button on my Army career was an insignificant price to pay when, more and more, I just wanted to quietly press the self-destruct button on my life.

Unsurprisingly, the shit hit the fan.

Over the following days, I received close to a hundred emails of support from the HAC rank and file – many of whom, it turned out, had been keeping quiet through gritted teeth about their own similar frustrations after being on tour.

But within two minutes of sending it, my squadron commander had left a voicemail on my phone.

He said I had let him down.

Though I could put down on paper the two words I immediately thought on listening to this message, there probably isn't any need.

My loyalties now lay only with my family, my fellow deployed soldiers, their families, and all those soldiers and families who would come after us.

I knew I would never go on tour again. The Army could now never be anything more than a part-time career, played at on weekends. So if the Army now wanted to take the fight to me, then so it would have to be.

In retrospect, there does not seem any doubt that I was still fighting, all these long months after Afghanistan. War had come home with me. But with no one left to fight but the ghosts haunting my waking hours and the demons hunting me in my dreams, now I had a self-destructively welcome, external enemy to take *jus ad bellum* arms against.

The fight would be worth it, ensuring that never again would HAC soldiers and their families be treated the way ours had.

But it would also be true that the added isolation of this fight would only help speed my fall into the last, dark depths of my own personal abyss.

I know my email reached the then head of the Army, General Sir Richard Dannatt, at least twice. I know it was printed out and enclosed within letters sent to him by both Tom's father and a close friend of my family.

And I know that as a result of this, an investigation into its contents was commissioned to be overseen by a major general, who in his day job oversaw all Army units in the London area. Stemming from this, both Tom and I were subsequently invited to raise official 'Service Complaints'.

This was a course of action that neither Tom nor I had any idea we could take against our senior HAC chain of command. I also learned that any disciplinary action to be taken against me for my email was to be put on ice until the investigation was completed.

But I was, however, informed by the senior HAC hierarchy that I personally was barred from entering the HAC barracks for the duration of the investigation – unless I phoned ahead for an 'escort', that is. However the thought of being physically escorted round the barracks by a member of the senior hierarchy I was now implicating actually did not appeal that much. These same HAC officers must have known this was an academic measure, as they knew I had PTSD and had been medically downgraded because of it, so was ineligible to join normal HAC training anyway.

I was sure as hell I did not need any physical protection from the ordinary rank and file, if that was indeed the official reason for this further isolation. And the further alienation I felt only hardened my resolve to fight.

*

In November 2008, I sat in another oak-panelled room. But this one was not at the HAC barracks off City Road. It was at the 'Headquarters London District' in Whitehall, not even a stone's throw from Downing Street and the Cenotaph honouring all our 'Glorious Dead'.

The major general spoke with me for nearly an hour. I thought he came across as an extremely intelligent, fair and reasonable man. He pulled me up on writing my open email, as much as he said he understood my reasons for it.

But in his subsequent letter to me outlining the findings of the investigation, he said he judged that I had been 'wronged by the lack of communication with your family while you were deployed, and by the imperfect way in which you were received back into the HAC on your return'.

And I had never seen any of this as his fault, but he said that he apologised 'on behalf of the Army' for what my family had been put through.

In redress, he said he was taking action to ensure that all units under his command assumed a role that ensured that the families of deployed personnel were communicated with – even if, in certain circumstances, communication was not by that unit. And he said that he had raised with the CO of the HAC the need to tighten procedures within the HAC with regard to personnel returning from operations.

On the issue of welfare, I could not ask for any more than that.

But in my complaint I had also taken the opportunity to raise the issue of arming drivers with pistols in addition to their long-barrelled personal weapons.

In his letter, the major general said that I had not been wronged in relation to the lack of issue of a pistol. Army policy was that personnel up to the rank of major were to deploy with long-barrelled personal weapons, and both the HAC and 19 Regiment had adhered to this policy. However, he said that he had read my rationale for arming drivers with pistols in addition to their personal weapons and recognised what I said. So he would be raising the issue with Headquarters Land Forces for evaluation.

As an insignificant TA lance sergeant, I knew I had no more hope of influencing Army policy than that. But some months later I will sit down with the new HAC CO for a second time. And for the second time, he will tell me how the HAC is improving its welfare out of recognition. And for the second time, with gentle sincerity he will ask the simple, heartbreaking question: 'How are you?'

With heartfelt appreciation, I will thank the new CO again for his and the new welfare officer's actions to revolutionise HAC welfare out of all recognition as much as I will thank him for his concern for my wellbeing.

But then I will ask him if he knows any more about my requests for drivers to be issued with pistols. He will say that, as yet, there had been no promulgation of policy from HQ Land Forces on that one. But what he could tell me was that it was his understanding that there had been a recent buy of 10,000 SIG Sauer pistols. And on the current tour in Afghanistan, it was also his understanding that not only every single driver, but also every single soldier on the ground there, now had the option of carrying a pistol in addition to their personal weapon, if he or she wished it.

I do not care if an insignificant TA lance sergeant had any or no influence over the arming of soldiers. Certainly it could never be acknowledged, even if he had. But now, every time on the news I see a driver with a pistol always attached to him, I afford myself the smallest of smiles. Because it is this result that I can see with my own eyes, along with the result of HAC soldiers' families never again having to endure what ours went through, that was all that ever mattered.

*

Before the new CO took over, I heard from the old CO one last time before he left the HAC.

I had put in an application for that year's HAC Winter Ball. I thought it would be good for me to come in from the cold.

But at this point I was still drafting my acceptance letter of the major general's findings.

In his letter, the CO instructed that my application be returned. He informed me that because the complaints process was ongoing and that I had not yet completed the required documentation, it would be inappropriate for me to attend a regimental function in any capacity. But he said that as soon as the matter was concluded, he or his successor would be pleased to write to me and set out the framework for my future service in the TA and HAC.

I thought I would wait until the new CO took over at the HAC before completing the required documentation.

*

In the same November that I sat down with a major general in an oak-panelled room, I also sat down with a human resources manager in the goldfish bowl of a glass-panelled office.

My sick leave was up. And now I was told of my future with the Bank.

I didn't have one.

If personal finances did not have to factor into the reckoning of this next imposition, then probably the only feeling to emerge through the haze of my emotional numbness would have been indifference.

Against the backdrop of a breaking crisis in the banking system, my sole consolation was that I did not have to whore my soul any more to an organisation whose counterparts, at least, were now threatening to implode as a direct result of their avarice – and doing their best to take the rest of the world with them.

But the near collapse of the banks and their bailouts only highlighted the pivotal place of money in this material, digital world that I found myself in again, after having grown accustomed to another world of living in mud huts, and killing.

By now, the Army deemed me to be 'totally disabled' from PTSD. And with this injury caused by my Army service, my bailout came in the form of 'disability allowance' from the Army – while I remained part of the Army.

But there was a 'but' – just as there usually is.

When TA soldiers are mobilised to go on tour, they receive a 'Reservist's Award' of open-ended denomination, which increases their basic TA rank salary to that of the civilian one they left behind. This, basically, is to ensure that the TA soldier can still pay the mortgage while he or she is away, without incurring any financial penalties for being mobilised.

If some Regs think this is a cushy number, then I would also ask these same Regs to remember that we in the TA never receive any generous, lifelong pension entitlements at the end of our service. We are cheap labour, and the Army knows this.

But now I had fulfilled my use on tour, the fact that I was subsequently incapable of doing my civilian career because of an injury attributable to that tour didn't seem to matter to my Army. Its rules stipulated that once a TA soldier was demobilised, and whether the injury was caused by your mobilised service or not, disability allowance was only paid at your basic TA rank salary.

So while I fight my demons with the added pressure of losing my civilian career, I now also stare down the barrel of losing £10,000 a year out of my life savings just to make ends meet financially.

As I watch my means to survive dying the death of a thousand cuts each month, with each cut slicing further stress into my degenerating mind, I also find myself staring down at the blank canvas of my arm. And for the first of what will be many times, slicing plain red cuts into that blank pink canvas now makes complete, logical sense.

It makes sense as a distraction from the pain inside. It makes sense as an expression of feeling, of that which I must fight to stop myself feeling. And it makes sense as an expression of control, over a life in which I have no control.

Now the banks were reaping the whirlwind of their excesses. And now I was reaping the personal whirlwind of mine.

My excesses were not born from a greed-driven, amoral desire for material gain, though. I had done murderously immoral things, but I told myself I had done them from the selfless moral high ground that a soldier has to live upon, where together he and his comrades must face killing or being killed.

But I had volunteered to serve my country in these ways. So you may condemn me, as I condemn myself.

Or you may consider that there are certain things that I did not volunteer either my family or myself for. And if you consider this, then you may feel some of the other pain that I do, in the solitude where I fight with my remaining sanity to keep this aftermath from overcoming me.

With Army policies being what they were, and bank decisions being what they will always be, I guess that I am not meant to feel betrayed.

But I do.

*

Since my first appointment with her in May 2008, Wendy had been doing everything she could to treat me.

Once a week, every week, I took the ten-minute drive to her psychologist's offices inside Woolwich Barracks' medical centre.

And for an hour every week, she recorded those symptoms I could recall over the past seven days. Together, we tried to delve into the root causes of these symptoms, within all the parts of my mind harbouring all the unprocessed memories bubbling up from my subconscious as all the flashbacks, nightmares and 'intrusive memories'.

As part of a strategy of 'Cognitive Behaviour Therapy', I undergo 'Trauma Focussed Therapy'.

We also try: 'Eye Movement Desensitisation and Reprocessing Therapy'.

And I know the psychological theories behind these lines of treatment; Wendy has explained them very well, very often.

In Trauma Focussed Therapy, the patient must force himself to recount in all visceral detail, using all his senses, everything that he does not want to recall. He must force himself to relive everything that fucked him up. This may sound counter-intuitive, maybe even masochistic. But the theory is that by forcing the brain to confront the memories it has clamped a subconscious lid on, by forcing the mind to feel what it shut off feeling at the time, then the patient can process these memories and come to peace with the past.

But there is a problem. And that problem is that, as much as I try, I cannot emotionally connect to the most painful and horror-filled of repressed memories as I try to recount them – even though I know full well from the projected imagery of my flashbacks that they are causing the PTSD.

This is not a conscious decision I take. Instead I find, just as it happened in Afghanistan, that at the critical moment of feeling the tip of an emotional iceberg, my subconscious just slams down the emotional shutters.

Throughout my battle with the HAC, past the termination of my career with the Bank and then into 2009, both Wendy and I try to get past this emotional walling-off. I know Wendy is doing everything right as a psychologist. I know it is I who am failing her and, by extension, myself.

But as soon as the feeling threatens to explode from me I always, automatically, shut down. I think this is for her safety as much as my own, because to give voice to these demons here in her office would be to tear her office apart. Although she tells me that she is prepared for this, I am not prepared for this. My mind will not let me.

So I feel an ever-growing frustration at myself, when all my adult life I have grown used to just *doing* things. There is nothing I want more than to give vent to the grief and the rage and just be *rid of them*.

But as soon as their blacknesses begin to boil from inside me, rushing up to my surface as scalding as searing steam, a singular, all-consuming black void suddenly reaches up to swallow them back down.

And then, just as suddenly, I find myself sitting on a chair, in an office, in Woolwich, staring blankly back at Wendy – without any words or memories or feelings to give voice to.

*

Failure is another emotion that I cannot stand to feel, because in adult life I have conditioned myself not to fail at anything. Failure takes me straight back to the feelings of worthlessness I grew up with as a stammering, reclusive little boy.

I cannot go back there. And I am tired of my life going nowhere. But as much as I consequently want to report improvement to Wendy, and as much as I want both her and myself to believe this is true, I know that I am lying to myself.

In September 2009, I try to force positive change in my life. I enrol in a part-time university course in Psychology. As a former graduate, I tell myself that a part-time course should not present any problems for an already tested intellect. And I tell myself that I know enough about PTSD now that maybe I could train to help other people like me.

But exactly the same thing happens as it did with the masses of unfamiliar, complex information that I encountered in my twilight weeks at the Bank.

Overlooking the frustration of now not being able to take on board anything that I am being taught, the most frustrating aspect of this intellectual failure is that I know intellectually why I am failing but cannot emotionally do anything about it.

Your brain is nothing but a series of synapses. In principle this series of binary on/off switches is exactly akin to a computer's CPU, with memory assigned to store and run applications such as Microsoft Word – or, in the case of your brain, the memory of how to click on this icon and tap your memories into the application that opens from it. Your computer must remember how to do other tasks, though, such as running the necessary evil of anti-virus software that keeps threats at bay. And you must also remember to look both ways before crossing the street – just as I must always stand as close as I can to anyone with a backpack on the underground and watch their hands as if my life and everyone else's depends upon it.

But sometimes you will just want to hurl your computer through the window, when it will not do what you tell it to do, or when it just seems to hang on some unseen background task using all of its processing power, when all you want to do is use its portal to get out there into the virtual universe it is supposed to connect you with. It whirs away on this unseen background task, leaving you incapable in the foreground.

This is what I know PTSD to be.

The emotional subconscious whirs away in your background as it tries to process gargantuan quarantined memories, while all the time your conscious tries to keep a lid on this past so it can mechanically operate in the here and now. The flashbacks, nightmares and 'intrusive memories' are just memory leaks into your foreground, bubbling up to the surface in front of your eyes.

With this, you know this past is now all you know. There is as much room left in your memory for new information as there is processing power left over in your mind to make use of it.

But on this university course, I determine to use every percentile of memory and processing power I have left in my mind. And with the bloody-minded determination that used to serve me so well, I push myself to the outer limits of what I can do.

With end-of-term exams approaching, I study full-time for what is only the introductory term of a part-time course. I attend every lecture and spend all my free time afterwards poring through notes.

Even in the lectures, though, I know something is wrong. I do not understand the messages that the spoken English sentences are trying to convey. So I try to write everything down that the lecturers say, so I can try to understand their words in my own time later. But I cannot write fast enough. And afterwards, my mind cannot even make sense of the bullet-pointed lecture slides downloaded from the university website.

In my study, I read and reread words. I piece them together into sentences. After a while, I highlight them to ram them home into memory. But when I turn over the page, I cannot even recall what the subject's title is, let alone any of the subject matter nested within its equally forgotten subheadings.

And immersed in this piling pressure, which should not be any pressure, the ghosts and the demons now come for me with a vengeance.

I feel like my home is haunted by the dead. But, of course, this house is only haunted by me.

To stand any chance of sleep, I must now lie in bed facing the closed bedroom door. I must do this with a claw hammer immediately to hand under my bed, so I can kill any night intruders before they kill me.

In the morning I must lock the bathroom door before I step naked and vulnerable into the shower. I know I am alone within a religiously locked house, but with the sound of the running water drowning out all other noise within the cubicle, I must always keep my eyes on the bathroom door.

I know this probably has something to do with the shrapnel-exposed showering facility at Inkerman. But this knowledge is of zero help.

Dressed and outside my house, I cannot stand the sensation of anyone walking unseen behind me. But this is a problem when I must walk along streets, stand on overcrowded underground trains and pass unseen through bustling university buildings.

Increasingly, I am not in any of these places. It only takes a pneumatic drill to sound in the street, or a happily innocent student to slam a door, and then I am back in Afghanistan.

Like a good soldier, I duck when I hear these *bangs*; my head snaps to face the threat and my right knee goes to ground first as my body instinctively kneels into a firing position. Surrounded by happy-go-lucky students, I cannot scream aloud as I feel the blood on my hands all over again and see those who died, dying and dead all over again.

Even without the flashback-inducing triggers of sudden bangs, I still see things.

I see blood in the blank canvas of snow, just as I saw blood in the pale sand of Afghanistan. I know I am hallucinating, but when I turn away and force myself to look again, it is still there.

Along with the flashbacks, the nightmares too increase in frequency and intensity, to the point where I feel like the walking dead even before the first lecture of each day begins.

Increasingly, I find myself waking beside the dead Taliban in that ditch.

So when you wake yourself up screaming in the middle of just another night, as drenched in sweat and immersed in horror as you were in Afghanistan; when you find yourself trying to ground your mind back to the house you are now sure you will lose; when you find yourself trying to resynchronise your mind with a new life over which you now have absolutely no control, then you know it is only a matter of time before something is going to give.

So I did not take the decision to walk away from university lightly in December 2009. But as much as I could not stand the thought of giving up at something, I knew that by exerting this extra pressure on my already overloaded mind, I was simply making the PTSD worse.

In selecting the battles I could win, versus those that were simply hopeless, I saw there was no point to my being in a classroom, let alone an exam room. And submitting my mind to unforgiving exams that I knew I would fail outright would only be a further failure enshrined by damning grades with which I would only further flagellate myself. I chose not to subject my loathsome frailty to this.

If you think I am a 'flake', as one peripheral 'friend' labelled me afterwards, despite everything he and now you know about me, then I too invite you to go away and do whatever it takes to give you the reality of Chronic Post Traumatic Stress Disorder.

Then I invite you to enrol at university.

And then you can come back to me on that one.

*

A new year began. And so did a new line of treatment.

Wendy administered neuropsychological tests on me. Although these apparently indicated a 'high level of intelligence' prior to the PTSD, they also revealed 'problems in immediate auditory and visual memory, working memory, sustained attention and cognitive flexibility'.

But now we were running out of treatment options. So to see if my memory and concentration problems could be specifically targeted, Wendy referred me to the Mild Traumatic Brain Injury department within the MOD rehabilitation centre at Headley Court.

There was a question mark over whether the same percussive impacts that had permanently damaged my hearing might also have caused mild physical damage to my brain. So I was thankful when a subsequent MRI scan revealed no physical damage to the watery mush between my ears. But this was not the reason why I was initially refused treatment at Headley Court.

I was turned away because I was a demobilised TA soldier.

I wrote an email back to the administrator responsible for turning me away, thanking him for his truly depressing email, and asking why I should be discriminated against just because I was no longer serving with the Regular Army.

If you don't ask, you don't get.

To Headley Court's complete credit, I got a phone call that afternoon asking when I could come in for treatment.

So once a fortnight for the next five months, I drove up and down the M25 to see a doctor called Clare. Here we went through 'problem-focussed coping and goal setting', 'sleep-management techniques', 'positive activity scheduling including increased social contact', 'compensatory strategies for attention and memory' and 'relaxation techniques'.

These techniques may well work for soldiers with mild, physical brain injuries. But, if only in my case, they did not work for a soldier with a severe, psychological injury.

I tried. God, I knew this was the last chance saloon.

But these techniques were only treating the knock-on effects to my life from the PTSD, not curing the root causes of the PTSD. So the PTSD symptoms did not go away. And neither did their knock-on effects to my life.

Treatment was concluded in September 2010, 'as it was agreed that he was unlikely to benefit from further input due to his ongoing mental health issues which were outside the remit of this service'.

Which was completely fair enough. The PTSD was the cause of the malaise, not any physical injury. And I will always be thankful to Clare for trying everything in her remit to heal me.

So I return to the care of Wendy. But now every avenue of treatment has been exhausted, I know that I am going to be medically discharged from the Army.

Wendy's focus changes to managing my day-to-day symptoms. But now I am dimly aware that the flashbacks, nightmares and resulting emotional walling-off are getting worse still, as I face the added stress of medical discharge from the Army.

Discharge will mean the cessation of my Army disability allowance. And the cessation of this allowance will mean that I will soon be in a position of dreaming about the time I was only losing £10,000 a year out of my life savings.

While I wait for the Army Medical Board that will discharge me, I fluctuate from complete emotional lockdown to flaring up in rage at the smallest irritation. A push-top bin that will not close because I tapped its lid down a couple of newtons too hard suddenly gets seven shades of shit knocked out of it. In retrospect, I probably would have made fantastic viewing if I had been incarcerated in the *Big Brother* house at this time, because there just would have been blood.

As always, though, Wendy does her best by me. But I am finding it increasingly hard to interact with the world around me. The front half of my car is ripped off by a speeding lorry as I am driving out of the med centre's gates. Wendy said she heard the bang all the way back in her office. I was just numbly picking up bits of wreckage from the road when she ran out to me. Somehow both of the insurance companies saw it as the other driver's fault. Fuck knows how.

After two years of therapy, Wendy continues to do everything she can to manage my spiralling, PTSD-twisted emotions. But now we both know that the severity of my symptoms and their resulting prognosis is not good. I know it is just a matter of looking facts in the face.

So I am persuaded to put in a claim to the Armed Forces Compensation Scheme (AFCS).

I know that maybe you will just read words here. But if you are anything like the person I was before, then maybe you will feel a trace of the frustration I feel now writing them.

In denial again of what happened at the Bank and at university, I had tried doing a PADI Open Water diving course. But, as much as I felt serenely disconnected from the real world above water, I could not take on board any of the theory in the books I was given.

I had also tried doing a British Military Fitness instructor's course in Cardiff, thinking I could maybe earn a crust beasting City-girl clients round the parks of London. But when the time came to plan all the practice lessons necessary for this qualification, I only found myself staring down at blank sheets of paper, with panic gripping at my chest.

One of the example exercises we were run through was a competitive elaboration of 'man down' drills, taught by the Army to extract dying soldiers from out of the line of fire.

I was not on a football field in Cardiff as the other students play-acted at war.

It turns out that this burden I have does not go away. And it turns out that just trying to will it away by trying to force positive change in my life only makes the burden heavier still.

My name is Jake Wood. And I have Post Traumatic Stress Disorder.

*

The reluctantly reached, considered prognosis for my PTSD was based on more than two years of psychological assessment by a certified psychologist.

And after more than two years of intensive treatment, with ultimately only a worsening of my PTSD, I know that I too must now face up to reality.

The prognosis for my 'severe' symptoms is that in all likelihood they will now be permanent.

I hate the word 'compensation' as much as anyone does. But I know that if I am to stand any chance of financial survival on discharge from the Army – and by extension stand any chance of physical survival in the material world beyond – then I now have no option but to submit a claim to the Armed Forces Compensation Scheme.

The AFCS is meant to ensure that debilitated soldiers discharged from the Army can financially survive in the outside world afterwards. But despite the fact that I am now due to be medically discharged from the Army specifically because of this prognosis, the AFCS refuses to accept it.

And they disagree with this prognosis despite the facts that the AFCS medical advisors assigned to my case have never even met me, have only Wendy's and Clare's reports to go on and, in the words of the AFCS themselves, 'are not specialists in any particular area of mental health or psychiatry'.

To back up their decision, they say that I successfully responded to treatment after my second tour of Iraq. They also refer to outdated reports from 2009, filed at a time when I was in a state of denial and desperate to force change in my life at university. It does not appear to make any difference to them that all this vain hope was blown out of the water.

Now I have lost my sanity, my civilian and Army careers and even my love life to the service of my country, the AFCS issues me with a single lump-sum payment of £9,075, 'for pain and suffering'.

I guess this means that when the Army discharges me, I will then be expected to go on the dole. Certainly, after medical discharge, the tens of pounds I might get each week from the standard state handout of 'Incapacity Benefit' will not pay any mortgage.

Now I have fulfilled my use to my country, I know I am just going to be dumped. And with spiralling anger, I do ask myself: 'How many other soldiers are they treating like this?'

But now all hope is lost, the fight inside me that my social worker had seen as a good thing in striving for new purpose to my life begins to turn in on myself. And now I have no prospect other than eking out an existence on the state handout of Incapacity Benefit and losing my home as a result, I reach only one conclusion in October 2010.

This conclusion is not one I suddenly jump to. It is a course of action that has been growing as a considerable comfort over the countless, endlessly long nights.

As I have lost control of my mind, I have lost control of my life. And the last shred of control I can exert over this twilight of life is simply to end it.

I hear Death calling me with his Siren song. I hear him promising the gentle release of escape. And I hear him promising final dignity.

I will hate my family now as much as I love them – because it is ultimately only my love for them which is stopping me from completing this journey.

I know I cannot do this to them.

But I do not want to live this shadow of a life any more. The ghosts and the demons never leave me alone. I cannot sleep. And I do not want to be a part of any life, any more, that is now just going to fade away into financial poverty, as a waning shade of my former self.

I do not see suicide just as an escape, though. I also see it as a devotion – for I do not think it is right how younger men, with whole lives to live, died when I survived. And I know this is labelled as 'survivor guilt', in just another of the listed symptoms of PTSD. But knowing intellectually what something is, as opposed to feeling the ever-accusing finger pointing at you, are two very different things.

Dave Hicks was still in his 20s when he was killed. Tony Rawson was nearly half my age. God alone knows how young the baby-faced Afghan soldier was. And I have no idea how old any of the people I killed were – any more than I have any idea of exactly how many of them there are to my name.

One is enough, in this afterwards.

But I think another of the reasons I always see Dave Hicks's dying face is what he represented to me – as an officer who would literally die for his men.

I had not seen this devotion in other officers on my return home. So as much as I rail against the death of Dave Hicks as a young man, I think I also rail against the death of what he represented to me.

All these feelings of betrayal at the hands of a now prior HAC now tap directly into all my feelings of despair and betrayal at the hands of the AFCS.

And it is when I go beyond despair, into the quiet abyss of certainty that I am simply going to drive up to the AFCS and take as many of them with me – before joining them all again in Hell – that I realise one of two things must now happen.

Either I do this, with the same cold, dislocated rage with which I killed in Afghanistan.

Or I cling onto the last vestiges of endurance within me, for the good of only my family, and pick up the phone, and tell someone of what I am going to do.

This is my soliloquy.

But Death does not scare me. I know him well now. And the thought of speeding his ever-coming, friendly embrace, all the way back home into the womb of oblivion, is nothing other than comfort.

And for the book I have been writing throughout all the years you are now familiar with, I can think of no more final resolution to it than the ending of the author's life.

11

VICISSITUDE

In that book which is my memory
Before which little can be read,
Appear the words 'Incipit vita nova':
Here begins the new life.

Dante Alighieri, La Vita Nuova

I did not know what to expect from the secure psychiatric wing of a hospital.

I thought it might be a place where you would undergo intensive treatment, to make you 'better again'.

But I found that it was no such place. It is just a place to put people.

You are body searched on admission. And then your shoelaces are taken from you as your bag is also searched for anything that might do harm to yourself or others. Lighters, razors, mirrors, every electrical item, anything with a cord, and even nail clippers – all gone.

And then you are just left, through all the waking hours of daylight into each dark night of the soul, with only your spiralling thoughts or the incoherent, babbling thoughts of other poor locked-away souls to keep you company.

Meals are the highlights of each day, served by stone-faced staff. And after tea, you are called one by one to a counter to take your pill for the day.

And that is your life, every day, on a secure psychiatric ward.

But there are deeper circles to this hell. And you can hear the tormented souls of even more tightly secured individuals screaming from them, late into the night.

I was just in an entry-level ward. On this ward I was one of a minority of patients, in that I had not been sectioned but had 'voluntarily' admitted myself under the direction of my GP and Wendy – for the safety of myself, and others.

Talking to a couple of completely lucid and surprisingly gentle girls with unspecified 'psychoses', however, I found out that getting in was the easy part. They had started out as voluntary patients too. But then, when they could not stand the mind-emptying, soul-destroying confinement of the ward any longer, they were told that if they tried to leave, they would be sectioned.

This made them angrier. And I'm no clinician, but I found myself agreeing, for reasons other than self-preservation, that this anger probably made their 'psychoses' worse. But now they were even angrier patients with an already diagnosed and underlying 'psychosis', they were now looking at not knowing whether they were going to be let out at all.

This was their Catch 22.

And now, with horror, I realised it was also mine.

If I said I wanted to leave, the staff could say I wasn't ready and section me.

But if I stayed much longer here, I knew my PTSD was going to morph into some kind of all-out, sympathetic, cabin-fevered madness mirroring that of my fellow inmates, which would mean I would have to be sectioned. And no one wants to be sectioned, because this is nothing other than open-ended imprisonment – though admittedly all for the direct good of the outside community.

Or as I only saw it at this time – for the indirect good of my family.

And my family will only learn of my time in this place when they read these words now.

So you may read these next words. But now I must apologise to my family for this deceit.

Please know that I did not tell you out of love. I just did not want to hurt you all over again, after everything I had already put you through.

*

Wendy came to see me.

I'd never been so pleased to see someone in all my life.

And, after speaking to both the hospital staff and me, she formed the opinion that I was fit to be discharged.

But this meant both of us had to sit in front of a panel of psychiatrists.

419

They questioned us both for an hour. If I were to 'go postal' following my release, after all, these psychiatrists would no doubt face their own questioning. I thought it diplomatic not to tell them my concerns that, looking forward, there was probably more chance of me going postal *because* I was banged up in there – on top of everything else. But Wendy told both them and me the good news from the HAC, who, upon hearing the news that one of their soldiers had been hospitalised, had looked with new urgency for new ways to help him.

We were told the British Legion could take up my case with the AFCS. This surprised me; I had not realised their Poppy Appeal funded such things for soldiers – though, now I heard it, it seemed to make sense.

As an alternative, we were also told about the wife of a long-past HAC CO who also happened to be a high-powered City lawyer. Apparently she had seen enough merit in my case to offer taking me on as a client – pro bono and completely free of charge – and taking the fight back to the AFCS for recognition of my wounds.

I was as cautious as I was thankful, though. By now, I knew that a ray of hope could be a dangerous thing to cling onto.

When I was released, the other ray of hope Wendy thought she could offer me – a stay in a dedicated, Regular Army-run rehabilitation centre for soldiers – was snuffed out. It turned out that because I was demobilised TA, I was ineligible for its treatment.

*

I did not know what to expect from the City of London branch of an international army of super-lawyers. From the outside, the offices of K & L Gates LLP were nothing but towering glass and shining steel, echoing that of any banking behemoth. The cavernous foyer, too, was all polished granite and harsh-echoing marble.

But, although polished, the lawyers I met were anything but harsh, at least with me. Jane, the wife of the long-previous HAC CO and a partner at K&L Gates, said they would do everything they could to help me. She said that she hoped they could lessen some of the strain on me by letting them take up the burden of dealing with the AFCS.

She cared.

The first lawyer she assigned to my case, Ben, cared as much as he was professional, too. In fact, he would later go on to take a probably massive pay cut, just so he could move jobs to work for a mental health charity.

And Ben's replacement, Rachel, who had just come back from advising on litigation in the High Courts and Supreme Court of India, would outstrip all plaudits imaginable.

I would trust them implicitly. But I did not trust the AFCS. So as my lawyers became overnight experts in the legislation governing the AFCS, I too tried to struggle my mind through its labyrinth of legal clauses.

But when this becomes too intellectually befuddling and too emotionally draining, I retreat into my singular, growing refuge: the book I have been trying to cathartically write all along. And when that in turn becomes too exhausting against the ever-present backdrop of the PTSD and the pervading fears of a future that I cannot run from, I just have to stop, period.

Ninety-minute sessions are spent with Wendy, who does everything she can to keep me as stable as I can hope to be.

And parts of other days are spent being assessed by other mental health professionals.

A second, seven-page-long, opinion of my condition is given by an eminent psychiatrist. And then for good measure, a third, eight-page-long, opinion is given by an equally eminent, PTSD-specialising psychologist.

This psychologist tells me of the higher occurrence of PTSD in Reservist soldiers, due to the dichotomy inherent to their lives. He tells me how this occurrence jumps dramatically, if the soldier has killed. He tells me it is when we are suddenly reimmersed in the cosy norms of civilian life again that different meaning is attached to the things we have done. And he tells me how feelings of abandonment, and betrayal, only exacerbate the resulting PTSD further.

These insights comfort me by making me feel a shade less mad. But both his and the psychiatrist's independent assessments and prognoses still echo Wendy's equally professional assessment and prognosis, all the way to the hilt.

My MOD social worker writes a report too. And even my patrol commander in Iraq, Alex, writes one from the perspective of both an officer and a close friend as to how he has seen the PTSD affect me after Afghanistan, turning me into a 'very different man' from the one I was before.

And Wendy herself emphasises all her findings in a whole new comprehensive report.

The lawyers collate all these reports into a ring binder. And in

February 2011, they send it to the AFCS with a doorstep of a legal letter, politely but firmly requesting both an appeal and a review of my case on a whole gamut of legal grounds.

Then there is nothing left to do but wait, all over again, for weeks – and then months – as the course of my life is decided by a faraway group of civil servants.

But, completely separate to this process, the Medical Board that will discharge me from the Army and its safety net of disability pay looms ever closer.

I guess that I am not meant to worry.

But the part of me that wants to live is going clean mad with worry.

And now my body reacts to the gathering crescendo of stress in my mind, by developing pompholyx eczema.

*

'Oxygen thief.'

I wonder if this is what one of my civilian friends truly thinks of me.

But, of course, this may say more about me than it does about him.

His emailed advice is long, but in my mind I boil it down to the points that I should 'seek employment' and 'talk to the Samaritans' whenever I feel suicidal.

I had only wanted a friend to talk to. But as much as I now think that through no fault of his personal life experience he will never be able to truly understand, I also wonder if I have just burned through all the goodwill he personally can offer me.

It probably does not help that his wife does not like me. She tells me that I have 'very serious issues with women'. And she tells me that the 'proof is in the pudding', with me being single.

But I think this overlooks the fact that I have issues with life itself.

I never thought I had a problem with women before she told me I had one. So I am thankful to those female friends who rally to me afterwards, who strive to nip in the bud this latest onslaught I am about to turn on myself. And I listen to them telling me with vigour that I am in no way the person she says I am, and that my friend's wife just needs to 'get a life'.

But, though they do not say it, I know only too well that I need to 'get a life'.

*

In the early hours of 14 March 2011, I got two hours of sleep, though this was not in any way unusual.

But when there was no more time to go through the motions of sleep, I fuelled myself with caffeine, climbed into my car and drove to a barracks in Colchester. And there, at the appointed hour, I sat in front of an Army Medical Board convened in my honour, staffed by three lieutenant colonel doctors.

Here I was put on the spot and gently asked to recount everything that had led me to sit there.

But I was not on my own. My always-supportive MOD social worker sat a few feet away from this spotlight – as did the new, concernedly helpful HAC welfare officer. And, just as he had been a raft of strength in Iraq and throughout this afterwards, Alex was there for me too.

They helped even the numbers.

The Army doctors said they had read Wendy's reports, along with all the others now sitting between them and me. And with the passage of each of their probing and confirmatory questions, I knew they were going to recommend my medical discharge from the Army.

And they did recommend my medical discharge from the Army.

Now I have reached the end of the most defining thread to my life, which has run throughout all my years since the seminal days when, as a very small boy, I looked up at my war-hero grandfather in wonder.

*

Before the old soldier faded first into Alzheimer's and then completely from this world, I sat down with him one Sunday afternoon so he could show me the photos of his life.

I was very young; I could not have been any older than eight. But I knew enough to know that Grandfather had been a soldier in two wars. And I knew enough from the glorified matinee war films I sat transfixed in front of during other Sundays at home to know that maybe this was why Grandfather was so very different from all the other relations my parents ferried me and my brother to see.

I did not know that there were wounds you could not see. I saw that Grandfather was gentle and kind and quiet. And I saw that when he spoke, everyone shut up and listened.

But he never, ever spoke about the wars.

It was no different when it was only he and I sitting together, though I was of course bursting to ask him. But I knew enough from instilled manners and growing shyness never to ask people questions about things they did not want to talk about it.

Instead he showed me pictures taken between the wars, when he was posted to places called Kenya, Mesopotamia and the North-West Frontier.

As he sifted through the peace of this past with me, there was no way for either of us to know that his young grandson would train for war in one of these places, and then see war in the other two.

Now he is gone. And now the eight-year-old is thirty-nine. But even now, I will still never be able to truly imagine what it would have been like to be a teenager, in the Machine Gun Corps, living and killing in the mud-, rat- and blood-filled trenches of the First World War.

And with British culture being what it was then, I am sure he could never imagine talking to anyone back Home of the things that he saw.

But I imagine, too, that he just wanted to keep the blissfully ignorant goodness of Home separate from the Horror. And if this was so, just with my own limited experience, I can understand this.

Of course, it is equally possible that, just as a human being, he wanted to leave all the Horror behind.

I will never know. But with the retrospect I am afforded now, I think his silence on the Horror was deafening.

Now there is only the heavy rack of medals left in his wake, accompanied only by the memory of silence as to how he earned them.

I was born into a later generation, though, that has been told of the value of exorcising the past by airing it. But just as a human being, I know that beyond these words I have forced myself to solitarily write, I will never want to talk of my Horror ever again.

This does not mean that I will ever forget, for this would never be right. But it does mean that one day, I can only pray to have a young, happily innocent grandson sitting on my knee, who I in turn will do everything in my power to shield from the Horror that men can do to one another.

And should I fade from this world before he is ready to know of such things, now there will be some explanatory, preparatory words to accompany his grandfather's own rack of medals.

*

I was still waiting for the wheels of Army bureaucracy to turn me out of the Army when the letter from the AFCS arrived in late June 2011.

It was a sparkling bright day, just like all the others in that whisper of a British summer. Sitting in the quiet sunshine on the steps outside my house, the brown envelope in my hands looked like all the manila others that had called me away to spend summers in hotter parts of the world.

Long ago, when he too was still alive, my father had taught me to 'hope for the best, but prepare for the worst'. So now, with my armour of light-headed, emotional numbness donned again in preparation, I took one last breath.

And then my fingers slowly ripped open the envelope.

> Dear Mr Wood
> We have recently reviewed the decision notified to you on 15/02/10 of your claim for compensation under the Armed Forces Compensation Scheme (AFCS).
> I am writing to tell you the outcome of this review.
> The decision on your case has been revised.

I look up. I know the fingers that lift the cigarette back to my lips are shaking. My whole body is shaking.

I take a long, deep drag. And then I force my eyes to look down again.

> You may also be aware that the Armed Forces Compensation Scheme was recently reviewed by Admiral The Lord Boyce, former Chief of the Defence Staff. The outcome of the Review was published in February 2010 and since then the MOD has been working to implement all of the improvements that Lord Boyce suggested to be made to the Scheme.
> As a direct result of implementing Lord Boyce's recommendations, the majority of previous awards made under the scheme are being increased. The amount payable for injury/illness has increased and therefore your previous award has been uplifted and we are pleased to inform you that you are due extra compensation.

I take another drag on the cigarette. And I slowly reread what I already have, just to make sure I really understand their words. And I have to read and reread the next words over and over again, just to begin to fathom their meaning and implications:

> As part of the Review an Independent Medical Group looked at some categories of injuries and illnesses to ensure that the scheme provided proper compensation in these cases. The types of

injuries/illnesses considered by the group were: hearing loss; injury to genitalia; non-freezing cold injury; paired injuries; brain and skull injuries; spinal injuries; and mental health.

As your previous award included an award for an injury/illness in this category the award descriptor and tariff level may have changed from that previously notified to you.

The additional payment due to you is £130,925. This will be paid into your bank account as soon as possible.

You were previously paid a lump sum of £9,075. Therefore the total lump sum received under the Armed Forces Compensation Scheme is £140,000.

The increase to your award means you will also receive a Guaranteed Income Payment (GIP) which will be paid monthly from the day after your discharge. This payment is tax free, and will be increased each year in line with inflation.

And it turns out that this GIP will be 75 per cent of my mobilised Afghanistan pay.

So maybe I can choose life now, because, in black and white, the letter tells me that: 'GIP is payable for life.'

Maybe this is why I now feel the sun shining gently down upon me. And, lost in this shattering moment, the heat and brightness of the day does not take me back to Afghanistan. I am just sitting bathed in the warmth of a fine English summer's day, on the steps of a home I will no longer lose.

I wish tears could roll down onto this letter in relief. But the only thing I can feel in this cataclysmic, resolution-filled, seminal moment is the numbness of shell shock.

But this, of course, is just another of the reasons I have been handed a financial lifeline by a country – which now, finally, I can begin to call my own again.

And with this I see that the very act of not ending an old life can itself be the first act of a new life.

*

I cannot express ample thanks to my lawyers. So I take them out for a thank-you lunch. And I give them a case of suitably expensive champagne each, to make up for my difficulties with expression.

But Rachel says she can only echo Jane's words: that my case was a 'privilege' to be involved with.

The least I can do after that is write a letter to their superiors, singing their praises.

But I will never be able to convey just how thankful I am. So I can only hope the message I had engraved on their champagne cases can begin to do so:

'Thank you. With every wish for your future, now you have afforded a future for me.'

*

The day after the AFCS letter arrived, I formally received my Afghan medals at the HAC.

Closure and Fate were as aligned as that.

Now, and as always when I go into the HAC, the new CO asks to see me. But this time he goes further, to tell me that not only will the HAC continue to be there for me when I leave the Army but that he personally will always be there for me too, when the time comes for him to leave the HAC.

I believe him.

And outside on the parade ground, surrounded by families and the entire regiment, I am placed in the dead centre of the front rank of soldiers just back from Afghanistan.

Individual citations are read out for every one of us. An official photographer takes pictures. And the general overseeing the ceremony commends each of us individually for our service, before collectively commending us as one – in front of all the hundreds standing around us.

And now I am proud to call myself a veteran member of the Honourable Artillery Company.

*

With financial survival, I know I can now entertain the dawning possibility of literal survival, in a new life that must be taken day by day.

The monthly income is a means to an end, nothing less than the financial means to physically survive while I begin down the unfamiliar road to a new, different life.

But what is of equal importance is the reason the money is given.

It is the recognition that is beyond price. Because, along with the healing recognition of a dedicated medals ceremony, it is this *recognition* of the wounds I carry – to such an extent that they now define *who I am* – which matters above all. The monthly income I now get, which in no way could be earned, whatever profit this book turns a first- and probably one-time author, is only the measure of that recognition.

I know that the story that this book carries will itself be the cause for no more words to be written beyond it.

So in the telling of this story, honesty has been the only way forward.

But I know some people may have a problem with this.

And my PTSD's hypervigilance waits with particular dread for the reaction it expects from the AFCS.

*

I wrote this story as I went along.

I wrote it as I lived it.

So the writing has taken ten years, just as the journey has taken ten of my years. And the act of its telling has come close to killing me, just as the journey itself did.

I kept journals. In Iraq, I took as many photos as any other soldier. And in Afghanistan I had a head cam strapped to my helmet, which remorselessly recorded all the bloody details my mind closed off from.

You will be the judge as to whether I have any raw talent for writing left over from the time before the PTSD. But in writing about the PTSD and everything that caused it, I have written about the only things that I now *know*.

So I ask you to see that there is a world of difference between writing about all your mind now knows, at the snail's pace your debilitated mind dictates, and dealing with any mass of unfamiliar information, in the professional, pressured environment inherent to any office, with its long, strictly regimented hours, performance assessment and never-ending, 'more-with-less' deadlines.

You can do the maths and work out how long it took me to write these final chapters.

During this period, there were days when I could write for a few hours. But there were unfathomably more when I could not even think, let alone write.

So I hope the AFCS will not begrudge this attempt to make sense of the only things now left in my mind. I hope they will not seek to financially punish me, by revising the godsend of a lifeline they have now given me.

And if they do, then I will, of course, have no option but to fight them. But as a word of warning, I cannot promise that the blood on my hands will not end up on theirs as a result.

This book is now my only chance of channelling the destruction of my past into something constructive for my present.

Maybe this will enable a future for me. Because as much as you may want resolution as a reader, I promise you that, as the writer, I need it more.

I know I have a 'sense of foreshortened future', listed as just another of the classic PTSD symptoms, but now I can dare to hope.

The precariousness of this hope does terrify me, but so does the idea of not living an ordinary family life in the future. So I have to dare to hope.

This flicker of hope has now moved me from the self-medication of cigarettes onto electronic cigarettes. Apparently they will not 'seriously harm you and others around you', as they deliver the same nicotine hit through the harmless medium of water vapour. And in choosing this life, it does not matter that some people I pass in the street, stare at the electronically glowing green tip of my 'cigarette' and in turn look at me like I am mad.

They don't know the half of it, after all.

But I do not seek any sympathy, for we both know that I made the decisions to serve my country as I did. I hope, though, that I can just be accepted for what I have given in service to my country.

So I am profoundly grateful to my country for handing me the means to survive beyond this service. And I hope I do not sound ungrateful, when I just state the fact that this pension will be index linked to the CPI rate of inflation, and not RPI. I accept that its relative value will slowly diminish with each passing year – just as I must accept that my country's public will slowly forget all the soldiers killed and injured in their name in Iraq and Afghanistan, with each passing year.

You may say that you won't. But over 600 British soldiers have died in the Iraq and Afghan conflicts I was in, with hundreds more injured.

More than a thousand British soldiers died protecting South Korea in the 1950s. And the veterans of this 'Forgotten War' still live among us now. So now I have been honest with you, I ask you in turn to be honest with yourself – for we are as guilty as each other.

Do you remember them?

*

The soldier walks out of the gates of the unit that he is no longer a soldier in.

He walks past the turning for Worship Street. He turns his back on where The Prophet used to be. It was consumed by fire while he was at war. And now not even a gutted shell of this journey's beginning exists. There is only empty space there now.

He walks past the '99 per cent' protestors camped out in Finsbury Square. He walks past their banners saying, 'Join us'. And he walks past their banners dreaming of 'Freedom, Unity, Peace and Love'.

He is not one of these 99 per cent. He knows the cost of their dreams.

But he never will be one of the 1 per cent they rally against, either.

He walks among the 100 per cent, merging into their whole. But he is apart from their sum of parts.

The heat of the day takes his mind to another place. And this place is not in the past, because the past lives on within him.

He sees the danger that is all around – draining into the space around him, as if a patch of blood-spattered sand is always beneath his feet.

He sees ghosts walking among the living.

But only he remembers these things, so only he sees these things. And only he knows what could happen, at any second, within this happy bubble encapsulating an oblivious City Road.

He carries this past with him now, just as he used to carry the weapon that was future and life in his hands.

But to glance at the soldier, this burden would be as invisible as him. And his shadow that is the same as everyone else's is likewise lost among the sea of others within the scurrying, sepia-grey streets.

He dissolves into the rush of humanity hurrying past him – who frown and talk and laugh and live, but who will never know, and so will never see.

On the train deep underground, he sits closeted opposite faceless strangers on buffeted banks of seats that mirror those of the helicopters he flew in.

And here he can never close his eyes, because this would mean he would never see the hand that reaches inside an explosives-filled rucksack. And if he were to close his eyes, then he would only feel the juddering fuselage skimming over the sand of a distant land, carrying him all the way back to those places he can never leave behind.

But it is already too late. He feels the weight of the helmet on his head and the heavy press of the body armour on his chest. And he feels the heavy, beautifully lethal purpose of the rifle in his sweating hands.

Now the strangers he sits opposite are faceless no more. Now he sees the faces of the dead.

And with this, he waits to see his own wraith joining them – passing unseen together through the herd of living making its way up to the world outside.

And as he waits for this release, his dead eyes that stare from so long ago and from so far away are alive to all that is threatened and could be. And as his body continues to mechanically mimic all the observed motions belonging to this borrowed life, he knows that the window through which his mind sees the world is clouded by ghosts.

He sees the past that will now always be present.

And sometimes he may think he sees a glimpse of the future, within the faraway eyes of another.

But no one sees him.

*

Before I became one of them, some Regular soldiers I served among saw me as a civilian.

But when I returned to be a civilian among civilians again, I saw that I remained a soldier.

So I know now that if I am to live, I must simply make room for the ghosts.

Wounds may heal. But scars will remain. And just as the 'acoustic blast trauma' tinnitus in my ears means I will never hear silence again, I know that this past will always be with me.

Martin will always be one of the closest friends I can truly talk to – because he is the only friend who was there in every single one of my Afghan footsteps with me. He has honoured this life friendship by making me godfather to his daughter. But the irony, of course, is that just the sight of the one resurrects the past for the other.

I look into the lives, the relationships, the marriages, the babies and the happiness of all my friends. And 'want' does not even begin to describe my view of what they have. The beautiful ordinariness that too many take for granted: I value this above all now I have lived through the dark flip side to life.

But, short of a woman who has the patience to see me for who I really am, past apparently good looks and underneath all that bubbles in my subconscious, I cannot have this life that others have.

In today's throwaway society, I feel myself labelled as a loony, a freak – and one that has 'very serious issues with women'.

A good woman is now all I want, though. I know there is a hidden well inside me that has so much to give. It cries to be released from the dark. It longs to become a spring with someone.

Someone who is not a Siren.

I just want someone I could learn to love, who could, in turn, learn to love me.

And now I have coldly taken life, I hope one day to be able to return life to the world, within the warmth of a long-lost thing called Love.

I hope.

When my friend Jules comes down to visit me in London, she brings her two young daughters with her. Isabelle is very young; she clings to her mother in the big, bad city. But Tabitha, at six, is a little older; she looks up at the tall city buildings in awe. And as we walk together through the wondrous city streets with all their amazing sights and sounds, Jules says to her, 'Hold Jake's hand, Tabitha . . . It's good for him.'

But Tabitha does not need telling. I make her squeal with laughter, after all. And, with warmth, Jules tells me that I am Tabitha's 'new favourite person in the whole world'.

How can you put into words what it is like to protectively hold the tiny hand of such a fragile, joyfully innocent little life when you know there is so much death inside you?

I carry her on my shoulders – and I 'run like the wind!' when she tells me to.

Her excited little laugh fills my ears. And her light makes the darkness go away.

When she cries and does not want to let go of Jake when the time comes to say goodbye to him, I hold her very gently and promise her that she'll see me again, real soon.

She does not know that my heart threatens to crack open on the spot. And she does not know that when I finally get home and close my front door, alone with empty silence once more, the well of tears that has been aching inside bursts forth. And I cry to the point where I do not know what I am crying about any more.

I want to live.

But the release of the tears enables me to see again. I see the tears are of grief born from death, with its 'survivor guilt' and 'killer guilt'. And I see the trigger for these tears is a little girl's own tears at having to say goodbye to me. But I think my tears are also born from having to say goodbye to the last traces of little boy's innocence I ever had.

But this is good, because it is in holding Tabitha's hand that I am reconnected to a part of me that would otherwise be dead.

And in the words of Wendy, when I punish myself I am also punishing the little boy inside me, who only ever wanted to be accepted, to be loved – and to live.

So weeks later, when Jules comes down with her daughters for Fireworks Night in London, I force myself out of the house.

And when I have finished being a 'scaredy cat' beneath all the BANGS, it is not my hand that holds Tabitha's, but her little hand that reaches up to hold mine.

And she says, 'Don't be scared, Jake,' as she takes all the Horror away.

*

Now, too, I am godfather to the tiny life that my friends Moxy and Clare have brought into this world.

Clare hands the tiny bundle of new life to me. And while I hold Sophia so very gently in my arms, with her only just sentient eyes fixed on mine, the death that I carry inside me goes away.

Moxy and Clare and Sophia give me hope, as I feel their goodness breaking something open deep inside of me, as I hold my helpless goddaughter to my chest.

And I know that I can only hope to hold such a tiny, perfect life of my own in the future.

I hope.

*

My most terrifying prospect used to be that of lying in my deathbed, 'holding my manhood cheap' as I regretted all the things I had not done.

I have not done everything I could with the Army, but I have done everything I wanted to have done. And so with who I was brought up to be, I can have no regrets. By the measures I placed on myself, I have lived.

But this cannot be the end.

I do not want to always inhabit that numb, grey limbo between Afghanistan and Home.

I know I must learn to let colours back in again. I know I must find those 'better angels of my nature', before darkness overcomes them.

I know I must strive to look outwards and forwards, where once I only looked inwards and backwards.

And now I have lived a life less ordinary, for the rest of my life I want only the ordinary – with all its extraordinary everyday miracles.

I know that I must remember the happily innocent, healing hand of a little girl. And I must remember the healing words of those therapists, family and friends who have always stayed loyal to me.

And against all hope, I know I must hope that Hope itself is not a threat.

So maybe our worlds will pass each other's on the street one day – though we will never know it.

Maybe you will see just another man holding the hand of just another woman. And just maybe, these two people may be cradling just another tiny new life brought into this world.

And maybe you will see just another husband and father, smiling.

I hope.

But as a Burmese author and former political prisoner now winning her own battles against previously hopeless odds has said, 'Hope must be joined to endeavour.'

And this book is my endeavour.

It is my ball of string out of my labyrinth.

I unravelled its length within journals as I crept deeper into the darkening, winding passages. I knew I would need their words to find my way out again.

But alive with the thrill of living, I stalked closer and closer to the prize of the Minotaur within. I could smell the promise of his blood in my nostrils and I did not care that I was lost.

And when the string ran out and it was so dark I was near blind, I came face to face with the Monster.

But in that moment turning everything black, I saw that the Monster was me.

So now you have read every sentence that is each one of my sword swings. And the final telling of this story is my last attempt to escape the maze I willingly entered.

As you read these last transcribed words, know that I have retraced my steps to reach the end of so long a thread, which so long ago marked a beginning.

And as my fingers reach for that final, unfamiliar door through which I think I entered, know that I hope to emerge blinking into the warmth of forgotten sunshine, and find myself standing on the border of another great unknown.

I can see cracks of light appearing as I push.

But now this story of years is done.

And now we both have seen this journey to its end, just maybe, it can now end – with a beginning.

EPILOGUE

I will always revere my grandfather, just as I will always revere those servicemen idolised in films of past wars. But now I do so because I know how some of them will have suffered.

This suffering will not die. The Ancients suffered as we do now. As long as we kill one another, as long as we do not evolve, we will suffer.

*

To those servicemen and servicewomen who have been injured in service to their country:

Arm yourself with some good lawyers, pro bono, or contact the British Legion, which has considerable experience representing injured soldiers – and does so free of charge.

You will need help, especially if you have PTSD. It is not weak to ask for allies; governments do so when they go to war. There is no need for you to stand alone against the machine of a government bureaucracy. And you may be surprised, as I was, as to how many people will want to help you.

But you personally will also have to be prepared to fight – just as you did in the service that gave you your wounds.

And you will know that some of it is about money – which is needed for nothing other than survival in this material world. But you will also know the deepest reason why you must fight, which is *recognition*.

You deserve to be recognised in full by this country, for everything that you have sacrificed for this country.

ACKNOWLEDGEMENTS

Profound thanks go to:

My mother, brother and father, for their love.

Toby, for giving me the space to live again.

My many true friends; I did not realise your number until the time came to count you here. So I hope you will forgive me if I give you my thanks in person.

All those professionals who did everything they could to treat me: Dr Niall Campbell, Dr Ashley Conway, Jane Lawrence, Rebecca Carter, Wendy, Dr Clare Eldred, Julia Broehling, Dr Mark Hinton, Dr Lakhan Basi, Amanda O'Donovan and Kate McLoughlin.

Jane Harte-Lovelace, Rachel Stephens and Ben Anstey at K&L Gates LLP, for doing nothing less than saving a life.

Patricia Rogers at the SPVA, and Martin Blythe, Daniel Isherwood and Carol Rigby at the AFCS, for listening.

The Right Honourable Nick Raynsford MP, for taking up my cause.

Tom Booker and Alex Ainslie, for their moral courage.

Captain Tom Cardwell at the HAC, for his enduring support, and Major Michael Joy, for fighting my corner.

Zoë Fairbairns and Caroline Natzler at the City Lit institute, for encouraging and honing my writing.

At Mainstream Publishing, Bill for believing in me, Seonaid, Graeme, Amanda Telfer and Fiona for their patience, and Karyn for her patient diligence, humour and, thankfully, considerable editing skills.

Nigel Davies at Davenport Lyons LLP, for having my interests at heart.

Suzanne Milligan, for her expertise and input.

Ian and Ellie, for introducing me to my agent.

And, for her belief and tireless support, to my agent, Claire Evans, without whom my writing would never have become my book.

Thank you.

GLOSSARY

2IC Second in command.

A-10 Single-seat, twin-engine, heavily armed and armoured jet aircraft, used by the USAF in close air support of ground troops.

AFCS Armed Forces Compensation Scheme.

AK Abbreviation for Kalashnikov: a Russian manufacturer of assault rifles.

AK-47 Kalashnikov automatic assault rifle, 7.62-mm calibre.

Ali Baba Colloquial Arabic term for a thief.

ANA Afghan National Army.

AO Area of operations.

Apache (Longbow) Two-seat, twin-engine attack helicopter. In service with US Army, with Longbow variant in service with British Army.

APC Armoured personnel carrier.

ASR Acute Stress Reaction.

B1-B Four-engine supersonic strategic bomber in service with the USAF.

Ba'athism An Arab nationalist ideology.

Badr Corps The armed wing of the Iraqi Islamic Supreme Council of Iraq (ISCI), an organisation run in exile within Iran during Saddam Hussein's rule of Iraq.

Bar mine An explosive charge laid against a wall, then detonated to gain access through it.

Battery A sub-unit of an artillery regiment, equivalent to an infantry company.

Beasting Intense physical exercise, sometimes spurred on by a certain style of Army motivation, usually involving a large number of decibels.

Bergan Large military rucksack.

Berm A raised bank of sand separating two areas.

Blue on blue Unintentional 'friendly fire', when friend fires on friend.

BRF Brigade Reconnaissance Force.

CamelBak A water bladder worn on a soldier's back, with attached drinking hose.

Camp Bastion The main British super-base in Helmand Province, Afghanistan (aka Bastion).

Carpe diem A Latin phrase meaning 'seize the day'.

Charybdis See 'Scylla and Charybdis'.

Chest rig A lightweight design of webbing useful to drivers, strapped to the soldier's chest and holding ammunition, pistol, personal radio and map.

Chinook Twin-engine, tandem rotor, large transport helicopter.

CIMC Civil-Military Cooperation. The buzz phrase that links the military with civilian agencies also active in a theatre of operations.

Civvies Civilian clothing, or plural of 'civvy'.

Civvy Civilian.

Civvy street The civilian world a soldier faces, once his/her employment by the military is concluded.

CLU The command launch unit of a Javelin missile, used in missile targeting. But useful in itself as thermal-imaging surveillance aid.

CO Commanding officer (usually in charge of a regiment).

CoC Chain of command.

Company A sub-unit of an infantry battalion, consisting of three platoons.

Contact Military term denoting incoming fire from, or an exchange of fire with, hostile forces.

Contact drill The fire and manoeuvre tactics employed on contact with hostile forces.

CPA Coalition Provisional Authority.

CPN Community psychiatric nurse.

CPU A computer's central processing unit.

Crap hat Derogatory term used to look down on another soldier from a different unit. Usually applied to a soldier who is not part of Airborne Forces (aka 'hat').

CSM Company sergeant major.

CTR Close target reconnaissance.

Debus Dismount from vehicle.

Dicker An individual acting as eyes and ears for the enemy.

Dioralyte A medicine that replaces salts and water lost by the body, usually from diarrhoea.

Dish-dash Clothing commonly worn by Middle Eastern males: a light single-piece robe stretching from neck to ankle.

DLR Docklands Light Railway.

Dole patrol A lifestyle in which an otherwise unemployed TA soldier seeks to earn all his income from the (usually part-time) Territorial Army.

Double tap Two shots fired in quick succession into the target's central mass or head.

DS Directing Staff: Army term for instructing staff.

DZ Drop zone.

ECM Electronic countermeasures.

F-15E Two-seat, twin-engine, multi-role jet aircraft, in service with the USAF.

FFD First field dressing: a bandage for dressing wounds, each absorbing a pint of blood.

Field dressing See 'FFD'.

Fifty Cal Heavy machine gun, 0.5-inch calibre (aka 'the Fifty').

Fire Team A four-man sub-unit of an infantry 'section'.

FOB Forward operating base.

FOO Forward observation officer: an artillery officer in a forward position, responsible for calling in artillery fire.

Four-tonner A flatbed Army lorry.

FPC Fire Planning Cell: a team based in a rear area, responsible for coordinating artillery assets.

FSG Fire Support Group: a sub-unit operating heavy weaponry in support of infantry company operations.

FST Fire Support Team: an artillery team attached to an infantry company, responsible for calling in artillery and close air support.

GMG Grenade Machine Gun: a belt-fed automatic grenade launcher, firing 40-mm high-explosive grenades at a rate of 340 rounds per minute.

GPMG General Purpose Machine Gun, 7.62-mm calibre (aka 'Jimpy').

Green Army Term coined for the large majority of the British Army by a minority of specialist soldiers within the British Army, some of whom work on 'black' operations.

Gucci Army slang for high-quality kit, often personally bought by the soldier.

Gun bunny An artillery soldier working directly on the artillery guns.

HAC Honourable Artillery Company.

Haram Arabic: activities/substances forbidden under Islamic sharia law.

Hard routine The practice of eating and drinking uncooked rations to eliminate sign of presence to the enemy from cooking.

Harrier Single-seat, single-engine, vertical/short take-off and landing, strike aircraft, in service with the RAF.

Hat Derogatory term used to look down on another soldier from a different unit. Usually applied to a soldier who is not part of Airborne Forces (aka 'crap hat').

Headshed A congregation of high-ranking military officers, usually in a headquarters or command post.

Hercules Four-turboprop engine, large military transport aircraft.

Hesco A flat-packed metal-cage container with heavy-duty fabric liner. When opened out, filled with sand and used in series, acts as an improvised, fortifying wall.

HLS Helicopter landing site.

ICDC Iraqi Civil Defence Corps: the interim Iraqi 'Army' after Saddam Hussein's Armed Forces were disbanded post-2003 invasion.

IED Improvised explosive device.

Imshi Arabic: 'Go away'.

In clip To be in a (usually physically) degraded state.

Inshallah Arabic: 'God willing'.

IPS Iraqi Police Service.

IRT Immediate Response Team: a team of medics scrambled in helicopter response to casualties on the ground.

ISAF International Security Assistance Force: the NATO-led security mission in Afghanistan since 2001.

Ismi Arabic: 'My name is'.

Javelin A man-portable, 'fire and forget' anti-tank missile.

Jimpy See 'GPMG'.

JNCO Junior non-commissioned officer.

JTAC Joint tactical air controller.

La Arabic: 'No'.

Lacuna A gap in a manuscript, chain of events or legal argument where some part has been lost or obliterated. (From the Latin for 'lake'.)

Laish Arabic: 'Why'.

LEWT Light Electronic Warfare Team.

Ma'a salama Arabic: 'Goodbye'.

Mag A weapon's detachable magazine, holding its bullets.

Mesopotamia The ancient Aramaic name for the land that will be named Iraq. (Translation: 'The land of rivers'.)

MFC Mortar fire controller.

MILF A 'mum I'd like to fuck'.

Mine tape A roll of non-adhesive high-visibility tape. Used as demarcation around unexploded ordnance.

Mini Maglite A toughened metal flashlight, 'mini' denoting the smallest size available.

Minimi A belt-fed light machine gun, 5.56-mm calibre.

Minotaur In Greek mythology, a monster that is part man and part bull, residing within a labyrinth. Theseus entered the labyrinth, unrolling a ball of string as he went along, before killing the Minotaur at the labyrinth's core and following the string back to escape. An interpretation of the myth is that the labyrinth represents the mind, with Theseus representing the 'noble' aspect of our psyche, battling against the bestial nature at the core of us all, represented by the Minotaur.

MOD Ministry of Defence.

Mortar A small artillery piece, firing high-explosive shells in a high arc onto a target.

Na'am Arabic: 'Yes'.

NBC Nuclear Biological Chemical.

OC Officer commanding (usually a unit smaller than a regiment, the difference in size denoting the difference between a CO and an OC).

OC's Tac An OC's 'Tactical Party': the small team that accompanies him into the field on operations.

OMLT Operational Mentor Liaison Team: a team of British Army soldiers, charged with mentoring Afghan National Army soldiers on operations.

OP Observation post.

OP Ack A forward observation officer's assistant, also trained in calling in artillery fire.

Oppo Military slang for a sidekick.

Ops Abbreviation for 'operations'.

Ops vest A waistcoat design of webbing, with pouches stitched to the front of torso for ammunition, pistol, grenades, water bottles and so on.

OPTAG Operational Training and Advisory Group: an entity responsible for soldiers' standard pre-deployment training.

ORBAT Order of Battle: the list of deploying units on an operation.

Padre An Army minister of God.

Para Paratrooper.

Pashtun(s) Ethnic Afghans, with a distinct, traditional set of customs and ethics.

PC Patrol commander.

Phys Abbreviation for 'physical training'.

Pinzgauer Six-wheel-drive military utility vehicle (aka 'Pinz').

PKM Russian-made, belt-fed general-purpose machine gun, 7.62-mm calibre.

Platoon A sub-unit of an infantry 'company', consisting of three 'sections'.

Presage A foreshadowing portent of future events.

Priory, The A British mental-healthcare provider. Famed for treating celebrities.

Pro bono An abbreviated Latin phrase used by lawyers, describing the circumstance where their services are offered free of charge to those who would be otherwise unable to afford them. (Translation: 'For the public good'.)

PRR Personal role radio: a short-range radio carried by every soldier for inter-patrol communication.

PSC Patrol Selection Course: a pass from which qualifies a soldier as a 'Special Observer' in the HAC.

PT Physical training.

PTSD Post Traumatic Stress Disorder.

QRF Quick Reaction Force.

R & R Rest and recreation: a mid-tour stay at home lasting no more than 14 days.

RAF Royal Air Force.

Ratpack The cardboard ration pack issued to British soldiers, containing 24 hours' worth of nutrition.

Recce Abbreviation for 'reconnaissance'.

Reg 1. Regular Army soldier, pronounced 'Regg'. 2. Abbreviation for 'Regiment', pronounced 'Rejj'.

REMF Rear-echelon motherfucker.

Respirator Gas mask.

RHA Royal Horse Artillery.

Roger In radioed voice procedure, a single word meaning: 'I have received and understood your last transmission.'

Rover Land Rover.

RPG Rocket-propelled grenade.

RSM Regimental sergeant major.

SA80 Standard-issue British Army automatic assault rifle, 5.56-mm calibre.

Sadeeq Arabic: 'Friend'.

Salaam alaykum Arabic greeting: 'Peace be upon you'.

Sand berm See 'Berm'.

Sandhurst The military academy where all British Army officers are initially trained.

Sanger A small position fortified with sandbags: usually one of a series within a larger position.

SAS Special Air Service.

Satphone Satellite phone.

Scoff Army slang for food, at whichever mealtime.

Scylla and Charybdis In Greek mythology, two sea monsters between which sailors had to navigate their ships. Scylla was a man-eating, six-headed hydra, while Charybdis was a ship-swallowing whirlpool.

Section An eight-man sub-unit of an infantry 'platoon', consisting of two 'fire teams'.

SH Support helicopter.

Shell scrape A trench dug to take cover in.

Shemagh A square piece of cloth with a checked pattern, wrapped round the head to cover the nose and mouth in sandstorms.

Shukran Arabic: 'Thank you'.

Signals Radio communications.

Siren In Greek mythology, murderous creatures in seductive female form who lured sailors' ships onto rocks with enchanting song.

Sitrep Situation report.

Slot Kill.

Slow time A slowed speed of marching, used in parades commemorating or repatriating the dead.

Snatch Lightly armoured British Army Land Rover.

SOPHIE A handheld thermal-imaging surveillance aid.

SPG-9 Tripod-mounted, man-portable recoilless gun firing rocket-assisted, high-explosive, armour-piercing projectiles, 73-mm calibre.

Squaddie Colloquial term for a British soldier.

STAB Stupid Territorial Army Bastard.

Stag A work shift: either on sentry, observing from an OP, or monitoring a radio.

SUSA A telescopic sight fitted to the Fifty Cal.

SUSAT Sight Unit Small Arms Trilux: the optical sight fitted to the SA80 rifle at this time.

TA Territorial Army.

Tab A 'tactical advance to battle': a fast walk/run carrying full equipment.

Terp Interpreter.

Terry The Taliban (aka 'Terry Taliban').

Threaders To have reached your wits' end with something.

TLA Three-letter acronym (really).

Tom Slang for a soldier of the lowest rank: private, trooper, gunner and so on. Derived from the poem 'Tommy' by Rudyard Kipling.

TriStar The RAF's version of an airliner.

TVR 1. A now dead British company, specialising in the manufacture of high-performance sports cars. 2. A cocktail comprised of tequila, vodka and Red Bull.

USAF United States Air Force.

VBIED Vehicle-borne improvised explosive device.

VCP Vehicle checkpoint.

Vector A lightly armoured variant of the Pinzgauer vehicle.

Vicissitude A change of fortune.

Wadi Arabic: a dry riverbed.

Wagguf Arabic: 'Stop'.

Webbing A yoke and belt worn by a soldier, with pouches attached to the belt for ammunition, water bottles and so on.

WMD Weapons of mass destruction.

WMIK Weapons mount installation kit: a cut-down version of the British Army Land Rover, fitted with roll cage, a weapon mount for a GPMG on the vehicle commander (front passenger) side, and a revolving weapon mount to the rear, usually fitted with either a Fifty Cal or a GMG.

Yomp Royal Marine term for a forced march. Known in the British Army as a 'tab'.

Zero Default radio callsign of a base/HQ controller, into which a patrol reports.

Zero Hour The appointed time for a planned action.